D1917206

Selected Papers from the 2006 Cyprus Syntaxfest

Selected Papers from the 2006 Cyprus Syntaxfest

Edited by

Kleanthes K. Grohmann and Phoevos Panagiotidis

CAMBRIDGE SCHOLARS
PUBLISHING

Selected Papers from the 2006 Cyprus Syntaxfest,
Edited by Kleanthes K. Grohmann and Phoevos Panagiotidis

This book first published 2009

Cambridge Scholars Publishing

12 Back Chapman Street, Newcastle upon Tyne, NE6 2XX, UK

British Library Cataloguing in Publication Data
A catalogue record for this book is available from the British Library

Copyright © 2009 by Kleanthes K. Grohmann and Phoevos Panagiotidis and contributors

All rights for this book reserved. No part of this book may be reproduced, stored in a retrieval system, or transmitted, in any form or by any means, electronic, mechanical, photocopying, recording or otherwise, without the prior permission of the copyright owner.

ISBN (10): 1-4438-0129-1, ISBN (13): 978-1-4438-0129-4

TABLE OF CONTENTS

ACKNOWLEDGEMENTS

The *2006 Cyprus Syntaxfest* refers to two conferences that were held back to back in Nicosia: *Edges in Syntax* (15-17 May 2006) and *InterPhases* (18-20 May 2006). The first conference was held at Cyprus College and organized by Phoevos Panagiotidis, then a member of the academic staff there. Kleanthes Grohmann organized the second conference at the University of Cyprus, with several side events, such as the prestigious Leventis Lecture delivered by Prof. Noam Chomsky and an Honorary Doctorate ceremony for Prof. Chomsky. The conference itself was held at Casteliotissa Hall in the Old Town of Nicosia. The *Syntaxfest* was rounded off with a conference party at the first editor's house.

We would like to use this opportunity to thank Cyprus College (now the European University Cyprus) and the University of Cyprus (where the second editor is now a member of the academic staff) for making all this possible with generous financial and administrative support. Furthermore, we extend our thanks to all the student helpers that ensured a smooth organization of the event (before, during, and after). And of course, we thank all academic participants in the two conferences for stimulating presentations and for being a great interactive audience. We also thank the contributors to this volume for their work, their patience, and their cooperation.

Lastly, we are grateful to Cambridge Scholars Publishing for getting as excited about this selected proceedings project as we are. Dealing with Carol Koulikourdi and Amanda Millar was a real pleasure, and the communication was great. Jointly we came up with an excellent product, we believe, that everyone involved can be very proud of.

Kleanthes K. Grohmann & Phoevos Panagiotidis
Nicosia, Cyprus — October 2008

List of Abbreviations

ΦP	Phi Phrase
ABIL	ability (marker)
ABL	ablative (case)
ACC	accusative (case)
ACD	antecedent-contained deletion
AdvP	Adverb Phrase
AP	Adjective Phrase
ARB	arbitrary
ASP	aspect
CL	clitic (chap. 11: classifier)
CLLD	clitic left dislocation
C	Complementizer
CG	Cypriot Greek
CP	Complementizer Phrase
CTM	copy theory of movement
D / Det	determiner
DAT	dative (case)
DEC	declarative (marker)
DEM	demonstrative
DP	Determiner Phrase
E	expressive
ec	empty category
ECM	Exceptional Case-Marking
EMPH	emphatic (marker)
EXPL	expletive
[F]	(formal) feature
FEM	feminine
[Fin]	(formal) finiteness-feature
FinP	Finiteness Phrase
[Foc]	(formal) focus-feature
FOC	focus (marker)
FocP	Focus Phrase
fP / FP	functional projection
FV	final vowel
GEN	genitive (case)
GER	gerund
HTLD	hanging topic left dislocation
[iFoc]	(formal) information focus-feature
IMP	imperative (marker)
IntP	Interrogative Phrase
IP	Inflection Phrase

L1	first language (acquisition)
L2	second language (acquisition)
LD	left dislocation
LF	Logical Form
MASC	masculine
ModP	Modifier Phrase
NEG	negative (marker)
NOM	nominative (case)
NP	Noun Phrase
NUM	numeral
NumP	Number Phrase
Op	operator
PF	Phonetic/Phonologial Form
PL	plural (marker)
PM	partial movement
Pred	predicate
PropP	Property Phrase
PRS	present tense (marker)
PRT	particle
PST	past tense (marker)
[Q]	(formal) question-feature
Q	question (marker / particle)
QP	Quantifier Phrase
QR	quantifier raising
REFL	reflexive (marker)
REL	relative (marker)
REP	repetitive (marker)
RP	resumptive pronoun
SA	speech act
SBJ	subjunctive
SG	singular (marker)
SMG	Standard Modern Greek
[SOP]	(formal) subject-of-predication feature
SP	simple past
Spec	specifier
SRefP	Speaker-Referential Phrase
T	Tense
t	trace
TOP	topic (marker)
TopP	Topic Phrase
TP	Tense Phrase
V2	verb second
*v*P	(light) Verb Phrase
VP	(lexical) Verb Phrase
[Wh]	(formal) *wh*-feature
WH	*wh*-phrase

LIST OF CONTRIBUTORS

Hee-Don Ahn
Konkuk University
Department of English
Seoul 143-701
Korea
e-mail: hdahn@konkuk.ac.kr

Ruixi Ressy Ai
Harvard University
Department of Linguistics
Boylston Hall, 3rd Floor
Cambridge, MA 02138
e-mail: ressy_ai@hotmail.com

Sungeun Cho
Yeungnam University
Department of English Education
214-1 Daedong Kyungsansi
Kyungsangbukdo, 712-749
Korea
e-mail: scho1007@ynu.ac.kr

Xuan Di
University of Tromsoe
CASTL
Box 134 CASTL
9037 Tromsoe
Norway
e-mail: xuan.di@hum.uit.no

Constantina Fotiou
University of Essex
Department of Language and Linguistics
Hawkins Quay H2/3/F
University Quays
Colchester CO2 8GY
United Kingdom
e-mail: cfotio@essex.ac.uk

Yukio Furukawa
McGill University
Dept. of Linguistics
1085 Dr. Penfield
Montreal, QC H3A1A7
Canada
e-mail: yfurukawa@tokai.or.jp

Kleanthes K. Grohmann
University of Cyprus
Department of English Studies
75 Kallipoleos
P.O. Box 20537
1678 Nicosia
Cyprus
e-mail: kleanthi@ucy.ac.cy

Rania Habib
Syracuse University
Department of Languages, Literatures, and Linguistics
325 H. B. Crouse
Syracuse, NY 13244
USA
e-mail: rhabib@syr.edu

Jeremy Hartman
Massachusetts Institute of Technology
Department of Linguistics and Philosophy
77 Massachusetts Ave.
Bldg. 32-D808
Cambridge, MA 02139
e-mail: hartmanj@mit.edu

Virginia Hill
University of New Brunswick & Concordia University
Department of Humanities and Languages
P.O. Box 5050
Saint John, NB E2L 4L5
Canada
e-mail: mota@unbsj.ca

Tabea Ihsane
University of Geneva
Department of Linguistics
2, rue de Candolle
1205 Geneva
Switzerland
e-mail: tabea.ihsane@unige.ch

Anna McNay
University of Oxford
Centre for Linguistics & Philology
Clarendon Press Institute
Walton Street
Oxford OX1 2HG
United Kingdom
e-mail: anna.mcnay@gmail.com

Sabine Mohr
Universität Stuttgart
Institut für Linguistik/Anglistik
Heilbronner Str. 7
70174 Stuttgart
Germany
e-mail: sabine@ifla.uni-stuttgart.de

Magda Oiry
University of Massachusetts, Amherst
Department of Linguistics
226 South College
150 Hicks Way
Amherst, MA 01003
USA
e-mail: magda.oiry@gmail.com

Phoevos Panagiotidis
University of Cyprus
Department of English Studies
75 Kallipoleos
P.O. Box 20537
1678 Nicosia
Cyprus
e-mail: phoevos@ucy.ac.cy

Tom Roeper
University of Massachusetts, Amherst
Department of Linguistics
226 South College
150 Hicks Way
Amherst, MA 01003
USA
e-mail: roeper@linguist.umass.edu

Introducing the Cyprus Syntaxfest

Kleanthes K. Grohmann &
Phoevos Panagiotidis

This volume brings together a selection of contributions that originated as presentations in the week-long *Cyprus Syntaxfest*. The Syntaxfest took place in the form of two conferences: *Edges in Syntax* (Cyprus College, 15-17 May 2006, organized by the second-named editor of this volume) and *InterPhases* (University of Cyprus, 18-20 May 2006, organized by the first), with a couple of hundred participants and remarkable overall appeal. The Syntaxfest brought together research in syntax by some of the most respected and prolific theoretical linguists from Europe, Asia, and the Americas. A total of almost 100 talks and posters were presented; given the sheer number of contributions, our intention as organizers, and joint editors of this volume, could therefore never have been to publish a comprehensive collection of conference proceedings.

However, when organizing the Syntaxfest we did not intend for it to serve as a generally-themed forum on syntactic theory and descriptive syntax, so it is far from accidental that the key topics of the two conferences comprising it thematically overlap. True, during the six days the Syntaxfest spanned over, work from a variety of viewpoints in modern generative grammar was presented, and the research discussed and debated over followed diverse methodological paths. And indeed, while a lot of the presentations revolved around foundational issues and matters pertaining to the architecture of grammar, in-depth discussion of typologically prominent or language-specific phenomena represented a good percentage of the cutting-edge, exciting, and insightful research aired in the two conferences.

As the titles of the two conferences indicate, the thematic focus was on (left) peripheries in linguistic structures and (their) interface interpretation. To wit, *Edges in Syntax* opened the floor examining the specifier-and-head edge of constituents in relation to their role in syntactic operations, including — but not limited to — edges as escape hatches for movement, issues of cyclicity, intervention/minimality effects, subject types, and so on. It also hosted work on the morphological realization of edge material and agreement, as well as on its LF interpretation: modification, tense, event and argument structure, topics, foci, specificity, definiteness, discourse effects. Against this background, the question of phase edges was inevitably also raised and discussed variously.

Now, *InterPhases* focused exactly on derivational sub-parts such as, most prominently, phases (and their edges), as interpretive and articulatory units — as the chunks of syntactic structure shipped off to the semantic and phonological interfaces of the language faculty with the conceptual-intentional and the articulatory-perceptual systems in the mind/brain, respectively. The themes dealt with in *InterPhases* were expectedly informed by recent theoretical insights in how syntactic derivations are sent to the interfaces: not at Spell-Out, a 'singular point' in the derivation (possibly a notational remnant of the S-Structure of old), but once a 'critical mass' of structure is reached — *phases* in the work of Chomsky (2000 *et seq.*) or some other kind of sub-structure, such as *command units* (Uriagereka 1999) and *prolific domains* (Grohmann 2003), among other suggestions. Given that every time phases are transferred to the interfaces, the derivational workspace is wiped *almost* clean (this is, *grosso modo*, the idea behind the Phase Impenetrability Condition of Chomsky 2000, 2001), a number of crucial matters were examined on how exactly this Transfer operation takes place.

Because of the thematic unity as well as the inherent interest of so many contributions to *Edges in Syntax* and *InterPhases*, we decided to select a number of expanded and written-up versions of some of the research presented in the two conferences, and to bring it together in the volume you are reading right now. We believe that the present selection of papers reflects first of all the variety of approaches discussed during the Syntaxfest; it also provides a glimpse of the rich sample of cross-linguistic data that perplexed, enlightened, and drove us to theory-building (and theory-revising) during those six days.

In a nutshell, this volume brings together eleven studies on clausal (and nominal) left-peripheral phenomena and their (role in) interpretation in a variety of typologically unrelated languages. More significantly, the current collection of eleven research contributions underscores the by now established importance and theoretical interest of studying the edge of constituents, whether they be phasal or not. In every chapter, the familiar workings of a single, relatively simple 'syntactic engine' (to use Marantz's 1997 metaphor) surface in analysis after analysis for language after language. Furthermore, the blueprint of a general interpretive hierarchy driving and constraining syntax is also retraced throughout — among many others, see, for example, Belletti (2004) for cartographic approaches to this, and Grohmann (2003) or Hegarty (2005) for more domain-centred approaches.

Let us now look at the individual chapters in more detail.

The volume opens with the chapter by Magda OIRY & Tom ROEPER on the acquisition of the *wh*-system, one of the prototypical edge phenomena. "How Language Acquisition Reveals Minimalist Symmetry in the *Wh*-System" investigates the role of *wh*-expletives in language development and their correlation with scope-marking partial *wh*-movement. It argues that children's acquisition paths can go through UG options not attested in their input language, and that acquisition data actually fills a gap among UG-sanctioned possibilities for scope-marking: that of permitting a scope-marking *empty wh*-operator in *root* clauses. The authors make their case by analyzing acquisition data in which children treat the first *wh*-word in an embedded context as a scope-marker for the second *wh*-word. The authors then extrapolate that examples such as (1) and (2) involve the same strategy, albeit with an *empty* initial scope-marking operator:

(1) You think what nut I am getting now? (picking nut out of a tin)
(2) You think where is Sophie? (hiding under table)

Building on a generalization by Fanselow & Mahajan (2000), OIRY & ROEPER further argue that, if a language possesses an empty *wh*-operator for use with root clauses, it will also display partial *wh*-movement with embedded clauses. Given that the role of such operators is to mark scope, they subsequently invoke acquisition data to argue that, in a grammar possessing empty scope-marking operators in root clauses, *overt* scope-markers should be possible as well.

In chapter two, "Non-Case-Marked *Wh*-Phrases and Left Dislocation", Hee-Don AHN & Sungeun CHO look into an interesting class of subject–object asymmetries in Korean affecting *wh*-elements, thus highlighting the interaction of complementizer edge phenomena with the properties of subjects — another major area of interest in the research on edges and their interpretation. In Korean, objects — but not subjects — may drop their Case-marker when they occur in their canonical positions. However, non-Case-marked *wh*-subjects are possible in sentence-initial position only as long as they are D(iscourse)-linked (in the sense of Pesetsky 1987). Still, no such restriction holds for *in-situ wh*-objects, unless they are also moved into a sentence-initial position; again, the fronted *wh*-object can be bare only if D-linked.

AHN & CHO argue against a pseudo-incorporation account of the above facts and, following Ahn (1999), they propose to analyse bare (non-Case-marked) arguments as left-dislocated, which goes some way towards capturing their D-linked interpretation, à la Boeckx & Grohmann (2004).

Simultaneously, bare objects remaining *in situ* undergo complex predicate formation with their verbs, which explains the absence of D-linking effects with them. In a parallel fashion, left-dislocated objects are also bare — otherwise they would strand their Case-marker behind, something banned by a version of the Stray Affix Filter (Lasnik 1981). Based on the evidence, they finally claim that Korean, next to Hanging Topics, allows a version of Clitic Left Dislocation (CLLD), thus *two* of the "possible subtype[s] of Left Dislocation derivable from UG species".

In "A Focus Account of Swiping", Jeremy HARTMAN & Ruixi Ressy AI discuss the type of ellipsis called 'swiping' as an edge phenomenon. 'Swiping' is actually an acronym coined by Merchant (2002) which describes structures such as the ones bracketed in the examples below:

(3) a. John went to the movies, but I can't remember [who with].
b. A: She got a package in the mail.
B: Really? [Who from]?

HARTMAN & AI develop an account according to which swiping should be analyzed as preposition stranding in a focus projection outside an elided IP: The entire PP moves to [Spec,FocP], the IP undergoes ellipsis, and then the *wh*-word moves to [Spec,CP], leaving the preposition behind in [Spec,FocP]. This account is compatible with peculiarities characterizing swiping: (i) the fact that prepositions in it must not have an antecedent, as they would not be foci; (ii) the fact that prepositions always receive stress (as foci); (iii) the requirement that the participating *wh*-expression must generally be a minimal *wh*-word, something linked to the incompatibility of focusing D-linked expressions such as *which low-fat cake*. Interestingly, their analysis can also capture the interaction of aggressively non-D-linked expressions, such as *what the hell*, with swiping, as well as cases of swiping *without* prepositions like the following:

(4) A: Mary made $10,000 in one week.
B: [What doing]?

Staying in the complementizer field and within focus investigations, the next chapter looks in detail into focus, and focusing in Cypriot Greek. The contribution "Focusing Strategies in Cypriot Greek" by Constantina FOTIOU does not primarily provide evidence for the existence and the workings of a clausal Focus Phrase, like the previous chapter, but attempts to shed light on different focus strategies by examining their function in Cypriot Greek. The focus system in this variety of Greek seems to make available three strategies: focus clefting, focus *in situ*, and focus movement. This immediately raises issues of economy and, consequently, possible interpretive differences among the three strategies.

FOTIOU embarks upon the task of addressing the problem by using questionnaires to elicit native intuitions, and she reaches the following conclusions: First, clefting is the preferred strategy with contrastive focus, whereas the *in-situ* strategy is the preferred one with information focus. Second, focus movement, to the extent that it is fully available in Cypriot Greek mental grammars (on which Fotiou makes some interesting socio-linguistic remarks), is also preferred in contrastive environments. Actually, the general tendency emerging from the questionnaire study was to interpret contrastively the constituents appearing in high focus positions. Third, there is an interesting discussion of a seemingly marginal structure, in which a constituent inside a cleft structure undergoes further movement higher up, with this second operation bearing the characteristics of A'-movement. The chapter concludes with a case for all focus being contrastive, with only the size of the set over which it ranges differing in each case.

Further insights into the nature of focus in the complementizer field are expanded upon in Sabine MOHR's chapter on Verb Second (V2) in German, "V2 as a Single-Edge Phenomenon". Mohr applies Rizzi's (1997) 'split-CP' proposal to German in order to argue that sentence-initial XPs in German declarative V2 clauses can be located either in the specifier of TopP/FocP or in [Spec,FinP] — depending on whether they carry topic/focus features or not. The merit of the analysis lies in its ability to account for a range of data that previous approaches to V2 fail to capture, namely that not all instances of V2 in German sound natural: Whereas subjects, dative objects of passives, experiencers of impersonal psych-verbs, and certain temporal and locative adverbs can be fronted to the first position with 'neutral' stress and in out-of-the-blue contexts, *all* other kinds of constituents can precede the verb in the second position only if they are topicalized or if they receive (contrastive) focus.

MOHR argues that [Spec,FinP] is the 'neutral' position for all constituents fronted in V2, a 'subject-of-predication' position, and to serve as the initial landing site for all of them; further movement operations to [Spec,FocP] or to [Spec,TopP] affect those constituents with the respective features and interpretations. This solution successfully subsumes the main insight behind 'asymmetric' analyses for V2, namely why fronted 'neutral' subjects in V2 (usually) behave differently than most of the other constituents.

Rania HABIB studies the edge positions between C and T in Arabic. As the chapter title "The Syntax of the Standard Arabic Particles *ʔan* and *ʔanna*" indicates, she provides accounts of the nature and position of two complementizer-like elements, *ʔan* and *ʔanna*, whose exact character and identity have been a matter of debate for some time.

HABIB, investigating in detail the functions and positions of these two elements, concludes that *ʔanna* is a bona fide complementizer that takes finite complements and assigns accusative to the subject, similar to English *for*, and not a T(ense)-element. For *ʔan* she puts forth the claim that it is a mood marker in the T-position, marking non-finiteness but being compatible with nominative — characteristics which bring it very close to mood elements like Greek *na*. In order to empirically support her claims, she utilizes tests employed in Stowell (1982) and Wurmbrand (2001), such as the behaviour of *ʔanna* in Exceptional Case-Marking (ECM) environments: Since ECM is only possible with CP-less infinitives, it is found to be compatible with *ʔan* (a mood marker) but not with *ʔanna* (a complementizer). The chapter winds into a detailed study of different CP-edge elements with respect to not just ECM, but also their interaction with negation and the Arabic infinitival marker *li-*.

"On a Conflict between Antecedent-Contained Deletion and the Copy Theory of Movement" by Yukio FURUKAWA looks into a puzzle regarding quantifier movement. This is illustrated by an example like the following:

(5) John [likes every boy that Mary does <gap>]

Given that the gap is created by VP ellipsis, it would be interpreted as a VP identical to "likes every boy that Mary does <gap>". This of course contains a gap, which would be interpreted as a gap-including VP — leading to infinite regress. Now, at LF, after quantifier movement applies, the structure would look something like this:

(6) John [every boy that Mary does <gap> [likes *t*]

If Quantifier Raising leaves a trace, a variable-type empty category (which was the received view until the early 1990s), then the problem of infinite regress is conveniently settled because the elided VP within the moved QP can now find a non-gap-containing antecedent VP that obeys the identity condition on ellipsis. However, under the current copy theory of movement, the situation is different because there still remains a silent copy of the QP containing a gapped relative in the object position of the matrix verb:

(7) John [every boy that Mary does <gap> [likes ~~every boy that Mary does <gap>~~]

This is the problem of Antecedent-Contained Deletion (ACD). Furukawa first presents a detailed criticism of Fox's (2002) solution to the infinite regress problem, he then proposes to solve it by extending it to Heim's (1982) analysis of indefinites as variables bound via unselective binding. FURUKAWA combines this idea with the hypothesis that composition of D with NP happens late in syntax: Therefore it is NPs, not DP arguments, that merge with V — as has been variously proposed and as suggested by Generalized Quantifier Theory.

Anna MCNAY opens her chapter "Information Structural Recursion at the Phase Level" with the question of what we are to make of a split CP in Germanic languages with V2: There is only one position before the verb (standardly argued to have head-moved to C) after all. In this respect, she attacks the same problem as MOHR's chapter, albeit in a more general way. She posits a feature [Link] and a specific phase edge projection, LinkP. This projection, recurring at the edge of every phase, encodes aspects of information structure and fulfils clearly defined feature checking roles within this edge domain. In other words, she substantiates the correlation between phases' edges and interface interpretation in the form of a specific feature, [Link], and of its head recursively projecting on every phase edge.

Building on research by Vallduví (1993), she then argues that none of the traditional bipartite divisions of the sentence (theme–rheme, old/given–new, topic–comment, ground–focus) actually works. Recasting this criticism, she puts Vallduvi's ideas to work by utilising [Link]: She therefore proposes dividing the sentence into Focus and Ground, with Ground consisting of a link (the material in [Spec,LinkP]) and a tail. Finally, the LinkP undertakes different interpretive roles depending on which phase's edge it appears. Thus, in the sentence-initial position [Link] can be related to Rizzi's (2004) [+aboutness] feature, whereas in the *v*P-phase it correlates with Rizzi's [+d-linking]; at the edge of the DP-phase, [Link] gets the interpretation of [+partitive] — a matter germane to the chapter by IHSANE on DP edges (see below).

Virginia HILL's contribution is another exploration of the edge of the complementizer field, but this time in its discourse-related interpretive function. In her chapter "Pragmatic Markers as Syntactic Heads: A Case Study from Romanian", she establishes discourse-oriented particles like Romanian *hai* as Speech Act functional heads. Descriptively speaking, pragmatic markers of speech acts are encoded as discourse features in the left periphery of the Romanian CP, merging above the Force (= C) Phrase. Such Speech Act heads are possible with indicative 'that'-clauses in root contexts, a fact shown to result from the impact of the pragmatic marker on the syntactic derivation, namely the marker's probing into the finite 'that'-clause.

Hill further argues that the Speech Act head is specified for a [V] feature clustered with a [speech act] feature, that it possesses selectional properties and that its different readings are correlated with the type of CP complement it selects (i.e., imperative vs. indicative 'that'-clauses).

"On the Edge of DP: Different Arguments, Different Edges" zooms into the relatively understudied area of nominal edges. In it, Tabea IHSANE investigates how a layered approach to the structure of the DP can capture facts about the interpretation of French indefinites. While the author follows a cartographic methodology, she justifies the various features and projections by tightly relating structure and interpretation in a fine-grained fashion. The chapter sets off from the empirical observation that argumental indefinite *un*-NPs and *du/des*-NPs in French may have three readings, and not two as customarily assumed: a referential, a quantificational, or a property-denoting reading.

These different readings are captured by IHSANE by taking the left periphery to be articulated into a Speaker Reference Phrase, a Quantifier Phrase, and a Property Phrase. Thus, superficially identical *un*-NPs and *du/des*-NPs result from different underlying structures involving movement of *un* and *du/des*. Quantifier scope interactions corroborate this analysis of the nominal left periphery, with the account arguing in favour of syntactic selection and not of selection in terms of semantic type. In a similar vein, the origin of *un* and *du/des* is traced inside the nominal inflectional domain, a nominal *Mittelfeld*, where features of [count], [quantity], and [number] are assigned a projection each, an analysis inspired by an overlapping with Borer (2005).

The final chapter of the volume, "Demonstratives, Numerals and Colour Terms in (Beijing) Mandarin", is by Xuan DI. Examining proximal demonstratives, colour terms, and numerals, DI makes a case for all parameters as choices in the lexicon. She conceives the complexity of lexical items as their derivational history, subscribing to Kayne's (2002) claim that UG imposes a maximum of one syntactic feature per syntactic head. The author argues that it is the complexity of lexical items that decides their syntactic distribution, against a primitive basic order or a fixed functional hierarchy; she further illustrates this point by looking at the relative distribution of the classifiers, numerals, and demonstratives.

This analysis is then applied to Mandarin colour terms, where a bimorphemic colour word needs the support of a *de* element, while a mono-morphemic colour word can modify an NP directly. In line with the above analysis, DI posits that an ordered set of movement operations affecting the different types of colour terms is sufficient for deriving the different structures involving demonstratives, numerals, and colour adjectives.

We would like to open the floor now to the interesting contributions just summarized with the obvious proviso that this volume does not constitute the final word on the matters addressed here. This not only concerns the individual proposals (but we might be wrong), which we hope will generate further research activities, but also the overarching theme of the 'triple *i*' — interface interpretation investigations of clausal and nominal edge phenomena (and here we are most certainly *not* wrong!). Rather, this volume should be seen as a (hopefully worthy) contribution to this thematic complex, inspiring researchers young and old to revisit, revise, and refine the observations, ideas, and analyses presented here and elsewhere.

References

Ahn, H-D. 1999. Notes on case deletion. In Y.-W. Kim, I.-K. Kim & J.-W. Park (eds.), *Linguistic Investigation: In Honor of In-Seok Yang*. Seoul: Hankuk Publishing Co., 1-16.

Belletti, A. (ed.). 2004. *Structures and Beyond: The Cartography of Syntactic Structures*, vol. 3. New York: Oxford University Press.

Boeckx, C. & K.K. Grohmann. 2004. SubMove: Towards a unified account of scrambling and D-linking. In D. Adger, C. de Cat & G. Tsoulas (eds.), *Peripheries*. Dordrecht: Kluwer, 241-257.

Borer, H. 2005. *In Name Only: Structuring Sense*, vol. I. Oxford: Oxford University Press.

Chomsky, N. 2000. Minimalist inquiries: The framework. In R. Martin, D. Michaels & J. Uriagereka (eds.), *Step by Step: Essays on Minimalist Syntax in Honor of Howard Lasnik*. Cambridge, MA: MIT Press, 89-155.

Chomsky, N. 2001. Derivation by phase. In M. Kenstowicz (ed.), *Ken Hale: A Life in Language*. Cambridge, MA: MIT Press, 1-52.

Fanselow, G. & A. Mahajan. 2000. Towards a minimalist theory of *wh*-expletives, *wh*-copying and successive cyclicity. In U. Lutz, G. Müller

& A. von Stechow (eds), Wh-*Scope Marking*. Amsterdam: John Benjamins, 195-230.

Fox, D. 2002. Antecedent-contained deletion and the copy theory of movement. *Linguistic Inquiry* 33, 63-96.

Grohmann, K.K. 2003. *Prolific Domains: On the Anti-Locality of Movement Dependencies*. Amsterdam: John Benjamins.

Hegarty, M. 2005. *A Feature-Based Syntax of Functional Categories*. Berlin: Mouton de Gruyter.

Heim, I. 1982. *The Semantics of Definite and Indefinite Noun Phrases*. Ph.D. diss., University of Massachusetts, Amherst.

Kayne, R.S. 2002. On some prepositions that look DP-internal: English *of* and French *de*. *Catalan Journal of Linguistics* 1, 71-115.

Lasnik, H. 1981. Restricting the theory of transformations: A case study. In N. Hornstein & D. Lightfoot (eds.), *Explanation in Linguistics*, London: Longman, 152-173.

Marantz, A. 1997. No escape from syntax: Don't try morphological analysis in the privacy of your own lexicon. *University of Pennsylvania Working Papers in Linguistics* 4.2, 201-225.

Merchant, J. 2002. Swiping in Germanic. In C.J.-W. Zwart & W. Abraham (eds.), *Studies in Comparative Germanic Syntax*. Amsterdam: John Benjamins, 295-321.

Rizzi, L. 1997. The fine structure of the left periphery. In L. Haegeman (ed.), *Elements of Grammar: Handbook of Generative Syntax*. Dordrecht: Kluwer, 281-337.

Rizzi, L. 2004. Locality and left periphery. In Belletti (2004), 223-251.

Stowell, T. 1982. The tense of infinitives. *Linguistic Inquiry* 13, 561-570.

Uriagereka, J. 1999. Multiple spell-out. In S.D. Epstein & N. Hornstein (eds.), *Working Minimalism*. Cambridge, MA: MIT Press, 251-282.

Vallduví, E. 1993. Information packaging: A survey. *HCRC Research Paper RP-44*. University of Edinburgh: Centre for Cognitive Science and Human Communication Research Centre.

Wurmbrand, S. 2001. *Infinitives: Restructuring and Clause Structure*. Berlin: Mouton de Gruyter.

CHAPTER ONE

HOW LANGUAGE ACQUISITION REVEALS MINIMALIST SYMMETRY IN THE *WH*-SYSTEM

Magda Oiry & Tom Roeper

1. Introduction

Linguistic theory has sought elegance through economy, locality, and a simple theory of transformation (movement). A natural form of elegance — a part of what makes a grammar 'perfect', in Chomsky's terms — should be, we argue, *symmetry* in the operations that cross structural types.

Recent work by Chomsky (2008) has taken a logical step in the theory of locality: Full Transfer (see below) should occur at the phase level. The idea, in brief, is that strict locality should lead — in the ideal form — to semantic, syntactic, and phonological Transfer of information to a cognitive/productive component at each phase boundary, such as the traditional clause, or CP, level. This then achieves an optimal interface between grammar and other mental systems.

We suggest that the system of feature satisfaction seeks to fulfil the interface goal of Full Transfer. In brief, Chomsky (2008) introduces the concept as the logical fulfilment of the concept of a phase: Information is transferred to phonological, syntactic, and semantic interfaces (as we discuss below). Therefore it is the concept of Transfer, not the notion of feature satisfaction itself, that drives the system and has the primary explanatory power. It provides an explanation for why, as we will show, *wh*-scope-marking appears spontaneously in acquisition in single clauses and why partial movement (PM) — that is, the occurrence of a partially moved *wh*-phrase in CP2, licensed by a scope marker in CP1 (as in German, for example) — appears spontaneously where it is not found in the target grammar.

This chapter first argues that the child's acquisition path can go through UG options found in other languages. Then we introduce how acquisition theory can adopt modern notions of Phrase Transfer and how other grammars exhibit PM and empty or covert operators, following a generalization by Fanselow & Mahajan (2000); we present evidence from a large corpus that supports the claim that empty operators correlate with PM in acquisition. Finally we show that acquisition data fills a logical UG possibility of a phonetically real empty operator in single clauses by examining how children respond to both *who bought what*-sentences and long-distance movement.

1.1. Scope-Marking Expletives

What happens when a grammar fails to fulfil derivational requirements? Here UG must provide options or the system will fail. A classic example of such a solution is the projection of semantically 'empty' expletives in overt positions, such as *there are three boys*, where *boys* moves invisibly to the subject, causing verb agreement, and where the expletive satisfies the case requirement. Our focus, scope-marking *wh*-expletives in PM-constructions, is seen the same way in a number of languages (see below): They mark landing sites for invisible movement. Thus expletives in general have evolved as conceptually marginal, 'elsewhere' conditions. However, as is often the case, what at first seems to be a marginal rescue device may reflect deep properties of grammar.

We claim in this chapter that *wh*-expletive insertion should appear at the same point as Transfer occurs following the same logic, maintaining symmetry among constructions. If true, it follows that scope-marking expletives should be possible in single-clause constructions as well as long-distance constructions. In particular, for a child, it can be a simplifying default delivering an interpretation for a comprehension challenge when the sentence spoken is not in the child's production grammar, which we will now explain.

1.2. The Acquisition Perspective on Linguistic Theory

How does acquisition reflect on fundamental properties of UG? Does it provide a unique avenue to UG? We argue here, what is implicit elsewhere, that, if the child cannot accommodate a sentence to his grammar, then the child will select from UG a 'default' to prevent the sentence from crashing. We argue that 'default' operations are reflections of *Initial State Options* that a child can use *without* any guiding input. In that sense, the term 'default' does not capture the important status of such operations well, and we prefer the term Initial State Options. We predict:

(1) Initial State Options appear 'spontaneously' in the acquisition process.

This prediction applies particularly in *comprehension* contexts where a child must respond to whatever an adult says whether or not it has an obvious analysis in the current child grammar. These Initial State Options should be perfect reflections of principles of economy, which in turn respond to the demands of interfaces:

(2) Initial State Options are direct indicators of the principles of interface economy. Initial State Options arise directly (i.e. 'spontaneously'), without specific input.

A consequence of this perspective is that children will pass through grammars that may reflect other non-target languages; see e.g. Roeper (1982, 1999, 2007), Yang (2000), Chomsky (2008). In an ideal system, such operations do not depend upon prior parametric decisions, but may require the identification of some lexical items (such as *wh*-words).

1.3. How Many Grammars Does UG Cover?

It is sometimes asserted that the extent of UG is revealed by the variation found in natural language. However, upon reflection it is obvious that UG could easily extend to grammars that do not exist, or once existed. Whatever biologically defines the set of possible grammars might not happen to appear in the set of grammars we know or happen to have studied. Imagine if one continent were not yet discovered, like Australia, then all of the insights that derive from Warlpiri for UG would not only not be known, but they would be defined as outside of UG, hence UG might easily be designed so as to exclude them. Excluding possibilities that should not be excluded has the effect of unnecessarily clouding — or making suspect — deeper principles. If predictable options appear in acquisition, then they can rectify what look like arbitrary restrictions in UG

Suppose we imagine that studied grammars constitute 1/100th (to be rather arbitrary) of possible human grammars supplied by biology, then it is not just possible but probable that children will pass through grammars that have not been revealed in other grammars, but are within the bounds of UG. Furthermore, the acquisition process might make that eventuality more likely — for instance, the absence of some lexical knowledge might lead to briefly eliciting a grammar that happens not to have appeared among the existing grammars and which disappears when more lexical knowledge is obtained. We will argue that precisely this is the case.

2. Transfer and the Place of Long-Distance Movement

Chomsky's (2008) notion of Transfer is the logical endpoint of a theory of locality:

(3) [T]here are Transfer operations: one hands the SO already constructed to the phonological component, which maps it to the SM interface ("Spell-Out"); the other hands SO to the semantic component, which maps it to the C-I interface. Call these SOs *phases*. Thus SMT entails that computation of expressions must be restricted to a single cyclic/compositional process with phases. In the best case, the phases will be the same for both Transfer operations. To my knowledge, there is no compelling evidence to the contrary. Let us assume, then, that the best-case conclusion can be sustained. It is also natural to expect that along with Transfer, all other operations will also apply at the phase level [...].
(p. 9 of the 2005 MIT ms., note omitted)

Why did this definition not emerge long ago? It was the implicit direction of grammatical theory once the locality of cyclic *wh*-movement became clear. However, Full Transfer is exactly what long-distance movement avoids, a topic which has stood in the centre of research for several decades. The Transfer Hypothesis reinforces the view that children avoid long-distance cyclic constructions if there is an option that preserves locality.[1]

If children mis-project grammars, what is the engine of change that shifts them to an adult grammar, particularly if their mis-projection fulfils locality requirements? A classic view, which we support, is that the addition of lexical features forces shifts in syntactic analysis. In particular, deVilliers, deVilliers & Roeper (to appear) argue that the child must learn exactly which verbs project indirect questions in order to move to the adult grammar.

2.1. Transfer, Partial Movement, and Feature Attraction

We argue that Transfer arises in instances of adult PM:

[1] Chomsky (2008) addresses the absence of articulation in adult English of *wh*-words at the CP-phase boundary (clause) with this observation: "We leave open the question of how, or whether, expression of the features on C relates to the CP-internal syntax" (p. 10, fn. 26 of the 2005 MIT ms.).

(4) **Was**$_i$ glaubt Hans **mit wem**$_i$ Jakob jetzt t_i spricht?
what believes Hans with who Jakob now talk
"With whom does Hans believe that Jakob is now talking?"

The scope marker *was* "what" in the higher clause is linked to the *wh*-phrase *mit wem* "with who(m)", in the lower clause. The expression *mit wem* occurs at the edge of the phase, where it has moved syntactically and been transferred to the phonology for pronunciation. The interpretation in terms of argument structure of the lower verb also occurs at this point.[2]

The last twenty years have seen a huge array of evidence on behalf of the claim that children spontaneously produce such sentences, which fits our claim. DeVilliers, Roeper & Vainikka (1990) found extensive evidence that children interpreted the medial *wh*-word as a contentful *wh*-expression and treated the initial one as a scope marker for both adjuncts and arguments:

(5) a. How did he learn what to bake? *adjunct-argument*
b. When did he learn how to bake? *adjunct-adjunct*

In both instances, the medial-WH is answered (*what*, *how*, etc.) just in case there is another WH in the higher clause (*what*, *how*, etc.). That word then functions as a *wh*-expletive scope-marker because it adds no argument structure content to the interpretation (see also Crain & Thornton 1998, Weissenborn, deVilliers & Roeper 1995).

Thornton (1990) showed that the effect could be elicited. She found examples of PM in L1 children elicited production, and analysed on par with German, along McDaniel's (1989) lines. According to Thornton, English children questions involve a scope marker (*what*) in [Spec,CP1] (the higher clause) which licenses the real *wh*-phrase (*which animal*) partially moved to [Spec,CP2] (the lower clause).

(6) ***What*** do you think ***which animal*** says "woof woof"?

(7) ***What*** do you think ***which Smurf*** really has roller skates?

Other studies of L2 children learners of English showed that PM occurred with second language learners as well. Gutierrez' (2005) production data

---

[2] See Rizzi (2006) for the development of the concept of 'criterial freezing' which suggests that children answer medial questions have the wrong criterion for the scope-discourse interpretation. Our proposal below can be seen as a proposal for *how that error occurs*.

are illustrated below in (8-9) (see also Schulz 2004).

(8) ***What*** do you think ***which baby*** had eaten the cake?

(9) ***What*** do you think ***who*** lived in the house?

The adult long-distance counterparts will be respectively:

(8') Which animal do you think had eaten the cake?

(9') Who do you think lived in the house ?

2.2. **Wh-*in-situ and Invisible Scope-Markers***

What happens in those languages which have *wh*-in-situ? Cheng & Rooryck (2000), based on Mathieu (1999), provide extensive arguments and evidence for the concept of an invisible scope marker, present in French and other languages, to account for *wh*-in-situ:

(10) $[_{CP}$ **Op**$_i$ $[_{IP}$ Jean aime $[_{VP}$ t_i **quoi**$_i$]]] (Mathieu 1999)
Q$_i$ John likes what
"What does John like?"

They also suggest that the underspecified morpheme is defective because it is ambiguous between a *wh*-phrase and *yes/no*-marker.

Oiry & Demirdache (2006) and Oiry (2008) show that the effect occurs in child French as well for long-distance movement, even though, predictable under our view, it is not found in the adult grammar. It does still appear in long-distance in situ environments, attested as being part of many French adult grammars (see also Strik 2003 from the protocol of Jakubowicz 2003). Data from children elicited production are illustrated in (11):[3]

(11) a. Q tu crois **quoi** qui est caché dans l'sac?
you believe what C is hidden in the-bag
"What do you believe/think is hidden in the bag?"

[3] Examples (11a-b) are taken from Oiry (2002), (11c-d) from Strik (2003). Two notes on the data from Oiry. First, according to Oiry & Demirdache (2006) and Oiry (2008), (11a) is ambiguous between a direct and an indirect dependency analysis; see their paper for more details. Second, # in (11b) indicates a phonological pause.

b. Tu penses ***quoi*** # que # Tinky Winky l'adore?
you think *what* C Tinky Winky CL.loves
"What do you believe/think Tinky Winky likes?"

c. Tu penses ***quoi*** que je lis?
you think *what* C I read
"What do you believe/think that I am reading?"

d. Tu penses ***qui qui*** me lit des histoires ?
you think *who C°* PR read the stories?
"Who do you think read me stories?"

Moreover, Oiry & Demirdache (2006) find that overt/covert operators co-exist in the grammars of children (from Oiry 2002, 2008), as in (12a), and (12b) showing respectively covert and overt markers:

(12) a. **Q** Tu penses **où** elle est cachée, l'assiette?
Q you think *where* she is hidden, the-plate
"Where do you think the plate is hidden?"

b. Est-ce que tu penses qu'est-ce qui est cache dans le lit?
ESK[4] you think what is hidden in the bed
"What do you think is hidden in the bed?"

Note that the absence of an overt scope marker in (12a) is not so surprising, given that, as illustrated in (10), French adult grammar exhibits this kind of scope marker.

Abdulkarim & Roeper (2003) also show that the effect of a matrix occurs in English with *whether* at the comprehension level. Children are asked the question in (13), to which many answered "no". This can only be an answer to (14):

(13) *Situation*
[She did brake the bike, but she said that she did not brake it.]
"Did she say <u>whether</u> she braked the bike?"

(14) a. whether she said whether she really broke the bike:
as if the truth of the lower *whether* were to be what she said

b. what did she say about whether she broke her bike.

The other alternatives lead to a "yes" answer to the question in (13). If

[4] ESK (*est-ce que*) is analyzed as a *yes/no*-scope marker in the French adult grammar — French children mis-analyze it as a potential licenser for the partially moved wh-phrase.

the child answers only the truth of the lower *whether*, then the answer is "yes", if child answers only upper say-whether, it is "yes" she did say something about whether she broke it Therefore they exhibit PM of whether to the medial CP, which gets a "yes" answer and covert movement over the verb "say" whether she told the truth, which is "no".

Yip & Matthews (2001) report covert movement in spontaneous speech with bilingual children acquiring Cantonese and English (children aged 4.01 and 5.03, respectively), as in (15a-b), and Wakabayachi & Okawara (2003) report it with children in Japanese learning English (15c):

(15) a. You think what nut I am getting now? (picking nut out of a tin)
b. You think where is Sophie? (hiding under table)
c. OP Do you know what is in the bag?

A covert scope marker checks the Wh-features of C^0 and marks the proposition as interrogative with scope over the matrix verb, *know* (it is arguable that the scope marker is overt if *do* itself can be analyzed as a scope-marker, but this perspective would require a full analysis of *do* in child grammar).

The options in child grammar are found in adult grammar cross-linguistically, such as Ancash Quechua, Bahasa Indonesia, and Kitharaka:

(16) *Ancash Quechua* (Cole & Hermon 1994)
(Qam) kreinki ***imata*** Maria munanqanta José rantinanta?
you think what Marie want José buy
"What do you think Maria wants José to buy?"

(17) *Bahasa Indonesia* (Saddy 1991)
Bill tahu ***siapa*** *yang* Tom cintai?
Bill knows who FOC Tom loves
"Who does Bill know that Tom loves?"

(18) *Kitharaka* (Muriungi 2004)
U-ri-thugania ati ***n-uu*** John a-ring-ir-e *t*?
2SG-T-think that *FOC-who* John SP-beat-T-FV[5]
"Who do you think that John beat?"

Fanselow & Mahajan (2000) and Fanselow (2006) then develop a far-

[5] The abbreviations for morphemes used in (18) are as follows: 2SG = second person singular, T = tense, FOC = focus, SP = simple past, and FV = final vowel.

reaching observation about the connection between *wh*-in-situ and PM, following them we suggest that:

(19) Every language with *one-clause covert operator* has partial movement in two clauses.

We have found new evidence that children spontaneously show exactly this pattern from a large experimental source, the DELV test, discussed below, with an important extension, dictated by the Transfer Hypothesis.

Now we are in a position to ask the question we asked at the outset, in terms of the full symmetry of the system:

(20) Do single clauses show the fully symmetrical range of options?

If they do, then we predict:

(21) *Symmetry Hypothesis*
A single clause should allow an overt-scope marker as well as a covert scope-marker by the logic of this account.

This is predicted for UG but not attested. Therefore we can ask whether it appears in children's grammar.

3. Disorders and the Symmetry Hypothesis: Experimental Evidence

In the development of a new instrument for language assessment (*DELV: Diagnostic Evaluation of Language Variation* - Seymour, Roeper & de Villiers 2005, copyright TPC, 2000) over 1,000 children were tested in advance on questions that involved both pair-list readings and embedded questions,

(22) *Pictures and sentences*
The father ate an apple and the boy ate a banana.
Who ate what?

and a scene and situation like the following,

(23) Mother watches TV and learns to bake a cake.
How did she learn *what* to bake? → "a cake" (not "from TV")

or a scene like this:

(24) A boy asks a man what to buy for his teacher.
"Bologna", the man answers.

(25) Who did he ask *what* to buy →
child answers: "Bologna" (not "Man" or "Teacher")

Medial-WH answers are/PM is found among a group of 297 children, 4-9yrs F (1,504) =29.94, p<.001, eta2=.137; age: F(5,975)=7/69, p<.001, eta2=.071). In response the pair-list questions an interesting phenomenon arose. The general results were:

(26) a. 4375 answers from 1400 children in full sample
b. 1125 → non-paired
c. 492 = object or adjunct
= 43,73% of the unexpected answers.

More precisely:

d. 20% of children answer only object
[*who ate what* → "an apple and banana"]

An age breakdown shows that the answer occurred most frequently with younger children:

(27) 80% came from children 5 years and under;
203 answers produced by 4-year-olds (41%);
48 answers by 5-year-olds;
80 answers by 6-year-olds (not equal numbers in each group).

This result is compatible with the notion that the children treat the first *wh*-word (*who*) as a scope marker for the second in comprehension.

(28) Hypothesis: first WH = scope marker
who ate what
scope real Q
←==========

This result then fills the missing niche in the symmetry prediction:

So children mis-analyze the *who*-form as a scope marker — instead of a scope marker neutral form expected such as *what*.

Now we can pursue the cross-linguistic parameter. The prediction is that the object-only answer will correlate with PM on an individual by individual basis. Consider again sentences like:

(29) Who_i did the boy ask t_i what_j PRO to buy t_j?
(medial answer/partial movement: "Bologna")

The result was a clear correlation for 20% of the children among 788 who gave PM responses:

(30) 172/788 (roughly 20%) children
→ both medial-WH and object-only in double-WH

Again there is an age effect with a significant correlation:

(31) 26 by 6-year-olds
101 produced by 5-year-olds
43 by 4-year-olds (fewer 2-year-olds involved)

The conclusion is that the correlation observed by Fanselow is found in the acquisition data, but extended to include overt scope markers in single clause environments.

4. Scope Marker Interpretation

There is some controversy over the semantic impact of the scope marker. Herburger (1994) and Lahiri (2002) have argued that PM imposes factivity on the lower clause[6]. In effect what is said must be true for the speaker, while in full long-distance movement the lower clause can be false, as in English:

(32) What did John say that he bought?

Under the Full Transfer account the factivity requirement would be natural because it means that the scope marker embeds the semantic

[6] See Oiry (2008); false or non-presupposed subordinate has strong effect on French children's production of long-distance questions.

content of the lower clause, but does not change its argument structure or its truth-value. The scope marker adds a further restriction, namely that the objects bought were also mentioned, but the notion that the truth value and argument structure can be transferred at the phase edge as the hypothesis predicts receives support. Dayal (2000) provides an analysis of PM as indirect-dependency which also entails that the lower clause receive a complete interpretation within its Phase. Abdulkarim (2001) and Oiry & Demirdache (2006) suggest that UG allows both and the acquisition sequence reflects a movement from indirect-dependency to covert movement to a scope marker. (See Oiry & Demirdache (2006) and Oiry (2008)) for exploration of this approach.) All of these analyses are compatible with the view that the PM reflects Transfer.

4.1. Explanatory Weight: Transfer and Feature Satisfaction

Our discussion has focussed on the conceptual force of Transfer. We have not addressed the role of feature attraction and satisfaction and how it can be fashioned to support our account. Two underlying issues are important:

(33) a. How does feature attraction work when cyclic movement is involved?
b. How does the child correctly identify the features to be satisfied when they are lexical projections from a higher verb?

Current theory has not fully resolved how to modify the highly restrictive notion of moving a feature in order to satisfy or value an identical feature when cyclic movement is involved. In principle, the feature is satisfied once, not twice. As usual, there are many technical options where it is not clear what their conceptual consequences are. Our focus is to make the theory naturally fit an acquisition path.

The natural upshot of a theory of feature satisfaction is that movement stops after one movement when a feature is satisfied. Chomsky has in fact proposed to explain PM on this basis, supporting a suggestion by Koster (2003) that Tense [T] originates in CP but is expressed in TP because the feature is inherited by the lower node which then executes agreement, when the T-element moves into it. Therefore it does not move all the way to the position where the T-feature [T] originates, but like PM, is expressed below its ultimate scope position.

It is natural then to suppose that PM results from a *wh*-movement that is frozen because agreement has occurred. Now however we have to ask exactly what the feature content of that node is such that we can both explain why it is frozen and why a child advances beyond it with additional knowledge.

The child must do three things:

(34) a. They have to identify the content of *wh*-words which does not exclude their still functioning as expletives (*what* or *how* in German or Russian)

b. They have to realize that some verbs project indirect questions.

c. And they have to realize the semantic force of indirect questions.

One device to capture this evolution is to imagine that there are two kinds of features: [Q(uestion)] and a second feature [I(ndirect) Q(uestion)] (see deVilliers, deVilliers & Roeper, in preparation for development of this approach and its connection to African-American English). Until the child realizes that the feature is an indirect question, they assume that it is a direct question. Because it is a direct question, it must be answered. This seems to be intuitively natural.

(35) [scope marker verb [CP [Q] … what]

←======

The initial *wh*-word can rescue the derivation by application of a default scope marker rule, which does not deny the interpretation that occurs at the point of Transfer.

How then would a child make this realization that the indirect question need not be answered? They could have an experience where they hear a sentence like (36),

(36) How did she learn what to bake?

and then hear the answer "from TV" from an adult and see that *what* is never answered.

Now, if we imagine that a Q-feature is associated with the matrix CP, then in Rizzi's (1997) terms of a Force Phrase, it carries exactly the notion of direct question ([Q]), and movement beyond the first phase could be motivated without answering the indirect question.

(37) [Q] verb [CP [… what]

If a child now hears (38),

(38) What did he say he bought?

which has no IQ-marker, it moves again to the higher clause with a Q-marker (for a direct question) where that feature is satisfied.

This account may be essentially correct, but it is seriously complicated by language diversity and the meaning of *wh*-words. Bošković (2000) has argued that Slavic languages have [Foc] and/or [Q] associated with *wh*-words. This allows multiple *wh*-fronting because both a Q-feature and a Foc-feature are available to be satisfied. Schulz (2004) has proposed that if [Foc] is projected in the lower clause, then it will motivate the existence of PM in those languages where it occurs. In those languages that have only [Q], no PM arises. The *wh*-word stops in the medial position because it satisfies the Foc-feature.

This is possible, but it leaves this problem: Children who pass through a [Foc] stage must somehow drop this feature in order to become English speakers.

It is neither entirely clear how to analyze Focus, nor clear how then a child would block [Foc]. However processes which involve de-topicalization, which may involve reanalysis of intonation patterns, could be involved. The problem is a part of an extending agenda in linguistics.

4.2. A Possible Trigger

Cheng & Rooryck (2000) have argued that *wh*-in-situ involves reference to a fixed set or we can use Bošković's term, a closed set.[7] That is, in Pesetsky (1987)'s term, when speaker and hearer have a fixed set of entities in mind which play a role in the discourse (D-linked elements).

Suppose we now argue that the child, when they hear an indirect question is forced to the realization, by virtue of the open nature of the higher verb, that no fixed set is involved, as in a sentence like:

(39) a. Ask Mom what to do.
b. Bill wondered where to go.

---

[7] Heizmann (2006) discusses how children learn 'exhaustivity' for cleft constructions which exhibit focus, hence a closed set.

Now the pure [IQ] form is realized. This blocks the [Foc]-reading unless it is reinstated by new structures of the kind found in Slavic languages, like *what, who bought*.

We leave this as a principal suggestion for how the acquisition path can be explained. A full answer would require that we explore how focus works, which engages multiple *wh*-expressions, clefted structures, and intonation.

Does the *wh*-scope-marking system also fit other types of Initial State Options? In the larger acquisition scheme we may ultimately find that scope-marking is a species of concord, as Felser (2004) has argued. It is well-known that children find negative concord easy to represent and often impose it on languages, like English, that do not show it.

5. Conclusion

We have argued that PM reflects the most basic form of minimalist symmetry: Each phase seeks an optimal interface with other systems as Chomsky has argued.

In rough terms, the fact that the *wh*-expression moves to the edge of the phase, is pronounced there, and interpreted at that point is all compatible with the acquisition data.

(40) Phonology (Spell-Out)
Syntax (local movement to phase edge)
Semantics (answer medial question)

This analysis has been made explicit in Chomsky's concept of Transfer. It is the logical endpoint of reasoning about locality: all interfaces are engaged at every phase edge. Much remains to be explored about such a strong hypothesis — for instance, the exact nature and force of indirect questions — but the prominence of PM in child grammar is a strong piece of evidence that the logic of locality is moving in the right direction. The fact that subtle support comes from outside the realm of intuitions and has both naturalistic and experimental support, provides one of the most important forms of 'independent' and converging evidence that linguistics can provide to future exploration in more biological terms.

To summarize the technical claims, we have argued that both one and two clause structures exhibit the full pattern of logical possibilities for overt and covert movement in UG.

(41) *who ate what* = *Invisible:*
single clause: [CP *wh*-OP verb what]
two clause: [CP1 *wh*-OP verb [CP2 what …]]
Visible:
1. *wh*-scope verb … [what …]
2. *wh*-scope verb what

The now irrefutable fact that these structures appear in comprehension and production in the acquisition of a wide languages and across many L1-L2 environments shows that the existence of *spontaneous* features of grammar — even those found in no adult grammar — are important strands in ultimately building a biological model of language ability.

Bibliography

Abdulkarim, L. 2001. *Complex Wh-Questions and Universal Grammars: New Evidence from the Acquisition of Negative Barriers*. Ph.D. diss., University of Massachusetts, Amherst.

Abdulkarim, L. & T. Roeper. 2003. From universal to language-specific grammars: How do children acquire embedded *yes/no*-questions in English? Ms., University of Massachusetts, Amherst.

Bošković, Ž. 2000. Sometimes in [Spec,CP], sometimes in situ. In R. Martin, D. Michaels & J. Uriagereka (eds.), *Step by Step: Essays on Minimalist Syntax in Honor of Howard Lasnik*. Cambridge, MA: MIT Press, 53-88.

Cheng, L.L.-S. & J. Rooryck. 2000. Licensing *wh*-in-situ. *Syntax* 3, 1-19.

Chomsky, N. 2008. On phases. In R. Freidin, C.P. Otero & M.L. Zubizarreta (eds.), *Foundational Issues in Linguistic Theory: Essays in Honor of Jean-Roger Vergnaud*. Cambridge, MA: MIT Press, 133-166.

Crain, S. & R. Thornton. 1998. *Investigations in Universal Grammar. A Guide to Experiments on the Acquisition of Syntax and Semantics*. Cambridge, MA: MIT Press.

Cole, P. & G. Hermon. 1994. Is there LF movement? *Linguistic Inquiry* 25, 239-262.

Dayal, V. 2000. Scope marking: Cross-linguistic variation in indirect dependency. In U. Lutz, G. Müller & A. von Stechow (eds.), Wh-*Scope Marking*. Amsterdam: John Benjamins, 157-193.

deVilliers, J., T. Roeper & A. Vainikka. 1990. The acquisition of long-distances rules. In L. Frazier & J. De Villiers (eds.), *Language Processing and Language Acquisition*. Dordrecht: Kluwer, 257-297.

deVilliers, J., T. Roeper, L. Bland-Stewart & B. Pearson. 2008. Answering hard questions: Wh-movement across dialects and disorder. *Applied Psycholinguistics* 29, 67–103.

deVilliers, J., P. deVilliers & T. Roeper. To appear. *Wh*-questions: Moving beyond the first phase. *Lingua*.

Fanselow, G. 2006. Partial movement. In M. Everaert & H. van Riemsdijk (eds.), *The Blackwell Companion to Syntax*, vol. III. Oxford: Blackwell, 437-492.

Fanselow, G. & A. Mahajan. 2000. Towards a minimalist theory of *wh*-expletives, *wh*-copying and successive cyclicity. In U. Lutz, G. Müller & A. von Stechow (eds.), Wh-*Scope Marking*.

Felser, C. 2004. Wh-copying, phases, and successive cyclicity. *Lingua* 114, 543-574.

Gutierrez, M.J. 2007. *The Acquisition of English LD* Wh-*Questions by Basque/Spanish Bilingual Subjects in a School Context*. Ph.D. diss., University of the Basque Country, Vitoria-Gasteiz.

Herburger, E. 1994. A semantic difference between full and partial *wh*-movement. Paper presented at the *1994 LSA Annual Meeting*, Boston.

Heizmann, T. 2006. Children's acquisition of exhaustivity in clefts. *Proceedings of the 31st BUCLD,* Cascadilla Press: 298-309.

Jakubowicz, C. 2004. Is movement costly? Paper presented at *JEL 2004 (Journées d'Etudes Linguistiques)*, University of Nantes.

Koster, J. 2003. All languages are tense second. In J. Koster & H. van Riemsdijk (eds.), *Germania et Alia: A Linguistic Webschrift for Hans den Besten*. [http://odur.let.rug.nl/~koster/DenBesten/contents.htm]

Lahiri, U. 2002. On the proper treatment of 'expletive *wh*' in Hindi. *Lingua* 112, 501-540.

McDaniel, D. 1989. Partial and multiple *wh*-movement. *Natural Language & Linguistic Theory* 7, 565-604.

Mathieu, E. 1999. French *wh*-in situ and the intervention effect. *UCL Working Papers in Linguistics* 11, 441-472.

Muriungi, P.K. 2004. *Wh*-movement in Kitharaka as focus movement. In *Proceedings of the Workshop on the Syntax, Semantics and Pragmatics of Questions (ESSLLI 16)*, 9-16.

Oiry, M. 2002. *Acquisition des questions à longue distance*. Master thesis. University of Nantes, France.

Oiry, M. & H. Demirdache. 2006. Evidence from L1 acquisition for the syntax of *wh*-scope marking in French. In , L. Escobar & V. Torrens (eds.), *The Acquisition of the Syntax of Romance Languages*.

Amsterdam: John Benjamins, 289-315.
Oiry, M. 2008. *Acquisition of Long-Distance Questions by French native speaker. Direct vs. Indirect strategies and alternative questions.* PhD Dissertation. University of Nantes, France.
Pesetsky, D. 1987. *Wh* in situ: Movement and unselective binding. In E. Reuland & A. ter Meulen (eds.), *The Representation of (In)definiteness*. Cambridge, MA: MIT Press. 98-129.
Rizzi, L. 2006. On the form of chains: Criterial positions and ECP effects. In L.L.-S. Cheng & N. Corver (eds.), Wh-*Movement Moving On*. Cambridge, MA: MIT Press, 97-134.
Roeper, T. 1982. The role of universals in the acquisition of gerunds. In L. Gleitman & E. Wanner (eds.), *Language Acquisition: The State of the Art*. Cambridge: Cambridge University Press, 267-287.
Roeper, T. 1999. Universal bi-lingualism. *Bilingualism* 2, 169-186.
Roeper, T. 2007. *The Prism of Grammar: How Child Language Illuminates Humanism*. Cambridge, MA: MIT Press.
Saddy, D. 1991. Wh-scope mechanisms in Bahasa Indonesia. *MIT Working Papers in Linguistics* 15, 183-218.
Seymour, H., T. Roeper & J. deVilliers. 2005. *Diagnostic Evaluation of Language Variation*. Psychological Corporation division of Harcourt San Antonio, Texas. [Copyright TPC, 2000]
Schulz, B. 2004. A minimalist account of partial *wh*-movement. In L. Clarito & T. McKamey (eds.), *Proceedings 2004: Selected Papers from the Eighth College-wide Conference for Students in Languages, Linguistics, and Literature*. Honolulu, HI: University of Hawaii Press.
Strik, N. 2003. Où tu as caché ton sac? Qu'est-ce que tu penses que je lis? Acquisition des questions *wh-* chez les enfants francophones de 3 à 6 ans. M.A. thesis, University of Paris 8.
Thornton, R. 1990. *Adventures in Long-Distance Moving: The Acquisition of Complex* Wh-*Questions*. Ph.D. diss., University of Connecticut, Storrs.
Wakabayachi, S. & I. Okawara. 2003. Japanese learners' errors on long distance *wh*-questions. In S. Wakabayachi (ed.), *Generative Approaches to the Acquisition of English by Native Speakers of Japanese*. Berlin: Mouton de Gruyter, 215-245.
Weissenborn, J., J. deVilliers & T. Roeper. 1995. *Wh*-features in French and German: Connections between case, *wh*-features, and unique triggers. *Recherches Linguistiques* 24, 125-157.
Yang, C. 2000. *Knowledge and Learning in Natural Language*. Oxford: Oxford University Press.
Yip, V. & S. Matthews. 2001. *Intermediate Cantonese: A Grammar and a Workbook*. London: Routledge.

CHAPTER TWO

NON-CASE-MARKED *WH*-PHRASES AND LEFT-DISLOCATION[*]

Hee-Don Ahn & Sungeun Cho

1. Introduction

This paper aims to explore subject-object asymmetries related to non-occurrence of case markers in Korean and capture close relation between absence of case markers on *wh*-phrases and interpretation.[1] It is widely observed that an accusative case marker [ACC] can be absent when nominals are in complement positions (Ahn 1988).

(1) Mary-ka   Sue-(lul)   manna-ss-e.
    Mary-NOM   Sue-(ACC)   meet-PST-DEC
    "Mary met Sue."

---

[*] This article develops and extends basic ideas in Ahn & Cho (2006a-c). Some of the material contained here was presented at *Seoul Linguistic Forum 2005* (Seoul National University), the *Workshop on Ellipsis in Korean* (Dongguk University), the *InterPhases* conference (University of Cyprus), the *2006 KALS-KASELL International Conference on English and Linguistics* (Pusan National University), and the *Syntax Lunch* (University of Maryland). An earlier version of this paper was published in the *University of Maryland Working Papers in Linguistics 16*. We are grateful to Ilan Hazout, Atakan Ince, Norbert Hornstein, Howard Lasnik, Jeff Lidz, Shin-ichi Tanigawa, Juan Uriagereka, and Masaya Yoshida for valuable inputs and discussions on earlier ideas of this paper. Special thanks to anonymous reviewers of *University of Maryland Working Papers in Linguistics 16* and of this volume for insightful comments that help us improve this paper. This work was supported by Konkuk University (first author).

[1] Some terminological remarks: We will use the term 'non-case-marked' throughout this paper. This term is different from case deletion, case drop, and case ellipsis the previous literature has used. The latter refer to the case where a case marker actually undergoes ellipsis. On the other hand, by using the former, we just refer to the phenomenon simply as non-occurrence of case and don't assume that a case marker undergoes deletion.

In (1), *Sue* and *Sue-lul* can freely occur as a complement of the verb.[2] A similar fact is pointed out for Japanese by Kuno (1972, 1973), Saito (1985), and others.

However, there is a relatively less well-known fact that absence of a nominative case marker [NOM] is more restricted than that of accusative. [NOM] in a 'canonical' subject position, i.e. [Spec,TP], cannot be absent, as (2) shows (Hong 1994, 2004, Ahn 1996, 1999, Y.-H. Kim 1998a,b, and Ahn & Cho 2005a,b):[3]

(2) Sue-lul **Mary-*(ka)** manna-ss-e.
Sue-ACC Mary-(NOM) meet-PST-DEC
"Mary met Sue."

It is plausible to assume that the subject *Mary-ka* in (2) is 'frozen' in the subject position, [Spec,TP], due to the scrambled object *John-ul*. Thus, (2) sharply contrasts with (1) in that nominative case must be marked unlike accusative.

Japanese seems to pattern with Korean. Kuno (1972, 1973) claims that nominative case *ga* in Japanese cannot be deleted. And he further argues, cited in (Saito 1985: 207), that the bare NP *John* in (3) functions not as a subject but as a topic and that the missing particle is not nominative *ga* but a topic marker *wa*.[4]

---

[2] It is not clear whether the presence/absence of an accusative marker has any bearing on semantic or pragmatic contributions. Ahn (1988) indicates some specificity effects on the overt accusative marker (see further evidence in D.-B. Kim 1993 and Lee & Cho 2003), while Jun (2005) claims that the overt ACC is an instance of a focus marker (see also E.-S. Ko 2000, S.-J. Ko 2002, 2004 for some semantic/pragmatic import of the overt cases in Korean). In this paper, space limitations force us to abstract away from the formal semantic/pragmatic details of pronouncing effects of case markers in Korean, but see the last section for some related discussion.

[3] Here we emphasize 'canonical' [Spec,TP] subject positions since in non-canonical subject positions, such as in sentence initial left-periphery positions like [Spec,CP], nominative case can be apparently absent, as seen in the following:

(i) Mary-(ka) wa-ss-ni?
Mary-(NOM) come-PST-Q
"Did Mary come?"

The status of bare subjects in non-canonical positions will be discussed in section 2.

[4] Kuno (1973) notes, cited in Masunaga (1988), the difference between *ga*-marked vs. *wa*-marked subject in the following:

(3) John kita no?
John came Q
"Did John come?"

Evidence of this analysis seems to be provided by the fact that in Japanese a bare *wh*-phrase shows distribution parallel to a *wh*-phrase with a topic marker *wa* as shown in (4), taken from Saito (1985: 208).[5]

(4) a. Dare-ga kita no?
who-NOM came Q
"Who came?"

(i) a. Taro-ga Osaka-ni itta.
b. Taro-wa Osaka-ni itta.
"Taro went to Osaka."

Kuno observes that (ia) means "It is Taro who went to Osaka" and *ga* yields an "exhaustive listing" reading, which is absent in (ib). *Wa* provides that Taro is the topic without the implication of an exhaustive listing reading (cited in Masunaga 1988: 145).

Kuno further indicates that the bare subject in the following sentence has the same meaning as (ib):

(ii) Taro Osaka-ni itta.
"Taro went to Osaka."

Thus, he concludes that the bare subject *Taro* in (ii) is derived by the deletion of *wa*. A similar observation is given in Kuno (1972: 283) with different examples.

[5] According to our Japanese informants (Shin-ichi Tanigawa and Masaya Yoshida, p.c.), if we set up the context with alternative sets as in the focus construction, even the one without D-linking as in (4b) sounds better.

(i) Dare-wa kite, dare-wa konakayya no?
who-TOP come.GER who-TOP didn't.come Q
"Who came, and who didn't?" Miyagawa (1987:186)

As shown in (i), *wh-wa* can occur in questions that severely restrict the set of referents. On the other hand, either D-linking or focus interpretation does not make a *wh*-phrase in (4c) better for most speakers that we consulted. There is, however, one Japanese speaker who we consulted gets similar contrasts that we get for Korean examples. That is, this speaker accepts (4c) with D-linked reading. We are not sure at this stage whether the status of (4c) may be subject to dialectal variation in Japanese. In fact, the judgments of the Korean counterpart of (4c) also give rise to some speaker variation, although most Korean informants that we consulted accepted it, contrary to Japanese.

b. * Dare-wa kita no?
who-TOP came Q

c. * Dare kita no?
who came Q

Several questions come up at this point. First, it's not clear why *wh*-topics are (semantically) ill-formed (see Wu 1999 for *wh*-topics in Chinese; see also Grohmann 2006 for cross-linguistic distribution of *wh*-topics).[6] Secondly, if *wh*-topics are not rare, then it's unclear whether the source of ill-formedness of (4c) correlates with (4b). Further, it's far less clear why only the topic marker *wa* can be deleted, but not the nominative case marker *ga* in Japanese: In fact, the syntactic marker *ga* is predicted to be more susceptible to deletion than the semantic/discourse marker *wa* in the light of recoverability of deletion if *wa* has more semantic/pragmatic content than *ga*.[7]

Regarding the absence of case markers, Korean exhibits interesting novel paradigms that might be lacking in Japanese: That is, bare *wh*-phrases are possible in sentence-initial positions, as in (5a). As noted by Ahn & Cho (2006a,b), (5a) is well-formed only if the non-case-marked subject *wh*-phrase *nwukwu* "who" has a D(iscourse)-linked interpretation in the sense of Pesetsky (1987).[8]

---

[6] Kuno (1973), cited in Masunaga (1988: 145), points out that *wh*-phrases cannot be construed as topics since *wh*-phrases are not compatible with the semantic properties of topics, namely, being generic or anaphoric. In fact, topicality is generally defined as specificity, definiteness, D-linking, and/or aboutness, and some of these features are not semantically incompatible with *wh*-phrases. See Ahn & Cho (2006a), Grohmann (2006), Jaeger (2003, 2004), and Rizzi (2006) for further discussion.

[7] Kuno (1972: 3) notes that *ga* is not a simple subject marker, but one that indicates that the subject conveys new information. That's why *ga* cannot be deleted. *Wa*, in contrast, indicates that the subject conveys old information. But this does not entail that *wa* itself can be deleted because it is a 'marker' of old information, for the overt realization of *wa* plays a significant role in marking semantic information. Under Kuno's strategy, we may offer a functional account for why *wa*-marked NPs can be deleted (since it can be recovered by context). However, we cannot account for the deletion of *wa* itself in this approach since it cannot be recovered functionally.

[8] The well-formedness of (5a) that we judge runs counter to most previous approaches such as Hong (1994, 2004), Y.-H. Kim (1998a,b), and Choi (2005), which consider (5a) ill-formed (S.-J. Ko 2002 is a notable exception, however). (5a) becomes more acceptable if the *wh*-phrase is modified by D-linking-inducing elements, as in (i).

(5) a. *only D-linked reading possible:*
Nwukwu Yenghi-lul manna-ss-ni?
who Yenghi-ACC meet-PST-Q
"Who is such that he/she met Yenghi?"
b. *non-D-linked reading possible:*
Nwu(kwu)-ka Yenghi-lul manna-ss-ni?[9]
who-NOM Yenghi-ACC meet-PST-Q
"Who met Yenghi?"

If the nominative case marker is present, no such semantic restriction obtains; hence, (5b) can be interpreted either as D-linked or non-D-linked.

By contrast, such restriction isn't observed in the case of object *wh*-phrases in (6). The 'bare' object *wh*-phrase in (6a) can be interpreted either as D-linked or non-D-linked, as well as the case-marked object *wh*-phrase in (6b) .

(6) a. *non-D-linked reading possible:*
Yenghi-ka **nwukwu** manna-ss-ni?
Yenghi-NOM who meet-PST-Q
b. *non-D-linked reading possible:*
Yenghi-ka **nwukwu-lul** manna-ss-ni?
Yenghi-NOM who-ACC meet-PST-Q
"Who did Yenghi meet?"

Further note that when a non-case-marked object *wh*-phrase occurs in sentence-initial position, only D-linked reading is induced, as indicated in the English translation in (7a).

(7) a. *only D-linked reading:*
Nwukwu Yenghi-ka manna-ss-ni?
who Yenghi-NOM meet-PST-Q
"Who is such that Yenghi meet (him/her)?"

(i) I cwung-eyse nwukwu Yenghi-lul manna-ss-ni?
this group-among who Yenghi-ACC meet-PST-Q
"Which person of this group met Yenghi?"

As a result of domain specification like *i cwungeyse* "among this group", (i) seems to be more natural than (5a). In both (5a) and (i), *wh*-phrases always have D-linked interpretations.

[9] *Nwukwu* normally reduces to *nwu* when it is marked with nominative case.

b. *non-D-linked reading possible*
Nwukwu-lul Yenghi-ka manna-ss-ni?
who-ACC Yenghi-NOM meet-PST-Q
"Who did Yenghi meet?"

However, if the case marker is present in the scrambled object *wh*-phrase, either D-linked or non-D-linked interpretation is possible, as shown in (7b).

In Japanese by contrast, as observed in Saito (1985: 267), when an object *wh*-phrase is scrambled out of its base-generated position, it seems to require an overt case marker, as shown in (8c).

(8) a. John-ga **dare(-o)** nagutta no?
John-NOM who-(ACC) hit Q
b. **Dare-o** John-ga nagutta no?
who-ACC John-NOM hit Q
c. ?* **Dare** John-ga nagutta no?
who John-NOM hit Q
"Who did John hit?"

As expected, *dare-wa* substituting the fronted *dare* in (8c) with a topic reading is also ruled out, so parallel account for deviance of (4c) can be given to (8c).[10]

In sum, the subject-object asymmetries and D-linking asymmetries with regard to non-case-marking mentioned so far are listed in Tables 1-2.

Table 1: Subject-object asymmetries on non-case-marking

Canonical	**Subjects**	**Objects**
Non-case-Marking	Impossible	Possible

Table 2: Asymmetries on non-case-marking and D-linking restriction

Non-case-Marked WH	**Subjects**	**Fronted Objects**	**In-Situ Objects**
D-linked Reading	Possible	Possible	Possible
Non-D-linked Reading	Impossible	Impossible	Possible

[10] Again, most of our Japanese informants rule out the dislocated bare WH, while they accept WH-*wa* with contrastive or focused interpretation only. However, the same informant who accepts (4c) also rules in (8c). Hence, there seem to be consistent judgment variations attested among Japanese informants.

Numerous questions arise, such as the following:

(i) How can nominals be bare in complement positions in Korean (and Japanese)?
(ii) Why are *wh*-subjects and dislocated *wh*-objects in Korean semantically restricted that way? (Namely, why do they yield only D-linked interpretation?)
(iii) Why can't *wh*-subjects and dislocated *wh*-objects be bare in Japanese for most speakers (unlike Korean)?

This chapter is organized as follows: In section 2 we attempt to answer the question (i). In sections 3 and 4, possible clues for the questions (ii) and (iii) will be explored. A summary and further implications will be provided in Section 5.

2. Bare Object NPs vs. Bare Subject/Dislocated NPs

The first question that is raised in the previous section concerns the well-known puzzles on subject/object asymmetry of bare NPs. We propose that bare NP object forms a 'syntactic' complex predicate with the subcategorizing verb. In other words, the bare NP object has a dual function: Namely, it fulfills as an argument of the subcategorizing verb, and it also forms a predicate with the selecting verb. This option is only available with bare NPs in Korean (but not DPs, for example).[11] Note that this option is not available if a bare NP takes place outside of V domain.[12]

[11] See related discussion of the dual status of a post-copular NP in English by Hazout (2004), on bare NPs in English by Uriagereka (2000), and on non-specific indefinite NP and bare NPs in Turkish by Cagri (2005) and Öztürk (2005).

[12] Under the analysis advanced here, what is crucial is not which kind of Case marker can be absent but where the Caseless nominal is placed. In this regard, non-occurrence possibility of nominative case marker on objects merits our attention. It seems that a nominative case on the object can be non-marked, as indicated in Ahn & Cho (2006c).

(i) Sue-ka ton-(i) pilyoha-yss-e.
Sue-NOM money-(NOM) need-PST-DEC
'Sue needed money."

Nominative can be unmarked in (i) since the bare object *ton* "money" in (i) which occurs in the complement position of the verb *pilyohaysse* can form a complex predicate with it. The judgment is similar with nominative *wh*-phrases in a

Hence, we get the contrast between (1) and (2), repeated here.

(1)	Mary-ka	Sue-(lul)	manna-ss-e.
	Mary-NOM	Sue-(ACC)	meet-PST-DEC
	"Mary met Sue."		

(2)	Sue-lul	**Mary-*(ka)**	manna-ss-e.
	Sue-ACC	Mary-(NOM)	meet-PST-DEC
	"Mary met Sue."		

Our proposal of bare object NPs essentially differs from incorporation-like analyses put forward in Hong (1994) and K.-S. Kim (1999). Incorporation analyses basically assume 'strict adjacency' between the object and the selecting verb. The incorporation analysis is empirically incorrect since bare object NPs can be non-adjacent to the selecting verbs via intervening adverbs (See Y.-J. Kim 1991, Y.-H. Kim 1998b).

(9)	a.	Chelswu-ka	**hakkyo-(lul)**	ohwu-ey/pesu-lo
		Chelswu-NOM	school-(ACC)	afternoon-in/bus-by
		ka-n-ta.		
		go-PRES-DEC		
		"Chelswu goes to school in the afternoon/by bus."		
	b.	Chelswu-ka	**ku chayk-(ul)**	ceycwuto-eyse
		Chelswu-NOM	the book-(ACC)	Jejudo-in
		sa-ss-ta.		
		buy-PST-DEC		
		"Chelswu bought the book in Jejudo."		

(Y.-H. Kim 1998b: fn. 15)

Cagri (2005) and Öztürk (2005) also note the problems of the incorporation analysis of bare NPs in Turkish, put forward in Kornfilt

---

complement position. To our ears, non-marking of nominative on *wh*-phrase in (ii) is also fully acceptable.

(ii)	Sue-ka	mwe-(ka)	pilyoha-yss-ni?
	Sue-NOM	what-(NOM)	need-PST-Q
	"What did Sue need?"		

Interestingly, there are two groups of native speakers in Japanese concerning non-Case-marking possibility of nominative *wh*-phrases; cf. Kuno (1973), Saito (1985), Ueda (1993), Ono (2001).

(2003). They suggest a pseudo-incorporation or complex predicate analysis for Turkish bare NPs, which basically is akin to our syntactic complex predicate analysis for bare Korean NPs.[13,14]

A syntactic complex predicate analysis can be indirectly supported by the so-called sub-scrambling in Turkish. The following examples show that sub-constituents of phrases can move only out of a bare NP; i.e. extraction out of case-marked DP as in (10b) results in ill-formedness (Kornfilt 2003: 132).

(10) a. ? Bir daha [e_i bir terzi] bul-a-ma-m [sen-in
one time a tailor find-ABIL-NEG-1SG you-GEN
gibi]$_i$.
like
"I won't ever be able to find a tailor like you again."

b. * Bir daha [e_i bir terzi]-yi bul-a-ma-m
one time a tailor-ACC find-ABIL-NEG-1SG
[sen-in gibi]$_i$.
you-GEN like

The intended meaning of (10b) is the same as for (10a), but the difference is that the object *bir terzi* "a tailor" is intended to have a [+specific] interpretation, which is [–specific] in (10a).

Note that specificity is not a crucial factor here to block sub-scrambling since nothing can move out of oblique case-marked phrases, irrespective of specificity, as observed in Kornfilt (2003: 135).

---

13 As observed in Kornfilt (2003), Cagri (2005), and Öztürk (2005), in Turkish, there is a correlation between the overt realization of accusative case on direct objects and genitive case on the subjects of nominalized embedded clauses on one hand, and of the specificity, on the other. Basically cases are overtly realized on specific DPs, while corresponding non-specific DPs do not bear overt cases. (Turkish seems to differ from Korean in this respect: As discussed in fn. 2, it is unclear that Korean bare NPs are necessarily non-specific.) Like Japanese, scrambled phrases in Turkish must be overtly Case-marked. Thus, Turkish seems to pattern more closely with Japanese than Korean concerning the behavior of bare NPs.

14 It is far from clear that the putative complex predicate formation in Korean morpho-syntactically and semantically parallels the so-called pseudo-incorporation in Hindi (cf. Dayal 2003) and Oceanic (cf. Massam 2001, Chung & Ladusaw 2003). Although there is a substantive overlap in behavior, Korean differs from these languages in various details. We leave further exploration in future research. We thank a reviewer for bringing these works to our attention.

(11) * [e_i bazi haydut-lar]-dan kac-mis–lar **[dev gibi]**$_i$.
some robber-PL-ABL flee-REP.PST-3PL giant like
"they reportedly fled from some robbers like (big) giants."

In (11), the robbers may be specific, marked [+specific], or non-specific, i.e. [–specific]. The Turkish sub-scrambling facts indirectly support our complex predicate analysis of bare NP complements since the bare NP is understood no longer as a barrier for movement of sub-constituents as a result of complex predicate formation.[15]

A similar fact is observed in Korean, as shown in (12). Consider the contrast between (12b) and (12d).

(12) a. Na-nun [sakwa seykay] mek-ess-e.
I-TOP apple three eat-PST-DEC
b. Sakwa$_i$ na-nun [t_i seykay] mek-ess-e.
apple I-TOP three eat-PST-DEC
c. Na-nun [sakwa seykay-lul] mek-ess-e.
I-TOP apple three-ACC eat-PST-DEC
d. ?* Sakwa$_i$ na-nun [t_i seykay-lul] mek-ess-e.
apple I-TOP three-ACC eat-PST-DEC
"I ate three apples."

Suppose the nominal *sakwa* "apple" forms a constituent with the numeral classifier *sey kay* "three". In (12b), the bare NP complement *sakwa seykay* "three apples" undergoes a complex predicate formation with the verb, and consequently the bare NP is no longer a barrier for movement of the subconstituent *sakwa* "apple". By contrast, in (12d), the case-marked phrase *sakwa seykay-lul* "apple three-ACC" is a DP, and hence it cannot undergo a complex predicate formation with the verb. Then, the subextraction of the nominal from DP is blocked, which results in the ill-formedness of (12d).

---

[15] Perhaps specificity effects in general can be reconsidered along these lines:

(i) a. Who did you see pictures of?
b. * Who did you see the pictures of?

In (ia), we may possibly assume that *see pictures* may form a complex predicate, so *see* [*pictures of who*] can be reanalyzed as *see-pictures* [*of who*]. Hence, no DP barrier occurs for the movement of *who*. In (ib), by contrast, *see the pictures* cannot form a complex predicate, and hence *who* cannot extract out of the DP barrier [*the pictures of who*].

Let us now consider the second question raised in the previous section: Namely, what causes *wh*-subjects and dislocated *wh*-objects in Korean semantically restricted as D-linked? We first adopt a proposal in Ahn (1999) that a bare NP subject without a nominative case marker in (13) can be analyzed as a left-dislocated (LDed) NP.

(13) Mary$_i$ *pro$_i$* ku chayk ilk-ess-ni?
Mary the book read-PST-Q
"Did Mary read that book?"

In (13), although *Mary* is not in a complement position of V, a nominative case marker can be absent. We analyze *Mary* in (13) as an LDed NP in a left-peripheral position with a null resumptive *pro* in its base-generated position.[16,17] Note that the LD option is not available for the analysis of the bare subject NP in (2), since LDed phrases cannot be embedded by other scrambled/moved elements cross-linguistically (see Grohmann 2003).

Note further that bare subjects cannot occur in embedded contexts such as relative clauses (14a) and subordinate clauses (14b) (Ahn 1999, Ahn & Cho 2006a):

(14) a. Na-nun ecey Mary-?*(ka) cohaha-nun
I-NOM yesterday Mary-(NOM) like-REL
yeca-lul manna-ss-ta.
woman-ACC meet-PST-DEC
"Yesterday I met the woman who Mary likes."

b. Na-nun cip-eyse Mary-?*(ka) John-ul ttaylye-se
I-TOP home-at Mary-NOM John-ACC hit-because
hwakana-ss-ta.
angry-PST-DEC
"I got angry because Mary hit John at home."

Dislocated bare objects in leftmost peripheries can also be treated along the similar lines: they too are LDed. Note that LDed phrases across languages are generally interpreted as specific and topical (see Grohmann

[16] In fact, a similar possibility is speculated in Saito (1985: 266): He states the possibility that a Caseless bare subject in Japanese, like *Mary* in (13), is simply uttered prior to the beginning of the sentence to create a discourse context, and this bare NP topic may not be treated as part of the sentence. He further mentions the possibility that the sentential-initial NP isn't generated by sentence grammar and it will differ from a topic marked by *wa* in this respect.

[17] We will return to the precise status of resumption in the next section.

2006). Hence, D-linked property of bare *wh*-phrases of (5a) and (7a) may follow: They are *wh*-topics in some broad sense (recall discussion in footnote 6). In the next section, we attempt to derive the D-linked property via syntactic operations SubMove.

3. Elaborations: SubMove Analysis of LD

Our analysis is based on the following articulated structure of nominal projections in Korean.[18]

(15)

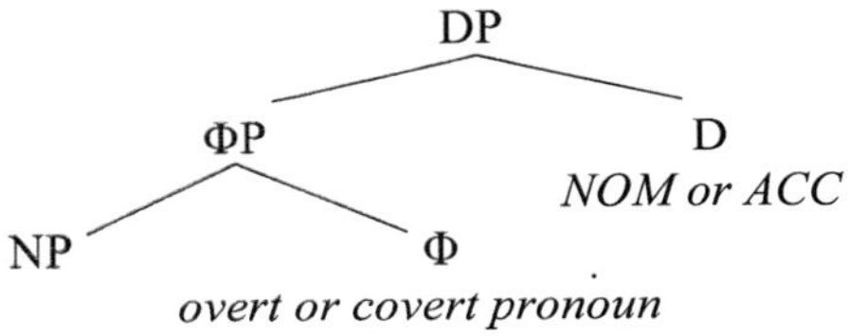

Note that there are three independent layers in (15): DP, ΦP, and NP.[19] Suppose that these layers can be freely projected, a null hypothesis. Then (15) may give rise to four possible nominal layouts: namely, NP, ΦP and DP with or without ΦP as an intermediate layer. The first possibility, NP layout, can only arise in complement positions, and it undergoes syntactic complex predicate formation with the selecting verb. The DP without ΦP is an instance of typical case-marked nominals: NP-*ka*, NP-*lul*. The projection of the DP with ΦP and the bare ΦP demand detailed discussion.

First, let us consider the outcome of projecting ΦP with a null *pro*. We suggest that ΦP, necessarily containing *pro* can be projected independently without DP layer, and it triggers movement of NP out of its domain stranding *pro* for theta-theoretic reasons.

The ΦP structure depicted in (15), hosting NP and Φ, is reminiscent of doubling constituents independently advanced by Kayne (2005) for a unified analysis of clitic doubling (16a), and antecedent-pronoun relation

---

[18] As pointed out by an anonymous reviewer, a similar analysis of a hierarchy of pronominal types (pronouns) has been popularized by Wiltschko & Déchaine (2002).

[19] In Korean, we assume that D is correlated with Case, following Ahn (1988). The correlation of D and Case is also found in other languages. For example, in German, the determiner alters its shape according to Case value: e.g. *der*-NOM/*den*-ACC/*dem*-DAT/*des*-GEN *Tag* "the day". We further assume that Φ is the projection of pronominal features such as number, person, gender, etc.

(17a).[20]

(16) a. **Cela** est-**il** vrai?
that is-it true
"Is that true?"
b. [cela il] est vrai
→ verb movement: est$_i$ [cela il] t_i vrai
→ movement of the double: cela$_j$ est$_i$ [t_j il] t_i vrai

(17) a. **John** thinks **he** is smart.
b. thinks [John he] is smart
→ movement of the double: John$_i$ thinks [t_i he] is smart

As shown in (16b), clitic and double are merged together underlyingly, and subsequently separated by the movement of the double. Similarly, the pronoun and its antecedent are merged together, and movement of the antecedent *John* captures the co-reference relation between *John* and *he* as shown in (17b). The movement of *John* is motivated for a theta theoretic reason since the theta role of the predicate *smart* is assigned to the larger constituent [*John he*], hence subsequently transferred to the head of doubling structure, *he*.[21] Given that the binder and the bindee start off as one constituent and split up in the course of derivation, the antecedent-pronoun relations are naturally captured without positing index convention that is independently barred by the Inclusiveness Condition put forward in Chomsky (1995, 2000, 2001).[22]

By the same token, we suggest that NP buried inside ΦP in (15) cannot be assigned a theta-role parallel to the double in (16-17). Hence, the NP is forced to seek a landing site in order to be properly interpreted. We

---

[20] See also Uriagereka (2000) for underlying inalienable possession structure for clitic doubling, and Hornstein (2001, 2006) for deriving interpretative mechanisms via movement conspiracies.

[21] Belletti (2005) has a different view that the theta role associated with the big DP reaches all its internal constituents. She shows that clitic left dislocation, right dislocation, and floating quantifier are all captured under the single big DP analysis and that the two parts in which the original constituent split are a lexical noun phrase and a functional word, either a clitic or a quantifier in all the cases. She argues that the possibility that two parts are both lexical noun phrases is excluded for a theta-theoretic reason.

[22] The Inclusiveness Condition basically states (Chomsky 2001:2):

(i) Do not introduce new elements (features) in the course of computation: bar-levels, traces, indices and similar descriptive technology.

propose that [Spec,CP] is one place where the NP can be interpreted, i.e. assigned a generalized theta-role 'aboutness'. Thus, movement of the NP out of ΦP (call this *SubMove*) is well-motivated on a par with movement of double in (17).

The next task is how to derive D-linked property of LDed nominals. Boeckx (2003, 2004) and Boeckx & Grohmann (2004) put forward that the peculiar property of LD hinges on the special type of movement.

(18) NP$_i$ … [$_{TP}$ … [$_{DP}$ RP [<NP$_i$>]] …]

In (18), a resumptive pronoun (RP) and its antecedent NP form a constituent and the resumptive chain is a result of sub-extraction of the NP. We assume with Boeckx (2003) that the resumptive chain results in D-linked interpretation. The particular derivational step is called SubMove (Boeckx & Grohmann 2004: 11). In line with this reasoning, we assume that (19) has the structures like (20).

(19) Nwukwu Yenghi-lul manna-ss-ni?
who Yenghi-ACC meet-PST-Q
"Who is such that he/she met Yenghi?"

(20)

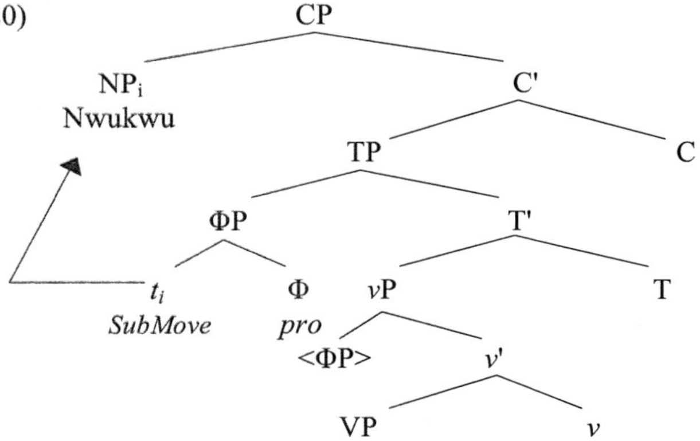

Movement of the bare NP to [Spec,CP] is triggered by the theta-theoretic requirement because the NP cannot obtain a theta-role in [Spec,*v*P].[23,24]

---

[23] We depart from Boeckx & Grohmann (2004) in that this kind of movement is related to theta-role assignment and the Φ-feature bearing element is Φ, not D.

[24] As gratefully pointed out by an anonymous reviewer of *University of Maryland Working Papers in Linguistics 16*, our analysis is compatible with both an Attract-

Note that *pro* and its antecedent are distinct syntactic entities and they form a constituent upon First Merge. The movement of ΦP to [Spec,TP] is triggered by Φ-features on T (Agree). Note further that the NP undergoes SubMove to [Spec,CP] where it gets a theta-role 'aboutness', so it fulfills Full Interpretation. Consequently, the chain <*nwukwu, pro*> induces only a D-linked reading like many other *wh*-resumption or *wh*-clitic doubling constructions (Boeckx 2003, Boeckx & Grohmann 2004, Grohmann 2006, Hirose 2003, Jaeger 2003, 2004, Kallulli 2005).[25]

A similar explanation is possible for (21). In (21), a non-case-marked object *wh*-phrase occurs in a left periphery position, and only D-linked interpretation is induced.

(21) Nwukwu Yenghi-ka manna-ss-ni?
who Yenghi-NOM meet-PST-Q
"Who is such that Yenghi meet (him/her)?"

Under our analysis, the object *wh*-phrase *nwukwu* in (21) is LDed. Then

---

and a Greed-based approach. If an Attract-based framework is assumed, movement in (20) is explained in the following way: CP attracts the closet nominal element. In this case, ΦP does not intervene: It is not active because it already has its theta-role. Under a Greed-based framework, movement in (20) is legitimate: The NP doesn't have a theta-role and hence it is greedy. Thus, it should undergo movement.

[25] *Wh*-phrases in Korean generally cannot variable-bind 'overt' pronouns (cf. Montalbetti 1984, Hong 1985, Boeckx 2004). Perhaps for this reason, a resumptive pronoun bound by the dislocated WH cannot be overt (but must be *pro*) in Korean, as shown in (i).

(i) * Nwukwu$_i$ ku-ka$_i$ Yenghi-lul manna-ss-ni?
who he-NOM Yenghi-ACC meet-PST-Q
"Who is such that he met Mary?"

The overt pronoun constraint seems to come into play in Greek CLLD, as observed in Alexopoulou, Doron & Heycock (2003: 342).

(ii) * **Pion** **ton** ides?
who.ACC.MASC CL.MASC saw.2.SG
"Who did you see (him)?"

CLLDed *wh*-phrases in Greek typically resist coindexing with resumptive pronouns shown in (ii). In fn. 6, however, the authors note that D-linking could improve the acceptability of clitics in *wh*-questions in Greek. Korean, in contrast, seems to differ from Greek in that even D-linked WH's do not allow an overt resumption, as shown in (i).

nwukwu undergoes SubMove, leaving *pro* in its base-generated position shown in (22), and the D-linked property of dislocated *wh*-object results.

(22) [$_{CP}$ [$_{NP}$ Nwukwu]$_i$ [$_{TP}$ Yenghi-ka$_j$ [$_{vP}$ t_j [t_i *pro*]…] T] C]

SubMove

Finally, let us consider the projection of the DP with ΦP. Here too, the bare NP should move for a theta-theoretic reason. However, if the NP SubMoves, it will result in stranding the affixal D, i.e. case marker, in Korean, and hence, it will yield Stray Affix Filter violation (Lasnik 1981), as seen in (23a).

(23) a. * [$_{CP}$ [$_{NP}$ Nwukwu]$_i$ [$_{TP}$ Yenghi-ka$_j$ [$_{T'}$ [$_{vP}$ [$_{v'}$ t_j [$_{DP}$ [$_{ΦP}$ t_i *pro*] **lul**]]] T]] C]

SubMove

b. * [$_{CP}$ [$_{DP}$ [$_{ΦP}$ [Nwukwu] *pro*]-lul]$_i$ [$_{TP}$ Yenghi-ka$_j$ [$_{T'}$ [$_{vP}$ t_j [$_{v'}$ t_i]] T]] C]

Move

Notice that pied-piping movement of the whole DP, as shown in (23b), results in theta-theoretic problems since *nwukwu* in (23b) cannot get a theta-role inside the DP. Thus, if a D is projected/pronounced, the ΦP layer cannot be projected even with the null Φ, i.e. *pro*. It implies that the nominal structures that project the DP with ΦP headed by a null *pro* are theoretically absent in Korean. Thus, the bare and only bare subject/dislocated-WHs are predicted to be enforced to be D-linked, while case-marked-WHs, lacking Φ-layer, are neutral for D-linking, as shown in (24).

(24) a. Nwukwu-lul Yenghi-ka manna-ss-ni?
who Yenghi-NOM meet-PST-Q
"Who did Yenghi meet?"

b. [$_{CP}$ [$_{DP}$ Nwukwu-lul]$_i$ [$_{TP}$ Yenghi-ka$_j$ [$_{T'}$ [$_{vP}$ t_j [$_{v'}$ t_i]] T]] C]

Move

As shown in (24b), the DP *nwukwu-lul* doesn't have a Φ-layer. Hence, non-D-linked reading of WH is also available when a case marker is present, a crucial contrast now we can derive naturally. Further, we can correctly capture the fact that Φ-layer with *pro* and overt cases are in complementary distribution, another welcome result.

4. Resumption Strategy and Dislocation Typology

4.1. Two Types of LD in Korean

A couple of questions arise at this point concerning the pronunciation possibility of Φ, namely, overt resumption. Suppose we pronounce Φ of a bare ΦP, then (25a) might result. However, this sentence is not acceptable in contrast with case-marked resumption of LD in (25b):

(25) a. ?* Mary, ne-nun ecey **kyay** po-ass-ni?
Mary you-TOP yesterday her see-PST-Q
b. Mary, ne-nun ecey **kyay-lul** po-ass-ni?
Mary you-TOP yesterday her-ACC see-PST-Q
lit. "Mary, did you see her?"

The deviance of bare overt resumption in (25a) is reminiscent of blocking resumption in the context where movement is possible, as noted in Hornstein (2006). He advances that resumption is possible only as a last resort where movement is blocked.[26] Along the similar lines, we propose that covert realization of the functional category Φ blocks its overt realization by economy considerations. Thus, (25a) seems to be blocked by its covert resumptive counterpart (26) where Φ is unpronounced and indicated as *pro*.

(26) Mary, ne-nun ecey *pro* po-ass-ni?
Mary you-TOP yesterday see-PST-Q
lit. "Mary, did you see her?"

(25b), on the other hand, is not blocked by (26) since the numeration is different:[27] Note that a D-projection is present in (25b) to host an

---

[26] Hornstein (2006) proposes that derivations with bound pronouns like (ib) compete with those containing reflexives like (ia):

(i) a. $John_1$ likes $himself_1$.
b. * $John_1$ likes him_1.

He suggests that (ia) and (ib) have a common numeration: namely, {*John*, *likes*}. Thus, (ia) and (ib) are comparable under the assumption that the reflexive/pronoun in his system cannot be part of the numeration of either sentence in (i).

[27] The analysis advanced here assumes that numeration contains lexical elements and 'categorical features'. Hornstein (2006: 64) notes that (ib) is blocked by (ia)

accusative case, which is lacking in (26).[28]

We, however, suggest that (25b) cannot be derived through SubMove of the bare NP *Mary* in the following fashion.

---

since they have the same numeration (NB: Obligatory control structure (ia) is derived via movement under Hornstein's analysis.)

(i) a. Harry hates [*PRO* kissing Mary]. = Harry$_1$ hates [t_1 kissing Mary].
 b. Harry$_1$ hates him$_1$ kissing Mary.

Hornstein (2006: fn. 26) further indicates that categorial difference may also yield separate numerations as shown in the following example which is not blocked by the convergent (ia).

(ii) John$_1$ hated his$_1$ having to leave the party.

Hornstein (2006), following Pires (2001), notes that ACC-ing gerunds are essentially clauses, while POSS-ings have an additional DP layer of structure. Further he suggests that this additional nominal layer is part of the numeration of POSS-ings but not PRO-gerunds, and hence PRO gerunds shouldn't block POSS-ings since these two constructions have two distinct numerations to compare. In line with this reasoning, D is essentially part of numeration in Korean, too. Hence, the example in (26) doesn't block the one in (25b).

[28] The following contrast is explained along the similar vein.

(i) Mary$_i$, na-nun *pro$_i$* coha.
 Mary I-TOP like
 "Mary, I like her."

(ii) a. *? Mary$_i$ na-nun ku papo$_i$ coha.
 Mary I-TOP that idiot like
 b. ? Mary$_i$ na-nun ku papo$_i$-ka coha.
 Mary I-TOP that idiot-NOM like
 "Mary, I like that idiot."

Ku papo "that idiot" in (ii) is an epithet and the covert realization like (i) blocks overt realization in (iia). In the case of (iib) the numeration is different since the resumptive epithet structure is a DP. (NB: The resumption structure in (i) is a bare ΦP.) Thus, (iib) is not blocked by (i) in contrast to (iia).

(27) *illicit derivation*

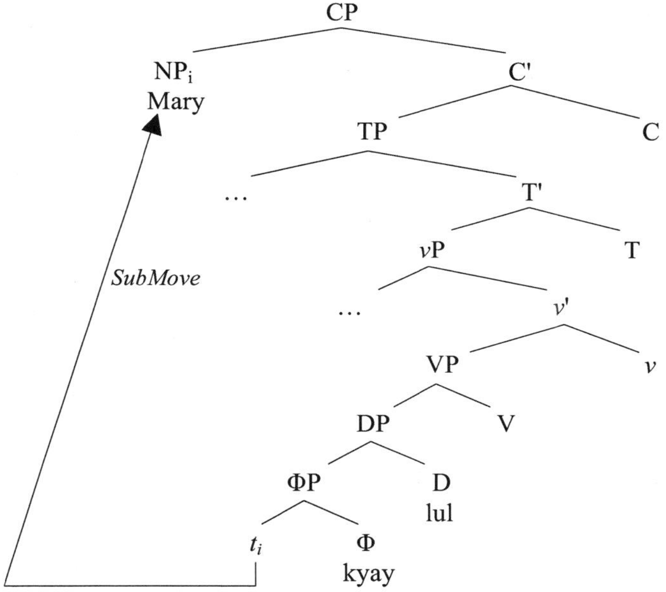

Following Howard Lasnik's suggestion (p.c.), we speculate that movement of an NP out of the DP shown in (27) is barred since DP is an inherited barrier by the blocking category ΦP.[29,30] Here, resumption as a last resort applies to save the illicit derivation in (27). (This is equivalent to intrusive pronouns or true resumption in previous literature; see Boeckx (2003) for extensive discussion.) Thus, the resumptive (or intrusive) pronoun *kyay* "he/she" is inserted in (25b), and the corresponding structural representation should be:

(27') $[_{CP}$ **[Mary$_i$]** ne-nun$_j$ $[_{TP}$ t_j $[_{T'}$ $[_{vP}$ t_j $[_{v'}$ $[_{DP}$ $[_{\Phi P}$ **kyay$_i$**]-lul]]] T]] C]

In (27'), *Mary* is base-generated in the left edge, linked to the resumption via binding. Thus, subextraction of an NP is not possible whenever a DP is

---

[29] See relevant details of barriers in Chomsky (1986). Note that ΦP doesn't seem to be L-marked inside DP since Case marker *lul* in Korean is not 'lexical' by assumption.

[30] Cyclic movements of NP via [Spec,ΦP] and [Spec,DP] might be barred by independent reasons. See Yoshida (2003) and Cho & Lee (2004) for related discussion.

layered, and the only licit option to license the dislocated NP is base-generation along with true resumption in-situ. This implies that overt resumptive LD in Korean can be a different kind in contrast to covert resumptive LD induced by Φ-projection.

There seem to be at least three distinct types of LD cross-linguistically: hanging topic LD (HTLD), contrastive LD (CLD), and clitic LD (CLLD), as illustrated below (see Grohmann 2003 and Alexiadou 2005).

(28) a. *Dutch HTLD* (van Riemsdijk 1997: 3)
Marie, dat wijf vermoord ik nog eens.
Mary that bitch killed I one day
"Mary, I killed that bitch one day."

b. *German CLD* (Grohmann 2003: 134)
Diesen Mann, den kenne ich nicht.
this.ACC man that-one.ACC know I not
"This man, I don't know [him]."

c. *Greek CLLD* (Alexiadou 2005: 669)
Ton Jani den ton ksero.
the.ACC John.ACC NEG CL.ACC know-1SG
"John, I don't know him."

Alexiadou (2005) points out that the resumptive element is crucial in the classification of LD across languages or even within a language. As can be seen in the HTLD construction (28a), the role of the resumptive element is performed by an epithet. By contrast, in the CLD construction, the resumptive element can be a regular personal pronoun or a demonstrative pronoun, as seen in (28b). In the CLLD construction, the resumptive element is a clitic pronoun, which is found in languages such as Italian, Romanian, Spanish, Hebrew, Arabic, and Greek. In addition to properties of resumptive elements, their positions and the presence of connectivity effects are also important issues in classifying LD constructions.

What kinds of LD are Korean ones among these types? First, consider the following two types of LD in Spanish. Escobar (1997: 233) analyzes (29a) as a discourse topic construction and, in contrast, (29b) as a sentence topic construction: That is, (29a) parallels HTLD, while (29b) parallels CLLD in Spanish.

(29) a. Juan, lo conozco.
"John, I know him."

b. A Juan, lo conozco.
"John, I know."

Note that the sentential topic must bear a case marker in Spanish shown in (29b). As indicated in Escobar (1997: 239), the *A*-marker in Spanish generally is a realization of an accusative case. Thus, the presence or absence of the *A*-marker explicitly discriminates the two constructions.[31] Evidence for the distinction is provided in (30): Only in the HTLD construction can the clitic be followed by a matching strong pronoun, as in (30a), but not in CLLD in (30b).

(30) a. Juan$_i$, lo conozco a él$_i$.
Juan CL know.1SG A him
b. * A Juan$_i$, lo conozco a él$_i$.
A Juan CL know.1SG A him
"John, I know him."

We propose that there are at least two types of LD in Korean: HTLD and CLLD.[32] If the resumption is overt as a pronoun or an epithet, it is HTLD, whereas when the resumption is covert, it should be CLLD in Korean on a par with two types of LD in Spanish, as seen in (29-30).[33] More specifically, dislocated NPs in CLLD are derived via SubMove leaving 'unpronounced' resumptive *pro* in Φ in Korean. CLLD in Korean displays typical movement properties such as (strong) island sensitivity.

---

[31] The default case in Spanish seems to be nominative, as indicated in the HTLD with dislocated pronouns (Escobar 1997: 271):

(i) a. * Mi, no me quieren.
me not me want
b. Yo, no me quieren.
I not me want
"Me, they don't want me."

In English LD, as shown in the English translation of (ib), the left-hand pronoun is accusative, which indicates default Case realization. In contrast, the left-hand pronoun in Spanish must be (default) nominative parallel to the German default Case (see Grohmann 2003).

[32] We set aside instances of C(ontrastive)LD in Korean here. We believe that *nun*-marked topicalization is the one (see Ahn & Cho 2006a and Hong 2005 for full discussion). We also sidestep the nature of scrambling operation in Korean. See Ahn & Cho (2005b) for some related discussion.

[33] We assume that the head of epithets and pronouns are base-generated in the head of ΦP based on the assumption that epithets are pronominal (cf. Jackendoff 1969, 1972, Dubinsky & Hamilton 1998 and others). Epithets can function as resumptives in other languages, too. See Boeckx (2003).

(31) *Island Sensitivity*[34]

* Nwukwu$_i$ ne-nun ecey Chelswu-ka t_i mannan
who you-TOP yesterday Chelswu-NOM met
sasil-ul alko sip-ni?
fact-ACC knew want-Q
"Who do you want to know the fact that Chelswu met?"

The ill-formedness in (31) implicates that bare *wh*-LD, namely, CLLD involves movement.

Connectivity effects further show that the bare WHs in left peripheral positions undergo movement from sentence-medial positions: Scope reconstruction (32) and binding reconstruction (33). Further note that although a part of idiomatic chunks is LDed (34), idiomatic interpretation is retained, which exhibits a movement property of (non-*wh*) CLLD.

(32) *Connectivity #1: Scope*

Mwe$_i$ nwu-ka t_i ilk-ess-ni? *what > who, who > what*
what who-NOM read-PST-Q
"Who read what?"

(33) *Connectivity #2: Binding*

[Selo$_i$-uy chinkwu]$_j$ nwu-ka t_j chingchanha-yss-ni?
each.other-GEN friend who-NOM praise-PST-Q
"Who praised each other's friend?"

---

[34] As noted in Hornstein (2006: 58), resumptive pronouns can ameliorate unacceptable sentences:

(i) a. * The man$_i$ who you told me that t_i was kissing a dog…
b. The man$_i$ who you told me that he$_i$ was kissing a dog…

A question that arises at this point is whether a resumptive pronoun can ameliorate island violation of (31). Consider (ii).

(ii) * Nwukwu$_i$ ne-nun ecey Chelswu-ka kyay$_i$ mannan
who you-TOP yesterday Chelswu-NOM him met
sasil-ul alko sip-ni?
fact-ACC knew want-Q
"Who do you want to know the fact that Chelswu met?"

The sentence (ii), however, is independently ruled out since *wh*-phrases in Korean cannot variable-bind overt resumptive pronouns as noted in fn. 25.

(34) *Connectivity #3: Idioms*
a. Son Yenghi cham khu-ta.
hand Yenghi really big-DEC
"Yenghi is generous."
b. Pal Yenghi cham nelp-ta.
foot Yenghi really wide-DEC
"Yenghi has a large acquaintance."

In sum, this type of LD including *wh*-LD in Korean patterns alike with clitic doubling and CLLD constructions in other languages, as discussed in Grohmann (2006).

By contrast, dislocated NPs in HTLD are claimed to be base-generated in Korean, and bind the resumptive pronoun. Non-*wh*-LD (i.e. referential LD) with overt resumption in Korean exhibits typical non-movement (i.e. base-generation) property of dislocated elements:

(35) *No Island Sensitivity*
? Yenghi$_i$ ne-nun ecey Chelswu-ka kyay$_i$-lul/
Yenghi you-TOP yesterday Chelswue-NOM he-ACC/
ku ai$_i$-lul mannan sasil-ul alko sip-ni?
the kid-ACC met fact-ACC knew want-Q
"As for Yenghi$_i$, do you want to know the fact that Chelswu met her$_i$?"

Island insensitivity in (35) supports our claim that in this type of LD, the sentence-initial NPs do not undergo movement.

Furthermore, observe that connectivity effects disappear in this type of LD, as shown in (36-38).

(36) *No Connectivity #1: Scope*
Manhun chayk$_i$ nwu-ka ku kestul$_i$-ul ilk-ess-ni?
many book who-NOM the thing-ACC read-PST-Q
"As for the many books, who read them?"

(Note that (36) only allows the scope interpretation *many* > WH.)

(37) *No Connectivity #2: Binding*
* [Selo$_1$-uy chinkwu]$_2$ nwu$_1$-ka kyaytul$_2$-ul chingchanha-yss-ni?
each.other-GEN friend who-NOM them-ACC praise-PST-Q
"As for each other's friend, who praised them?"

(38) *No Connectivity #1: Idioms*

a. * Son Yenghi ku ke-ka cham khu-ta.
hand Yenghi the thing-NOM really big-DEC
"Yenghi is generous." ← *impossible reading*

b. * Pal Yenghi ku ke-ka cham nelp-ta.
foot Yenghi the thing-NOM really wide-DEC
"Yenghi has a large acquaintance." ← *impossible reading*

Thus, (36) is not ambiguous, namely the fronted QP takes widest scope, binding reconstruction doesn't occur in (37), and idiom chunks cannot be separated as in (38).

This type of LD functions more like a discourse-topic, as speculated by Saito (1985).[35,36] Absence of multiplicity shown in (39) and restriction to root contexts in (40) further support our analysis that this type LD exhibits HTLD property.

---

[35] Non-*wh*-LD (i.e. referential LD) without overt resumption in Korean, however, may give rise to a dual status of movement and base-generation. For example, in an island context, connectivity effects may not occur, as shown in (i) (see Aoun, Choueiri & Hornstein 2001 for related phenomena in Lebanese Arabic).

(i) ?* [Selo$_i$–uy chinkwu]$_j$ ne-nun ecey Chelswu-wa
each.other-GEN friend you-TOP yesterday Chelswu-and
Yenghi$_i$-ka t_j mannan sasil-ul alko sip-ni?
Yengi-NOM met fact-ACC knew want-Q
"Do you want to know the fact that Chelswu and Yenghi met each other's friend?"

This indicates that non-*wh*-LD with *pro* resumption can be either HTLD or CLLD in Korean.

[36] The *wh*-LD in Korean seems to exhibit radical reconstruction effects in the sense of Saito (1989): Namely, *wh*-LD in Korean patterns with long-distance *wh*-scrambling in one crucial respect (in many respects, however, they do not parallel scrambling).

(i) a. Mwe$_i$-lul Chelswu-nun [Yenghi-ka t_i sa-ss-nunci]
what-ACC Chelswu-TOP Yenghi-NOM buy-PST-QC
alkoiss-ta.
knew-DEC
"Chelswu knew what Yenghi bought."

b. Mwe$_i$ Chelswu-nun [Yenghi-ka t_i sa-ss-nunci] alkoiss-ta.
what Chelswu-TOP Yenghi-NOM buy-PST-QC knew-DEC
"Chelswu knew what Yenghi bought."

(39) *No Multiplicity*
* Ku chayk$_i$ Yenghi nay-ka ecey ku ke$_i$-lul cwuess-ni?
the book Yenghi I-NOM yesterday the thing-ACC gave-Q?
"As for the book, did I give it to Yenghi?"

(40) *No Embedded Dislocation*
* Ne-nun Yenghi Chelswu-ka kyay-lul mannassta-ko
you-TOP Yenghi Chelswu-NOM her-ACC met-C
sayngkakha-ni?
think-Q
intended "Do you think that as for Yenghi, Chelswu met her?"

Under the assumption that the position for the HTLD in Korean is restricted to one base-generated position per sentence, the absence of multiplicity in (39) and ban on embedded dislocation in (40) are accounted for.[37]

4.2. Difference between Japanese LD and Korean LD

In this sub-section, we discuss impossibility of bare *wh*-subjects and dislocated *wh*-objects in Japanese. Japanese LD seems to pattern with Spanish CLLD at least in one respect: Only (overtly) case-marked NP can be dislocated as shown in (41) (recall the obligatory presence of *A*-marker in Spanish CLLD as discussed in (29)).

(41) **Dare-?*(o)** John-ga nagutta no?
who-(ACC) John-NOM hit Q
"Who did John hit?"

[37] By contrast, CLLD in Korean shows multiplicity:

(i) Ku chayk$_i$ nwukwu$_j$ ney-ka ecey t_j t_i cwu-ess-ni?
the book who you-NOM yesterday give-PST-Q
"As for the book, to whom did you give it?"

Further, CLLD in Korean can also selectively take place in some non-root contexts:

(ii) Ne-nun nwukwu$_i$ Chelswu-ka ecey t_i mannan sasil-ul
you-TOP who Chelswu-NOM yesterday met fact-ACC
alkoiss-ni?
know-Q
intended "Who do you know the fact that Chelswu met yesterday?"

In other words, if a case marker is not realized on a left-hand phrase, the construction must be HTLD in Japanese. Thus, apparent case marker drop in subjects and dislocated phrases in Japanese can all be treated as instances of HTLD. However, *wh*-phrases cannot be hanging (discourse) topics for semantic reasons, and hence they must always bear overt cases in Japanese (and perhaps in Spanish, too). By contrast, in Korean LD, dislocated NPs must be bare whether they are HTLD or CLLD.

Saito (1985: chapter 4) observes that in Japanese, NP-topicalization (NP-*wa*) can be base-generated while PP-topicalization (PP-*wa*) always exhibits movement properties. He suggests that only NP-topic can be related to *pro* in-situ, while this option may not be available for PP-topic since PP-*pro* might not exist in Japanese.[38] We may reinterpret this asymmetry in the following way. SubMove is available only for NP-topic (presumably movement of a bare NP to [Spec,ToP] (*wa*); see Kayne 1994 and Whitman 2001 for *wa*-projection), but not PP-topic since ΦP, hence Φ-*pro*, is licensed only with the NP-layer it selects (this idea obviously recaptures the presence/absence of NP-*pro*/PP-*pro* advanced in Saito 1985).

Another correlated interesting observation is made by Hoji (1990: chapter 5). He observes that a bare NP-cleft in Japanese does not exhibit movement properties, whereas case-marked NP-cleft does (see Fukaya & Hoji 1999 for further discussion). He suggests that the bare NP-cleft is associated with *pro* in-situ. We can also reinterpret this fact in following fashion: the bare and only bare NP-cleft seems to be a partial instance of SubMove, and hence, it only displays limited movement properties in Japanese since the construction is ambivalent for HTLD and CLLD in Japanese. Korean cleft constructions below, however, do not appear to display this kind of asymmetry since case-marked NP-cleft is generally barred in Korean.

(42) Chelswu-ka ecey manna-n kes-un Yenghi-(*lul) ita.
Chelswu-NOM yesterday meet-REL thing-TOP Yenghi-(ACC) is
"It was Yenghi who Chelswu met yesterday."

Thus, there's another difference lying between Korean and Japanese with respect to presence/absence of case markers in Clefts.

[38] See, however, Watanabe (2003) and Nishigauchi & Fujii (2006) for alternative treatments.

5. Summary and Further Implications

To recap, we attempt to give a new analysis of distribution of subject-object asymmetries on absence of case markers in Korean. We argue that bare NPs can occur in the complement position of V since it can be a part of a syntactic complex predicate. As a result, a non-case-marked object nominal can freely occur without any semantic restriction whether it is *wh* or non-*wh*. We postulate a ΦP layer within the nominal structure of the Korean DP. With this fine structure of nominals, we account for the following novel facts: subject *wh* and dislocated object *wh* without case markers must have D-linked interpretations. We claim that bare *wh*-phases in derived positions are CLLDed nominals which undergo SubMove leaving unpronounced resumptive *pro* that heads Φ-projection. Our proposal may correlate with the new typology of dislocation in Korean: namely, HTLD vs. CLLD in connection to the pronunciation of resumption. HTLD (true resumption) emerges only when CLLD (resumption-by-stranding in the sense of Boeckx 2003) is blocked. Thus, the instances of Korean LD are not special at all, but they are just possible subtypes of LD derivable from UG species.

There are some implications of our proposal. First, our analysis crucially takes a step against postulation of a null D in Korean. One may possibly postulate a null D to account for the asymmetries of overt/covert distinction of cases in Korean. One possible candidate (as suggested by Masaya Yoshida, p.c.) is positing a null D that has a feature [+specific]. Thus, in Korean under this view, there are two sorts of Ds: overt D is neutral for specificity, while covert D is argued to be always specific (putting aside the status of a bare NP in complement positions). Hence, the bare dislocated/subject-*wh* in Korean is predicted to be D-linked under this view since it is linked to [+specific] D which is always phonetically null.

However, this view encounters at least two problems: one is empirical, and the other is theoretical. Empirically, unlike our LD analysis, this null D view cannot account for the deviance in (2) repeated here. Note that it is not obvious why a [+specific] null D cannot occur here on this subject.

(2) Sue-lul **Mary-*(ka)** manna-ss-e.
Sue-ACC Mary-(NOM) meet-PST-DEC
"Mary met Sue."

Theoretically, the null D approach bears a burden to explain why null Ds in Korean pattern differently from the ones in other languages. As widely catalogued in Landau (2005), the distribution of null Ds (in fact, null X^0 in general including null P and C) in many languages is heavily restricted: Namely, they cannot occur in subject/dislocated positions. Note that under the null D view of Korean, [+specific] null Ds must take place only in the environment of subjects (leaving aside the counterexample in (2)) and dislocated positions, which is exactly contrary to the facts in other languages. Why, then, is Korean so special in this regard? We see no convincing reasons to take the opposite route for Korean unless there is some compelling independent evidence.

The structural difference between bare NP subjects and bare NP objects correctly predicts the high occurrence rate of bare NPs in complement positions, as observed in the wide range of conversational data (H. Lee 2006). Given that bare NPs in a complement position can freely occur as part of a syntactic predicate, it is not conditioned by any discourse restrictions. By contrast, bare NPs in non-complement positions that are derived through movement are conditioned by discourse constraints. If bare NPs function as base-generated sentence-topic, their distribution is closely conditioned by their information factors. Hence, unlike bare NPs in complement position, those in derived positions are distributionally more restricted (see D.-Y. Lee 2002, Ohara 2001, Shimojo 2006). The LD analysis of bare NPs in non-complement positions also predicts that bare NP subjects are sensitive to person information (H. Lee 2006). Given that 1st and 2nd person subjects are given information in the discourse, they are more likely to function as LDed nominals that trigger D-linked or topical reading, compared with 3rd person subjects. This analysis further explains the fact that definite subjects exhibit the higher rate of case deletion than low definite ones (see H. Lee 2006, K. Lee 2002, Masunaga 1988, Ono et al. 2000, Yatabe 1999) since definite expressions referring to individuals already known to the hearer are more likely to function as sentence topics or as LDed nominals.

This analysis also makes a correct prediction about bare NP subjects in specific/non-specific contexts.

(43) (Yeytnaley) han/etten namca-*(ka) sal-ass-ta.
long.time.ago a/a.certain man-(NOM) live-PST-DEC
"(A long time ago) there was a man lived."

In (43), nominative case marker must be pronounced since the modifier *han/etten* can license only non-specific nominals. This is predicted under our analysis since LDed subject, i.e. bare NP subject, which is inherently specific or D-linked cannot co-occur with non-specific marker semantically.

Note, however, that this restriction doesn't apply to the non-occurrence of accusative case. Thus, in the following example, accusative case on the object can be freely missing with non-specific modifier.

(44) (Yeytnaley) Mary-ka han/etten namca-(lul) manna-ass-ta.
long.time.ago Mary-NOM a/a.certain man-(ACC) meet-PST-DEC
"(Long time ago) Mary met a man."

Note also that as observed in previous discourse studies, overt realization of accusative case in (44) may induce a 'focal' reading (Jun 2005, E.-S. Ko 2000, S.Lee2006, Matsuda 1995). By contrast, overt realization of NOM in (43) does not necessarily give rise to a focal interpretation. This minimal difference may imply that our syntactic treatment of NOM/ACC asymmetry is on the right track. In other words, the presence of NOM in (43) is compulsory under our analysis unlike that of ACC in (44), and hence overt NOM should cover wider range of discourse information in contrast to overt ACC considering pragmatic division of labor.

Similar contrasts seem to be found in ACC variation in Kannada. Lidz (2006) observes that ACC-marked objects receive a specific interpretation, but only when this morphological marking is optional (this is the case with inanimate direct objects). When the ACC morpheme is obligatory, specificity effects are positional and are not due to the presence of the morpheme (this is the case with animate direct objects, for instance). In this case, additional morphology is required in order to achieve the specific interpretation. In Korean, the morphological marker *nun* (often called Topic marker) is widely employed in subject positions to make semantic/pragmatic distinction from NOM, instead of overt/covert NOM distinction. The morphological marker *nun*, however, occurs only in certain very limited contexts (often called Contrastive Focus) in object positions since we can exploit overt/covert ACC distinction here quite freely for semantic/pragmatic purposes.

In sum, our main concern in this paper was two-fold. First, we tried to tie some seemingly unrelated phenomena in Korean with other languages, namely, non-case-marked (subject/dislocated) WHs in Korean and *wh*-resumption or *wh*-clitic doubling in other languages. Second, we attempted to build up a UG-based approach to account for the nature of these new phenomena in Korean via the operation SubMove and finer nominal structures postulating a Φ-layer under DP. Our analysis sheds fresh light on parametric language variations (Korean vs. Japanese on the distribution of bare *wh*-NPs, for example) along with new insights on semantic/pragmatic implications concerning presence and absence of case markers.

References

Ahn, H.-D. 1988. Preliminary remarks on Korean NP. In E.-J. Baek (ed.), *Papers from the Sixth International Conference on Korean Linguistics*. Seoul: Hanshin Publishing Co., 1-15.

Ahn, H.-D. 1996. A study of syntactic word-formation. In H.-D. Ahn, M.-Y. Kang, Y.-S. Kim & S. Lee (eds.), *Morphosyntax in Generative Grammar*. Seoul: Hankuk Publishing Co., 1-21.

Ahn, H.-D. 1999. Notes on case deletion. In Y.-W. Kim, I.-K. Kim & J.-W. Park (eds.), *Linguistic Investigation: In Honor of In-Seok Yang*. Seoul: Hankuk Publishing Co., 1-16.

Ahn, H.-D. & S. Cho. 2005a. The emergence of silent Cs and Ds in Korean: Distribution and licensing. In K. Choi & C. Yim (eds.), *Ellipsis in Minimalism*. Seoul: Hankuk Publishing Co., 1-12.

Ahn, H.-D. & S. Cho. 2005b. On scope asymmetries in fragments. *Studies in Generative Grammar* 15, 661-678.

Ahn, H.-D. & S. Cho. 2006a. *Wh*-topics and unpronounced case markers. *Studies in Generative Grammar* 16. 61-90.

Ahn, H.-D. & S. Cho. 2006b. Unpronounced case markers and apparent subject-object asymmetry. *Studies in Modern Grammar* 43, 55-80.

Ahn, H. & S. Cho. 2006c. Layered nominal structures: implications for caseless nominals. *Korean Journal of Linguistics* 31, 165-185.

Alexiadou. A. 2005. Left dislocation including CLLD. In M. Everaert & H. van Riemsdijk (eds.), *Blackwell Companion to Syntax* vol. 2. Malden, MA: Blackwell, 669-699.

Alexopoulou, T., E. Doron & C. Heycock. 2003. Broad subjects and clitic left dislocation. In D. Adger, C. de Cat & G. Tsoulas (eds.), *Peripheries*. Dordrecht: Kluwer, 329-358.

Anagnostopoulou, E., H. van Riemsdijk & F. Zwarts (eds.). 1997. *Materials on Left Dislocation*. Amsterdam: John Benjamins.

Aoun, J., L. Choueiri & N. Hornstein. 2001. Resumption, movement, and derivational economy. *Linguistic Inquiry* 32, 371-403.

Aydemir. Y. 2004. Are Turkish preverbal bare nouns syntactic arguments? *Linguistic Inquiry* 35, 465-474.

Beck, S. & S.-S. Kim. 1997. On wh- and operator scope in Korean. *Journal of East Asian Linguistics* 6, 339-384.

Belletti, A. 2005. Extend doubling and the VP periphery. *Probus* 17, 1-36.

Boeckx, C. 2003. *Islands and Chains*. Amsterdam: John Benjamins.

Boeckx, C. 2004. Free word order in minimalist syntax. *Folia Linguistics* 37, 77-102.

Boeckx, C. & K.K. Grohmann. 2004. SubMove: Towards a unified account of scrambling and D-linking. In D. Adger, C. de Cat & G. Tsoulas (eds.), *Peripheries*. Dordrecht: Kluwer, 241-257.

Cagri, I. 2005. *Minimality and Turkish Relative Clauses*. Ph.D. diss., University of Maryland, College Park.

Cho, S. & W. Lee. 2004. Extraction from NPs. *Studies in Modern Grammar* 37, 77-92.

Choi, K. 2005. Unrealization of case [in Korean]. Ms., Kwangwoon University.

Chomsky, N. 1986. *Barriers*. Cambridge, MA: MIT Press.

Chomsky, N. 1995. *The Minimalist Program*. Cambridge, MA: MIT Press.

Chomsky, N. 2000. Minimalist inquiries: The framework. In R. Martin, D. Michaels & J. Uriagereka (eds.), *Step by Step: Essays on Minimalist Syntax in Honor of Howard Lasnik*. Cambridge, MA: MIT Press, 89-155.

Chomsky, N. 2001. Derivation by phase. In M. Kenstowicz (ed.), *Ken Hale: A Life in Language*. Cambridge, MA: MIT Press, 1-52.

Chung, S. & W. Ladusaw. 2003. *Restriction and Saturation*. Cambridge, MA: MIT Press.

Dayal, V. 2003. A semantics for pseudo-incorporation. Ms., Rutgers University, New Brunswick, NJ.

Dubinsky, S. & R. Hamilton. 1998. Epithets as antilogophoric pronouns. *Linguistic Inquiry* 29, 685-693.

Escobar, L. 1997. Clitic left dislocation and other relatives. In E. Anagnostopoulou, H. van Riemsdijk & F. Zwarts (eds.), *Materials on Left Dislocation*. Amsterdam: John Benjamins, 233-273.

Fukaya, T. & H. Hoji. 1999. Stripping and sluicing in Japanese and some implications. *Proceedings of WCCFL* 18, 145-158.

Grohmann, K.K. 2003. *Prolific Domains*. Amsterdam: John Benjamins.

Grohmann, K.K. 2006. Top issues in questions: Topics – topicalization – topicalizabilty. In L.L.-S. Cheng & N. Corver (ed.), Wh-*Movement Moving On*. Cambridge, MA: MIT Press, 249-288.

Hazout, I. 2004. The syntax of existential constructions. *Linguistic Inquiry* 35, 393-430.

Hirose, T. 2003. The syntax of D-linking. *Linguistic Inquiry* 34, 499-506.

Hoji, H. 1990. Theories of anaphora and aspects of Japanese syntax. Ms, University of Southern California, Los Angeles.

Hong, S. 1985. *A and A' Binding in Korean and English: Government-Binding Parameters*. Ph.D. diss., University of Connecticut, Storrs.

Hong, Y.-T. 1994. Incorporation theory and the distribution of case morphemes. *Studies in Generative Grammar* 4, 1-43.

Hong, Y.-T. 2004. Omission and absence of case morpheme in Korean [in

Korean]. *French Language Education* 18, 295-314.
Hong, Y.-T. 2005. A unified approach to the so-called topic particle "nun" morphemes [in Korean]. *Studies in Generative Grammar* 15, 397-413.
Hornstein, N. 2001. *Move! A Minimalist Theory of Construal*. Malden, MA: Blackwell.
Hornstein, N. 2006. Pronouns in a minimalist setting. *University of Maryland Working Papers in Linguistics* 14, 47-80.
Jackendoff, R. 1969. *Some Rules of Semantic Interpretation for English*. Ph.D. diss., MIT, Cambridge.
Jackendoff, R. 1972. *Semantic Interpretation in Generative Grammar*. Cambridge: MIT Press.
Jaeger, T.F. 2003. Topics first! In- and outside of Bulgarian *wh*-interrogatives. *Proceedings of the 10th International Conference on HPSG*, 181-202.
Jaeger, T.F. 2004. Topicality and superiority in Bulgarian *wh*-questions. *Proceedings of FASL* 12, 207-228.
Jun, Y. 2005. On so-called specificity markers in Korean [in Korean]. *Korean Journal of Linguistics* 30, 715-743.
Kallulli, D. 2005. D-linking, resumption and null objects. Paper presented at the conference *Sound of Silence: Empty Elements in Syntax and Phonology*, University of Tilburg.
Kayne, R. 1994. *The Antisymmetry of Syntax*. Cambridge, MA: MIT Press.
Kayne, R. 2005. *Movement and Silence*. New York: Oxford University Press.
Kim, D.-B. 1993. *The Specificity/Non-Specificity Distinction and Scrambling Theory*. Seoul: Taehaksa.
Kim, K.-S. 1999. Case-deletion in Korean. *WECOL* 9, 225-236.
Kim, Y.-H. 1998a. Overt case and covert case in Korean. *Studies in Generative Grammar* 8, 177-240.
Kim, Y.-H. 1998b. *A Minimalist Approach to Case and Word Order in Korean* [in Korean]. Ph.D. diss., Keimyung University.
Kim, Y.-J. 1991. Nominative case marking in Korean. *Studies in Generative Grammar* 2, 113-148.
Ko, E.-S. 2000. A discourse analysis of the realization of objects in Korean. *Japanese/Korean Linguistics* 9, 195-208.
Ko, S.-J. 2002. On the meaning of *ka* [in Korean]. *Korean Linguistics* 40, 221-246.
Ko, S.-J. 2004. *A Study of Particles in Modern Korean* [in Korean]. Seoul: Hankuk Publishing Co.
Kornfilt, J. 2003. Scrambling, subscrambling, and case in Turkish. In S. Karimi (ed.), *Word Order and Scrambling*. Malden, MA: Blackwell,

125-155.

Kuno, S. 1972. Functional sentence perspective: A case study from Japanese and English. *Linguistic Inquiry* 3, 269-320.

Kuno, S. 1973. *Nihon-bunpoo kenkyuu*. Tokyo: Taisyukan.

Landau, I. 2005. EPP extensions. Ms., Ben Gurion University.

Lasnik, H. 1981. Restricting the theory of transformations: A case study. In N. Hornstein & D. Lightfoot (eds.), *Explanation in Linguistics*. London: Longman, 152-173.

Lee, D.-Y. 2002. The function of the zero particle with special reference to spoken Japanese. *Journal of Pragmatics* 34, 645-682.

Lee, H. 2006. Parallel optimization in case systems: Evidence from case ellipsis in Korean. *Journal of East Asian Linguistics* 15, 69-96.

Lee, K. 2002. Nominative case marker deletion in spoken Japanese: An analysis from the perspective of information structure. *Journal of Pragmatics* 34, 683-709.

Lee, S. 2006. A pragmatic analysis of accusative case-marker deletion. *Discourse and Cognition* 13, 69-89.

Lee, W. & S. Cho. 2003. Argument scrambling and object shift. *Studies in Generative Grammar* 13, 39-59.

Lidz, J. 2006. The grammar of accusative case in Kannada. *Language* 82, 10-32.

Massam, D. 2001. Pseudo Noun Incorporation in Niuean. *Natural Language & Linguistic Theory* 19, 153-197.

Masunaga, K. 1988. Case deletion and discourse context. In W.J. Poser (ed.), *Papers from the Second International Workshop on Japanese Syntax*. Stanford, CA: CSLI Publications, 145-156.

Matsuda, K. 1995. *Variable Zero-Marking of (o) in Tokyo Japanese*. Ph.D. diss., University of Pennsylvania, Philadelphia.

Miyagawa, S. 1987. *Wa* and the *wh*-phrase. In J. Hinds, S.K. Maynard & S. Iwasaki (eds.), *Perspectives on Topicalization: The Case of Japanese "wa"*. Amsterdam: John Benjamins, 185-217.

Montalbetti, M. 1984. *After Binding: On the Interpretation of Pronouns*. Ph.D. diss., MIT, Cambridge.

Nishigauchi, T. & T. Fujii. 2006. Short answers: Ellipsis, connectivity, and island repair. Ms., Kobe Shoin Graduate School & University of Maryland, College Park.

Ohara, M. 2001. Configurationality in Japanese: How grammatical functions are determined. Ms., Shimane University.

Ono, H. 2001. EPP-driven XP Movement in Japanese. *Proceedings of WECOL '99*.

Ono, T., S. Thompson & R. Suzuki. 2000. The pragmatic nature of the so-called subject marker *ga* in Japanese: Evidence from conversation. *Discourse Studies* 2, 55-84.

Öztürk, B. 2005. *Case, Referentiality and Phrase Structure*. Amsterdam: John Benjamins.

Pesetsky, D. 1987. *Wh* in situ: Movement and unselective binding. In E. Reuland & A. ter Meulen (eds.), *The Representation of (In)definiteness*. Cambridge, MA: MIT Press, 98-129.

Pires, A. 2001. *The Syntax of Gerunds and Infinitive: Subjects, Case and Control*. Ph.D. diss., University of Maryland, College Park.

van Riemsdijk, H. 1997. Left dislocation. In E. Anagnostopoulou, H. van Riemsdijk & F. Zwarts (eds.), *Materials on Left Dislocation*. Amsterdam: John Benjamins, 1-10.

Rizzi, L. 2006. On the form of chains: Criterial positions and ECP effects. In L.L.-S. Cheng & N. Corver (eds.), Wh-*Movement Moving On*. Cambridge, MA: MIT Press, 97-134.

Saito, M. 1985. *Some Asymmetries in Japanese and Their Theoretical Implications*. Ph.D. diss., MIT, Cambridge.

Saito, M. 1989. Scrambling as semantically vacuous A'-movement. In M. Baltin & A. Kroch (eds.), *Alternative Conceptions of Phrase Structure*. Chicago: University of Chicago Press, 182-200.

Ueda, M. 1993. On the phrase structure of Japanese and English clauses. In Nobuko Hasegawa (ed.), *Japanese Syntax in Comparative Grammar*. Tokyo: Kuroshio, 9-44.

Uriagereka, J. 2000. Doubling and possession. In B. Gerlach & J. Grijzenhout (eds.), *Clitics in Phonology, Morphology and Syntax*. Amsterdam: John Benjamins, 405-431.

Watanabe, A. 2003. *Wh* and operator constructions in Japanese. *Lingua* 113, 519-558.

Whitman, J. 2001. Kayne 1994: p. 143, fn. 3. In G. Alexandrova (ed.), *The Minimalist Parameter*. Amsterdam: John Benjamins, 77-100.

Wiltschko, M. & R.-M. Déchaine. 2002. Decomposing pronouns. *Linguistic Inquiry* 33, 409-442.

Wu, J. 1999. *Syntax and Semantics of Quantification in Chinese*. Ph.D. diss., University of Maryland, College Park.

Yoshida, M. 2003. The specificity condition: PF-condition or LF-condition? Paper presented at *WCCFL XXII*, University of California, San Diego.

CHAPTER THREE

FOCUSING STRATEGIES IN CYPRIOT GREEK*

Constantina Fotiou

1. Introducing the Puzzle

This paper will investigate the expression of focus in Cypriot Greek. I will concentrate on a description of the focus system in Cypriot Greek (CG) and put it into perspective by comparing it with Standard Modern Greek (SMG), of which it might just be a variant.[1]

---

* I am particularly grateful to Kleanthes Grohmann for his supervision and support of this project, and to Ianthi-Maria Tsimpli for her interest in the issues and help with the empirical data gathering part. Cedric Boeckx and Anna Roussou also deserve my gratitude for taking out some of their valuable time to discuss some of these issues with me and providing me with very useful comments, which I was only partially able to integrate. I would like to use this opportunity to also thank the participants of the questionnaire that came out of that, which is briefly presented in the Appendix.

[1] CG is mainly a spoken language; it can be seen written in poems or text messages, but it is never used in formal writing. Some people do not even categorize it as a language at all; for them it is just a dialect of SMG. (Within generative grammar, such a distinction is largely moot, of course; nevertheless, a lot of work remains to be done on this issue, such as adequately describing CG grammar.) The situation in Cyprus is very interesting from a linguistic point of view, since, although Cypriots speak in CG, they learn to read and write in SMG. News, magazines, newspapers, speeches, and formal events are also in SMG. In these cases the use of SMG is demanded. There are also cases where it may not be demanded but nevertheless be preferable. In those cases the people who use it are considered to be more well-mannered than others who do not. Generally speaking the case in Cyprus is that people speak in CG and code-switch to SMG in several occasions.

However, there is a considerable number of people who refuse to speak CG since they consider it the language of the lower class, people from the suburbs or uneducated people. As Papapavlou (1997) observes: "Contrary to linguistic evidence, which stipulates that all languages and varieties are 'equal', and that none is inherently better than any other, people still believe that some languages are more 'precise', 'beautiful' and 'expressive' and that some dialects are

Speakers of Cypriot Greek employ three different strategies — though not necessarily to the same extent — to express focus: by clefting the focus constituent ('focus cleft', (1)), by leaving it in situ ('focus in-situ', (2)), or by fronting it ('focus movement', (3)).

(1) En ESENA pu agapo. *focus cleft*
be.3SG you.ACC that love.1SG
lit. "It is you that I love."

(2) Agapo ESENA. *focus in-situ*
love.1SG you.ACC
lit. "I love you."

(3) ESENA agapo. *focus movement*
you.ACC love.1SG
lit. "You I love."

The puzzle these data introduce is the fact that all three strategies converge in one meaning —in this case the meaning of the equivalent English sentence *I love you* with focus on the direct object (capitals). In order to explain, and in the end solve, this puzzle, two hypotheses can be formulated. According to the first, the three strategies co-exist as part of the CG focus system; I call this *Hypothesis I* as in (4). According to the second, referred to from now on as *Hypothesis II*, CG only employs clefts and focus in-situ as mechanisms of the focus system, whereas focus movement is an SMG strategy and is used in the context of CG focus formation due to the interaction of CG and SMG speakers, as formulated in (5).

'inferior', 'inexpressive' and 'incomplete'" (quoted from Papapavlou & Pavlou 1998: 215). He investigated through sociolinguistic experiments attitudes of CG speakers towards both CG and SMG. "The results clearly showed that Greek Cypriots hold more favorable attitudes (i.e. have more positive feelings) towards SMG than towards the Cypriot dialect which they use in their daily interactions. Specifically, those who use SMG are thought of as being more attractive, ambitious, intelligent, educated, interesting, modern, dependable and pleasant than those who use the Cypriot dialect. However, the judges did not feel that SMG speakers were more sincere, friendlier, kinder or more humorous than the Cypriot speakers" (Papapavlou & Pavlou 1998: 216). I leave the treatment of CG and/versus SMG at this level. More (socio)linguistic work needs to be done to validate the hunches expressed elsewhere in this paper and to treat this important issue appropriately. For my purposes, I will assume a CG grammar of which I will investigate the focus system.

(4) *Hypothesis I*
The focus system of CG makes available three strategies (*prima facie* of equal status): (i) focus cleft, (ii) focus in situ, and (iii) focus movement.

(5) *Hypothesis II*
The focus system of CG makes available two strategies (*prima facie* of equal status): (i) focus cleft and (ii) focus in situ — (iii) focus movement is transfer from SMG.

This paper will first examine the three strategies and then discuss the two hypotheses in order to decide which of the two is to be preferred.[2]

However, first let me provide some relevant background on the expression of focus and past syntactic approaches. In the generative tradition, Jackendoff (1972) first divided sentences formally into two semantic parts, presupposition and focus. He defines the presupposition of a sentence as "the information that is assumed by the speaker to be shared by him and the hearer," while the focus of a sentence is "the information in the sentence that is assumed by the speaker *not* to be shared by him and the hearer" (p. 230). The focus might involve a single word or a phrase, or in some cases even the entire sentence. And the focus might be more or less emphatic, depending on the conversational context (e.g., whether the new information is particularly surprising or important, or whether it contrasts with previously introduced information, etc.).

Furthermore, it is widely accepted that there are two types of focus, what is often called 'information focus' and 'contrastive focus'. We speak of information focus when the focused constituent simply introduces new, non-presupposed information without contrasting it with any other type of information, either old or new. Contrastive focus, on the other hand, refers to a situation in which the new information is viewed in specific contrast to other (old or new) information. Here the clause actually contradicts what is asserted in previous context (see Georgiafentis 2003, who I draw from heavily, for SMG, as well as Ambar 1999 and Brunetti 2003, among many others).

It must be pointed out however, that focus is neither just a syntactic

[2] The interaction of CG and SMG is present in the mind of the same speaker who happens to know both varieties; language contact presumably has an effect on the internalized grammar of the individual (referred to as 'I-language' in Chomsky 1965). There is cross-dialectal influence not only from SMG to CG, as Hypothesis II explicitly presumes by calling it 'transfer' (whether or not this is the correct characterization), but also the other way around.

phenomenon nor simply a prosodic one. Phonology, syntax, semantics, and pragmatics all play a role in expressing focus. This paper concentrates on syntactic approaches to the phenomenon of focus, so next I will briefly review the major proposals in the literature. To begin with, Brody (1990) first observed that Hungarian focus is syntactically marked in a specific sense:

(6) JANOSSAL vittem le a szemetet.
John.with took.I down the rubbish.ACC
"I took down the rubbish with JOHN."

Brody proposed the existence of a focus projection FP (these days, in the wake of Rizzi 1997, often called FocP) in the left periphery of the clause whose specifier is filled by the focused item and whose head attracts the verb. The verb moves to the focus head to assign a feature to the XP in its specifier.

Following Brody, Agouraki (1990) suggests that focus creates its own maximal projection in Greek as well (that is, SMG). Here the idea is that there is a focus feature [FOC] which is assigned by the verb. When the verb itself is focused, it absorbs the feature. In addition, she argues that when there is phonological focus-marking, it is only at LF that the focused phrase moves to [Spec,FocP]. What she ends up with is an analysis according to which SMG makes available both orders presented below in (7).

(7) a. $[_{FocP}$ Spec Foc^0 $[_{CP}$ Spec C^0 ...]]
b. $[_{CP}$ Spec C^0 $[_{FocP}$ Spec Foc^0 ...]]

To continue with studies on focus in the Greek language, Tsimpli (1990, 1995) argues that focused phrases are assigned the feature [FOC] in their D-structure position. Moreover, she claims that focus movement always occurs; while focused phrases *may* raise overtly, they must raise by LF. However, in later work, more compatible with the minimalist assumption that D-structure can be dispensed with (Chomsky 1995), she investigates the possibility of in-situ focusing as being distinct from focus movement (Tsimpli 1998). Consider (8):

(8) a. TI MARIA sinandise (oxi tin Eleni).
b. Sinadise TI MARIA (oxi tin Eleni).
met.3SG the Mary (not the Eleni)
"He met MARY, not Helen."

For these data (from Tsimpli 1998) she argues that focus in-situ (8b) is ambiguous between a presentational (or information focus) and a contrastive reading, whereas a preposed focus phrase (i.e. focus movement), as in (8a), cannot be construed as presentational. She concludes that the ambiguity between a presentational and a contrastive reading in the in-situ focusing is a valid reason for keeping the two strategies apart.

More specifically, Lekakou (2000) suggests that movement of the focused constituent is used when the context permits it to guide the interpretation process. Focus movement marks the material across which the movement takes place as presupposed, i.e. discourse given. Thus the difference between focus movement and focus in-situ has to do with the status of the material that follows and precedes it, respectively. In focus movement, what follows the preposed focus phrase is discourse given and marked as such. In focus in-situ no marking takes place and what precedes the focused constituent can either be presupposed or not. Each syntactic structure has a different pragmatic effect, and the option of moving the focused phrase is exploited whenever the pragmatic value that obtains by a moved focus phrase needs, in the speaker's view, to be highlighted. Under this analysis no formal feature needs to be checked (under either version of Checking Theory presented in Chomsky 1995, for example).

Next, I will lay out the three focus strategies illustrated in (1) to (3) above. Each type of focusing strategy will be discussed in a separate sub-section with data drawn primarily from Greek (both CG and SMG). I will start with focus clefts in section 2. Section 3 will address focus movement in CG and contain a novel analysis for some incalcitrant cases. In section 4 I will treat focus in-situ and section 5, where I will put forward my specific proposal for the CG focus system, will bring the major issues together. Section 6 briefly concludes with an outlook for future research.

2. Focus Clefts

2.1. Clefts under Contrastive and Information Reading

When constructing focus in CG it is important to note that this variety of Greek makes heavy use of the clefting strategy, unlike SMG which disallows it, in this form, completely.[3] In a first study of the phenomenon,

---

[3] However, Ianthi Tsimpli (p.c.) has pointed out to me that clefts are acceptable in SMG, but with some interesting differences. This makes the SMG construction

Grohmann et al. (2006) claim that CG uses cleft structures in lieu of syntactic focus movement.[4] In this way, they seem to subscribe to *Hypothesis II* (5).

Clefts in CG are used mainly for contrastive reading. One example is the following:

(9)	En	EGO	pu	enna	pao	sto	party.
	be.3SG	I.NOM	that	will.1SG	go	to.the	party

"I will go to the party."
lit. "It is me that will go to the party."

According to a questionnaire that was carried out (see Appendix for details about the scenarios), example (9) is, under a contrastive reading, acceptable enough for 26% of the speakers and very acceptable for 67%. There is no doubt that the majority of CG speakers express contrastive focus with clefting constructions. Other examples are the following (for expository purposes, they are all translated as clefts):

(10) a.
En be.3SG / TI MARIA the Maria / pu that / agapa love.3SG / o the / Petros Peter
(, oi tin Eleni).
not the Eleni
"It is Maria that Peter loves, not Helen."

b.
En be.3SG / TO VIVLIO the book / pu that / mu me / arese like.3.PST / (, oi ti tenia). not the movie
"It is the book that I liked, not the movie."

However, there are cases where clefting is employed in a non-contrastive setting, as an answer to a wh-question, for example, as in (11):

(11) A:
Pian who / agapa love.3SG / o the / Petros? Peter
"Who does Peter love?"

B:
Nomizo think.1SG / en be.3SG / TI the / MARIA Maria.ACC / pu that / agapa. love.3SG
"I think it is Maria that he loves."

---

somewhat similar to what I later call 'unusual movement' for CG (see section 3.2).

[4] While I disagree with some of Grohmann et al.'s findings, it must be noted in all fairness that their main concern was *wh*-question formation in CG. They only discuss non-interrogative clefting in passing, pending further research. This article, alongside Koursarou & Christodoulou (2005), attempts to fill some of these gaps.

Or in the case when someone knocks on a friend's door unexpectedly:

(12) A: Pcos?
"Who?"
B: En EGO pu ime.
be.3SG I.NOM that be.1SG
"It's me (that's here)."

(12) was part of the questionnaire in Scenario 3 (see Appendix). Although (12B) was not the most preferred answer to (12A), there was a considerable number of people who would use it. In fact, 14% of the people asked considered it to be very acceptable, 16% thought it to be acceptable enough, 26% to be so-so (i.e. neither liked nor hated it), and 16% to be little acceptable. It has to be pointed out though, that the remaining 26% who considered it to be unacceptable is a relatively high percentage.

However, as Ianthi Tsimpli (p.c.) brought to my attention, the reason why (12B) sounds bad to many speakers might be due to the personal pronoun coupled with the copula in the main clause (and the cleft). Consider another example that was part of the questionnaire in scenario 2, which is also a non-contrastive scenario:

(13) En I KOKINOMALA pu mu aresi.
be.3SG the.NOM redhead that me like.3SG.PRS
"It is the redhead that I like."

Here the percentage of people who considered it to be unacceptable was "only" 13%. 17% thought it to be little acceptable, 22% to be so-so, 25% to be acceptable enough, and 13% to be very acceptable. After comparing these results with the results of the previous example, the conclusion is that half the people that considered (12) unacceptable also consider (13) unacceptable. The other half is added in the percentage of people who took it to be acceptable enough. The other percentages are relatively the same. Clearly, there is some preference for (13) in contrast to (12), although both were answers to a wh-question.

2.2. Clefts and Quantifiers

As quoted in Brunetti (2003), Benincà et al. (1988: 219) argue that when focusing a quantifier in Italian, clefts become unavailable whereas Brunetti (2003: 101) casts some doubt on this claim and provides relevant data. Maybe the reason that quantifiers are not expected to be acceptable with clefts is that they are not referential, whereas clefts supposedly express, what É. Kiss (1998) calls, identificational focus. She argues that identificational focus, and not information focus, expresses exhaustive identification in which the "focused constituent identifies a unique referent from the context to be interpreted as focus" (quoted from Brunetti 2003: 88). Brunetti concludes that Italian clefts do not express exhaustive identification.

It seems that this also extends to clefts in CG, since, for whatever reasons (which cannot be treated exhaustively here), focus clefting is perfectly fine in CG for most quantifiers.[5] The data in (14) illustrate:

(14) a. En ULLI pu enna rtun sto party.
be.3SG everybody that will.1SG come to.the party
"It is everybody that will come to the party."

b. En ULLI MERA pu eperpatusa.
be.3SG all day that walk.1SG.PST
"Is all day that I was walking."

c. Enen KANENAS pu ftei.
be.3SG.NEG nobody that blame.3SG
"There is nobody to blame."
lit. "It is nobody that is to blame."

d. En i PARAPANO (PU EMAS) pu apetixan.
be.3SG the most (of us) that fail.3PL.PST
"It is most (of us) that failed."

e. En LII pu irtan.
be.3SG few that come.3PL.PST
"It is few that came."

f. En POLLES FORES pu efien trexontas.
be.3SG many times that leave.3SG.PST run.GER
"It is many times that he left running."

g. En PARAPANO/LIOTERI PU DEKA ANDRES
be.3SG more/less than ten men.NOM
pu efian.
that leave.3PL.PST
"It is more/less than ten men that left."

[5] In examples such as (14a), the negative operator *en* (the CG equivalent of SMG *den*) is attached to the copula part of the cleft. Here, *kanenas* can also be unstressed, which will result in a different interpretation. I will discuss this presently.

There are cases, though, in which clefts with quantifiers are completely unacceptable (certainly all instances with *o kathenas* "each"):

(15) a. * En o kathenas pu exi to provlima tu.
be.3SG the each that have.3SG the problem.ACC his
"It is each with his problem."
b. * En otidipote pu xriazese na ertis se mena.
be.3SG anything that need.2SG SBJ come.2SG to me
"It is anything you need come to me."

It might be interesting to note that there are cases in which clefting with quantifiers is allowed, but it results in a different meaning than expected. Consider the following:

(16) a. Enen kati/tipote pu me anisixi.
be.3SG.NEG something that me worry.3SG
"It is not something that worries me."
b. En kapios pu thelo.
be.3SG someone that want.1SG
"It is someone that I want."
c. Enen kanenas pu troi polla.
be.3SG.NEG nobody that eat.3PL much.
"It is not somebody/nobody that eats much."

In the examples in (16) there is always something specific, known both to the speaker and the hearer, that the speaker is referring to. To make things clearer, consider a scenario in which Peter has an exam the next day and someone asks him how he feels about it. He replies:

(17) Oi, enen kati/tipote pu me anisixi.
no be.3SG.NEG something that me worry.3SG
"No, it is not something that worries me."

Here *kati/tipote* refers to the event of the exam.

What the examples in (16) have in common is the fact that the quantifiers are not stressed, whereas in (14) they all are. As Anna Roussou (p.c.) notes, the examples in (16a,c) include polarity items (namely, *kanenas* and *tipote*). She points out that Tsimpli & Roussou (1996) argued that phonological stress on these items changes their quantificational force, that is, when focused they are negative polarity items, whereas when unstressed they are existential polarity items.

For reasons of space, I will not discuss this interesting connection, or the relevance to the current set of data, any further. However, the fact that the quantifiers in (16) are not stressed seems a good enough reason to suggest that these sentences are not actually clefts, or at least focus clefts as discussed here. In a focus cleft construction, phonological stress is applied to the focused material. These sentences could then, in fact, be analyzed as standard copular sentences with a subject null pronoun and a relative clause, which would explain the lack of stress on the quantifiers.

To conclude this section, I present the following example, which is translated from the acceptable Italian data provided by Brunetti (2003: 101). In CG, however, (18B) is not a good answer to (18A). A preferable answer would be (18B'), which employs focus in-situ.

(18) A: Perimenis to leoforio?
wait.2SG the bus
"Are you waiting for the bus?"
B: #Oi, en kapio pu perimeno.
no be.3SG someone that wait.1SG
"No, it is someone that I am waiting for."
B': Oi, perimeno kapio.
no wait.1SG someone
"No, I am waiting for someone."

What (18) demonstrates is that, although both CG and Italian allow focus clefts with quantifiers, they nevertheless exhibit some differences.

3. Movement in CG

3.1. Movement as Usual

A first assumption, in line with Hypothesis II from (5) above, is that CG does not utilize movement so much because it utilizes clefts — and that focus movement is taken to be a strategy restricted to SMG. However, the results of my questionnaire seem to suggest otherwise. Consider (19):

(19) EGO enna pao sto party.
I.NOM will go to.the party
"I will go to the party."

Example (19) presumably employs focus movement of the subject under the assumption that *ego* originates in [Spec,*v*P] and that [Spec,TP] is not filled in null subject languages like Greek, at least not by an overt subject (see e.g. Alexiadou & Anagnostopoulou 2001). Thus the subject seems to be fronted to [Spec,CP] or [Spec,FocP]. This example was used in the contrastive scenario 1 and only 4% of the people asked thought it to be unacceptable, while 34% considered it acceptable enough and 51% very acceptable.

The results were approximately the same for the following example (20) as well; the difference being that it was used in the non-contrastive scenario 3. Only 2% considered it unacceptable, whereas 24% acceptable enough and 54% very acceptable.

(20) EGO ime.
I.NOM be.1SG
"It is me."

In this context, consider (21):

(21) ESENA agapo.
you.ACC love.1SG
"You I love."

Example (21) was used in a contrastive scenario. Here 9% of the participants considered it unacceptable, 21% acceptable enough, and 56% very acceptable. The numbers speak for themselves. CG utilizes movement under both contrastive and non-contrastive settings, and it is acceptable for the majority of CG speakers.

Moreover, example (21), and the following example (22), sound more like SMG than CG to my ears as a native speaker of CG, while (19) and (20) sound better as far as I am concerned. Although there are arguably Cypriots who use (21) and (22), there is something distinctively unnatural about these structures as concerns "speaking dialect" (see also fn. 1 for more information as well as a general disclaimer about such "feelings").

(22) TI MARIA agapa o Petros.
the Maria.ACC love.3SG the Petros
"It is Maria that Peter loves."

(23) * TI MARIA o Petros agapa.
the Maria.ACC the Petros love.3SG
"Maria Peter loves."

Furthermore, example (23) is ungrammatical due to the adjacency condition (Tsimpli 1990, Agouraki 1990), which states that when the focused constituent moves overtly, the verb must immediately follow, moving to the head of FocP.

It is evident that movement in CG is very acceptable, although there are cases like (21) and (22) when it does not sound so good. Moreover, movement is used mainly for a contrastive reading, but it can also be interpreted informationally (see (20)). Contrary to Tsimpli (1998), who argues that a preposed element in SMG can not be construed as signaling presentational focus, experimental evidence from Georgiafentis & Sfakianaki (2004) seems to suggest that preposed focus with an information reading does exist in SMG. The following examples are taken from Georgiafentis (2003):

(24) a. Pjos djavazi to vivlio?
who read.3SG the book
"Who is reading the book?"
b. O JANIS djavazi to vivlio.
the Janis read.3SG the book
"John is reading the book."

Whether focus movement is an SMG strategy used in CG (Hypothesis II) or whether CG employs the movement strategy proper (Hypothesis I) shall not matter for the moment. Either way I conclude that a moved focused constituent can have both information and contrastive readings. Just consider example (20) above, which was an answer to a wh-question in scenario 3 of the questionnaire (see Appendix): According to 54% of the Greek Cypriots questioned, this is a very acceptable answer.

3.2. An Unusual Movement

In CG there is a construction, exemplified by the data below, which I will refer to from now on as 'unusual movement'. Although many speakers might not like as much, its existence can not be denied. There are two issues to be addressed as far as this construction is concerned. First of all, its (un)acceptability and secondly, whether it is a true movement construction or just another type of cleft as some claim.

Examples of what I call unusual movement are provided in (25)-(27):

(25) TI MARIA en pu thelo.
the Maria be.3SG that want.1SG
"I want MARY."
lit "Mary it is that I want."

(26) ESI en pu thelis jatro.
you be.3SG that want.2SG doctor
"You want a doctor."
lit "It is you that wants a doctor."

(27) I KOKINOMALA en pu mu areski.
the redhead be.3SG that me like.3SG
"I like the redhead."
lit "It is the redhead that I like."

According to Grohmann et al. (2006), such examples would be derived from moving within the cleft, which is supposedly disallowed, and they thus judge it ungrammatical. Their example is given here (my capitals):

(28) * O XAMBIS en pu efie.
the Hambis be.3SG that left.3SG
"It is Hambis that left."
lit. "Hambis it is that left."

I disagree with Grohmann et al. (2006), and also the related Tsiplakou et al. (in press) which contains slightly more discussion of cleft structures in Greek, because, although sentences like (25)-(27) may not be widely acceptable, they are nevertheless used by a large number of speakers.

In order to be more specific, I will discuss example (27), which appeared in the questionnaire as an answer to a wh-question in scenario 2 (see Appendix). The results showed that 21% of the people asked considered it to be unacceptable, 12% little acceptable, 32% so-so, 27% acceptable enough, and 6% very acceptable. It seems that the majority of speakers range from unacceptable to acceptable enough. This shows that this construction is used, but that speakers do not favor it over others and may be a little puzzled about it. Let us not forget that as a construction it may be used in speech, but because of its peculiarity when written down on paper (as in the questionnaire), it may have confused the speakers.

Moreover, example (28) sounds perfectly fine to me, especially as an answer to wh-questions such as the following, where *en pu* (the copula-complementizer complex akin to English "(it) is that") is present:

(29) Pcos en pu efie?
who be.3SG that left.3SG
"Who is it that left?"

What I find interesting to note here is that, as Ianthi Tsimpli (p.c.) points out to me, constructions of the type presented in (25)-(27) can be used in SMG. Tsimpli calls them clefts, although SMG apparently disallows clefts. The interesting difference between SMG and CG is that in the CG examples, the copula is always 3rd person (as in English), whereas in SMG, it inflects and agrees with the clefted constituent. CG (and English) clefts assume a 3rd person (null) subject instead. The example below is the equivalent of (26) in SMG:

(26′) ESI ise pu thelis jatro.
you be.2SG that want.2SG doctor.ACC
"You are the one that wants a doctor."

This difference between CG and SMG is relevant to my claim that the CG examples are a movement construction, and not movement within a cleft. I will come back to this in the next section, when I further address the syntactic status of clefts.

Moving on, according to Gryllia & Lekakou (2006), sentences like the examples (25)-(27) are cleft structures which utilize what they call "movement within the cleft." They argue that there are two orders for clefts; the [*en*–clefted XP] order and [clefted XP–*en*], and that there are two different focus projections to host the clefted constituent of each order. There is a low FocP in the IP area (cf. Belletti 2004), and this is where the clefted constituent moves to in clefts where the clefted XP stays below the copula, [*en*–clefted XP]. There is also a higher FocP, in the left periphery of the clause (with Rizzi 1997 and work cited in section 1), and this position hosts the clefted constituent in 'movement within the cleft'-structures, i.e. [clefted XP–*en*]. They claim that the different focus projections reflect the different discourse properties of the clefts in CG, namely, that in [*en*–clefted XP] orders the interpretation is contrastive focus and in [clefted XP–*en*] orders it is that of new information focus.

Their examples are provided below:

(30) A: Pjos epessen pu tes skales?
who fell.3SG from the stairs
"Who fell down the stairs?"

B: En o mitsis pu epessen pu tes skales.
be.3SG the young that fell.3SG from the stairs
"It is the young one that fell down the stairs."
B′: O mitsis en pu epessen pu tes skales.
the young be.3SG that fell.3SG from the stairs
"It is the young one that fell down the stairs."

(31) A: Yati ise stenaxorimeni?
why be.2SG upset
"Why are you upset?"
B: En o mitsis pu epessen pu tes skales.
is the young that fell.3SG from the stairs
"It is the young one that fell down the stairs."
B′:#O mitsis en pu epessen pu tes skales.
the young is that fell.3SG from the stairs
"It is the young one that fell down the stairs."

However, I have already demonstrated that clefts of the [*en*–clefted XP] order are acceptable in both a contrastive and an informational reading (section 2.1). This is also shown in Gryllia & Lekakou's example. The interpretation of (31B), which is an [*en*–clefted XP], can not be — as an answer to a wh-question — that of contrastive focus. Now, what is the interpretation of what they call a [clefted XP–*en*] order? Is it that of new information only or can it have a contrastive reading as well? If it has only an informative reading then their claim about the existence of two different FocP is valid. In this light, consider the following example:

(32) A: Akousa oti epesse i Maria pu tis skales, en kala?
"I heard that Maria fell down the stairs, is she ok?"
B: O GIORGOS en pu epesse pu tes
the Giorgos be.3SG that fall.3SG.PST from the
skales, oi i Maria.
stairs not the Maria
"It is Giorgos that fell from the stairs, not Maria."
B′: En O GIORGOS pu epesse pu tes
be.3SG the Giorgos that fall.3SG.PST from the
skales, oi i Maria.
stairs not the Maria
"It is Giorgos that fell from the stairs, not Maria."

Both (32B) and (32B′) are acceptable answers to (32A), although the latter sounds a little bit better. Anyhow, what matters here is that it is not unacceptable under the contrastive reading.[6] Therefore, the presence of two different focus projections for cleft constructions in CG is uneconomical — if it is supposed to be justified by the distinction of contrastive focus and information focus that each order is supposed to represent.[7]

However, as Gryllia & Lekakou also indicate there does exist a difference between the two orders as far as the distinction between type A clefts and type B clefts is concerned.[8] In type A clefts the clefted constituent bears new, often contrastive information, while the cleft clause bears known or old information; there is nuclear accent on the clefted constituent, whereas the cleft clause is weakly stressed. In type B clefts the information borne by the clefted constituent is frequently old or anaphoric, while the cleft clause bears information that is new to the hearer; the cleft clause is strongly stressed and as a result, it cannot be deleted.

Their argument is that clefts in example (30) belong to the type A cleft whereas clefts in example (31) to the type B cleft. Moreover, they successfully demonstrate that 'movement within the cleft' is allowed *only* in type A clefts, that is why (31B′) is unacceptable. The interpretation that I get from (31B) as an answer to (31A) is one in which the speakers means: "Because the young one fell down the stairs, that is why I am upset".

Lastly, it is worth mentioning that Gryllia & Lekakou argue that CG utilizes focus movement along with cleft structures. It seems that their analysis is along the lines of Hypothesis I (4). Under their assumption we do not only have focus movement and in-situ focus in CG but we also

---

[6] It is unfortunate that I had not included any examples similar to (32) in my questionnaire; the comments I make here are my own and of some other native speakers that I have consulted afterwards.

[7] Economy in (pre)minimalist syntactic theorizing goes back to Chomsky (1991, 1993) and played a big role in the mid 1990s (Chomsky 1995). In their recent introduction to minimalism, Hornstein et al. (2005: 7-9) distinguish methodological economy (Occam's razor: less is better, fewer principles outweigh more, and so on) from substantive economy (least effort: fewer steps, shorter movement, and other such technical considerations). It could be argued that the uneconomical nature of having different positions for CG clefts, while pertaining to the grammar, is in fact a methodological consequence that should be pushed further.

[8] They cite other labels for these distinction as well: Stressed-Focus vs. Informative-Presupposition clefts (Prince 1978), Topic-Clause vs. Comment-Clause clefts (Hedberg 2000) and Focus-Ground vs. Broad-Focus clefts (Doetjes et al. 2004)

have two kinds of clefts structures in which the clefted constituent hosts a different position each time. This system appears to me to be highly uneconomical. Finally, isn't it strange that while *usually* the higher FocP in the left periphery is utilized mainly for contrastive focus under their analysis the high Foc position is utilized by the [clefted XP–*en*] orders whose interpretation they argue is that of new information focus?

3.3. A New Proposal

Since CG and SMG interact the way they do, a mixture of the two becomes inevitable.[9] In my analysis, examples like (25)-(27) are not clefts of any sort but employ a movement strategy adopted from SMG to CG. Example (34) is the SMG equivalent of CG (27), which is repeated here as (33), and (35) is another instance of an apparent cleft structure in SMG:

(33) I KOKINOMALA en pu mu areski.
the redhead be.3SG that me like.3SG
"The redhead is that I like."

(34) I KOKINOMALA mu aresi.
the redhead me like.3SG
"The redhead I like."

(35) ESI ise pu thelis jatro.
you be.2SG that want.2SG doctor.ACC
"You are the one that wants a doctor."

Example (33) is, in my view, a movement construction since, unlike in clefts, the clefted constituent moves to a position above the copula. Moreover, I do not consider it a cleft of another order as Gryllia & Lekakou (2006) do since, as I have already demonstrated, I consider their proposal uneconomical (see previous section). Furthermore, as mentioned above, I find the difference between (33) and (35) crucial for my proposal. As noted in the previous section the copula in CG clefts, such as (33), is always 3rd person singular, whereas in the SMG, as in (35), it inflects with the focused element. The fact that in the former the clefted XP does not

[9]As Ianthi Tsimpli (p.c.) points out, in the case of bilingualism a mixture between the two languages that the speaker masters is not (necessarily) inevitable. In fact, children seem to be able to keep the two languages in question apart by the age of two. The interaction of CG and SMG is a different case, however, since CG and SMG are not two entirely different languages. See also fn. 1 for discussion.

agree with the verb does not require it to be below the copula and above the main verb at some point in the derivation. Thus, a direct movement of it from its generated position to above the copula is possible.

The reason I call this movement unusual is because of the presence of *en pu*. The use of *en pu* or *embu*, referred to by Grohmann et al. (2006) as the '*embu*-strategy', appears in wh-questions in CG and is absent in SMG. Their examples are provided below:

(36) Pcos embu efie?
who.NOM is.that left.3SG
lit. "Who is it that left?"

(37) Pcon embu idhes?
who.ACC is.that saw.2SG
lit. "Who is it that you saw?"

Since wh-movement with *en pu* (*embu*) is grammatical, why isn't focus movement with *en pu*? In this line of thinking, example (28) — repeated here as (38) — is not ungrammatical at all (see also the discussion of (27)).

(38) O XAMBIS en pu efie.
the Hambis be.3SG that left.3SG
"It is Hambis that left."

This *unusual movement* is imported from SMG into CG, and CG differentiates it from SMG through the use of the '*embu*-strategy'. The existence of it reinforces Hypothesis II (see (5)), which states that focus movement in CG is in fact an SMG strategy. If it wasn't, then why would CG have two different ways of forming focus movement, the usual and the unusual one? It would not be economical since each one does not elicit its own interpretation but they are both able to express both contrastive and information focus despite the fact that unusual movement is more preferred as an answer to a wh-question.

4. Focus In-Situ

In addition, CG has the option of focusing a constituent by leaving it in situ. Here it is usually stressed; hence this is also called phonological focus marking.[10] Examples are:

(39) O Petros agapa TI MARIA.
the Petros love.3SG the Maria
"Peter loves Maria."

(40) Agapo ESENA.
love.1SG you.ACC
"I love you."

In SMG, in-situ focus is ambiguous between a presentational and a contrastive reading (Tsimpli 1995), contrary to what É. Kiss (1998) argues (see Lekakou 2000 for discussion). This is the case for Italian as well (Rizzi 1997). The same goes for CG. Example (39) can have either a presentational reading, where Maria is not contrasted with anyone, or a contrastive reading, where Maria is contrasted with Eleni, as in the following example:

(41) O Petros agapa TI MARIA, oi tin Eleni.
the Petros love.3SG the Maria, not the Eleni
"Peter loves Maria, not Helen."

Also, as Lekakou (2000) suggests, if we add *mono* "only", which forces an exhaustive contrastive reading on the constituent it modifies, then an in-situ focalized element can also have a contrastive reading.

(42) O Petros agapa MONO TI MARIA.
the Petros love.3SG only the Maria
"Peter loves only Maria."

Finally, if we take a look at the following example and the results of the questionnaire, there is no doubt that speakers utilize in-situ focusing for contrastive reasons as well.

---

[10] In this paper, I will refrain from discussing movement approaches to in-situ focus, such as Belletti's (2004), among others, whether within the cartographic approach to syntax or on any other grounds. In other words, I work from the assumption that a dedicated focus projection may be in the left periphery, but not in the lower IP area (see also Grohmann 2003 for principled justification in terms of a dedicated discourse domain).

(43) Sto party enna pao EGO.
to.the party will.1SG go I.NOM
"I will go to the party."

Although it was not the most preferred choice in scenario 1, no one can doubt that it is used under a contrastive reading. Only 6% of the people asked considered it unacceptable, 14% little acceptable and 24% so-so while 30% thought it to be acceptable enough and the remainder (26%) very acceptable.

5. The Focus System in CG

5.1. The Problem

This is the picture for CG so far:

(44) a. FOCUS CLEFT → Information Focus / Contrastive Focus

b. FOCUS IN-SITU → Information Focus / Contrastive Focus

c. FOCUS MOVEMENT → Information Focus / Contrastive Focus

It is undoubtedly uneconomical to assume that the above is representative of the focus system of CG. If we were to accept it, then we would adopt *Hypothesis I* which supports the co-existence of the three strategies. Except for the fact that it may be the easy way out, there is no other reason to support this hypothesis. Why should CG have three different strategies instead of two (like Italian, SMG etc. do)? Moreover, we have to consider the fact that there are languages like Hungarian which exemplify only one strategy; movement in this case (Brody 1990).

One question that has remained unanswered until this point is the following: Since CG employs clefts as a focus mechanism, why is it that it is claimed to employ focus movement as well? The answer lies in the relationship between the two languages have (see also fn. 1). No one can doubt that the influence from SMG is *inevitable* in CG. Thus, along with clefting constructions, CG speakers employ focus movement as well. As a result I would argue that focus movement is an SMG focus strategy "imported" to CG. People use it because they hear it so often in schools and in TV programs and they see it written in books, magazines, newspapers and so on. Nevertheless, there are cases, like example (24), which do not sound so good in CG but rather sound like SMG; yet, they are not considered unacceptable by the Cypriot speakers.

Since I rejected Hypothesis I (4), I will adopt Hypothesis II (5), which I repeat here in simplified form: *CG only employs clefts and focus in-situ as focus mechanisms.*

(45) a. FOCUS CLEFT → Information Focus / Contrastive Focus

b. FOCUS IN-SITU → Information Focus / Contrastive Focus

(At least) one problem remains, however. Why are there two different mechanisms, the in-situ strategy and clefting, used for both types of focus, information (or presentational) and contrastive focus? Even if we accept Hypothesis II, as represented above, the system still seems uneconomical.

5.2. A Solution

As I mentioned in section 1 above, most analyses of focus claim the existence of two *types* of focus: information focus and contrastive focus. One argument to support this distinction is the fact that while focus in-situ can express both, left peripheral focus can only express contrastive focus. However, as I have already demonstrated, left peripheral focus can also express information focus.

A second argument refers to the prosodic differences the two types of focus bear. Georgiafentis (2004), citing Donati & Nespor (2003), refers to two different kinds of prominence, neutral and emphatic. They differ in two points. To begin with, neutral prominence concerns the word bearing main prominence and can also be extended to the projection(s) dominating the constituent bearing pitch accent. This extension is only available in information focus and not in contrastive focus. Secondly, emphatic prominence and not neutral prominence, generates the insertion of an intonational phrase boundary at its right edge. Let us test if these two points hold for CG as well:

(46) Enna agoraso Foc^0 kithara.
will buy.1SG guitar
"I will buy a guitar."

Georgiafentis (2004: 238-239) has already demonstrated that both points hold for SMG. I will follow *his* steps using my examples to demonstrate that the same happens with CG:

(47) A: Ti enna agorasis?
what will buy.2SG
"What will you buy?"
B: Enna agoraso Foc^0 [kithara].
will buy.1SG guitar
"I will buy a guitar."

(48) A: Ti enna kamis avrio?
what will do.2SG tomorrow
"What will you do tomorrow?"
B: Avrio enna Foc^0 [agoraso kithara].
tomorrow will buy.1SG guitar
"Tomorrow I will buy a guitar."

(49) A: Giati ise enthusiasmenos?
why be.2SG excited
"Why are you excited?"
B: Foc^0 [avrio enna agoraso kithara].
tomorrow will buy.1SG guitar
"Tomorrow I will buy a guitar."

While the DP *kithara* "guitar" is the focused object in the B answers, the domain of focus can nevertheless be larger than just that DP as the above examples demonstrate. Can this happen with the following example as well? The answer is negative.

(50) En Foc^0 [kithara] pu enna agoraso, oi motora.
be.3SG guitar that will buy.1SG, not motorbike
"It is a guitar that I will buy, not a motorbike."

A: En motora pu enna agorasis?
be.3SG motorbike that will buy.2SG
"Is it a motorbike that you will buy?"
B:*Foc^0 [en kithara pu enna agoraso, oi motora].
be.3SG guitar that will buy.1SG, not motorbike
"It is a guitar that I will buy, not a motorbike."

The following examples test if the second point holds for CG, with the subscripted I indicating the intonational phrase:

(51) a. [Thelo esena na ertis mazi mu]$_I$.
want.1SG you.ACC SBJ come.2SG with me
"I want you to come with me."
b. [En esena]$_I$ [pu thelo na ertis
be.3SG you.ACC that want.1SG SBJ come.2SG
mazi mu].
with me
"It is you that I want to come with me."

Pending a more careful investigation, it seems that in terms of prosody the distinction between information and contrastive focus holds for CG as it does for SMG. But, while the distinction is clear in terms of prosody, it is not clear in terms of syntax[11]. As a consequence and for reasons that I will discuss shortly, I suggest that the distinction between 'contrastive' and 'information' focus does not hold. On the contrary, focus is always contrastive[12]; when we focus something, we always focus it in contrast to

---

[11] The work of Haidou (2006) might be relevant here. Her approach to information structure units such as topic and foci rejects 'syntactocentrism' and the hypothesis that there is no direct interaction between PF and LF. She claims that we should allow PF to access Lf directly and vice versa and leave narrow syntax free from semantics of discourse notions such as topic and focus. Particularly, as far as SMG is concerned "the idea of in-situ focus equaling new information focus and ex-situ focus equaling exhaustive-identificational properties can not be sustained for Greek" (p. 211). She successfully demonstrates that there is no one-to-one correlation between word order and information structure in SMG since one word order can realize different information structures and a certain information structure can be realized by a range of word orders. She goes on to argue that focus is a uniform phenomenon with a uniform interpretation; that of new information. The exhaustive interpretation of focus is just the outcome of the interaction between the semantic component and the discourse component (context).

[12] Incidentally, my suggestion is supported by Brunetti (2003), who cites personal communication with Irene Heim and Rita Manzini. Her claim is that Focus is

all the other possible entities that could take its place. For example:

(52) Enna pio FRAPE.
will.1SG drink frappé
"I will drink frappé."

(53) Agapo ton PETRO.
love.1SG the Peter
"I love Peter."

In example (52) *frappé* is focused and contrasted with every other possible drinkable object there is to choose from. Similarly, in example (53) Peter is focused and contrasted with every other man or woman —depending on one's sexual preferences— that there is to love. Both examples are instances of focus in-situ, for which I showed earlier that they can either be 'information' or 'contrastive' focus. The following example is a cleft which usually expresses 'contrastive' focus:

(54) En TI MARIA pu aghapa o Petros, (oi tin Eleni).
be.3sg the Maria that love.3SG the Peter (not the Helen)
"It is Maria that Peter loves (, not Helen)."

No one can question the fact that in the above example, Maria is contrasted with Eleni. The difference in this case from example (53) is that the focused phrase is contrasted with something *specific,* known in the discourse context within the utterance is spoken.

É. Kiss (1998) assumes that there is a contrastive feature and Focus is [+contrastive] "if it operates on a closed set of entities whose members are known to the participants of the discourse" (p. 267). I would suggest that focus always operates on a set of entities which is sometimes closed and sometimes not, and as a consequence its members are *sometimes known and sometimes unknown to the participants of the discourse* accordingly. Thus focus is always contrastive.

Do we have a '+contrastive feature' under this analysis? The answer is negative since, if focus is always contrastive, the existence of a '+contrastive feature' is redundant and not economical in any way.

However there are a few questions left unanswered. If focus is always

---

always contrastive. Brunetti concludes that Focus always identifies a referent for a variable. Contrast is not a matter of Focus but the result of the discourse context in which focus occurs.

contrastive, why are there two strategies instead of one? Note also that the movement of the focused item in cleft constructions is a costly operation.

(55) a. FOCUS CLEFT → Contrastive reading
b. FOCUS IN-SITU → Contrastive reading

From the examples given in this paper it appears that clefts were *mainly* used for 'contrastive' reading and in-situ focusing *mainly* for 'informational' reading. Therefore, a difference between the two must hold. I suggest that, as a tendency, clefts are *mainly* used when focus operates on a set of entities whose members are known to the participants of the discourse, whereas in-situ focusing is used when focus operates on a set of entities whose members are not known. Consider the following data:

(56) Thelo KOTOPOULO gia dipno.
want.1SG chicken for dinner
"I want chicken for dinner."

(57) En KOTOPOULO pu thelo gia dipno.
be.3SG chicken that want.1SG for dinner
"It is chicken that I want for dinner."

The difference is that in (56) *kotopoulo* "chicken" is contrasted with every other possible food but not something specific or known to the participants of the discourse, while in (57) *kotopoulo* is likely to be contrasted with something previously mentioned in the discourse, like pork, for example. In this case the contrast is highlighted since it is obvious to the hearer of the utterance.

Lastly, I would like to address two questions:

(Q1) Why are clefts used when focus operates on a set of entities whose members are known to the participants of the discourse, while in-situ-focusing is used when the members are not known?

In response to (Q1) an assumption is that when the members of the set of entities are known, the contrast is much stronger or emphatic than in the case in which they are not. In order to demonstrate this strength/emphasis clefts are employed, which require movement of the focused element. In the case in which the members of the set of entities are unknown, there is no need of the costly operation of movement, therefore the focused element remains in situ.

(Q2) What does '*mainly*' mean?

At this time, I do not yet have a clear or satisfactory answer for this question. A working hypothesis I intend to pursue further in future work is that, regardless of the familiarity with the members that the focused element is contrasted, every speaker chooses the strategy which s/he employs depending on how *much* focus s/he wants. If the assumption made in response to (Q1) is valid, clefts demonstrate an emphasis of the focused element which is not demonstrated in in-situ focusing.

6. Concluding Remarks

This paper explored the mechanisms of focus strategies employed in CG, the (primarily oral and colloquial) variety of Modern Greek spoken in Cyprus. The main assumption is that focus movement is an SMG strategy imported to CG (possibly due to the constant interaction between the two languages). The labels 'contrastive' and 'information' focus used throughout this paper have been dropped at the end, since focus is claimed to be always contrastive. Finally, two assumptions are provided in effort to answer to the existence of two mechanisms for one type of focus. The two assumptions do not necessarily have to exclude one another.

Appendix

One hundred people aged 18–50 years from all geographical areas of Cyprus participated in a questionnaire I conducted. The questionnaire was based on four scenarios, two in a 'contrastive' setting and two in an 'information' setting. For each scenario the participants were given ten statements and asked to rate them from 1-5 corresponding to 'unacceptable', 'little acceptable', 'so-so', 'acceptable enough' and 'very acceptable', respectively. These statements concerned only subject and object focus. Unfortunately, mostly young people took part in this questionnaire therefore interesting results in regard of the age factor can not be obtained. Moreover, the educational level of the participants was not required from them for methodological reasons and again conclusions regarding this factor cannot be obtained.

The four scenarios were the following:

Scenario one:
Take a situation where you are 15 years old and you ask your mum if you can go to a party. The day of the party you ask her if you can go, and she says: "Isn't it your sister who is going to that party?"

Scenario two:
You go to a party and your best friend asks you: "Who do you like best in here?"

Scenario three:
You go to a friend's house unexpectedly, knock at the door and your friend asks: "Who's that?"

Scenario four:
Your girlfriend/boyfriend doubts your love. S/he thinks you love someone else. What do you say to convince her/him that this is not the case?

The detailed analysis of the responses and full range of data can be obtained from the author.

References

Agouraki, Y. 1990. On the proposition of maximal categories: The case of CP and FP in Modern Greek. *UCL Working Papers in Linguistics* 2, 183-200.

Ambar, M. 1999. Aspects of the syntax of focus in Portuguese. In G. Rebuschi & L. Tuller (eds.), *The Grammar of Focus*. Amsterdam: John Benjamins, 23-53.

Belletti, A. 2004. Aspects of the low IP area. In L. Rizzi (ed.), *The Structure of CP and IP: The Cartography of Syntactic Structures*, vol. 2. Oxford: Oxford University Press, 16-51.

Benincà, P., G. Salvi & L. Frison. 1988. L'ordine degli elementi della frase e le costruzioni marcate. In L. Renzi & G. Salvi (eds.), *Grande grammatica italiana di consultazione*, vol. I. Bologna: II Mulino, 115-225.

Brody, M. 1990. Some remarks on the focus field in Hungarian. *UCL*

Working Papers in Linguistics 2, 201-225.
Brunetti, L. 2003. *A Unification of Focus*. Ph.D. diss., University of Florence.
Chomsky, N. 1991. Some notes on economy of derivation and representation. In R. Freidin (ed.), *Principles and Parameters in Generative Grammar*. Cambridge, MA: MIT Press, 417-454.
Chomsky, N. 1993. A minimalist program for linguistic theory. In K. Hale & S.J. Keyser (eds.), *The View from Building 20: Essays in Honor of Sylvain Bromberger*. Cambridge, MA: MIT Press, 1-52.
Chomsky, N. 1995. *The Minimalist Program*. Cambridge, MA: MIT Press.
Donati, C. & M. Nespor. 2003. From focus to syntax. *Lingua* 113, 1119-1142.
Doetjes, J., G. Rebuschi & A. Rialland. 2004. Cleft sentences. In F. Corblin & H. de Swart (eds.), *Handbook of French Semantics*. Stanford, CA: CSLI Publications, 53-69.
Georgiafentis, M. & A. Sfakianaki. 2004. Syntax interacts with prosody: The VOS order in Greek. *Lingua* 114, 935-961.
Georgiafentis, M. 2004. *Focus and Word Variation in Greek*. Ph.D. diss., University of Reading.
Grohmann, K.K. 2003. *Prolific Domains: On the Anti-Locality of Movement Dependencies*. Amsterdam: John Benjamins.
Grohmann, K.K., P. Panagiotidis & S. Tsiplakou. 2007. Properties of *wh*-question formation in Cypriot Greek. In M. Janse, B. Joseph & A. Ralli (eds.), *Proceedings of the 2nd International Conference on Modern Greek Dialects and Linguistic Theory (Mytilene, Greece: 30 September–3 October 2004)*. Patras: University of Patras, 83-98.
Gryllia, S. & M. Lekakou. 2006. Syntax reflects information structure: Evidence from Cypriot Greek. Paper presented at the *27th Annual Meeting of the Department of Linguistics*, Aristotle University of Thessaloniki.
Haidou, K. 2006. On the syntax and pragmatic interface: Left-peripheral, medial and right-peripheral focus in Greek. *SOAS Working Papers in Linguistics* 14, 283-308.
Hedberg, N. 2000. The referential status of clefts. *Language* 76, 891–920.
Hornstein, N., J. Nunes & K.K. Grohmann. 2005. *Understanding Minimalism*. Cambridge: Cambridge University Press.
Jackendoff, R. 1972. *Semantic Interpretation in Generative Grammar*. Cambridge, MA: MIT Press.
É. Kiss, K. 1998. Identificational focus versus information focus. *Language* 74, 245-273.
Koursarou, E. & C. Christodoulou. 2005. Focus and clefting in Cypriot

Greek. Ms., University of Cyprus, Nicosia.

Lekakou, M. 2000. Focus in Modern Greek. MA thesis, University College London.

Papapavlou, A. 1997. Attitudes towards the Greek Cypriot dialect: Sociocultural implications. *Proceedings of the 10th International Symposium on Theoretical and Applied Linguistics*. Aristotle University of Thessaloniki: School of English, 173-193.

Papapavlou, A. & P. Pavlou. 1998. A review of the sociolinguistic aspects of the Greek Cypriot dialect. *Journal of Multilingual and Multicultural Development* 19, 212-220.

Prince, E. 1978. A comparison of *wh*-clefts and *it*-clefts in discourse. *Language* 54: 883-906.

Rizzi, L. 1997. The fine structure of the left periphery. In L. Haegeman (ed.), *Elements of Grammar: Handbook in Generative Syntax*. Dordrecht: Kluwer, 281-337.

Tsimpli, I.-M. 1990. The clause structure and word order in Modern Greek. *UCL Working Papers in Linguistics* 2, 226-255.

Tsimpli, I.-M. 1995. Focusing in Modern Greek. In K. É. Kiss (ed.), *Discourse Configurational Languages*. Oxford: Oxford University Press, 176-206.

Tsimpli, I.-M. 1998. Individual and functional readings for focus, *wh*- and negative operators: Evidence from Greek. In B.D. Joseph, G.C. Horrocks & I. Philippaki-Warburton (eds.), *Themes in Greek Linguistics II*. Amsterdam: John Benjamins, 197-228.

Tsiplakou, S., P. Panagiotidis & K.K. Grohmann. In press. Properties of Cypriot Greek wh-question formation. In G. Tsoulas (ed.), *Proceedings of the 7th International Conference on Greek Linguistics*. York: University of York, Department of Language and Linguistic Science (electronic and CD-ROM publication).

CHAPTER FOUR

A FOCUS ACCOUNT OF SWIPING*

Jeremy Hartman & Ruixi Ressy Ai

1. Introduction

This paper investigates *swiping*, the obscure but intriguing ellipsis phenomenon that has been the subject of recent work by Merchant (2002) and van Craenenbroeck (2004). Of specific interest here is the interaction between swiping and information focus. We show that this interaction straightforwardly explains several properties of swiping that have motivated unneeded complications to previous accounts, or else eluded these accounts entirely. To provide the syntactic scaffolding that supports this explanation, we propose that swiping should be analyzed as preposition-stranding in a focus projection outside an elided IP.[1] This has the theoretical consequence that *wh*-phrases in sluicing undergo *two* movement operations — an initial move to [Spec,FocP] to check a focus-based feature [Foc], and a subsequent move to [Spec,ForceP/CP] to check the more familiar *wh*-feature [Wh]. Our aim is essentially to show that, given this syntactic analysis, the various properties of swiping fall out completely from the conditions governing focused elements and their behaviour with respect to ellipsis. No extra theoretical material is required.

In terms of background, the general theory of sluicing assumed here is that of Merchant (2001): The ellipsis site has an internal structure, and sluicing is *wh*-extraction followed by IP-deletion at PF. Additionally, the

---

* This paper grew out of a seminar on ellipsis offered at Harvard in the fall of 2004. We thank Cedric Boeckx, James Huang, and Andrew Nevins for discussion and encouragement. Parts of this paper have also been presented at the UNC Spring Colloquium (2006) and we thank the participants there for their comments and suggestions. All remaining errors are ours.

[1] Previous analyses of swiping as stranding can be found in Kim (1997), Richards (2001), and, in much greater detail, van Craenenbroeck (2004). It is worth noting that the core ideas in this paper were formulated before we had knowledge of the recent latter work, and that accordingly we have re-centred our investigation to emphasize the points on which van Craenenbroeck's account contrasts with ours.

FocP in our analysis is more or less the FocP in the Split-CP framework of Rizzi (1997), and is assumed to have the location and relevant properties attributed to it therein. Namely: (i) the FocP lies above IP but below ForceP/CP, whose specifier is the eventual landing site of extracted *wh*-phrases, and (ii) the head of FocP hosts an (information) focus feature which checks the matching feature of a focused element in the clause.

The paper is organized as follows. Section 1 introduces swiping and briefly reviews its four main established properties, drawn from Merchant (2002) and van Craenenbroeck (2004), which, while not without precedent, are unquestionably the two most thorough discussions of the phenomenon to date.[2] Section 2 introduces the present account and explains how it deals simply with three of these four properties. Section 3 examines the last property, the 'minimal *wh*-condition', argues that it is not what it appears to be, and shows how the present account can explain some crucial new data. Section 4 shows how the present account can additionally explain the interaction of swiping with 'aggressively non-D-linked' *wh*-phrases. Section 5 discusses a previously unnoted phenomenon, 'swiping with *doing*', and demonstrates how it lends support to the present account. Section 6 reviews and critiques the two previous accounts mentioned above. Finally, a concluding section sums up the accomplishments of the present account.

2. Swiping: Background

Merchant (2002) discusses a peculiarity found in some Germanic languages whereby prepositions may invert with sluiced *wh*-words. He terms this phenomenon *swiping*[3]:

(1) a. John went to the prom, but I don't know with who.
b. John went to the prom, but I don't know *who with*.
→ *swiping*

Despite its quirkiness from a syntactic point of view, swiping is fairly

[2] See also Ross (1969), Rosen (1976), van Riemsdijk (1978a,b), and Lobeck (1995).

[3] The word itself, presumably an allusion to the inversion process, and possibly an homage to the idiosyncratic coinages of John Ross, is Merchant's own clever acronym. It stands for **S**luiced ***Wh***-word **I**nversion with **P**repositions **I**n **N**orthern **G**ermanic.

common in written and spoken English. The following are examples taken from Merchant (2002):

(2) a. Lois was talking, but I don't know who to.
 b. They were arguing; God only knows what about.
 c. A: She got a package in the mail.
 B: Really? Who from?
 d. He'll be at the Red Room, but I don't know when till.
 e. Bees are getting into the house, but we can't figure out where from.
 f. He sold his farm and moved away, but no-one knows where to.
 g. Abby quit and got a new job—guess what as!
 h. She bought a robe, but God knows who for.
 i. She fixed it, but she wouldn't let us in on what with.
 j. Lisa wants Bart to get involved, but what in isn't exactly clear.
 k. Tests indicate the megalith was constructed, but not what of.
 l. Although we don't yet know who from, we know she received a package last Monday with instructions on bomb assembly.

(Merchant 2002: (17))

Merchant (2002) and van Craenenbroeck (2004) both identify four properties of swiping that serve as the basic explananda for any account. They are as follows:

(A) Swiping only occurs in sluicing

(3) a. He's giving a speech, but I don't know what about.
 b. * I don't know what about he's giving a speech.

(4) a. She's dancing, and wait till you hear who with.
 b. * Wait till you hear who with she's dancing.

(5) a. A: I'm getting dressed up.
 B: What for?
 b. * What for are you getting dressed up?

(6) a. I got this present, and you'll never guess who from.
 b. * Guess who from I got this present.

(7) a. A: I'm writing my dissertation.
B: Really? What on?
b. * What on are you writing your dissertation?

Merchant (2002) calls this the 'sluicing condition'. The above examples demonstrate the sluicing condition for both embedded and matrix questions. Van Craenenbroeck (2004) notes that swiping is additionally disallowed in a number of other *wh*-constructions (relative clauses, clefts, pseudo-clefts, echo questions, and in situ *wh*-questions) but these seem less relevant, since they do not allow sluiced counterparts for comparison.

(B) Swiping targets only minimal wh-*elements*

(8) a. Lois was talking, but I don't know who to.
b. * Lois was talking, but I don't know which person to.
(van Craenenbroeck 2004: Part One (43))

(9) a. * She bought a robe for one of her nephews, but God knows which (one) for.
b. * They were arguing about animals, but we couldn't figure out what kind about.
c. * This opera was written by an Italian composer in the 19th century, but we're not sure which (composer / one) by.
d. * She's driving, but God knows what town to.
e. * They were riding in somebody's car, but I don't know whose in.
(Merchant 2002: (22a-c,f,h))

Merchant (2002) refers to this as the 'minimality condition', but to avoid confusion with the more prevalent use of that term, we will refer to it here as the 'minimal *wh*-condition'. The generalization is that minimal *wh*-operators, defined more or less as simple heads, may engage in swiping, whereas phrasal or otherwise morphologically complex *wh*-operators may not. Merchant notes two apparent exceptions to this rule, which cover both logical possibilities. The first exception involves *which* and *whose*, *wh*-words that appear to be minimal but may not engage in swiping (cf. (9a,c,e)). The second exception involves morphologically complex *wh*-phrases like *how much* and *how many*, which are marginally and variably acceptable in swiping. We will discuss these exceptions at greater length below.

(C) In swiping, the preposition is always given stress.

(10) a. John's going to the prom, but I'm not sure who WITH / *WHO with.
b. Mary's got flowers in the mail. Guess who FROM / *WHO from.
c. A: I need to talk to you.
B: What ABOUT? / *WHAT about?
d. A: He has a PhD, you know.
B: What IN? / *WHAT in?
e. A: Can you give me a ride?
B: Where TO? / *WHERE to?

If the *wh*-word is given stress instead of the preposition, the result is unacceptable.

(D) Swiping only affects PPs which have no antecedent.[4]

(11) a. We were with somebody. I forget who (*with).
(Merchant 2002: (44a))
b. I'm thinking about something. Guess what (*about).
c. A: I have to buy a birthday present for someone.
B: Who (*for)?
d. A: I have to accompany my sister to somewhere.
B: Where (*to)?

For completeness, observe the following contrasts:

---

[4] Merchant maintains that swiping with an antecedent preposition is sometimes acceptable, citing the following sentence (i); van Craenenbroeck repeats the claim, using this example (in ii):

(i) She fixed it with something, but God only knows what with.

(ii) Howard shares the apartment with someone, but I have no idea who with.

However, of three out of four native English speakers consulted (plus the one who is co-author of this article) consider these two examples to be no better than any of the starred sentences in (11)-(14). (In a footnote, van Craenenbroeck (2004: 28) relays a similar finding by Howard Lasnik.) One speaker judged them (along with (11c-d) and (13b)) to be marginally better, but still degraded. Unfortunately, we have no light to shed on this speaker variation. For our purposes here, it will be assumed that the ban on antecedent prepositions holds without exception.

(12) a. She has a date tonight, but she won't tell me who with.
b. * She has a date with some guy, but she won't tell me who with.

(13) a. A: I managed to borrow a ladder.
B: Really? Who from?
b. A: I managed to borrow a ladder from someone.
* B: Really? Who from?

(14) a. A: We talked for hours.
B: What about?
b. A: We talked for hours about a topic of mutual concern.
* B: What about?

In summary, then, the four basic properties of swiping are as follows: (A) swiping only occurs in sluicing; (B) swiping targets only minimal *wh*-elements; (C) the swiped preposition is always given stress; and (D) swiping only affects PPs without antecedents.

3. The Present Account

(15)

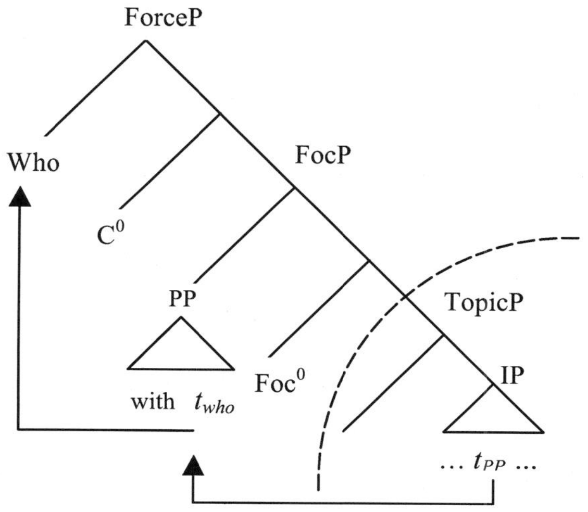

(15) sketches the syntactic analysis serving as foundation for our account.

The one-sentence summary of this analysis is as follows: First the entire PP escapes the ellipsis site by moving to [Spec,FocP], and then the *wh*-word moves alone to [Spec,ForceP/CP], stranding the preposition and deriving the inverted word order. A full explication of (15) and how it can ultimately account for the properties of swiping starts with a closer look at the first movement and what motivates it.

Let us start out by adopting a few assumptions that have already been introduced in the literature. Following Rizzi (1997), we will assume that [Spec,FocP] is the position targeted by (information) focus movement. Following Merchant (2001), we will further assume that IP-ellipsis is driven by an 'E-feature' and that the distribution of this feature is governed by certain information-structural properties of the sentence, embodied in the notion of E-GIVENness (roughly, presence of an antecedent):

(16) E-GIVEN:
An expression E counts as E-GIVEN iff E has a salient antecedent A and, modulo □-type shifting,
(i) A entails F-clo(E), and
(ii) E entails F-clo(A).
(Merchant 2001: ch. 1 (42))

The head of an E-GIVEN phrase bears an E-feature, which marks the head's maximal projection as available for deletion at PF.[5] As applied to IP-deletion (sluicing), these assumptions about the E-feature (that it is governed by the E-GIVENness property and that it is what allows deletion at PF) produce the following constraint:

(17) An IP α can be deleted only if α is E-GIVEN.

Clearly related to this constraint is Merchant's (2001: 26, fn. 9) generalization that "a deleted constituent will not contain any F[ocus]-marked material; material extracted from the ellipsis site, on the other hand, will often, though not always, be F-marked." To capture this generalization, we propose that there is an [*i*Foc] (information focus) feature which marks elements containing antecedent-less information as

[5] This is the revised E-feature analysis used in Gengel (2005). Merchant's (2001) original E-feature analysis was rather more complex; it involved I-to-C feature raising, which meant the relation of the feature-bearing head to the deleted IP was given as head-complement, instead of head-maximal projection. The differences between these two versions are not of consequence here.

focused in the context of E-GIVEN material.[6] Specifically, the generalization is jointly captured by (18), which states the distribution of the [*i*Foc] feature, and (19), which describes its behaviour with respect to ellipsis.

(18) Assign an [*i*Foc] feature only to a *non*-E-GIVEN element which is dominated by an E-GIVEN constituent.

(19) A deleted constituent may not contain an [*i*Foc] feature.

In (18) we have a nice formulation of the intuition that the [*i*Foc] feature should pick out the 'new' material from the old. On the assumption that, at the very least, an [*i*Foc] feature marks its bearer for stress, (18) is demonstrated in the following examples:

(20) a. Bill's coming, but I'm not sure WHEN$_{[i\text{Foc}]}$ he's coming.
b. * Bill's coming, but I'm not sure when HE's$_{[i\text{Foc}]}$ coming.
c. * Bill's coming, but I'm not sure when he's COMING$_{[i\text{Foc}]}$.

(21) a. He keeps telling us he's writing a book. He just won't tell us what he's writing a book ABOUT$_{[i\text{Foc}]}$.
b. He keeps telling us he's writing a book about something. He just won't tell us WHAT$_{[i\text{Foc}]}$ he's writing a book about.
c. * He keeps telling us he's writing a book about something. He just won't tell us what he's writing a book ABOUT$_{[i\text{Foc}]}$.
d. * He keeps telling us he's writing a book. He just won't tell us WHAT$_{[i\text{Foc}]}$ he's writing a book about.

In (20), *when* is not E-GIVEN, so it can bear an [*i*Foc] feature, but *he* and *coming* are both E-GIVEN and thus cannot bear [*i*Foc] features. The examples in (21) are a bit more complex. In (21a) the PP is not E-GIVEN, so its head, *about*, bears an [*i*Foc] feature. In (21b) *what* is not E-GIVEN (its only antecedent is an indefinite), so it bears an [*i*Foc] feature. In (21c) the PP is indeed E-GIVEN, so the [*i*Foc] feature on *about* is unlicensed and

[6] The [*i*Foc] feature is so named to distinguish it from other proposed focus-marking features, such as the [contrastive] feature introduced in Gengel's (2005) account of pseudogapping. Note that in general swiping is acceptable only with informationally focused PPs, not contrastively focused ones:

(i) ??/*The senator voted for the tax cut, but I don't know what AGAINST.
(ii) ??/*The senator voted against the tax cut, but I don't know what FOR.

the sentence is unacceptable. In (21d) the PP is not E-GIVEN, so it should bear an [*i*Foc] feature, but it does not, rendering the sentence is unacceptable. Note that the examples containing an unlicensed [*i*Foc] ((20a-b) and (21c)) have a distinctly redundant character, suggestive of their status as violations of the rules of focus assignment.

Having stated in (18) the principles that govern the distribution of the [*i*Foc] feature, let us now turn to the condition given in (19), and examine the interaction of [*i*Foc] with ellipsis. (19) states that no deleted constituent may contain an [*i*Foc] feature. How is this requirement met? What happens to [*i*Foc] within an E-GIVEN constituent targeted for deletion? We propose that, when threatened with deletion, the [*i*Foc] feature triggers an overt extraction that 'rescues' new information from the ellipsis site, thereby preventing a violation of the condition stated in (19). This rescue consists of movement to [Spec,FocP], driven by a matching [*i*Foc] on the Foc-head[7] (cf. the tree in (15) above). Note that this (overt) movement to [Spec,FocP] is motivated entirely by the constraint in (19), and thus only occurs in ellipsis environments; when no deletion occurs, there is nothing to rescue, and the [*i*Foc] feature is presumably checked covertly, resulting in mere stress (as in, e.g., (21a)).

To review: So far we have lain down the following principles governing the [*i*Foc] feature and its behaviour under ellipsis.

THE FOCUS ASSIGNMENT RULE (18):
Assign an [*i*Foc] feature only to a *non*-E-GIVEN element which is dominated by an E-GIVEN constituent.

THE FOCUS DELETION BAN (19):
A deleted constituent may not contain an [*i*Foc] feature.

THE FOCUS MOVEMENT RULE:
A. Only elements that bear [*i*Foc] may move to [Spec,FocP].
B. This movement only occurs overtly if it is independently compelled to do so in order to rescue [*i*Foc] from IP-deletion at PF.

We have also proposed the following syntactic analysis of swiping and the following constraint that is its logical consequence (after all, you cannot get stranded somewhere unless you are there in the first place):

---

[7] See Ai (2006a,b) and Gengel (2005) for analyses of gapping and pseudogapping that follow similar lines of reasoning.

THE SWIPING-AS-STRANDING ANALYSIS & CONSEQUENT CONSTRAINT:

A. Swiping is preposition-stranding in [Spec,FocP].

B. Consequently, no preposition may appear in swiping unless it has moved to [Spec,FocP].

What we would now like to argue is that all four main properties of swiping can be derived from these principles alone. Two of these four properties can be given fairly brief explanation, and the other two require more discussion. Let us begin with the two briefer explanations, which are to some degree intuitively connected.

In swiping, the preposition is always given stress.

On the Swiping-as-Stranding Analysis, this property simply follows from the position in which the preposition is stranded, given widely accepted assumptions about the correlation between focus and stress. If focused elements are as a rule given stress, and only focused elements can move to [Spec,FocP], then anything stranded [Spec,FocP] should be given stress. Since swiping is assumed to be preposition-stranding in [Spec, FocP], it is natural that the preposition should always bear stress.

Swiping only affects prepositions which have no antecedent.

This property is accounted for by the distribution of the [*i*Foc] feature, coupled with the fact that it is this feature that triggers movement to [Spec, FocP]. Put differently, this property results from the interaction between the Focus Assignment Rule and the Focus Movement Rule. A step-by-step derivation of the property runs as follows:

i. Only non-E-GIVEN prepositions may receive an [*i*Foc] feature. (*FOCUS ASSIGNMENT RULE*)
ii. Only prepositions without antecedents may bear an [*i*Foc] feature. (Definition of E-GIVENness)
iii. Only prepositions which bear [*i*Foc] may move to [Spec,FocP]. (*FOCUS MOVEMENT RULE*)
iv. Only prepositions without antecedents can move to [Spec,FocP]. (ii) & (iii)
v. No preposition may appear in swiping unless moved to [Spec,FocP]. (*SWIPING-AS-STRANDING*)
vi. Only prepositions without antecedents can appear in swiping. (iv) & (v)

Swiping only occurs in sluicing.

This property, the so-called 'sluicing condition', is practically a restatement of the second part of the Focus Movement Rule. Recall that [*i*Foc] triggers overt movement only when threatened with deletion. Thus, focus movement (by hypothesis a prerequisite for swiping) is only motivated when there is a deletion site to extract from. At the risk of formalizing the obvious, here is a step-by-step derivation of the sluicing condition:

i. Swiping is contingent on (overt) movement of a PP to [Spec,FocP]. (*SWIPING-AS-STRANDING ANALYSIS*)
ii. (Overt) movement to [Spec, FocP] only occurs if it is required in order to rescue an [*i*Foc] feature from IP-deletion at PF. (*FOCUS MOVEMENT RULE*)
iii. Swiping is contingent on IP-deletion at PF. (i) & (ii)
iv. Swiping is contingent on (only occurs in) sluicing. (Definition of sluicing)

One troubling objection presents itself here. According to the Focus Deletion Ban in (19), there is no reason why IP-deletion should be the only type of ellipsis that necessitates a rescue of the [*i*Foc] feature. VP-deletion should work just as well to trigger movement of the focused PP to [Spec, FocP] and thus allow swiping. The question, then, is: why do we have a 'sluicing condition' and not a general 'ellipsis condition' which would include VP-ellipsis? Specifically, why aren't the 'swiping' examples in (22) acceptable?

(22) a. * He went to the prom, but I don't know who with he did ~~go to the prom $t_{witch\ who}$~~.
b. A: They were arguing.
* B: What about were they ~~arguing $t_{about\ what}$~~?
c. * Mary got chocolates in the mail, but you'll never guess who from she did ~~get chocolates in the mail $t_{from\ who}$~~.
d. A: I sent a package today.
* B: Who to did you ~~send a package $t_{to\ who}$~~?

Merchant (2002) voices a version of this objection, using it to challenge Richards' earlier (2001) swiping-as-stranding account. It is unclear, however, whether swiping is really the source of the ungrammaticality in (22). Indeed, the force of these examples is quite muted because the problem does not seem to be specific to swiping. The sentences in (22) are not salvaged when swiping is removed from the equation:[8]

(23) a. ??/* He went to the prom, but I don't know with who he did ~~go to the prom $t_{with\ who}$~~.
b. A: They were arguing.
* B: About what were they ~~arguing $t_{about\ what}$~~?
c. ??/* Mary got chocolates in the mail, but you'll never guess from who she did ~~get chocolates in the mail $t_{from\ who}$~~.
d. A: I sent a package today.
* B: To who did you ~~send a package $t_{to\ who}$~~?

Note that, like those in (22), the sentences in (23) would be perfectly grammatical if the entire IP were deleted. Furthermore, not only is the ungrammaticality in (22) unspecific to swiping, it is not even specific to PP focus movement or pied-piping of prepositions. It appears to be part of a larger phenomenon which prohibits the extraction of argument *wh*-words out of VP-ellipsis sites.[9]

(24) a. A: I kissed someone tonight.
* B: Who did you ~~kiss t_{wo}~~?
b. * I need to buy something, but I forget what I do ~~need to buy t_{hat}~~.
c. * Ed was driving somewhere, but I'm not sure where he was ~~driving t_{here}~~.
d. A: Bill fired someone.
* B: Really? Who did he ~~fire t_{wo}~~?

Again, note that all the sentences in (24) are perfectly fine if the entire IP is deleted. It seems, then, that the unavailability of swiping with VP-

---

[8] As indicated above, some speakers find embedded examples of this type slightly better than non-embedded examples. We have no account for this variation.

[9] Curiously, the extraction of adjunct *wh*-words out of VP-ellipsis sites is generally unproblematic:

(i) Mary's baking a cake, but I'm not sure WHY she is ~~baking a cake t_{why}~~.

(ii) The prisoners escaped. We're just trying to figure out WHEN they did ~~escape t_{hen}~~.

ellipsis does not constitute an objection to our account of the sluicing condition, because movement of argument *wh*-words (or PPs containing them) out of VP-ellipsis sites is prohibited independently of swiping. At present, we cannot offer any explanation of this very intriguing phenomenon.[10]

4. The Minimal *Wh*-Condition Reconsidered

This final property of swiping requires a bit more thought, and, eventually, a bit of tweaking to get the facts right. A closer look at the initial evidence for the 'minimal *wh*-condition' should immediately prompt some scepticism. Of the five examples in (9) above, four are already violations of the ban on antecedent PPs. When we attempt to remove these violations in order to legitimately test the minimal *wh*-condition, we run up against the true nature of the minimal *wh*-condition. (9a), (9b) and (9e) are repeated here in (25). In (26) they have been modified by removing the antecedent PP.

(25) a. * She bought a robe for one of her nephews, but God knows which (one) for.
b. * They were arguing about animals, but we couldn't figure out what kind about.
c. * They were riding in somebody's car, but I don't know whose in.

---

[10] One idea worth pursuing is that this phenomenon follows from a principle stating that no E-GIVEN constituent may be deleted if it lies within a larger E-GIVEN constituent. In other words, if the deletion option is chosen, it must apply to the largest possible E-GIVEN constituent (cf. the principle of 'MaxElide' proposed by Takahashi & Fox, 2005). The examples in (22), (23) and (24) all violate this principle, since only the VP is deleted even though the full IP is E-GIVEN. Standard 'contrastive subject' VP-ellipsis, on the other hand, is allowed because the subject is new material. In the following example, the subject has no antecedent, hence the IP is not E-GIVEN, and the VP is the largest E-GIVEN constituent:

(i) Mary's eating cake, and BILL is ~~eating cake~~, too.

Of course, more needs to be said, because the argument *wh*-extraction ban appears even in 'contrastive subject' VP-ellipsis:

(ii) a. * Mary's eating cake, but I don't know what BILL is ~~eating t_{what}~~.
b. * Mary loves Bill. Who does SALLY ~~love t_{who}~~?

(26) a. * She bought a robe, but God knows which (one/nephew) for.
b. * They were arguing, but we couldn't figure out what kind about.
c. * They were riding, but I don't know whose in.

The sentences in (26) are still ungrammatical, but for a new reason. Now the intuition is that the non-minimal *wh*-phrases *which (one/nephew)*, *what kind*, and *whose (car)* are unlicensed because they lack the proper antecedent context. This intuition is explained once we recognize a fairly conspicuous fact about non-minimal *wh*-phrases, but one that has thus far escaped mention in discussions of swiping. To wit: Non-minimal *wh*-operators are always 'D(discourse)-linked' in the sense of Pesetsky (1987). In other words, a question with a non-minimal *wh*-phrase such as [*which x, what x, whose x*] requires a presupposition in the discourse that there exists some x with the properties ascribed to it in the question. For instance, the questions in the a-examples require the presuppositions in the b-examples:

(27) a. Which dress did Mary end up buying?
b. ∃x.x is a dress, Mary ended up buying x
"Mary ended up buying a dress."

(28) a. Whose jacket are you wearing?
b. ∃x.x is a jacket, you are wearing x
"You are wearing a [necessarily someone's] jacket."

Crucially for our purposes, this means that if the property ascribed to the non-minimal *wh*-phrase involves placing the *wh*-phrase within a PP, then the discourse presupposition, in order to provide the required informational context, must also contain this same PP:

(29) a. Which dress did Mary pay $300 for?
b. ∃x.x is a dress, Mary paid $300 for x
"Mary paid $300 *for a dress*."

(30) a. Whose dissertation is everybody talking about?
b. ∃x.x is a dissertation, everybody is talking about x
"Everybody is talking *about a [necessarily someone's] dissertation*."

Thus, whenever a non-minimal *wh*-phrase is generated within a PP, that PP must have an antecedent in the discourse. But we have already seen in the last section that, due to the principles of focus assignment and focus movement, swiping *prohibits* PP antecedents. This produces a clash, and we are now in a position to view the apparent 'minimal *wh*-condition' as nothing more than this clash, merely a by-product of the interaction between the licensing of D-linked *wh*-phrases and the licensing of focused elements.

If this reasoning is correct, it makes a surprising prediction: the generalization embodied in the minimal *wh*-condition should not hold absolutely. This is because the aforementioned clash between D-linking requirements and focus requirements is not absolute. Focus requirements (cf. the *FOCUS ASSIGNMENT RULE* established in the previous section, and the definition of E-GIVEN in (16)) in effect deny focus to PPs with *overt* antecedents. Presuppositional D-linking requirements strongly favour overt antecedents, but do not absolutely require them. Under specific circumstances, as Pesetsky (1987) observed, the discourse antecedent can come in the form of contextual implication. Thus, scarce exceptions to the minimal *wh*-condition are predicted to exist under the rare circumstances where an antecedent clause does not contain an overt PP, but strongly implies one.

In fact, this prediction is borne out. It turns out there are indeed examples where the semantics of the antecedent clause implies a given restricted set of options, satisfying both the focus and D-linking requirements, and allowing swiping even though the *wh*-phrase is not minimal:

(31) a. He fought in the civil war, but I don't know which side for.
b. Pierre is an illegal immigrant. He's originally from France, but came here from Canada. He'll definitely be deported, but it's not clear which country to.
c. A: He plays shortstop.
B: Which team for?
d. It appears to have been translated, but I can't tell what language from.

Speakers' judgments on these vary somewhat, but importantly, they are always judged to be more acceptable than the sentences in (9). Furthermore, hundreds of individually verified examples collected from internet searches attest to the wide acceptability of sentences like this. Here is a small sampling, a fraction of the total examples found.

(32) a. It doesn't matter where in the world you work or **what company for**, bosses are all the same and for the life of you, you just can't work out how the hell they got to be boss in the first place.

b. Fiat will keep on buying GM's 1.8-liter for six models in its current range, while the American company admitted, on the other hand, that it will purchase Fiat's 1.2-liter F.I.R.E. engine. But GM has not said so far **what product for**, but it seems clear that it is the subcompact Celta, Chevrolet's best seller.

c. Will you be going into town to buy it on release day? If so, **which store from?**

d. Chrissy, nice to meet you, I recognize your name, not sure **what site from**, but that doesn't matter, nice to meet you regardless.

e. … but 1st how do you tell who it was composed by and **what instrument for**, and what title best suits the piece etc. ... I've guessed some of them.

f. A complete breakdown of how Brown has scored his points and **which teams against** is as follows:

g. I'm definitely buying Megaman, but am not sure **what system for** yet.

h. And yeah, it's open late. Not sure **what time til**, but late.

i. He is now a professional Quidditch player but I can't remember **what team for**.

j. And I won more tickets, but I don't know **what day for**, so I might be going twice.

In sum, the present account of swiping can explain the overwhelming appearance of a 'minimal *wh*-condition' as well as the rare but crucial exceptions to it. Additionally, since the present account invokes D-linking instead of strict phrasal character, it can deal straightforwardly with bare *which* and *whose*, the aforementioned apparent exceptions to the minimal *wh*-condition. Because *which* and *whose* are just as D-linked when they are bare as when they head phrases, these 'exceptions' turn out not to be exceptions at all, and are correctly predicted not to appear in swiping.

Finally, the present account also suggests a solution to another of swiping's unsolved mysteries — why it is available with some prepositions but not with others (cf. Merchant 2002: n. 5):

(33) A: I was arguing with Bill.
B: What about? (*before, *during, *despite, etc.)

Perhaps the prepositions which never appear in swiping (*between*, *before*, *underneath*, *despite*, *during*, etc.) are simply those prepositions for which it is virtually impossible to conceive of an antecedent that carries the unequivocal implication of the appropriate PP. For instance, the preposition *about* is very amenable to swiping, because there is no shortage of antecedents which, for all practical purposes, imply a PP headed by *about*; many things and actions can be automatically assumed to be about something. If Mary tells you she was arguing with Bill, it makes sense to ask her, without further context, what she was arguing with Bill *about*. On the other hand, it would make very little sense to ask her, without further context, what she was arguing with Bill *before*, or what she was arguing with him *despite*, *during*, or *underneath*, even though she might well have been arguing with him before lunch, during a movie, underneath a pine tree, or despite her promise not to. It is not that PPs headed by these prepositions are incompatible with the antecedent; it is simply that they are not *implied* by the antecedent, and thus they do not appear in swiping.

5. Swiping and Aggressively Non-D-Linked *Wh*-Phrases

As it happens, turning the spotlight on the discourse status of non-minimal *wh*-phrases also serves to illuminate a less-discussed property of swiping regarding *wh*-phrases with the exact opposite discourse status. Pesetsky (1987) proposed that at the other end of the D-linking spectrum are so-called 'aggressively non-D-linked *wh*-phrases' like *what the hell*, *who on earth, where the devil*, etc. (for more recent discussion of these, see also den Dikken & Giannakidou, 2002).

Swiping has the ability to 'save' aggressively non-D-linked *wh*-phrases, which are otherwise flatly unacceptable under sluicing.

(34) a. John's talking about something, but I don't know what.
b. * John's talking about something, but I don't know what the hell.

(35) a. John's talking, but I don't know about what.
b. * John's talking, but I don't know about what the hell.

(36) a. John's talking, but I don't know what about.
b. √ John's talking, but I don't know what the hell about.

(37) a. A: I borrowed a strobe light for the party.
B: Who on earth from?
b. A: Is there a way you could get me on board the *Dallas*?
B: What the hell for? (from *The Hunt for Red October*)
c. Mary went dancing but you'll never guess who the hell with.
d. A: I'm getting married.
B: Who the hell to? (from *Arrested Development*)

Other *wh*-phrases may appear with or without swiping, but aggressively non-D-linked *wh*-phrases are restricted to swiping. The explanation we will propose here is that, for reasons related to their aggressively non-D-linked status, these *wh*-phrases cannot bear [*i*Foc] features, and thus the only way they can move to [Spec,FocP] is to be moved as part of a larger constituent which *does* bear an [*i*Foc] feature. The PP plays the role of this larger constituent.

Recall that D-linked *wh*-phrases require an antecedent presupposition with certain informational properties (cf. (27)-(30)). The essential property of aggressively non-D-linked *wh*-phrases, then, is that they *prohibit* antecedent presuppositions of this type. A moment's reflection reveals an important consequence of this prohibition: aggressively non-D-linked *wh*-phrases cannot be dominated by E-GIVEN material, and thus cannot receive an [*i*Foc] feature, given the FOCUS ASSIGNMENT RULE established in Section 2. This is demonstrated in the following examples:

(38) a. ??/* He's writing something, he just won't tell me WHAT THE HELL$_{[i\text{Foc}]}$ he's writing.[11]
b. ??/* Mary kissed someone tonight, but I have no idea WHO ON EARTH$_{[i\text{Foc}]}$ she kissed.
c. ??/* The prisoners escaped, but we can't figure out HOW THE HELL$_{[i\text{Foc}]}$ they escaped.
d. ??/* I know you already ate. I'm asking WHAT IN THE WORLD$_{[i\text{Foc}]}$ you ate!

Observe in (39) that garden-variety *wh*-words have no trouble receiving an [*i*Foc] feature in these exact same sentences, and in (40) that

[11] Here we are capitalizing the aggressively non-D-linked phrases in this peculiar way in order to indicate that they are bad regardless of their internal prosodic structure (*what the HELL*, *WHAT the hell*, *who on EARTH*, *WHO on earth*, etc.).

aggressively non-D-linked *wh*-phrases are perfectly acceptable in the same sentences as long as there is no discourse antecedent:

(39) He's writing something, he just won't tell me WHAT$_{[i\text{Foc}]}$ he's writing.

(40) What the hell are you writing?

The issue, then, is simply that aggressively non-D-linked *wh*-phrases cannot receive an [*i*Foc] feature, for the reason stated above. (The distribution of the [*i*Foc] feature clashes with the distribution of aggressively non-D-linked phrases; the former must be dominated by an E-GIVEN constituent, whereas the latter must not be.)

The logical path towards an explanation of the data in (34)-(37) should now be reasonably clear. Since aggressively non-D-linked *wh*-phrases cannot bear an [*i*Foc] feature, it follows that they cannot engage in movement to [Spec, FocP], as per the *FOCUS MOVEMENT RULE* established in Section 2. If, however, an aggressively non-D-linked *wh*-phrase is contained within a PP whose head bears an [*i*Foc] feature, this feature can trigger movement of the entire PP (including the *wh*-phrase) to [Spec, FocP]. The aggressively non-D-linked *wh*-phrase can then move to [Spec, CP] to satisfy its [Wh]-feature, stranding its preposition in [Spec,FocP], and producing swiping:

(41)

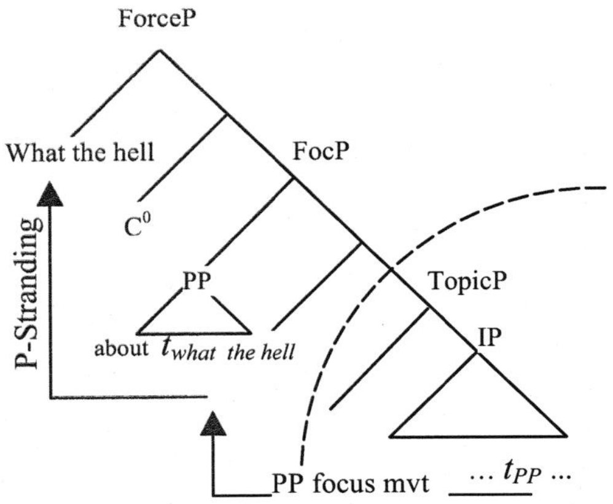

Looking back at the paradigm in (34)-(36), one question remains. We have explained how (36b) is ruled in, but we have not explained how (35b)

is ruled out. Once the entire PP has been moved to [Spec,FocP], we might expect the aggressively non-D-linked *wh*-phrase to be able to pied-pipe the preposition along to [Spec,CP], retaining the usual word order, as in (35a). What prevents a non-stranding version of the derivation in (41)? We propose that this version is ruled out by an independent restriction on pied-piping for aggressively non-D-linked phrases: Aggressively non-D-linked *wh*-phrases cannot pied-pipe. They must strand their prepositions.

(42) a. What the hell did you fix it with?
b. * With what the hell did you fix it?

(43) a. Who on earth is he talking to?
b. * To who on earth is he talking?

Thus, *what the hell* must strand its preposition in [Spec,FocP] while it moves on to [Spec,CP], giving us (36b) but ruling out (35b), because pied-piping is prohibited with aggressively non-D-linked phrases. (35a) and (36a), on the other hand, are both acceptable because garden-variety *wh*-words have no such restriction. They may either strand or pied-pipe. Thus, the present analysis of swiping successfully accounts for its interaction with aggressively non-D-linked *wh*-phrases.

6. Swiping with *Doing*

This section introduces a hitherto unmentioned variant of swiping, which we will call 'swiping with *doing*':

(44) a. A: I spent the entire day at the mall.
B: Really? What doing?
b. John has a job, but he won't tell me what doing.
c. A: I threw my back out the other day.
B: What doing?
d. A: Mary made $10,000 in one week.
B: What doing?
e. He's been here for hours, God only knows what doing.

We propose that these have a structure and two-part derivation analogous to prepositional swiping. *Doing what* is first focus-marked and moved to [Spec,FocP] to avoid deletion, and then *doing* is stranded in that position, obtaining the surface word order, as in (45):

(45) $[_{CP}\ \text{what}_i\ [_{FocP}\ \text{DOING}\ t_i]_j\ [_{IP} \ldots [\ t_j\ ]]]$

Swiping with *doing* can thus be seen as the elliptical version of 'stranding with *doing*' (exemplified in (46)), which we take to be related to constructions of the type exemplified in (47):

(46) a. What did you spend your summer doing?
b. Guess what I got a job doing
c. They don't care what we do. They care what we get photographed doing. (from *Casino Royale*)

(47) a. I spent the entire day at the mall buying clothes.
b. John has a job mowing lawns.
c. I threw my back out trying to lift the sofa.
d. Mary made $10,000 selling stocks.
e. He's been here for hours fiddling with the thermostat.

Swiping with *doing* is somewhat less common than swiping with prepositions, but is still fairly prevalent, as demonstrated by the following examples from literature:

(48) a. "I had a nice evening," she said, in the bathroom.
"**What doing**?" (from Ray Bradbury, *Fahrenheit 451*)
b. "The basement joint on Wells Street?" asked Jimmy.
"Sure I know it."
"Well that's where I got you a job," said the Lizard.
"**What doing**?" asked Jimmy.
(from Edgard Rice Burroughs, *The Efficiency Expert*)
c. Q. Were you over there at the factory on May 3d?
A. Yes, in the morning.
Q. **What doing**?
(from the transcript of the Sacco and Vanzetti trial)
d. "What are you doing in New Haven, Weagle?"
"I'm working here. Got a job in the Connecticut Inn."
"Oh. **What doing**?"
(from Sinclair Lewis, *Work of Art*)
e. "They were caught with Simon Moonan and Tusker Boyle in the square one night." The fellows looked at him and asked:
"Caught? **What doing**?"
(from James Joyce, *Portrait of the Artist as a Young Man*)

f. My Dear Tommy, – The mail is just about to leave us, so I write to let you know where I am and **what doing**.
(from R.M. Ballantyne, *The Lifeboat*)

g. "I've been here ever since you came."
"**What in the world doing**?"
"Oh, enjoying myself."
(from William Dean Howells, *Dr. Breen's Practice*)

A large number of individually verified examples collected from the internet also attest to the swiping with *doing* phenomenon. A few samples are provided below:

(49) a. Questions as to where I'd been and **what doing** stopped as I began dumping cigarettes out of the pockets of the several layers of ragged summer uniforms I was wearing.

b. And he said, you want a job? And I said, **what doing**? He said dumping coal…

c. A: I have a list there of employers, did you work for Bechara and Son?
B: I work with him, yes.
A: **What doing**?

d. Another time I was by myself (I forget **what doing**).

e. A: Spent 6 hours at the mall yesterday.
B: **What on earth doing**? Hanging out? Girl-watching? Shopping? Eating? Catching a movie?

f. Dave's got a job now too, though I don't know **what doing** or where.

Swiping with *doing* exhibits counterparts to all the relevant properties of normal swiping. It obeys a sluicing condition (50), a ban on antecedent instances of *doing* (51), and a requirement that *doing* must bear stress (52):

(50) a. A: Bill's at the library.
B: What doing?

b. * What doing is Bill at the library?

(51) a. A: Bill's at the library
B: What doing?

b. A: Bill's at the library doing something.
* B: What doing?

(52) A: Bill's at the library.
B: What DOING? / *WHAT doing?

It is certainly difficult to argue that *doing* is a preposition.[12] Thus, the existence of swiping with *doing* has important consequences for analyses of swiping, since it shows that the principles that interact to produce swiping are not limited to PPs.

Other constituents, such as VPs, may engage in swiping-like constructions, but only if they meet the requirements for an [*i*Foc] feature (in effect, only if they are unambiguously implied, but not overtly stated, by an antecedent). This requirement also serves to explain why *doing* is the only verb that regularly works this way.

(53) A: I've been here for hours.
B: What doing? (*eating, *singing, *building, etc.) (cf. (33))

Put bluntly, people are usually *doing* something, hence many antecedents carry an obvious implication that subject was doing something; on the other hand, virtually no antecedents (or only carefully contrived antecedents[13]) carry an obvious implication that the subject was, e.g., building something, or singing something, etc. (cf. the similar discussion of why some prepositions never appear in swiping, at the end of section 4).

---

[12] Although it seems intuitively off the mark, one could conceivably claim that *doing* belongs to the small class of verbally derived pseudo-prepositions like *regarding* and *concerning*, which often do behave like prepositions. Unlike this class however, *doing* does not show preposition-like behaviour. For instance, it is unable to pied-pipe its complement (**Doing what did you spend your summer?*)

[13] For instance, some speakers will accept sentences along the lines of (i). Less explicably, however, we also get the attested example in (ii), courtesy of Gilbert & Sullivan:

(i) A: Last week John made a thousand dollars going door to door.
B: Really? What selling?

(ii) Josephine: Remember who you are and whom addressing.
(from *H.M.S. Pinafore* (1878), Act. I, No. 11)

Note that this example (like (48f) and (49a) above) is particularly odd, since the elided material exhibits only phonological identity, not semantic identity, to its antecedent. In *Remember who you are*, the *are* is predicative, but in *whom ~~you are~~ addressing,* the *are* is an auxiliary.

7. Two Previous Accounts

This section will briefly review two previous accounts of swiping, and show that neither of them is entirely satisfactory. We will turn first to Merchant (2002), who analyzes swiping as head-movement at PF:

(54)

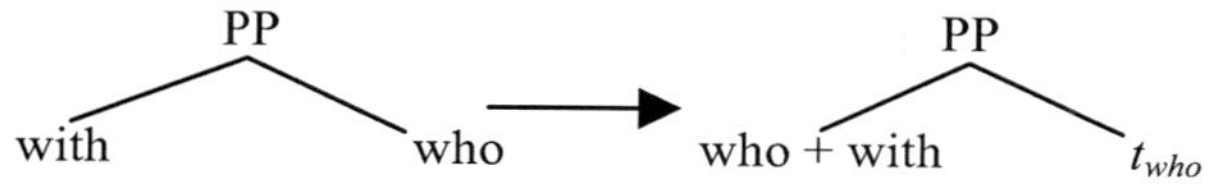

Thus, (1b) is derived from (1a) by a simple, PP-internal operation. These sentences are repeated here as (55a) and (55b),

(55) a. John went to the prom, but I don't know with who.
b. John went to the prom, but I don't know who with.

Let us see how this analysis deals with the four main properties of swiping. The major accomplishment of Merchant's account is that it is able to offer a clear-cut explanation for the (apparent) minimal *wh*-condition. On the standard assumption that phrases cannot adjoin to heads, the following variation on the derivation in (56) is ruled out:[14]

(56)

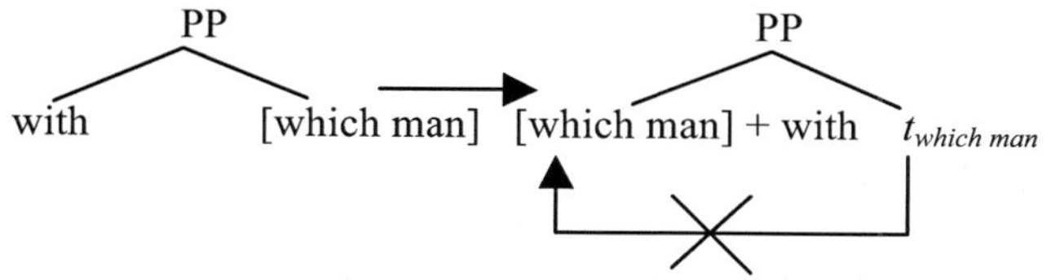

As for the two aforementioned exceptions to the minimal *wh*-condition (bare *which* and *whose*, the apparent heads that act like phrases; and *how much*, *how long*, etc., the apparent phrases that act like heads), Merchant explanation consists, unsurprisingly, of arguing that appearances are deceiving, and that the former are in fact phrases, and the latter in fact heads. Essentially, bare *which* and *whose* actually have elided NP complements, making them phrasal. And elements like *how much*, despite being polymorphemic, are "presumably subject to varying degrees of reanalysis" as heads (Merchant 2002:297).

[14] Another possibility would be to have the D head alone adjoin to the preposition, stranding its NP complement. Merchant rules this out by invoking the general ban on D-excorporation in English (see Baker 1995).

The fact that swiped prepositions must receive focus, Merchant attributes to "general head-final prominence algorithms operative in English" (Merchant 2002:305). This constraint, HEADFINAL, interacts with another constraint from the realm of focus, Schwarzschild's (1999) AVOIDF, to derive the third main property of swiping, that swiping only affects PPs which have no antecedent. AVOIDF states that a GIVEN element (one with a salient antecedent) should not receive focus. Taken together with HEADFINAL, AVOIDF effectively prohibits swiping when there is a prepositional antecedent. The reasoning runs as follows, but see Merchant (2002: 304-309) for more detail.

i. HEADFINAL dictates that swiped prepositions should receive focus.
ii. AVOIDF dictates that GIVEN elements should *not* receive focus.
iii. Therefore, if a preposition GIVEN, it should not appear in swiping.

Merchant's (2002) treatment of the 'sluicing condition' is somewhat opaque. In the expository portion of that article, it clearly held up as an explanandum, yet in later sections (pp. 304-309) it is recast as a premise and used to argue that the head-movement in swiping occurs at PF. The suggestion is presumably that the sluicing condition is in some way tied to the fact that IP-deletion and (this particular) head-movement are both PF phenomena. It is not at all obvious, though, how this might lead to an explanation of the sluicing condition, which goes beyond stating that swiping and IP-ellipsis are merely linked in terms of where in the derivation they take place, to state that swiping cannot occur except under sluicing. From the fact that two syntactic operations both occur after spell-out it certainly does not follow that one is contingent on the other.[15]

This issue aside, Merchant's account is unsatisfactory for four reasons. First, it cannot explain the exceptions to the minimal *wh*-condition. Since it assumes that it is the phrasal nature of the *wh*-element, not its discourse status, that determines acceptability in swiping, Merchant's account predicts phrasal *wh*-elements to be unacceptable in swiping without exception (i.e., altering the information-structural context should in no way alter the acceptability of swiping.) After all, an element like *which country* is phrasal regardless of information-structural context, so the data in section 3 present Merchant's account with a major obstacle.

Second, Merchant's account is unable to account for the striking cross-linguistic correlation between swiping and preposition-stranding. As

[15] Van Craenenbroeck (2004: 105) appears to share our scepticism towards Merchant's treatment of the sluicing condition.

Merchant (2002) notes, swiping exists only in (a subset of) those languages that allow preposition stranding: Danish, Norwegian, and English. If swiping simply *is* preposition stranding, this particular cross-linguistic distribution is not surprising. If swiping is head-movement, its cross-linguistic distribution is quite a coincidence indeed.

Third, since it assumes that swiping is a PP-specific operation, Merchant's account cannot explain the existence of swiping with *doing*, unless *doing* is claimed to be a preposition (a hard sell; see fn. 12 above).

Fourth, and perhaps most problematically, a head-movement analysis cannot account for the fact that swiping can apparently occur across higher clauses (a fact noted by van Craenenbroeck (2004)). The following examples, collected from the internet, show that higher interrogative clauses can intervene between the preposition and the *wh*-word in swiping:

(57) a. A: He wants us.
B: What do you suppose for?
b. Besides, Jisao was "invited" here. Who do you think by?
c. It looks like he's thinking pretty hard in the last two poses, what do you suppose about?
d. Will I get married, and if so, who do you think with?
e. Do Polynesians feel that they originated on the Islands of Polynesia, or do they think that they sailed there? If they sailed there, where do you think from?

Examples like these pose an obvious problem for a head-movement analysis. If *who by* is derived from *by who* with a simple PP-internal operation, it is unclear how any material could intervene, let alone an entire clause. In contrast, the present account of swiping has no difficulty with the data in (57): After the *wh*-word has stranded the preposition in [Spec,FocP] of the lower clause and moved on to [Spec,ForceP] of the lower clause, it simply undergoes another movement [Spec,ForceP] of the higher clause, no differently from usual multi-clause *wh*-movement without a preposition.

Let us now turn to van Craenenbroeck (2004), whose analysis of swiping is syntactically very similar to ours. He proposes that swiping is preposition-stranding in an iterated CP (the same CP targeted by focus movement), as shown below:

(57)

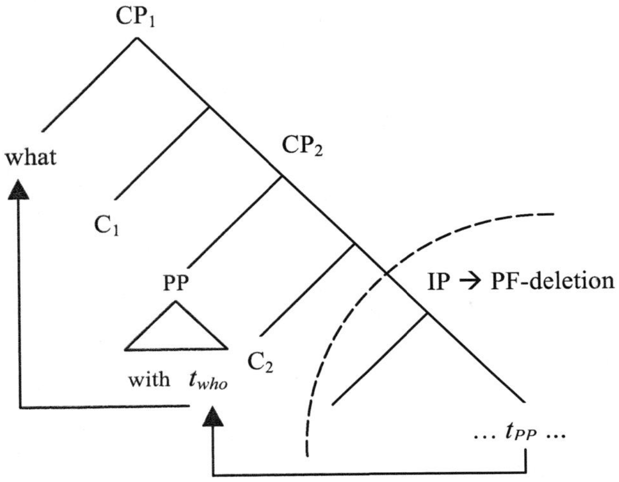

The fact that swiping stresses the preposition and the fact that swiping affects only PPs without antecedents are explained in virtually the same way as in the present account, so we will not dwell on them here. As in our account, the former is taken to follow from the position in which the preposition is stranded and the latter from the interaction of focus with the presence or absence of antecedents (see van Craenenbroeck 2004: 75 for details).

The sluicing condition, it is argued, reduces to the fact that the derivation of swiping in (57) entails a violation of the conditions of chain formation, and that, crucially, this violation can be repaired by ellipsis. The violation in question concerns the Chain Uniformity condition (see Chomsky 1995), which requires that successive-cyclic movement chains be uniform with respect to syntactic category (DP, PP, etc.). The derivation in (57) does not satisfy Chain Uniformity, because the chain's three members are not of the same syntactic category. The two higher members of the chain are DPs, but the bottom one is a PP. Assuming, as van Craenenbroeck does, that Chain Uniformity must be respected at PF, it is not difficult to see how IP-deletion at PF repairs the violation in (57). After sluicing, the chain has only two members at PF, and they are both DPs. Chain Uniformity is thus respected only in the case of IP-deletion, and the sluicing condition appears to receive a clever explanation.

To explain the minimal *wh*-condition, van Craenenbroeck argues that non-minimal (he uses the term 'complex') *wh*-elements differ syntactically from minimal *wh*-elements in that they are base-generated above IP, in [Spec,CP].[16] This proposal has consequences for the movement of the two types of *wh*-elements: "While minimal *wh*-phrases move from their IP-internal base position via [Spec,CP_2] (where they check an operator feature) on to [Spec,CP_1] (where they check a clause-typing feature), complex *wh*-phrases are base-generated in [Spec,CP_1] (and check a clause-typing there) and an empty operator moves from the IP-internal base position into [Spec,CP_2] (to check the operator feature and create an operator/variable-dependency)" (van Craenenbroeck 2004:32).

From these assumptions, coupled with the claim that swiping is stranding in an intermediate projection, the minimal *wh*-condition follows quite clearly. Non-minimal *wh*-phrases cannot occur in swiping because they never have the opportunity to be stranded in the intermediate projection. This is because they are generated above it, so they are never there in the first place.

Van Craenenbroeck's account offers several appealing solutions, but is unsatisfactory for two main reasons. First, its treatment of the minimal *wh*-condition is inadequate. Like Merchant's account, it cannot handle the exceptions the to minimal *wh*-condition, because it uses structural complexity rather than discourse status as its operative notion.[17] For van Craenenbroeck, all structurally complex *wh*-phrases are base-generated above in [Spec,CP_1], and are as such unavailable in swiping. The *wh*-phrases in the good swiping examples in (31) are no less structurally complex than those in the bad swiping examples in (9), and thus van Craenenbroeck's account fails to capture the difference in acceptability.

Second, the explanation given for the sluicing condition suffers from a lack of clarity on two points and is as such subject to two damaging objections. For chain uniformity to be violated in the non-ellipsis cases, van Craenenbroeck must (and does) assume there is a single movement chain consisting of three members, of which the lowest is a PP and the higher two are DPs. However, it is not at all clear how this single-chain

---

[16] More specifically, van Craenenbroeck uses a simplified split-CP framework consisting of a CP_1 and a CP_2. Complex *wh*-phrases are assumed to be generated in [Spec,CP_1], which is for the present purposes functionally equivalent to [Spec, ForceP] in our framework. [Spec,CP_2] is functionally equivalent to [Spec,FocP] in the present context.

[17] Van Craenenbroeck (2004: 45-47) does give a nod to the occasional ability of D-linking to trump structural complexity of *wh*-words in other contexts (namely, superiority violations), but he proposes to "ignore these complications" and makes it clear that in his account of swiping "the distinction between the two types of wh-phrases is a purely structural one."

analysis holds true, since we are not dealing with successive-cyclic movement of a single element, but rather with separate movement operations, the first involving a PP and the second involving a DP extracted out of that PP. On this more natural analysis, there are really two two-member movement chains, both of which trivially satisfy Chain Uniformity. Additionally, even if we accept van Craenenbroeck's single-chain assumption, along with his stipulation that Chain Uniformity most be satisfied at PF, it seems that his repair-by-deletion explanation of the sluicing condition does not succeed. PF-deletion of the chain's lowest member is not enough to render the sentence grammatical, because even under deletion Chain Uniformity will still be violated at LF. Van Craenenbroeck is quite clear that his PF application of Chain Uniformity is an *additional* requirement: "Assume now that the notion of Chain Uniformity (in the sense of Chomsky 1995: 91) applies *not only* at LF, but *also* at PF" (van Craenenbroeck 2004: 74, our italics — JH & RRA). Consequently, if we accept all of van Craenenbroeck's assumptions, swiping should be ruled out even under sluicing.

Thus, both of the most thorough previous accounts of swiping leave something to be desired. Both propose vague and problematic explanations of the sluicing condition, and both present self-contained explanations of the minimal *wh*-condition that make false predictions. By contrast, the present account, which assumes nothing above and beyond the independently motivated principles of discourse linking and focus assignment, can explain both the overwhelming appearance of a minimal *wh*-condition, as well as the rare exceptions to it.

Additionally, it should be noted that neither Merchant's nor van Craenenbroeck's account has anything direct or detailed to say about the interaction of swiping with aggressively non-D-linked *wh*-phrases. This is not necessarily a fault, though, because it might very well be possible to give an independent account of this interaction in strictly prosodic terms (see, for example, Sprouse 2006).

8. Conclusion

In this paper, we have argued that swiping is best analyzed as preposition-stranding in the specifier of a FocP intermediate between the elided IP and the final landing spot of the *wh*-phrase. We have proposed that the initial movement to [Spec,FocP] is driven by an information focus feature, [*i*Foc], whose distribution and ellipsis-related behaviour are governed by specific information-structural principles and constraints.

Most importantly, we have shown how these principles and constraints interact to explain — without extra assumptions — all previously noted properties of swiping, as well as a few new issues unmentioned in earlier accounts. These new issues include a crucially revised 'minimal *wh*-condition', the ability of swiping to save aggressively non-D-linked *wh*-phrases in sluicing, and the existence of swiping with *doing*.

The theoretical import of this account extends in principle beyond swiping to sluicing in general. If the focus-movement derivation is not merely an anomalous quirk of swiping, we must assume that all sluicing (in English, at least) consists in fact of two movement operations — first a move to [Spec,FocP] to check [*i*Foc] on the ellipsis remnant, and then a second move to [Spec,ForceP] to check [Wh]. In normal sluicing, the bearer of [*i*Foc] (and hence the ellipsis remnant) is simply a *wh*-phrase. What is special about swiping is simply that the bearer of the [*i*Foc] feature (and hence the ellipsis remnant) is a PP *containing* a *wh*-phrase. While we have shown that, when it comes to swiping, this analysis avoids the problematic assumptions and empirical deficiencies of previous explanations, many open questions remain. In particular, the cross-linguistic viability of this focus-movement analysis of sluicing is an issue ripe for further research. Perhaps the observations made herein will serve as fodder for future investigation.

References

Ai, R.-X. 2006a. Topic-comment structure, focus movement and gapping formation. *Proceedings of NELS 36*, 103-114.

Ai, R.-X. 2006b. *Elliptical Predicate Constructions in Mandarin*. Ph.D. diss., Harvard University, Cambridge, MA.

Baker, M. 1995. Lexical and nonlexical noun incorporation. In U. Egli, P.E. Pause, C. Schwarze, A. von Stechow & G. Wienold (eds.), *Lexical Knowledge in the Organization of Language*. Amsterdam: John Benjamins, 3-33.

Chomsky, N. 1995. *The Minimalist Program*. Cambridge, MA: MIT Press.

van Craenenbroeck, J. 2004. *Ellipsis in Dutch Dialects*. Ph.D. diss., Leiden University.

den Dikken, M. & A. Giannakidou. 2002. From hell to polarity: Aggressively non-D-linked *wh*-phrases as polarity items. *Linguistic Inquiry* 33, 31-61.

Gengel, K. 2005. Contrastivity and ellipsis. *Proceedings of LingO 2005*. [http://www.ling-phil.ox.ac.uk/events/lingo2005/proceedings.html]

Kim, J.-S. 1997. *Syntactic Focus Movement and Ellipsis: A Minimalist Approach*. Ph.D. diss., University of Connecticut, Storrs.

Lobeck, A. 1995. *Ellipsis: Functional Heads, Licensing and Identification*, Oxford: Oxford University Press.

Merchant, J. 2001. *The Syntax of Silence: Sluicing, Islands, and Identity in Ellipsis*. New York: Oxford University Press.

Merchant, J. 2002. Swiping in Germanic. In C.J.-W. Zwart & W. Abraham (eds.), *Studies in Comparative Germanic Syntax*. Amsterdam: John Benjamins, 295-321.

Pesetsky, D. 1987. *Wh* in situ: Movement and unselective binding. In E. Reuland & A. ter Meulen (eds.), *The Representation of (In)definiteness*. Cambridge, MA: MIT Press. 98-129.

Richards, N. 2001. *Movement in Language: Interactions and Architectures*. Oxford: Oxford University Press.

van Riemsdijk, H. 1978a. *A Case Study in Syntactic Markedness: the Binding Nature of Prepositional Phrase*. Dordrecht: Foris.

van Riemsdijk, H. 1978b. On the diagnostic of *wh*-movement. In S.J. Keyser (ed.), *Transformational Studies in European Languages*. Cambridge, MA: MIT Press, 189-206.

Rizzi, L. 1997. The fine structure of the left periphery. In L. Haegeman (ed.), *Elements of Grammar*. Dordrecht: Kluwer, 281-337.

Rosen, C. 1976. Guess what about? *Papers from the Sixth Meeting of the North Eastern Linguistic Society — Montreal Working Papers in Linguistics*, 205-211.

Ross, J.R. 1969. Guess who? *Papers from the Fifth Regional Meeting of the Chicago Linguistic Society*, 252-286.

Schwarzschild. R. 1999. GIVENness, AVOID-F, and other constraints on the placement of accent. *Natural Language Semantics* 7, 141-177.

Sprouse, J. 2006. The accent projection principle: Why the hell not? *Proceedings of the 29th Penn Linguistics Colloquium — University of Pennsylvania Working Papers in Linguistics* 12.1, 349-359.

Takahashi, S. & D. Fox. 2005. MaxElide and the re-binding problem. In E. Georgala & J. Howell (eds.), *Proceedings of Semantics and Linguistic Theory 15*. Ithaca, NY: CLC Publications, 223-240.

CHAPTER FIVE

ON A CONFLICT BETWEEN ANTECEDENT-CONTAINED DELETION AND THE COPY THEORY OF MOVEMENT*

Yukio Furukawa

1. A Conflict between ACD and the CTM

This article uses quantifier phrase (QP)-movement as a neutral term; it does not refer to a particular kind of movement involving a QP, such as quantifier raising (QR), object shift of a QP, extraposition of a QP, and so on. The reason why I use this term is in part because all analyses that rely on movement operations to resolve the problem of infinite regress in antecedent-contained deletion (ACD) seem to face the conflict mentioned in the following discussion. Note that, due to presentational reasons, the following discussion mentions one particular analysis that critically depends on QR to handle ACD.

In one view of ACD, the well-formedness of (1a) seems to be considered as a piece of evidence for QP-movement. Assuming that ACD involves VP ellipsis (May 1985, Sag 1976),[1] without any further operation, the elided VP is contained within the antecedent VP, and hence, the problem of infinite regress arises in ACD. It is often claimed that the QP-movement analysis of ACD can avoid the problem of infinite regress:

---

* Materials discussed in this chapter were also partly presented at the Workshop 'Consequences of the Copy Theory of Movement' (*23rd Annual Meeting of the Japan English Linguistic Society*, Kyushu University, November 2005). I'd like to thank Asaf Bachrach, Jeroen van Craenenbroeck, Naomi Harada, Kyle Johnson, Hirohisa Kiguchi, Hilda Koopman, Takashi Munakata, Masanori Nakamura, Jon Nissenbaum, Maira Noonan, Kayono Shiobara, and Dominique Sportiche for helpful comments and suggestions. Any remaining error belongs to me.

[1] Jacobson (1992, 1998, 2004) does not assume this; she assumes that, in (1a), the gap in the relative clause has the matrix verb *likes* as its antecedent that does not include any of its arguments such as its direct object NP. Hence, no antecedent containment occurs in her analysis.

The movement operation in (1b) raises the object QP with the gapped relative clause out of the domain of the antecedent VP. Assuming that a trace of QP-movement corresponds to a variable that the raised QP must bind (May 1977), the elided VP can find its antecedent VP that obeys the identity condition on ellipsis.[2]

(1) a. John [$_{VP}$ likes every boy Mary does <gap>].
         └──── *antecedent VP* ────┘

b. [every boy Mary does <*likes t*>]
   John *likes t* (Fox 2002)

The copy theory of movement (CTM), which is assumed in the Minimalist Program (Chomsky 1993 et seq.), threatens the QP-movement analysis of ACD: If movement is a copy operation, it does no longer resolve the problem of infinite regress since a gapped relative clause still remains in the object position of the matrix verb (see (2)).

---

[2] Fox (2002) assumes a strict identity condition on ellipsis, i.e., an elided VP must be identical to an antecedent VP at Logical Form (LF). Although this article adopts his view on the identity condition, whether or not this assumption is a valid assumption seems unclear.

As pointed out by Jacobson (1992, 1998), if the elided constituent of the ACD sentence in (i) is a VP, it cannot be identical to its antecedent VP due to the presence of the relational noun *mother* in the head noun of the relative clause. Note that, the well-formedness in (i) apparently suggests that the names of the variables left behind as the object arguments in the two VPs are ignorable. Things are not so simple, however.

Kennedy (2003) reports that, although the object NPs of the two VPs share the same restriction, it is impossible for (iia) to be used as ACD as shown in the unacceptability in (iib). Its unacceptability may suggest that the names of the variables are not ignorable. The contrast between (i) and (iib) raises a more complicated problem: It seems hard to define an identity condition that can rescue (i) but, at the same time, exclude (iib).

(i) John loves every woman the mother of whom Bill does. (Jacobson 1998)

(ii) a. Nicholas touched every circle above a circle that Julian touched.
b. * Nicholas touched every circle above a circle that Julian did.
(Kennedy 2003)

Since the issue of the identity condition on ellipsis is a naïve issue that I believe should be discussed in a larger context of ellipsis (see Dalrymple et al. 1991, Fiengo & May 1994, Hardt 1993, Merchant 2001, and many others), I postpone its discussion to another occasion.

(2) [every boy Mary does <gap>] (Fox 2002)
John [likes [every boy Mary does <gap>]]
└──── *antecedent VP* ────┘

Fox (2002) notes that this problem has already been recognized by Lasnik (1993) and Hornstein (1994, 1995). However, most of the studies of ACD after them have not discussed the problem seriously; they either ignore the conflict or avoid assuming CTM. For example, Abe & Hoshi (1999) and Tanaka (2005) seem to consider that ACD involves a type of movement that does not leave a copy. As far as I can see, only Fox (2002) challenges the conflict and provides a solution (see also Fox 1995). The following sections mainly discuss his analysis. Section 2 briefly summarizes his proposal, and section 3 raises three major problems in his analysis. Then, section 4 proposes an alternative analysis.

2. Fox (2002)

Fox (2002) uses QR to resolve the problem of infinite regress (see also Fox 1995, 2003). At the same time, he assumes that QR obeys CTM. Hence, his analysis faces the problem mentioned above. To solve the problem, he gives up two assumptions that are often assumed, i.e. the directionality of QR and the timing of merger.

2.1. Semantics: The Interpretation of Copies of a QP

Fox's analysis of ACD has a prerequisite, i.e. interpretation of the copies of a QP. Before mentioning the heart of his analysis, let me mention the prerequisite. It is well-known that, without any further operation, a QP in the object position such as *every boy* in (3a) is uninterpretable (see Heim & Kratzer 1998). Fox assumes QR to interpret such a QP. If QR is an instance of movement operation that obeys CTM, however, at least two problems arise. First, as a result of the copying operation, QR of *every boy* leaves an additional and unnecessary *every boy* in the base position (as indicated by *every boy* in the original position of (3b)). Due to the presence of this additional *every boy*, a meaning may be derived that is not intended by (3a).

(3) a. A girl talked to every boy.
b. **every boy** a girl talked to **every boy**

Second, as shown in (3b), QR obeying CTM leaves a copy of *every boy* in the object of *talked to*. Due to the reason mentioned above, this copy is uninterpretable. To interpret (3b), further QR of this copy is necessary. However, such QR still leaves a copy of this *every boy* in the object position, and hence, may induce another infinite regress.

(4) *Trace Conversion* (Fox 2002)
 a. Variable Insertion:
 (Det) Pred → (Det) [Pred λy(y=x)]
 b. Determiner Replacement:
 (Det) [Pred λy(y=x)] → the [Pred λy(y=x)]

In order for a QP to be interpreted in terms of movement such as QR, at least the original copy of a QP must be shifted to a type <e> object, i.e. a variable that the raised QP must bind. To solve the problem, Fox proposes Trace Conversion (4). Determiner Replacement converts the original copy of a QP to a *the NP*. Variable Insertion introduces the variable that the QP binds, and this variable is identified with the value of *the NP*. Then, as a result of Trace Conversion, (3b), repeated in (5a), is interpreted as the converted structure (5b).

(5) a. **every boy** a girl talked to **every boy**
 b. **every boy** λx [a girl talked to **the boy x**] (Fox 2002)

2.2. Syntax

The heart of Fox's analysis of ACD is late merger of the gapped relative clause; the gap is not contained in the antecedent VP due to its merging out of the domain of the antecedent VP (see (6b) in the underlying structure for (6a). I will come back to details of (6b), later in this subsection).

(6) a. John likes every boy that Mary does.
 b. [John [[$_{VP}$ likes every boy]
 [$_{NP}$ *every boy* **that Mary does <gap>**]]]
 └── *late merger* ──┘
 (Fox 2002)

Let me mention his motivation for its late merger, first. As a piece of evidence, he appeals to the obviation of the Condition C effect in ACD. Several studies (Fiengo & May 1994, Fox 1995, 2002, 2003, Pesetsky

2000) assume that the unacceptability of (7a) is due to a Condition C effect: At a certain stage, the R-expression *John* is c-commanded by the offending pronoun. Given this, consider (7b). Its well-formedness seems to suggest that, once a gap is created in the relative clause, the Condition C effect observed in (7a) disappears.

(7) a. ?? You introduce him$_i$ to everyone John$_i$ wanted you to meet.
b. You introduce him$_i$ to everyone John$_i$ wanted you to <gap>.
(Fox 2002)

Adopting Lebeaux's (1988) analysis of the obviation of the Condition C effect in an adjunct clause, Fox assumes (i) that restrictive relative clauses are adjuncts, and (ii) that it is not necessary for the gapped relative clause in (7b) to be associated with its head noun *everyone* at the base-generated position, i.e. an argument position of the matrix verb. He proposes that, as shown in (8), the gapped relative clause containing the R-expression *John* is associated after raising of the head noun, and hence, it never enters the domain that the offending pronoun c-commands.

(8)

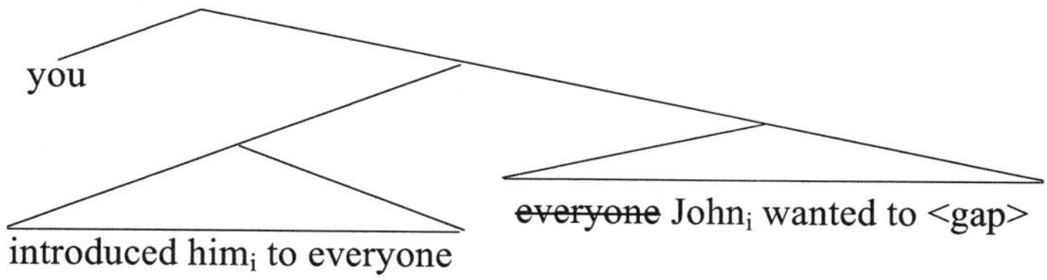

Due to the late merger of the gapped relative clause, his analysis can resolve the problem of infinite regress in ACD and predicts the obviation of its Condition C effect in (7b). However, it has at least two problems. As mentioned above, he assumes that a restrictive relative clause is an adjunct, and hence, can be inserted in a later stage of the derivation. Basically, his late merger analysis does not exclude any possibility of the late merger of the non-gapped relative clause in (7a), and hence, the obviation of the Condition C effect is wrongly predicted, contrary to its unacceptability. Section 3.3 further discusses this problem.

The second problem concerns the driving force behind raising the head noun. As far as I can see, there seems to be two influential theories of restrictive relative clauses, i.e. the movement theory (Kayne 1994) and the matching theory (Sauerland 1998).[3] It seems, however, that both assume

[3] Fox adopts the matching theory (see Fox 2002).

that a restrictive relative clause has to form a constituent with its head noun in a certain stage of derivation. The question is, in what way is the head noun raised to the position where it accommodates the late-merged relative clause?

(9) John likes every boy that Mary does.

(10) a. [$_{VP}$ John likes **every boy**]

b. [[$_{VP}$ John likes *every boy*] **every boy**]
└ *DP-movement (QR)*┘

c. [[$_{VP}$ John likes every boy] every boy **that Mary does**]
└ *late merger*┘

(Fox 2002)

To accommodate the gapped relative clause in a higher position, *every boy* in (9) must be raised to the right. However, since May (1977), QR is usually considered as an instance of leftward movement. If this is assumed, the gapped relative clause in (9) has no chance to be associated with its head noun by QR. Fox gives up this assumption. He proposes rightward QR; as shown in (10b), QR raises *every boy* in (10a) to a right adjoined position.[4] He claims that the raised *every boy* accommodates the gapped relative clause in this QRed (or extraposed) position, and its original copy in the object position is processed by Trace Conversion (see (11)).

(11) [every boy λx.Mary does <likes the boy x>]
λy.John likes the boy y (Fox 2002)

2.3. *Interim Summary*

Fox's analysis successfully eliminates a gapped relative clause from the domain of the antecedent VP by appealing to its late merger. As implied in the previous subsection, his analysis is very similar to Baltin's (1987) extraposition analysis in that both of the analyses crucially use rightward movement, and also, predict that antecedent containment never happens. In fact, Fox himself admits that his analysis is similar to Baltin's analysis.[5]

---

[4] Fox seems to regard QR as an instance of movement similar to extraposition or heavy NP shift. Note that, he assumes that not the copy of a QP in the raised position but its original copy is pronounced in rightward QR.

[5] Those who are familiar with the history of the research on ACD may be aware of the following; Larson & May (1990) raise several problems in Baltin's

Note that, adopting Lebeaux's view, Fox assumes that Condition C is an anywhere condition, and, with this assumption, his analysis can predict the obviation of the Condition C effect. Without this assumption, however, it is not necessary for the late merger of a gapped relative clause to be evidenced by its obviation. In fact, there is no unified view on the Condition C effect,[6] and whether or not this assumption is tenable is less clear. If Condition C is a condition on a representation in a later stage of the derivation and, in the representation, the copy of the gapped relative clause is ignored (or deleted) in the antecedent VP, the base-generated position of the gapped relative clause does not seem to be specified by the obviation of the Condition C effect in (7b). Since the main issue of this article does not concern binding conditions and I have no particular theory of the Condition C effect, I postpone any discussion about the well-formedness of (7b).

3. Problems in Fox's Late Merger Analysis

Although Fox's analysis can avoid antecedent containment, and also, can predict the obviation of the Condition C effect in ACD, his analysis faces several problems. The following mentions three major problems in his analysis. One is about his Trace Conversion. The other two are about the rightward movement of the head noun and the late merger of the gapped relative clause.

3.1. Problem 1: About Trace Conversion

As mentioned earlier, in order to interpret the copies of a QP after QR, Trace Conversion (4), repeated in (12), converts the original copy of a QP to a *the NP* whose value is identified with the value of the variable that the raised QP binds.

(12) *Trace Conversion* (Fox 2002)

a. Variable Insertion:
(Det) Pred → (Det) [Pred λy(y=x)]

---

extraposition analysis. Fox admits that one of the problems is also relevant to Fox's analysis. That is, so-called the problem of 'sandwiched' ACD. Section 3.2 mentions details of the problem and Fox's solution.

[6] For example, Pesetsky (2000) does not assume this assumption. Furthermore, Reinhart (1983) considers that Condition C is a pragmatic condition.

b. Determiner Replacement:
(Det) [Pred λy(y=x)] → the [Pred λy(y=x)]

Trace Conversion, however, makes a wrong prediction about the truth of (13a). It seems that (13a) is true (see also von Fintel 2004). Its truth may not be predicted by his Trace Conversion due to the presupposition failure of the scope of (13b): Determiner Replacement postulates a definite expression *the king of France* in its scope.

(13) a. No king of France had dinner with Yukio last night.
b. *no king of France* λx [**the king of France x** had dinner with…]

3.2. Problem 2: Abused Rightward Movement

So-called 'sandwiched' ACD is one of the major problems in Baltin's extraposition analysis (Baltin 1987, Larson & May 1990). Under his extraposition analysis, the gapped relative clause is extraposed to an adjoined position of the antecedent VP. He seems to assume that an extraposed relative clause is the rightmost constituent. Given this, consider (14). Its gapped relative clause, which is associated with the direct object, is followed by an argument of the matrix predicate, i.e. *to Mary*. The gapped relative clause is apparently sandwiched by arguments of the matrix verb.[7]

(14) I gave a book on linguistics that you did <gap> to Mary. (Fox 2002)

It seems hard to assume that *to Mary* in (14) is base-generated in an adjoined position of the VP. To derive its order, one might think that *to Mary* is additionally extraposed. In fact, to account for the well-formedness in (14), Fox admits string vacuous multiple rightward movement; he claims that *to Mary* is extraposed after the merger of the gapped relative clause, as shown in (15d).

---

[7] An anonymous reviewer finds that it is impossible for (14) to be construed in the way intended by Fox. At this stage, however, I have no idea about the variability of judgments (though the reviewer's judgment is not so surprising). Due to presentational convenience, the discussion here adopts Fox's judgment. For further details of the problem of 'sandwiched' ACD, I refer readers to Larson & May (1990) and Fox (2002).

(15) a. I [gave a book on linguistics to Mary]
b. *QR or extraposition/heavy NP shift*
I [[gave *a book on linguistics* to Mary]
a book on linguistics]
c. *late merger of the gapped relative clause*
I [[gave a book on linguistics to Mary]
a book on linguistics **that you did <gap>**]
d. *additional extraposition*
I [[[gave ~~a book on linguistics~~ ~~*to Mary*~~]
a book on linguistics that you did <gap>] **to Mary**]
(Fox 2002)

Given these, consider (16) and (17). While the gapped relative clause cannot be 'directly' associated with the subject QP of the embedded clause (see (16b), (17b)), it can be 'visibly' extraposed, as shown in the acceptability of (16a) and (17a).

(16) a. I expect that everyone will visit Mary that you do <gap>.
b. * I expect that everyone that you do <gap> will visit Mary.
(Fox 2002; see also Tiedeman 1995 and Wilder 1995)

(17) a. John wants for everyone to have fun that you do <gap>.
b. * John wants for everyone you do <gap> to have fun.
(Fox 2002)

If string vacuous multiple extraposition is freely allowed, acceptability in (16b) and (17b) may be wrongly predicted (see (18b)). To account for their unacceptability, Fox stipulates that a predicate extraposition (such as the extraposition of *will visit Mary* in (18b)) is somehow prohibited.

(18) a. I [[expected that everyone will visit Mary]
~~everyone~~ that you do <gap>].
b. * I [[[expected that ~~everyone will visit Mary~~]
everyone that you do <gap>] will visit Mary].
(Fox 2002)

Once this is stipulated, however, the acceptability of (19b) is not predictable anymore. To avoid the antecedent containment, the gapped relative clause must be inserted after the extraposition of *everyone* in his analysis. Then, without extraposing the predicate of its embedded clause, i.e. *(to) be a genius*, the order of (19b) may not be derivable. In fact, the contrast between (17b) and (19b) raises a complicated problem. It seems hard to find a condition on the predicate extraposition that can exclude (17b) but rescue (19b): The unacceptability in (17b) seems to suggest that the non-finiteness of the embedded clause does not play any role in extraposing its predicate.

(19) a. * John believed (that) everyone you did <gap> was a genius.
b. ? John believed everyone you did <gap> to be a genius.
(Larson & May 1990)

3.3. Problem 3: Unobviated Condition C Effects

As briefly mentioned earlier, Fox assumes that, since a restrictive relative clause is an adjunct, it can be inserted in a later stage of the derivation. Given this, the obviation of the Condition C effect is wrongly predicted in (7a), repeated in (20a), contrary to its unacceptability: Basically, his analysis does not exclude any possibility of the late merger of its non-gapped relative clause. To prohibit late merger, Fox speculates that a parser can postulate an extraposed structure only in the case of (20b) to avoid infinite regress by antecedent containment (cf. Fox 1995).[8]

(20) a. ?? You introduce him$_i$ to everyone John$_i$ wanted you to meet.
b. You introduce him$_i$ to everyone John$_i$ wanted you to <gap>.
(Fox 2002)

However, this stipulation has a serious flaw. Fox crucially assumes that the source of the problem of infinite regress in ACD is a violation of parallelism/ identity: Identity between two VPs is never established (see fn. 2). Then, unless he answers the following questions, his stipulation does not work at all to account for the contrast in (20) (and the answer to (21a) seems negative).

(21) a. Is it possible for a parser to know that two items are identical?

---

[8] In Fox (1995), he tries to reduce the difference between (20a) and (20b) to an economy reason. He assumes that the extraposition of *everyone* and the late merger of the relative clause are additional operations, and hence, he claims that economy prohibits them in (20a).

On the other hand, he claims that these operations are allowed in (20b): Without these operations, (20b) ends up with infinite regress, and hence, its derivation crashes.

b. How can a parser anticipate a violation of parallelism/ identity simply by encountering the VP gap in the relative clause in (20b)?

c. If both infinite regress by antecedent containment and a Condition C violation are matters of identity between two items, why and how can a parser only repair the former?

4. An Alternative Analysis

The following presents an alternative analysis that I have generated. As far as I can see, any QP-movement analysis of ACD that assumes operator variable binding for the interpretation of a quantifier faces the conflict between ACD and CTM. To resolve this conflict, perhaps, we have to give up several crucial assumptions in the grammar (and Fox gives up the assumption about the timing of merger as shown earlier). I give up one of the assumptions about the architecture of a VP, that is, the predication/functional application between verbal and nominal expressions. The presence of a 'Heimian variable' casts doubt on this assumption.

4.1. Heimian Variables

Free variables introduced by indefinites are often called 'Heimian variables', whose presence seems to be indicated by the contrast in (22). Descriptively speaking, an adverb of quantification *always* requires either a stage-level predicate or an indefinite in a sentence. According to the research on genericity (see Carlson & Pelletier 1995), due to the presence of *always*, the indefinite subjects in (22a-b) can bear universal readings. Then, in one view of adverbs of quantification (see Lewis 1975 and Kratzer 1995; cf. de Swart 1991), *always* is considered as an unselective binder that can quantify over an indefinite subject of an individual-level predicate: under this view, the individual-level predicate, i.e. *knows French*, lacks a situational variable, and hence, the only variable that *always* can bind is the variable provided by the indefinite subjects. Note that, the previous studies consider (22c) as an instance of vacuous quantification: Since neither its subject *John* nor its individual-level predicate provides a variable, *always* has no variable it can bind.

(22) a. A Moroccan always knows French.
b. Moroccans always know French.

c. John (??always) knows French.

d. John always speaks French. (Chierchia 1995)

However, it is well-known that the presence of a 'Heimian variable' induces a problem in compositionality (see Groenendijk & Stokhof 1990). If *a Moroccan* in (22a) is defined as a variable with restriction such as λx.Moroccan(x), it is not applicable to its predicate whose denotation should be defined as λy.know(y,French): Both are type <e,t> objects (see (23)).

(23)

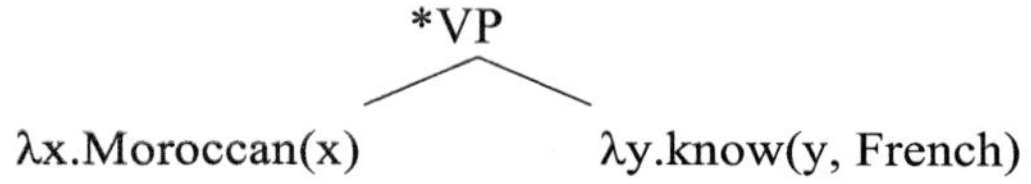

On the other hand, if *a Moroccan* is simply defined as a variable such as *x*, the compositionality problem does not arise. However, its restriction, i.e. the property of being a Moroccan, follows from nowhere (see (24)). Thus, the sentence with the structure (24) would fail to convey its intended meaning.

(24)

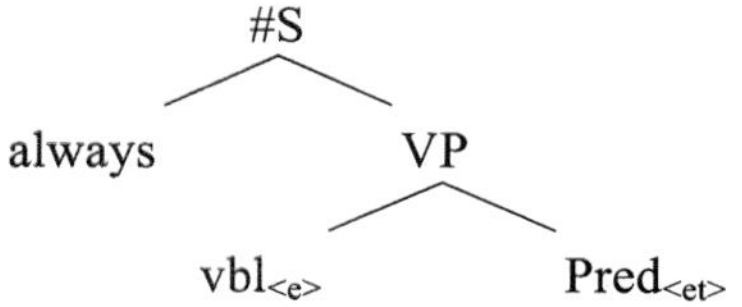

Compared to the compositionality problem in (23), the problem in (24) seems fatal: (24) has no way to recover the restriction unless it is lexically postulated. Moreover, it is not unreasonable to think that *a Moroccan* in (22a) and *Moroccans* in (22b) have their own restrictions. Therefore, the denotation of *a Moroccan* and *Moroccans* should be described as Moroccan(x) (or λx.Moroccan(x)), which is exactly the same as the denotation of a common noun (or an NP) *Moroccan* (cf. Percus 1998).

In fact, a phenomenon called determiner sharing (25) seems to suggest that Ds and NPs are not generated as constituents within VPs (see also Sportiche 1997). At this stage, I give up any predication/functional application in the level of VP.

(25) a. Too many Irish setters are named Kelly, ~~too many~~ German shepherds ~~are named~~ Fritz, and ~~too many~~ Huskies ~~are named~~ Nanook.

b. The duck is dry and ~~the~~ mussels ~~are~~ tough, but Bocuse D'Or rehearsal goes well for chef Bumbaris.

c. Mary will eat the pizza on Monday and ~~the~~ tofu on Tuesday. (Lin 2000)

4.2. Proposal 1: Syntax

Following Harada (2005), Johnson & Tomioka (1997), Lin (2000), and Sportiche (1997), I propose that not a DP but an NP is base generated in the VP level (see (26a)). Second, in order for an NP (e.g. *boy*) to become a DP (e.g. *every boy*), it has to be raised to the domain of a functional projection fP to merge with a determiner *every* (see (26b)).[9]

(26) a.

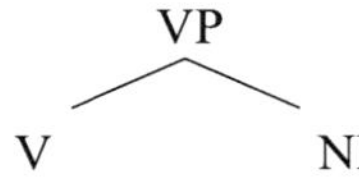

b.

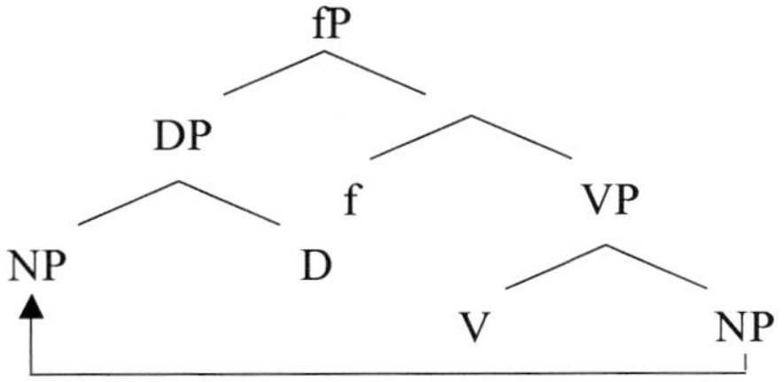

4.3. Proposal 2: Semantics

I assume that, in the VP level, two characteristic functions such as like(x, y) and boy(z) (or two formulas such as $[[\text{like}]]^g$ and $[[\text{boy}]]^g$) are lexically inserted as the values of V and NP, respectively. Assuming that an NP denotes a property, it is not applicable to a predicate that requires an individual as its argument. I claim that they are intersectively/ conjunctively combined with each other in terms of the same variable assignment or by identifying their variables (see (27a)).[10]

[9] Due to presentational convenience, the subject argument is temporarily ignored in (26) (see also fn. 12). Also, in this preliminary version of my proposal, I do not want to specify what f in (26b) is, due to the lack of decisive evidence. One of the candidates for it may be a projection related to Case.

[10] Again, due to presentational convenience, the subject argument is temporarily ignored in (27) (see also fn. 12).

(27) a. $[[\text{like}]]^{g[x\to a][y\to b]}\&[[\text{boy}]]^{g[x\to a]}$

$[[\text{like}]]^{g}$ $[[\text{boy}]]^{g}$

b. $[[\text{every}_x]]^{g}([[\text{boy}]]^{g[x\to a]})([[\text{like}]]^{g[x\to a][y\to b]}\&[[\text{boy}]]^{g[x\to a]})$

$[[\text{every}_x]]^{g[z\to c]}\ ([[\text{boy}]]^{g[z\to c]})$

f $[[\text{like}]]^{g[x\to a][y\to b]}\&[[\text{boy}]]^{g[x\to a]}$

$[[\text{boy}]]^{g}$ $[[\text{every}_x]]^{g}$

$[[\text{like}]]^{g}$ $[[\text{boy}]]^{g}$

After accommodating the raised NP formula (i.e. $[[\text{boy}]]^{g[x\to a]}$), the determiner *every* takes two formulas (see (27b)), namely $[[\text{boy}]]^{g[x\to a]}$ and $[[\text{like}]]^{g[x\to a][y\to b]}\&[[\text{boy}]]^{g[x\to a]}$. According to the study of generalized quantifiers, natural language determiners are (i) relational terms between two properties, and (ii), in most cases, conservative.[11] Then, (27b) is interpreted as (28).

(28) a. $[[\text{every}_x\ \psi\varphi]]^{g} = 1$ iff $[[\varphi]]^{g[x\to a]} = 1$
for every a such that
$[[\psi]]^{g[x\to a]} = 1$. (Heim 1997)

b. $[[\text{every}_x]]^{g}([[\text{boy}]]^{g[x\to a]})([[\text{like}]]^{g[x\to a][y\to b]}\&[[\text{boy}]]^{g[x\to a]})$
is equivalent to
$[[\text{every}_x]]^{g}([[\text{boy}]]^{g[x\to a]})([[\text{like}]]^{g[x\to a][y\to b]})$
due to conservativity.

4.4. *Proposal 3: ACD*

Assuming that restrictive relative clauses are also interpreted intersectively (Sauerland 1998), it is not necessary to postulate an identical VP in the gap of the relative clause; due to the same variable assignment by intersection (or after conjunction), positing a matrix verb (e.g. $[[\text{like}]]^{g}$ in (29)[12]) in the gap has the same effect as VP-recovering. Moreover, once

---

[11] D is conservative iff, for all α, β in the universe, Dα β = Dα α∩β (Keenan & Westernståhl 1997).

[12] Heim (1997) and Rooth (1992) report that contrastive focus marking, illustrated by F in (29a), is necessary on the subject of the relative clause. I assume this focus marking, which enables the identity of the two subjects to be ignored in the variable assignment.

such a verb formula is postulated, no antecedent containment happens, and hence, the problem of infinite regress is automatically avoided (see also Jacobson 1992, 1998).

(29) a. John likes every boy Mary^F does <gap>.

b.

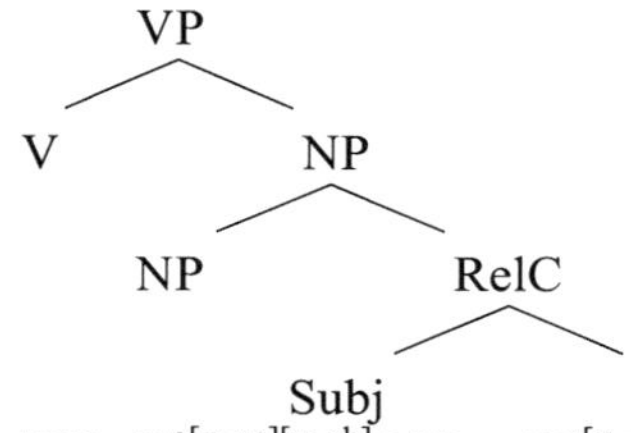

c.

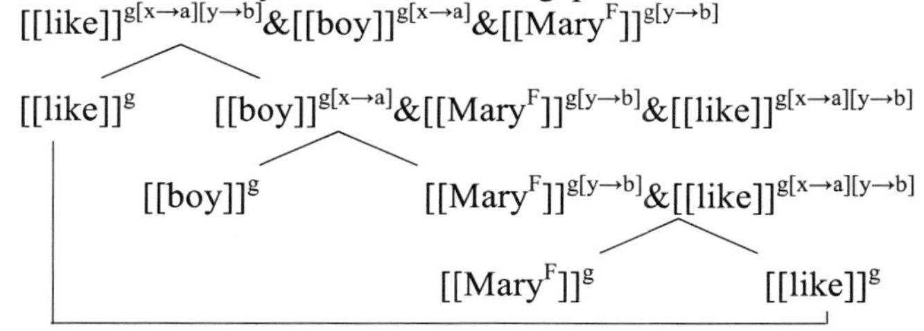

5. Summary and Implications

This article first spelt out the conflict between ACD and CTM, and then, critically reviewed Fox's (2002) study, which, to the best of my knowledge, presents the only challenge to the conflict. Alternatively, I proposed a non-compositional analysis based on the nature of indefinites and determiners. However, I do not think that the proposal here handles all cases that are considered as ACD. One of the problems in this analysis is the acceptability in (30) (Jacobson 1992, 1998). Since the verb with the same variable assignment is copied to the gap, the direct object of the matrix verb is identical to the direct object of the copied verb, as shown in (29c). However, the former cannot be identical to the latter due to the presence of the relational noun *mother* in the head noun of the relative clause (see also fn. 2). At this stage, I leave it as future research.

(30) John loves every woman the mother of whom Bill does.
(Jacobson 1998)

Note that, this analysis has an implication. Since May (1977), it has been assumed that QP-movement has two properties, i.e. variable creation and scope shifting. One of the robust characteristics of the former is that there is no fundamental explanation for why and how traces/copies (in the base positions) are replaced by variables. By positing a variable on each lexical item (such as NP, V, and so on), however, we can maintain QP-movement simply as a scope shifting operation.

References

Abe, J. & H. Hoshi. 1999. A generalized rightward movement analysis of antecedent contained deletion. *Journal of Linguistics* 33, 451-487.

Baltin, M. 1987. Do antecedent-contained deletions exist? *Linguistic Inquiry* 18, 579-595.

Carlson, G.N. & F.J. Pelletier (eds.). 1995. *The Generic Book*. Chicago: University of Chicago Press.

Chierchia, G. 1995. Individual-level predicates as inherent generics. In Carlson & Pelletier (eds.), 176-223.

Chomsky, N. 1993. A minimalist program for linguistic theory. In K. Hale & S.J. Keyser (eds.), *The View from Building 20*. Cambridge, MA: MIT Press, 1-52.

Dalrymple, M., S.M. Shieber & F.C.N. Pereira. 1991. Ellipsis and higher-order unification. *Linguistics & Philosophy* 14, 399-452.

Fiengo, R. & R. May. 1994. *Indices and Identity*. Cambridge, MA: MIT Press.

von Fintel, K. 2004. Would you believe it? The King of France is back! In A. Bezuidenhout & M. Reimer (eds.), *Descriptions and Beyond*. Oxford: Oxford University Press, 315-341.

Fox, D. 1995. Condition C effects in ACD. *Papers on Minimalist Syntax — MIT Working Papers in Linguistics* 27, 105-119.

Fox, D. 2002. Antecedent-contained deletion and the copy theory of movement. *Linguistic Inquiry* 33, 63-96.

Fox, D. 2003. On logical form. In R. Hendrick (ed.), *Minimalist Syntax*. Malden, MA: Blackwell, 82-123.

Groenendijk, J. & M. Stokhof. 1990. Dynamic Montague grammar. In L. Kalman & L. Polos (eds.), *Papers from the Second Symposium on Logic and Grammar*. Budapest: Akademiai Kiado, 3-48.

Harada, N. 2005. A reconstruction and raising-to-object. Paper presented at the *23rd Annual Meeting of the Japan English Linguistic Society*, workshop *Consequences of the Copy Theory of Movement*.

Hardt, D. 1993. *Verb Phrase Ellipsis: Form, Meaning and Processing*. Ph.D. diss., University of Pennsylvania, Philadelphia.

Heim, I. 1982. *The Semantics of Definite and Indefinite Noun Phrases*. Ph.D. diss., University of Massachusetts, Amherst,.

Heim, I. 1997. Predicates or formulas? Evidence from ellipsis. In A. Lawson & E. Cho (ed.), *Proceedings of Semantics and Linguistic Theory VII*. Ithaca, NY: CLC Publications, 197-221.

Heim, I. & A. Kratzer. 1998. *Semantics in Generative Grammar*. Oxford: Blackwell.

Hornstein, N. 1994. An argument for minimalism: The case of antecedent contained deletion. *Linguistic Inquiry* 25, 662-688.

Hornstein, N. 1995. *Logical Form: From GB to Minimalism*. Malden, MA: Blackwell.

Jacobson, P. 1992. Antecedent contained deletion in a variable free semantics. In C. Barker & D. Dowty (eds.), *Proceedings of Semantics and Linguistic Theory II*. Columbus, OH: OSU Working Papers in Linguistics, 193-213.

Jacobson, P. 1998. Antecedent contained deletion and pied-piping: evidence for a variable free semantics. In D. Strolovitch & A. Lawson (eds.), *Proceedings of Semantics and Linguistic Theory VIII*. Ithaca, NY: CLC Publications, 74-91.

Jacobson, P. 2004. Kennedy's puzzle: What I'm named or who I am? In R.B. Young (ed.), *Proceedings of Semantics and Linguistic Theory XIV*. Ithaca, NY: CLC Publications, 145-162.

Johnson, K. & S. Tomioka. 1997. Lowering and mid-size clauses. In G. Katz, S.-S. Kim & H. Winhart (eds.), *Proceedings of the Tübingen Workshop on Reconstruction*. Tübingen: University of Tübingen, 185-205.

Kayne, R. 1994. *The Antisymmetry of Syntax*. Cambridge, MA: MIT Press.

Keenan E.L. & D. Westerståhl. 1997. Generalized quantifiers. In J. van Benthem & A. ter Meulen (eds.), *Handbook of Logic and Language*. Amsterdam: Elsevier, 837-893.

Kennedy, C. 1994. Argument contained ellipsis. *Linguistics Research Center Report LRC-94-03*, University of California, Santa Cruz.

Kennedy, C. 1997. Antecedent-contained deletion and the syntax of quantifiers. *Linguistic Inquiry* 28, 662-688.

Kennedy, C. 2003. Argument contained ellipsis revisited. Ms., Northwestern University, Evanston, IL.

Kratzer, A. 1995. Stage-level and individual-level predicates. In Carlson & Pelletier, 125-175.

Larson, R. & R. May. 1990. Antecedent containment or vacuous movement: A reply to Baltin. *Linguistic Inquiry* 21, 103-122.

Lasnik, H. 1993. *Lectures on Minimalist Syntax – University of Connecticut Occasional Papers in Linguistics 1*. Cambridge, MA: MIT Working Papers in Linguistics. [Revised version appeared in Lasnik, H. 1999. *Minimalist Analysis*. Malden, MA: Blackwell.]

Lebeaux, D. 1988. *Language Acquisition and the Form of Grammar*. Ph.D. diss., University of Massachusetts, Amherst.

Lewis, D. 1975. Adverbs of quantification. In E. Keenan (ed.), *Formal Semantics of Natural Languages*. Cambridge: Cambridge University Press, 3-15.

Lin, V. Determiner sharing. 2000. *Proceedings of the 19th West Coast Conference on Formal Linguistics*, 274-287.

May, R. 1977. *The Grammar of Quantification*. Ph.D. diss., MIT, Cambridge.

May, R. 1985. *Logical Form*. Cambridge, MA: MIT Press.

Merchant, J. 2001. *The Syntax of Silence*. Oxford: Oxford University Press.

Percus, O. 1998. A somewhat more definite article. In D. Strolovitch & A. Lawson (eds.), *Proceedings of Semantics and Linguistic Theory VIII*. Ithaca, NY: CLC Publications, 185-201.

Pesetsky, D. 2000. *Phrasal Movement and Its Kin*. Cambridge, MA: MIT Press.

Reinhart, T. 1983. Coreference and bound anaphora: A restatement of the anaphora question. *Linguistics & Philosophy* 6, 47-88.

Rooth, M. 1992. Ellipsis redundancy and reduction redundancy. In S. Berman & A. Hestvik (eds.), *Proceedings of the Stuttgart Ellipsis Workshop: Report Series Sprachtheoretische Grundlagen no.29, SFB 340*. Heidelberg: IBM, 1-26.

Sag, I. 1976. *Deletion and Logical Form*. Ph.D. diss., MIT, Cambridge.

Sauerland, U. 1998. *The Meaning of Chains*. Ph.D. diss., MIT, Cambridge.

Sportiche, D. 1997. Reconstruction and constituent structure. Paper presented at MIT and elsewhere.

de Swart, H. 1991. Adverbs of quantification: A generalized quantifiers approach. Ph.D. diss., University of Groningen,.

Tanaka, H. 2005. Antecedent-contained deletion without quantifier raising. *York Working Papers in Linguistics* 3, 173-184.

Tiedeman, R. 1995. Some remarks on antecedent contained deletion. In S. Haraguchi & M. Funaki (eds.), *Minimalism and Linguistic Theory*. Tokyo: Hituzi, 67-103.

Wilder, C. 1995. Antecedent containment and ellipsis. *FAS Papers in Linguistics* 4, 132-165.

CHAPTER SIX

V2 AS A SINGLE-EDGE PHENOMENON*

Sabine Mohr

1. Introduction

In this paper I revisit the question of the structural position of the sentence-initial XP in Verb Second (V2) clauses, with special emphasis on German. In all Germanic languages except for English, which has only a few constructions that feature the so-called 'residual Verb Second',[1] declarative main clauses are subject to the V2 requirement.[2] The V2 requirement means that the finite verb of a clause is preceded by exactly one XP as in (1), or more abstractly formulated, that the clauses in question have the structure XP–V_{fin}–ZP.... Thus in sentences with an initial adverb, for example, the subject appears in a position following the finite verb, whereas in English the SVO word order remains unchanged if an adverb is put in sentence-initial position (see translations of (1a) vs. (1b)). (All data are taken from German, unless indicated otherwise.))

(1) a. Peter hat dieses Buch gestern gelesen.
Peter has this book yesterday read
"Peter read this book yesterday."

---

* Earlier versions of this paper were presented at the workshop "Sentence-initial and sentence-final positions" at the *38th SLE Conference*, Valencia, 2005 and at the conference *Edges in Syntax*, Nicosia, 2006. I'd like to thank the audiences of these meetings for their comments and questions, especially Liliane Haegeman, André Meinunger, Matthew Pearson, Susan Pintzuk, Roberta D'Alessandro, Anna McNay, and Luigi Rizzi, as well as Tom McFadden and an anonymous reviewer for their helpful criticism. All errors are, of course, mine.

[1] This term reflects the assumption that in older stages of the language English, too, had V2. It has, however, been shown that Old English 'V2' is not identical to the V2 discussed here (e.g. Fischer et al. 2000, Haeberli 1999, 2002a,b).

[2] In this paper I only consider declarative main clauses.

b. Gestern hat Peter dieses Buch gelesen.
yesterday has Peter this book read
"Yesterday Peter read this book."

However, most Germanic V2 languages are characterized by the so-called root-embedded asymmetry, i.e. main clauses are subject to the V2 requirement while in embedded clauses the finite verb usually stays lower down in the structure as is illustrated in (2) vs. (1a).

(2) ... dass Peter dieses Buch gestern gelesen hat.
that Peter this book yesterday read has
"... that Peter read this book yesterday."

There have been various suggestions as regards the syntactic structure of V2 clauses in German and the other Germanic languages (for some suggestions see section 2). To my knowledge, however, none of the structures proposed has really considered discourse functions (for a first step see Haegeman 1996). To be more precise, Frey (2000), for example, suggested that the V2 requirement could be satisfied in three ways, namely (i) by merger of an expletive, (ii) by stylistic fronting and (iii) by semantically/pragmatically triggered fronting of an XP, so that in (iii) discourse functions do come into play. These discourse functions, however, are simply encoded by different features, such as [fok] or [link],[3] which appear on one and the same head (C^0).

The aim of this paper is to incorporate discourse functions into the syntactic structure of V2 clauses. More precisely, I will show that Rizzi's (1997) assumptions about the Left Periphery can be extended to German and can account for the findings concerning the discourse functions of the sentence-initial XPs of V2 clauses.

2. Previous Accounts

2.1. Asymmetric Approaches

In the literature (e.g. Travis 1984, Zwart 1997) we often find that V2 clauses

[3] The feature [fok] stands for *Fokus* "focus" and is therefore checked by constituents that receive a certain (mainly contrastive) focus, while [link] is checked by elements that are 'familiarity-topics' (as opposed to 'aboutness-topics') and establish a link to the previous discourse.

are analyzed differently depending on whether they are subject-initial or have another type of XP in the clause-initial position. Thus subject-initial clauses are simply analyzed as IPs (or their respective modern equivalents) because the subject occupies the canonical subject position, [Spec,IP], while in all other clauses (e.g. object-initial or adverb-initial clauses) the sentence-initial element is topicalized which means that the clause is a CP. In particular the fact that a weak pronoun in sentence-initial position is fine if it is the subject of the clause but ungrammatical if it is an object ((3b) vs. (4b)) is taken as evidence that subject-initial and object-initial V2 clauses have a different structure. In other words, weak pronouns are fine in [Spec,IP] but not in [Spec,CP].

(3) a. Das große Kind hat sich gewaschen.
the big child has itself washed
"The big child has washed itself."
b. Es hat sich gewaschen.
it has itself washed
"It has washed itself."

(4) a. Das kleine Kind hat der Vater gewaschen.
[the small child].ACC has [the father].NOM washed
"The father has washed the small child."
b. * Es hat der Vater gewaschen.
it has the father washed
intended "The father has washed it."

According to Zwart, this asymmetric approach to V2 is also supported by the different agreement patterns in the examples in (5).[4] Following his analysis, the *–t* ending is chosen when the verb is in I^0, while the *–e* ending is chosen when the verb is in C^0.

(5) a. Wy speult. *Eastern Dutch* (Zwart 1997)
we play
b. … datte wy speult.
that we play

---

[4] Exactly the same pattern can be found in Swabian, a dialect spoken in Southern Germany. The Swabian equivalents of the Dutch examples are *M'r spielet./…dass m'r spielet./Spiele m'r?*. Tom McFadden (p.c.) pointed out to me that, similarly, the Old English plural endings *-aþ*, *-on* and *-en* of strong verbs could be reduced to *-e* when followed by a pronoun of the 1st or 2nd person.

c. Speule wy? [as well as all other inversion constructions]
play we

2.2. *Symmetric Approaches*

The proponents of the symmetric approaches (among them den Besten 1983, Holmberg & Platzack 1995, Vikner 1995, Schwartz & Vikner 1996, Frey 2000, Roberts & Roussou 2002, Roberts 2005), on the other hand, advocate the idea that all kinds of sentence-initial XPs of V2 clauses target the specifier of the same phrase, CP in most analyses.[5]

Den Besten (1983) was the first to suggest that V2 clauses are (what is now called) CPs. He argued that the root-embedded asymmetry found in most V2 languages is due to the fact that in declarative main clauses the verb moves to C^0, while in embedded clauses this position is occupied by the complementizer so that the verb has to stay further down in the clause.

Holmberg & Platzack (1995) and Roberts & Roussou (2002) amend this idea and introduce a parameter. Holmberg & Platzack's parameter requires the finiteness feature [Fin] (their [+F]) to be located in C^0 in V2 languages (but in I^0 in non-V2 languages) and Roberts & Roussou's one requires tense to be spelt out in C^0 in the case of V2 (but in the IP domain otherwise).

With respect to empirical evidence, most advocates of the symmetric approach refer to den Besten (1983) and to Schwartz & Vikner (1996), although these lines of argumentation have their shortcomings. For example, concerning den Besten's argumentation, it is now widely known that only in German, Dutch, and Standard Afrikaans are complementizers and V2 in complementary distribution.[6]

---

[5] Haider (1993) goes even one step further than the other proponents of the symmetric approach and claims that there is no (independent) IP in German as, according to him, there is no compelling evidence to assume this category in German. Therefore V2 is a phenomenon of the combined CP/IP in German.

[6] Schwartz & Vikner (1996) argue that a uniform treatment of all V2 clauses is preferable over the asymmetric approach as subject-initial and non-subject-initial clauses pattern exactly alike with respect to a number of phenomena such as placement of adverbials and extraction from embedded V2 clauses. Unfortunately, all the arguments put forth by Schwartz & Vikner (1996) can be questioned as easily as the adverb placement one. There, Schwartz & Vikner (1996) argue as follows.

(i) a. … dass bis gestern kein Mensch dieses Buch gelesen hatte.
that till yesterday no human.being this book read had
"… that no-one had read this book till yesterday."

Van Craenenbroeck & Haegeman (2007), however, show that in Wambeek Dutch object clitics follow the complementizer in embedded clauses (6a) and precede the subject in non-subject initial V2 clauses (6b). They suggest that this object clitic is adjoined to a functional head F^0 lower than C^0 and higher than T^0. Since the object clitic follows the finite verb also in subject-initial V2 sentences (6c), van Craenenbroeck & Haegeman conclude that subject-initial V2 clauses are CPs as well.[7]

(6) a. ... dan-t Marie al wetj. *Wambeek Dutch*
that-it Marie already knows
"... that Marie already knows it."
b. Nou wenj-t Marie al.
now knows-it Marie already
"Now, Marie already knows it."
c. Marie wenj-t al.
Marie knows-it already.

Schwartz & Vikner (1996), contrary to van Craenenbroeck & Haegeman (2007), maintain that the symmetric approach cannot provide a satisfactory explanation as regards, for example, the distribution of weak pronouns in sentence-initial position where subject pronouns are fine but object pronouns are not, as shown in (3) and (4). I will return to this problem in section 4.

---

b. * Bis gestern kein Mensch hatte dieses Buch gelesen.
till yesterday no human.being had this book read
c. * Bis gestern dieses Buch hatte kein Mensch gelesen.
till yesterday this book had no human.being read

(ia) shows that adverbials can adjoin to IP, and if subject-initial main clauses were really just IPs, adjunction of an adverbial should be possible here as well. This prediction, however, turns out to be wrong (cf. (ib)). Instead, subject-initial main clauses behave exactly like object-initial main clauses (ic) and do not allow for adjunction. This behaviour is predicted if both subject-initial and non-subject-initial main clauses are CPs.

Schwartz & Vikner (1996), however, do not consider the possibility that (ib) could simply be ruled out because the V2 requirement (which — in the case of subject-initial clauses — would have to be satisfied in the I-system) is violated, and that, in OT terms, the V2 constraint is ranked higher than the constraint regulating adjunction (although I do not necessarily subscribe to this theory).

[7] Van Craenenbroeck & Haegeman (2007) apply the same line of argumentation to clauses featuring the particle *tet* in the West Flemish dialect of Lapscheure, which is taken to realize an affective head F^0 in the left periphery.

In the discussion below, I will follow the symmetric approach insofar as I assume that all V2 clauses are CPs, but I will argue that we need a finer-grained structure, namely a Split-CP à la Rizzi (1997) to account for all the data. Thus we reach a kind of synthesis of the symmetric and the asymmetric approach, where the different types of XP target different specifier positions of the Split-CP. In other words, I will argue that the V2 phenomenon is located in a single 'extended edge' (the Split-CP), instead of involving two different edges, IP and CP.

3. A Closer Look at German Data

Contrary to the distinction drawn in the asymmetric approaches (i.e. subject-initial vs. non-subject-initial clauses), the data in (7) show that many more types of XP pattern with subjects.

(7) a. Alle Studenten lieben Syntax.
all students love syntax.
b. Einer alten Frau wurde die Handtasche gestohlen.
[an old woman].DAT was the handbag stolen
roughly "Someone stole the handbag of an old lady."
c. Mir war gestern fürchterlich heiß.
Me.DAT was yesterday terribly hot
"I felt terribly hot yesterday."
d. Morgen kommt der Weihnachtsmann.
tomorrow comes the Santa.Claus
"Santa Claus is coming tomorrow."

In addition to subjects (7a), also dative object DPs in passives (7b), experiencer DPs of impersonal psych-verbs (7c), and certain temporal and locative adverbs that create a setting (7d) can occur in sentence-initial position with 'neutral stress and interpretation'.[8] This means that all of the sentences in (7) can be used as out-of-the-blue utterances. In fact, with respect to (7d) only the word order given here is contextually neutral and sounds natural in an out-of-the-blue context.

[8] These adverbs seem to be all the adverbs that fall into Frey & Pittner's (1998) categories of *Bereichsadverbiale* (e.g. *aus medizinischer Sicht* "from a medical perspective") and *Frame-Adverbiale* (e.g. *im Mittelalter* "in the Middles Ages") which mark the frame within which the truth value of the rest of the proposition is evaluated.

The subject-initial version given in (8), on the other hand, is marked insofar as either *morgen* "tomorrow" or *der Weihnachtsmann* "Santa Claus" is focused. Of course, all of the sentence-initial XPs in (7) CAN be stressed, focused or topicalized as well.

(8) Der Weihnachtsmann kommt morgen.
the Santa.Claus comes tomorrow
"Santa Claus is coming tomorrow."

All other object DPs, PPs, adverbials and VPs, on the other hand, can only appear in sentence-initial position if they are topicalized, link up with the preceding sentence or receive (contrastive) focus.

(9) a. Diesen Minister hat die Presse schon lange kritisiert.
this.ACC minister has the media already long criticised
"The media has criticised this minister for a long time."

b. * Einen Minister hat die Presse schon lange kritisiert.
a.ACC minister has the media already long criticised
intended "The media has criticised a minister for a long time."

c. EINEN Minister hat die Presse schon lange kritisiert
a.ACC minister has the media already long criticised
(aber nicht alle).
(but not all)
"The media has criticised one minister for a long time (but not all)."

d. Einen MINISTER hat die Presse schon lange kritisiert
a.ACC minister has the media already long criticised
(aber nicht den Kanzler).
(but not the chancellor)
"The media has criticised a MINISTER for a long time (but not the chancellor)."

In (9a) the demonstrative *diesen* "this-ACC" indicates that the minister we are talking about must have been mentioned in the preceding sentence. Hence the sentence-initial object DP establishes a link between the two sentences and is thus topicalized or contrastively focused. (9b) illustrates that an object that is newly introduced into the discourse (indicated by the use of the indefinite article) — and therefore calls for neutral stress and interpretation — cannot occur sentence-initially. It can only do so if it (or rather some part of it) receives contrastive focus, as can be seen in (9c) and (9d).

However, as the examples in (10) show, sometimes not even focalization alone makes an object a licit sentence-initial element. (10a) and (10b) will always be interpreted with *Peter* being the subject and *Maria* the object. To turn *Peter* into the object we have to use the definite article with the name (a construction that is usually only found in some German dialects or in the spoken language) to mark the DP morphologically as accusative.

(10) a. Peter liebt Maria.
Peter loves Maria.
b. PETER liebt Maria.
c. Den Peter liebt Maria.
the.ACC Peter loves Maria.
"Maria loves Peter."

The same holds for dative object DPs in active clauses, as is illustrated in (11).

(11) a. Dem Peter hat Maria ihre Liebe gestanden.
the.ACC Peter has Maria her love confessed
"To Peter, Maria confessed her love."
b. ?? Peter hat Maria ihre Liebe gestanden.
Peter has Maria her love confessed

In the version without the article (11b), not even the possessive pronoun which unambiguously refers to *Maria* helps to turn *Peter* into the object. It rather leads to high marginality, if not ungrammaticality.

The fact that PPs, just like adverbials that do not create a setting, have to be focused or topicalized is illustrated by the following example from the *Stuttgarter Zeitung*, 4 April 2005 which comments on Pope John Paul II, who had just died. Here, the fronted PP *vom Westen* "by the West" contrasts with the PP *im Osten* "in the East" of the first conjunct.

(12) Er hat geholfen, die Regime im Osten zu beseitigen, aber
He has helped the regimes in.the East to get.rid.of but
vom Westen ließ er sich nie vereinnahmen.
by.the West let he himself never take.in
"He helped to get rid of the regimes in the East but he would never let himself be used by the West."

Last but not least, (remnant) VPs in sentence-initial position have to make reference to some aforementioned event, element etc. or be contrastively focused, as can be seen in (13). Here we might think of a discussion of possible consequences of a political scandal, the resignation of the minister (i.e. the option given by the fronted remnant VP) (not) being one of them.

(13) Zurücktreten wird der Minister deswegen wohl nicht.
resign will the minister because.of.that probably not
"The minister probably won't resign because of that."

Table 1 summarizes which XPs can show up in sentence-initial position with neutral stress and interpretation (but can also have a special discourse function) and which XPs always have to be associated with a special discourse function to be able to occur sentence-initially.

Table 1: Sentence-initial XPs and discourse function

	neutral	**special discourse function**
subject DPs	✓	✓
dative objects in passives	✓	✓
experiencer DPs of impersonal psych-verbs	✓	✓
temporal and locative adverb-(ial)s that create a setting	✓	✓
other object DPs	X	✓
other adverb(ial)s	X	✓
PPs	X	✓
(remnant) VPs	X	✓

4. Discourse Functions and the Split-CP

In his seminal paper on the fine structure of the left periphery, Rizzi (1997) suggested that the CP be split into (at least) the following categories: *ForceP*, where the clause-type is determined, *TopP*, targeted by topicalizations, *FocP*, targeted by focused elements and *wh*-elements, and *FinP*, where finiteness is encoded.[9] This minimally split CP has the structure given in (14).[10]

[9] Rizzi (1997) suggests that the Split-CP can contain more than one TopP.
[10] Fin^0 selects the topmost category of the Split-IP as its complement. If the category

(14)

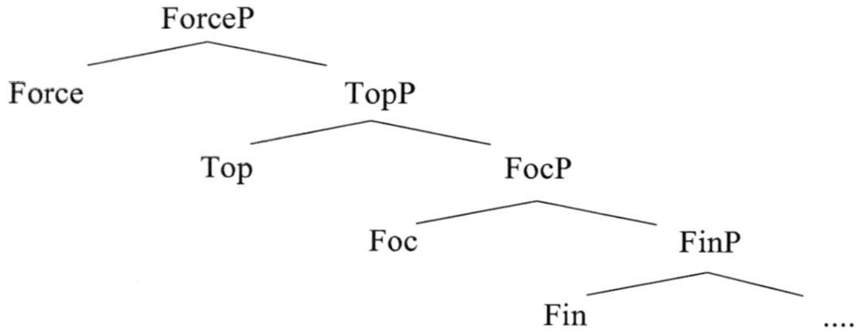

Assuming that German, too, does not simply have a CP but such a finer-grained structure and that the sentence-initial XPs of V2 clauses target different specifier positions within this Split-CP, the above observations can easily be accounted for. I suggest that all kinds of XPs that can occur in sentence-initial position with neutral stress and interpretation are merged in or move to [Spec,FinP]. All the other kinds of XP, however, have to be associated with a topic or focus feature to be able to occur sentence-initially in a V2 clause. This means that these XPs move to [Spec,TopP] or [Spec,FocP], respectively and check their semantic feature against the respective head. The same applies to XPs of the 'neutral group' if they are contrastively focused or topicalized.

This analysis thus complements and extends the discussion in Fanselow (2002). There, Fanselow, too points out that several other kinds of XP pattern with subject DPs when it comes to the sentence-initial position of V2 clauses, and although he does touch on the question of a Split-CP he does not really develop the idea. He rather focuses on the various 'subject'-like elements and argues for an abolition of the notion 'subject'. If one, however, adopts an extended left periphery in which subject-like and non-subject-like XPs target different positions, and in which subject-hood is defined in different terms (see below), Fanselow's observations can be captured satisfactorily.

Whether an XP can end up in [Spec,FinP] or whether it has to have a special discourse function is determined by economy and locality. If the numeration still contains an expletive *es*[11] or an adverb that creates a setting

---

selected by Fin^0 varies, it can be either some adverb-related category (cf. Cinque 1999), a TopP or FocP as in constructions involving Scrambling (cf. Mohr 2004, 2005), or a category hosting a subject position.

11 Expletive *es* can be found in presentational sentences (i) and impersonal passives (ii); for a detailed discussion see Mohr (2004, 2005).

(and thus has the right featural make-up to check the subject-of-predication feature, see below) once the derivation has reached FinP, this element will be merged in [Spec,FinP] because merger is less costly than movement of an XP. This is why (7d) with the adverb *morgen* "tomorrow" merged in [Spec,FinP] is much more natural than the subject-initial version *Der Weihnachtsmann kommt morgen*, which requires movement of the subject DP because the adverb (which, in this case, has a different featural make-up) has been merged at an earlier stage of the derivation. If, as in the example just given, all material is used up by the time the derivation reaches FinP, the default case is to move the XP closest to Fin^0 to [Spec,FinP].[12] This XP is usually the subject. In the case of impersonal psych-verb constructions there is no subject and therefore the structurally highest or only argument of the verb, namely the experiencer DP, moves to [Spec,FinP] (unless the numeration still contains an adverb).

Contextually neutral movement of the dative DP of a passive to [Spec,FinP] can be explained in two ways, both of which require an extra assumption. The dative DP is the highest argument in the *v*P/VP as the syntactic subject is underlyingly a direct object, and one could assume that the hierarchy of the arguments has to be preserved in the Split-IP as well (cf. Fanselow 2002).[13] In this case the experiencer DP would be closest to

---

(i) Es hat soeben der Kanzler die Bühne betreten.
EXPL has just the chancellor the platform entered
"In this moment, the chancellor has mounted the platform."

(ii) Es wird gesungen, getanzt und gelacht.
EXPL is sung, danced and laughed
"People are singing, dancing and laughing."

[12] Of course, the topmost XP of the Split-IP (e.g. TP) would be closer to [Spec, FinP] than argumental XPs, but the topmost XP does not qualify as a candidate for movement to [Spec,FinP]. If [Spec,FinP] is associated with a subject-of-predication feature (see below) this restriction becomes plausible because the topmost XP is the predication rather than the subject of the predication.

[13] Fanselow (2002), among others, bases his assumption on the observation that in the embedded version of (15), too, it is the order dative object > subject (ia) and not the subject-initial order (ib) that receives a neutral reading. See also fn. 15.

(i) a. … dass einem Kind das Fahrrad gestohlen wurde.
that a.DAT child the bike stolen was
"… that someone stole the bike of a child."

b. … dass das Fahrrad einem Kind gestohlen wurde.
that the bike a.DAT child stolen was
"… that someone stole the bike of a CHILD."

FinP and therefore the natural candidate for movement to [Spec,FinP]. In Mohr (2004, 2005), however, I have argued that definite subject DPs occupy a fairly high position in the I-system, a position that is structurally higher than the dative DP. According to this analysis, the dative DP in sentences like (15), must be associated with a feature that allows it to move across the definite subject to [Spec,FinP] without violating any locality constraints.

(15) Einem Kind wurde das Fahrrad gestohlen.
a.DAT child was the bike stolen
roughly "Someone stole the bike of a child."

Thus I suggest that even the neutral position [Spec,FinP] is associated with the checking of a feature, which I assume to be a subject-of-predication feature — [SOP], for short. This means that movement to [Spec,FinP] is not simply triggered by an EPP-feature, but by the need to check the SOP-feature. What makes this idea of [SOP] in Fin^0 particularly attractive is the fact that we can account for why [Spec,FinP] behaves in many respects like a subject position but nevertheless displays properties different from [Spec,IP]/[Spec,TP]. The element in [Spec,FinP] is thus not necessarily the syntactic subject but the semantic subject of the predication. In addition, [Spec,FinP] is not restricted to nominative subject DPs because [Spec,FinP] is not a Case position. Therefore not only subject DPs but also experiencer DPs of psych-verbs, dative objects of passives, and certain adverbs make good subjects of predication and can thus occupy [Spec,FinP].[14,15]

The argumentation that it is usually the closest XP that moves to [Spec,FinP] predicts that, if we have an object that has scrambled over an indefinite subject, this subject can only show up in sentence-initial position if it is topicalized or focused because it is not the element closest to

[14] If an adverb is merged in [Spec,FinP], it will check the SOP-feature although it will set the frame of the predication rather than constitute the subject of predication.

[15] I assume that in declarative main clauses of V2 languages the SOP-feature is located in Fin^0 while in non-V2 languages it is located in some head of the I-system. However, it remains to be determined where the SOP-feature sits in embedded clauses in V2 languages. It cannot be in Fin^0 as this is the position where the complementizer is merged (at least in German).

If, in embedded clauses, the SOP-feature is located in some position at the edge of the I-system we can also account for Fanselow's observation that the dative experiencer precedes the nominative subject in embedded clauses as well (cf. fn. 13). For then the SOP-feature makes sure that the dative object moves across the definite subject to the edge of the I-system in embedded clauses.

[Spec,FinP] in this case. The example in (16) confirms this prediction because the subject *ein Kind* "a child" has to be focused.[16]

(16) *Context:*
Irgendjemand hat giftige Köder ausgelegt und schon mehrere Hunde und Katzen sind daran eingegangen.
Someone has laid out poisoned bait and several dogs and cats have died.
Ein KIND hat einen solchen Köder glücklicherweise noch nicht
a child has a such bait fortunately yet not
gegessen.
eaten
"Fortunately, no child has eaten such a bait yet."

This association with a topic or focus feature is the default case when it comes to objects, more complex adverbials, PPs, and VPs. As these XPs are usually not closest to the C-system, they have to carry a feature that has to be checked against the head of one of the discourse related projections of the Split-CP to be able to move across the subject DP which would be the default candidate for the sentence-initial position. One possible solution would be that this discourse-related feature makes sure that the XP is brought to (a [Spec,TopP] or [Spec,FocP] at) the edge of the Split-IP and therefore *is* the element closest to FinP. This device resembles the phase-based approach although IP/TP is standardly not considered to be a phase (Chomsky 1999 et seq.; but see Butler 2004 for an alternative view). As I assume, however, that all XPs have to move through [Spec, FinP] (an A-position in my system) before targeting [Spec,TopP] or [Spec,FocP] of the C-system (see below), movement through the edge of the I-system would result in improper movement. Therefore I suggest that the semantic feature allows the XP to move across the subject directly to the C-system — an assumption that does not create any problems if IP/TP is not a phase.

Thus the entries in Table 1 can directly be translated into structural positions in which the respective XPs can occur as can be seen in Table 2.

[16] This argumentation relies on Frey's (2000) assumption that the sentence adverb *glücklicherweise* "fortunately" marks the right edge of the (upper) topic area of the I-system.

Table 2: structural position of sentence-initial XPs

	neutral	special discourse function	[Spec,FinP]	[Spec,FocP]/ [Spec,TopP]
subject DPs	✓	✓	✓	✓
dative objects in passives	✓	✓	✓	✓
experiencer DPs of impersonal psych-verbs	✓	✓	✓	✓
temporal and locative adverb(ial)s that create a setting	✓	✓	✓	✓
other object DPs	X	✓	X	✓
other adverb(ial)s	X	✓	X	✓
PPs	X	✓	X	✓
(remnant) VPs	X	✓	X	✓

As it is never the case that more than one specifier of the Split-CP is used, it could be argued that an unsplit CP where topic and focus come in as features of C^0 would suffice for German (Gereon Müller, p.c.) and this is exactly what Frey (2000) proposes. Apart from the fact that he assumes an unsplit CP, Frey's system is very similar to mine. He suggests that [Spec,CP] could simply be filled by merger of an expletive or by what he calls 'stylistic fronting'. In the latter case, which just serves to satisfy the V2 requirement, the phrase that is highest in the *Mittelfeld* is fronted to the sentence-initial position and this operation is completely unmarked and 'contextually neutral'. It usually applies to subjects, dative DPs of passive constructions and temporal and frame adverbials (Frey & Pittner 1998), and it cannot apply whenever there is a sentence topic, which marks the left edge of the I-system.

This definition of 'stylistic fronting' describes in slightly different words exactly what I have said about the group of XPs that can occupy [Spec,FinP]. On the other hand, C^0 can also be associated with a semantic or pragmatic feature, such as [fok] or [link], according to Frey. Fronting of an XP to check these features results in the sentence not being contextually neutral any more but having a certain semantic or pragmatic effect. This option corresponds to movement to [Spec,FocP] and [Spec,TopP] in my system.

As a reply to this scepticism against a Split-CP in German, I argue that the reason why we cannot have a 'neutral' XP together with e.g. a topic XP is that the topic always passes through [Spec,FinP] on its way to [Spec,TopP]. This idea is expressed in slightly different words also by Rizzi's (2006) suggestion that subjects are specified for [+aboutness] and topics for [+aboutness] and [+D-linking]. [+aboutness] easily translates into my subject-of-predication feature [SOP] and thus the feature specification of topics explains why topics move through [Spec,FinP] to [Spec,TopP]. This analysis is supported by doubling structures like the one in (17) where, on its way to [Spec,TopP], the complex DP [$_{DP2}$ *den* [$_{DP1}$ *diesen Satz*]] (cf. Belletti 2003) leaves the resumptive pronoun behind in [Spec,FinP].

(17) Diesen Satz, den mag ich einfach nicht.
this.ACC sentence, that.ACC like I simply not
"This sentence, I simply don't like (it)."

Therefore I assume that any topicalized or focused XP[17] moves through [Spec,FinP] first before it moves on to its final destination. This means that FinP constitutes a sort of bottleneck which is responsible for the fact that only one XP can reach the C-system even though theoretically there are several specifier positions available there. In addition, (17) illustrates that the verb does not move to a higher head position in the Split-CP but stays in Fin^0.

Last but not least, the structure proposed here, namely the assumption of a Split-CP for German, too, has the advantage that it can account for the data in (18) and (19) (and those in (3) and (4)) that proved problematic for Schwartz & Vikner (1996).

(18) a. Das Kind hat das Buch gelesen.
the child has the book read
"The child has read the book."
b. Es hat das Buch gelesen.
it has the book read
"It has read the book."

---

[17] One might object that focused XPs, contrary to topicalized XPs, are associated with new information and should therefore not be able to check the SOP-feature. Butler (2004), however, points out that "the stress marking found on external focused elements [= focused elements in the left periphery — SM] corresponds not to the new information reading of post-verbal subjects, but rather to a contrastive reading".

(19) a. Dieses Buch hat das Kind gelesen.
this book has the child read
"This book, the child has read."
b. * Es hat das Kind gelesen.
it has the child read

Es, being a weak, unstressed pronoun, cannot be topicalized or focused, or in other words, it cannot occur in sentence-initial position if it stands for an object DP because an object DP always has to target a discourse-related projection of the Split-CP. This analysis is supported by the fact that, if we choose the strong pronoun *das* "this" instead of *es* "it", the sentence-initial pronominal object becomes grammatical (cf. (20)). If *es* stands for a subject DP in [Spec,FinP], however, no problem arises.

(20) Das hat das Kind gelesen.
this has the child read
"This one, the child has read."

Thus my analysis comes close to Travis' (1984) asymmetric account which relied on the assumption that objects but not subjects carry focal stress and move to [Spec,CP].

5. Conclusion and Outlook

In this chapter which brings together assumptions about the left periphery of clauses, the impact of discourse functions on clausal architecture and different approaches to the structure of V2 clauses, I argue that declarative V2 clauses uniformly target the C-system as advocated by the symmetric approaches to V2. On the other hand I suggest, as the use of the term C-system indicates, that German has a Split-CP and that the sentence-initial XPs of V2 clauses target different specifier positions within this Split-CP, depending on their discourse function. Subjects, expletives, adverb(ial)s that create a setting, dative object DPs of passives, and experiencer DPs of impersonal psych-verbs, i.e. all the XPs that can show up in sentence-initial position with neutral stress and interpretation, end up in [Spec,FinP], while all the other XPs can only appear sentence-initially if they fulfil a special discourse function and therefore move to [Spec,TopP] or [Spec,FocP].

Thus this analysis combines the advantages of the symmetric and the asymmetric approaches because it confines the V2 phenomenon to the C-domain and can nevertheless account for the fact that there are some differences in behaviour with respect to the different kinds of XPs in sentence-initial position.

In this paper I have only looked at the structure of V2 clauses in German. Ideally, the other Germanic V2 languages should pattern alike. It seems, however, that at least Icelandic has some further requirements, in addition to the "pure" V2 requirement. First, definite subjects seem to have to go into the sentence-initial position and second (or rather following from the first) some speakers of Icelandic seem to disfavour topicalizations (Gunnar Hrafnbjargarson, p.c.). As regards the different agreement patterns found in Dutch (cf. (5)), van Craenenbroeck & Haegeman (2007) suggest that *speule* sits in C^0 while *speult* ends up in Fin^0, both C^0 and Fin^0 being part of a minimally split CP which consists only of CP and FinP, but it remains to be seen whether Dutch patterns like German with respect to the kinds of XP that can occur in [Spec,FinP] and how the distributional facts can be combined with the analysis offered by van Craenenbroeck & Haegeman. These cross-linguistic questions will be left for further research.

References

Belletti, A. 2003. Extended doubling and the VP periphery. Paper presented at the Universität Stuttgart.

den Besten, H. 1983. On the interaction of root transformations and lexical deletive rules. In W. Abraham (ed.), *On the Formal Syntax of Westgermania*. Amsterdam: John Benjamins, 47-131.

Butler, J. 2004. *Phase Structure, Phrase Structure, and Quantification.* Ph.D. diss., University of York.

Cinque, G. 1999. *Adverbs and Functional Heads: A Cross-Linguistic Perspective*. New York: Oxford University Press.

van Craenenbroeck, J. & L. Haegeman. 2007. The derivation of subject-initial V2. *Linguistic Inquiry* 38, 167-178.

Fanselow, G. 2002. Quirky 'subjects' and other specifiers. In B. Kaufmann & B. Stiebels (eds.), *More Than Words*. Berlin: Akademie-Verlag, 227-250.

Fischer, O., A. van Kemenade & W. Koopman. 2000. *The Syntax of Early English*. Cambridge: Cambridge University Press.

Frey, W. 2000. Über die syntaktische Position des Satztopiks im Deutschen. *ZAS Papers in Linguistics* 20, 137-172.

Frey, W. & K. Pittner 1998. Zur Positionierung der Adverbiale im deutschen Mittelfeld. *Linguistische Berichte* 176, 489-534.

Haeberli, E. 1999. *Features, Categories and the Syntax of A-Positions: Synchronic and Diachronic Variation in the Germanic Languages*. Ph.D. diss., University of Geneva.

Haeberli, E. 2002a Inflectional morphology and the loss of verb-second in English. In D. Lightfoot (ed.), *Syntactic Effects of Morphological Change*. Oxford: Oxford University Press, 88-106.

Haeberli, E. 2002b. Observations on the loss of verb second in the history of English. In C.J.-W. Zwart & W. Abraham (eds.), *Studies in Comparative Germanic Syntax*. Amsterdam: John Benjamins, 247-275.

Haegeman, L. 1996. Verb second, the split CP and null subjects in early Dutch finite clauses. *Geneva Generative Papers* 4, 133-175.

Haider, H. 1993. *Deutsche Syntax — generativ*. Tübingen: Narr.

Holmberg, A. & C. Platzack. 1995. *The Role of Inflection in Scandinavian Syntax*. Oxford: Oxford University Press.

Mohr, S. 2004. *Clausal Architecture and Subject Positions: Impersonal Constructions in the Germanic Languages*. Ph.D. diss., Universität Stuttgart.

Mohr, S. 2005. *Clausal Architecture and Subject Positions*. Amsterdam: John Benjamins.

Rizzi, L. 1997. The fine structure of the left periphery. In L. Haegeman (ed.), *Elements of Grammar*. Dordrecht: Kluwer, 281-337.

Rizzi, L. 2006. On the form of chains: Criterial positions and ECP effects. In L.L.-S. Cheng & N. Corver (eds.), Wh-*Movement Moving On*. Cambridge, MA: MIT Press, 97-134.

Roberts, I. 2005. *Principles and Parameters in a VSO Language: A Case Study in Welsh*. New York: Oxford University Press.

Roberts, I. & A. Roussou. 2002. The extended projection principle as a condition on the tense-dependency. In P. Svenonius (ed.), *Subjects, Expletives, and the EPP*. New York: Oxford University Press, 125-156.

Schwartz, B.D. & S. Vikner. 1996. The verb always leaves IP in V2 clauses. In A. Belletti & L. Rizzi (eds.), *Parameters and Functional Heads*. New York: Oxford University Press, 11-62.

Travis, L. 1984. *Parameters and Effects of Word Order Variation*. Ph.D. diss., MIT, Cambridge.

Vikner, S. 1995. *Verb Movement and Expletive Subjects in the Germanic Languages*. New York: Oxford University Press.

Zwart, C.J.-W. 1997. *Morphosyntax of Verb Movement: A Minimalist Approach to the Syntax of Dutch*. Dordrecht: Kluwer.

CHAPTER SEVEN

THE SYNTAX OF THE STANDARD ARABIC PARTICLES *ʔAN* AND *ʔANNA*

Rania Habib

1. Introduction

ʔan "ʔan" and *ʔanna* "that"[1] are only two of the many particles that behave as complement clause subordinators or introducers in Standard Arabic (SA). *ʔan* is one particle of a set of subjunctive markers, such as *kay* "for"', *li-* "to", and *lan* "not", which precede verbs in verbal sentences (i.e. VSO) and assign those verbs subjunctive mood. *ʔanna* is one of the sisters[2] of *ʔinna* "emphatic that", which precede subjects in nominal sentences (i.e. SVO or small clauses) and assign those subjects accusative Case in place of their default nominative case (Ouhalla 1994). Other sisters of *ʔinna* are *lakinna* "but", *kaʔanna* "as if", *laʕalla* "maybe, perhaps", and *layta* "if only". While Arabic is a VSO language, which is the order found after *ʔan*, the order SVO, which is the order found after *ʔanna*, is very common. VSO is established by raising the verb from V to T (Ouhalla 1994), i.e. a VSO order is derived of an underlying SVO order, where the subject DP is in [Spec,*v*P]. The SVO order, on the other hand, is derived by raising the subject DP from [Spec,*v*P] to [Spec,TP]. The latter is presumed by many to be a Topic position in Arabic (e.g. Badawi et al. 2004, Brustad 2000, and Salih 1985), i.e. an A′-position, but the possibility of having an expletive in this position that alters with an overt subject DP questions this presumption. We will leave this for further research.

---

[1] *ʔan* will be glossed throughout the paper as *ʔan* because this paper argues against a complementizer analysis of *ʔan*, whereas *ʔanna* will be glossed as *that* since it is considered a complementizer in this paper.

[2] This is the traditional label that is given to *ʔanna* and other particles mentioned in the text, all of which behave in the same way; they precede a nominal sentence and assign an accusative case to the subject in place of its default nominative case.

Despite their different behavior on what can follow in the sentence, *ʔan* and *ʔanna* have often been viewed as complementizers (see e.g. Salih 1985 and Persson 2002). Persson, for instance, asserts that *ʔan* and *ʔanna* are complementizers that head a sentence-like complement and "link complements and matrix clauses together" (p. 81). She further indicates that the embedded subject is not deleted after *ʔanna*, whereas it is deleted after *ʔan*, i.e. assuming the same structure for *ʔan* and *ʔanna*. Traditionally, *ʔan* and *ʔanna* were considered by Sirafi (III, 119) to be relative pronouns whose position in current syntax is well known to be [Spec,CP]. Some researchers, such as Ouhalla & Shlonsky (2002: 18), indicate their uncertainty of whether *ʔan* is really a complementizer or "a functional category that encodes (subjunctive) mood."

The purpose of this study is to eliminate this uncertainty and to show that *ʔan* and *ʔanna* are different with respect to their syntax. *ʔan* is followed by a verb in the subjunctive mood in spite of the free word order that is characteristic of SA, (1a). *ʔanna*, on the other hand, must always be followed by an overt subject DP, either a noun or a pronoun, in the accusative Case, (2a). A number of arguments will be presented to support my proposal that *ʔan* is not a complementizer, rather it is a functional head analogous to the infinitival *to* in English, i.e. it assigns the subjunctive mood to the following verb. It heads a TP complement, occupying T (*contra* Ben Ayad 2003)[3]. Following Chomsky (1993, 1995) and Roberts & Roussou (2002), the verb raises and incorporates with *ʔan* in T to check the strong uninterpretable subjunctive feature, [*u*SUBJ*], on T, in a local head-head configuration, as (1a) is schematized in (1b).

(1) a. yu-riid-u ʔan ya-ʔkul-a
3SG.M.IMP-want-IND ʔan 3SG.M.IMP-eat-SUBJ
raami t-tufaħat-a.
Rami the-apple-ACC

[3] Ben Ayad (2003) deviates from the traditional view that *ʔan* is a complementizer, but she suggests in analogy to Greek *na* and Balkan equivalents (Romanian *să* and Bulgarian *da*) that *ʔan* heads a Modal Phrase projected higher than TP, checking verbal mood morphology through the operation *Agree*. Terzi (1997) also proposes that the Greek subjunctive marker *na* heads a Mood Phrase that is higher than TP but considers it comparable to the English infinitival *to* (Chomsky & Lansik 1993). Other researchers have proposed that subjunctive markers in Greek and Balkan languages are not complementizers, rather they head an MP (Ingria 1981, Rivero 1994, Terzi 1991, and Tsimpli 1990 for Greek; Rudin 1983 for Bulgarian; Rivero 1994 and Motapanyane 1991 for Rumanian; Terzi 1992 for Albanian).

b. [$_{VP}$ [$_{V'}$ yu-riid-u [$_{TP}$ [$_{T'}$ ʔan+ya-ʔkul-a$_i$ [$_{vP}$ raami [$_{v'}$ t$_i$ [$_{VP}$ [$_{V'}$ t$_i$ [$_{DP}$ t-tufaħat-a]]]]]]]]]
"He wants Rami to eat the apple."

In contrast, *ʔanna* is a complementizer that assigns an accusative Case to the following overt DP. It heads a CP complement and the overt DP that follows *ʔanna* raises from [Spec,*v*P] to [Spec,TP] to check the strong uninterpretable accusative Case feature, [*u*ACC*], of C, assuming that C transfers its features to T (Chomsky 2006, 2008). Hence, C transfers its [*u*ACC*] to T, and the moved subject DP checks this strong feature in a local Spec-head configuration between [Spec,TP] and T, as (2a) is derived in (2b). That makes it analogous to the English complementizer *for* that assigns an accusative Case to the following DP.

(2) a. ya-bduu ʔanna ħusaam-a
3SG.M.IMP-seem that Husam-ACC
yu-ħibb-u ṭ-ṭaʕaam-a.
3SG.M.IMP-like-IND the-food-ACC

b. [$_{VP}$ [$_{V'}$ ya-bduu [$_{CP}$ [$_{C'}$ ʔanna [$_{TP}$ ħusaam-a$_i$ [$_{T'}$ [$_{vP}$ t$_i$ [$_{v'}$ [$_{VP}$ [$_{V'}$ yu-ħibb-u [$_{DP}$ ṭ-ṭaʕaam-a]]]]]]]]]]
"It seems that Husam likes the food."

Feature checking is assumed to be the main mechanism that accounts for each structure; establishing locality with the strong feature that each of *ʔan* and *ʔanna* carries is inevitable. The strength of the features [*u*SUBJ*] and [*u*ACC*] on *ʔan* and *ʔanna*, respectively, is evident in what each of *ʔan* and *ʔanna* selects for. In addition to feature checking, this study presents empirical evidence that the syntax of *ʔan* and *ʔanna* is not the same, exploring features of *ʔan* and *ʔanna* and tests adopted from Wurmbrand (2001) that determine whether the complement of a verb is a CP or a TP.

The study is organized as follows: section 2 presents some similarities between *ʔan* and *ʔanna*. Section 3 presents an analysis of *ʔanna* as a complementizer, arguing against a TP analysis, while section 4 presents an analysis of *ʔan* as T, arguing against a CP analysis. Then section 5 implements diagnostics that show that the *ʔan*-complement of the matrix verb is a reduced non-restructuring structure, i.e. a TP, while the *ʔanna*-complement is a full non-restructuring structures, i.e. a CP. And section 6, finally, concludes the paper, raising a number of issues.

2. Similarities between *ʔan* and *ʔanna*

The similarities that exist between *ʔan* and *ʔanna* can easily tempt one to give a unified syntactic analysis of these two particles, misleading us into equal interpretation of their position in the syntax, i.e. considering both of them either Cs or Ts. First, they are both complement clause subordinators that introduce an embedded clause and link it to the matrix clause as in (1) and (2) above.

Second, both *ʔan* and *ʔanna* prohibit long passive/long object movement which, according to Wurmbrand (2001), is an impossible operation with both a TP and a CP complement. Long passive or long object movement refers to passivization of the matrix verb, where the embedded object is raised to the matrix subject position. Note that passivization in SA also involves morphological change of the verb being passivized to agree with the moved object and deletion of the original matrix subject. (3b) shows that long passive is not possible with *ʔan*:

(3) a. rafaɖ-a ħusaam-un ʔan ya-ktub-a
refused-PRF Husam-NOM ʔan 3SG.M.IMP-write-SUBJ
r-risaalat-a.
the-letter-ACC
"Husam refused to write the letter (himself)."

b. * rufiɖ-a-t r-risaalat-u ʔan
was.refused-PRF-3SG.F the-letter-NOM ʔan
ya-ktub-a.
3SG.M.IMP-write-SUBJ
*"The letter was refused that he writes."

Long object movement/long passive is also not compatible with *ʔanna*, as (4b) illustrates:

(4) a. ʕarif-a ħusaam-un ʔanna raami saaʕad-a ranaa.
knew-PRFHusam-NOM that Rami helped-PRF Rana
"Husam knew that Rami helped Rana."

b. * ʕurif-a-t ranaa ʔanna raami saaʕad-a-haa.
was.known-PRF-3SG.F Rana that Rami helped-PRF-her
"Rana was known that Rami helped her."

Third, both *ʔan* and *ʔanna* allow only embedded negation interpretation in the presence of a negative word in the embedded clause, which is the only interpretation permitted with both a TP and a CP complement (Wurmbrand 2001). (5) shows that only embedded negation meaning is allowed with *ʔan* when the negative word *laa* is present:

(5) rafaḍ-a ħusaam-un ʔan laa ya-ktub-a
refused-PRF Husam-NOM ʔan not 3SG.M.IMP-write-SUBJ
r-risaalat-a.
the-letter-ACC
"Husam refused not to write the letter."
"*Husam did not refuse to write the letter."

Similarly, only embedded negation interpretation is possible with *ʔanna* in the presence of the negative word *maa*, as in (6):

(6) ʕarif-a ħusaam-un ʔanna raami maa saaʕad-a ranaa.
knew-PRFHusam-NOM that Rami not helped-PRF Rana
"Husam knew that Rami did not help Rana."
*"Husam did not know that Rami helped Rana."

Another similar feature between *ʔan* and *ʔanna* is their coalescence with the element that follows them. The notion of coalescence means that the two elements cannot be separated. The idea that *ʔan* is coalesced with the subjunctive verb that follows goes back to Sībawayhi (Baalbaki 1999: 89). The reason that particles like *ʔan* "ʔan" and *kay* "for, to" are considered as one word with the verb that follows is that they can be substituted for by a *masdar* (a 'deverbal noun'), an active participle, or a preposition and its genitive. This is what is referred to by Wurmbrand (2001: 104) as the IPP ("infinitive for participle") effect. The IPP effect is an expression used to describe constructions in which the matrix verb that semantically corresponds to a participle appears in the form of infinitive (Wurmbrand 2001: 162). In other words, the IPP effect is only compatible with a TP structure, not a CP one. In our case, the *masdar* which is analogous to present participle or gerund in English can be replaced by *ʔan* + verb. Example (7) shows that *ʔan* + verb can replace a deverbal noun in the subject position:

(7) a. ʕalay-ka kitaabat-u waaʒib-i-ka.
on-you writing-NOM homework-GEN-your
"You have to write your homework."

b. ʕalay-ka ʔan ta-ktub-a waaʒib-a-ka.
on-you ʔan 2SG.M.IMP-write-SUBJ homework-ACC-your
"You have to write your homework."

It is also possible for *ʔan* + verb to replace a deverbal noun in the object position, e.g.:

(8) a. rafaḍ-a ħusaam-un kitaabat-a
Husam-NOM writing-ACC homework-GEN-his
waaʒib-i-hi.
refused-PRF
"Husam refused writing his homework."
b. rafaḍ-a ħusaam-un ʔan ya-ktub-a
refused-PRF Husam-NOM ʔan 3SG.M.IMP-write-SUBJ
waaʒib-a-hu.
homework-ACC-his
"Husam refused to write his homework."

This inseparability from the following form is considered as an *idafa* 'genitive' (Baalbaki 1999: 95) or what is referred to as the 'construct state' in Semitic (Hebrew and Arabic), which is equal to interpretive possessive structures in English, i.e. the *of*-structure.

Traditionally, the idea of coalescence also applied to *ʔanna*, i.e. it is considered with the pronominal that follows one noun (Baalbaki 1999: 103, adopted from Sirafi, SharH, in Kitab's margin III, 119). Letourneau (1993), for example, argues that pronominal subject clitics are incorporated into their complementizers. This coalescence feature of *ʔanna* is also supported in this study (section 3.2).

However, closer examination of the compatibility of *ʔanna* with the IPP effect raises doubt about its equality to *ʔan* with respect to their syntax. The IPP effect is incompatible with overt complementizers (Wurmbrand 2001: 104). This is exactly what we discover when we try to replace *ʔanna* + DP with a *masdar* in SA, (9b). Replacing *ʔanna* + DP in (9a) with a deverbal noun in (9b) results in a completely different meaning and *Rami* is deleted altogether. Because of the resultant different semantic interpretation, sentence (9b) is assigned an asterisk.

(9) a. ʕarif-a ħusaam-un ʔanna raami saaʕad-a ranaa.
knew-PRFHusam-NOM that Rami helped-PRF Rana
"Husam knew that Rami helped Rana."

b. * ʕarif-a ħusaam-un ʕan musaaʕadat-i ranaa.
knew-PRFHusam-NOM about helping-GEN Rana
"Husam knew about the helping of Rana."

This disparity between *ʔan* and *ʔanna* with regards to their coalescence with the following element and their (in)compatibility with the IPP effect highlights the uncertainty about the syntactic structure of each one of them. Since *ʔan* + V can replace a deverbal noun in the subject and object position, then they should constitute a TP complement in accordance with Wurmbrand's (2001) theory. The inability to substitute for a deverbal noun with *ʔanna* + DP is an indication that *ʔanna* has a different syntactic structure from *ʔan*. Following Wurmbrand's (2001) assumption, *ʔanna* should be a complementizer because it is incompatible with the IPP effect. This prompts us to lead a closer investigation of the structure of *ʔan* and *ʔanna* to provide evidence and show that despite their various similarities, they have different syntax.

3. Analysis of *ʔanna*

This section presents argument against a TP analysis of the *ʔanna*-complement and support for a CP analysis of it. In both analyses, I assume that Case is checked rather than assigned, following Chomsky (1993). I also assume that *ʔanna* carries a strong uninterpretable accusative Case feature, [*u*ACC*], that must be checked by the following subject DP that must be assigned an accusative Case in the presence of *ʔanna*.

A TP analysis of the *ʔanna*-complement would suggest that *ʔanna* is a functional head that occupies T rather than C, since [Spec,*v*P] could be an excellent host for the following subject DP. The subject DP after *ʔanna* merges in [Spec,*v*P] and the verb does not have to raise higher than the subject DP because it receives a default indicative mood in situ.[4] In this case, the [*u*ACC*] on T is checked by the following subject DP in a non-canonical configuration. Strong features should be checked in a local configuration (Chomsky 1993, 1995 and Roberts & Roussou 2002): head-head or Spec-head. According to this analysis, a sentence such as (2) repeated here in (10) is derived as in (11):

---

[4] I assume that indicative mood in Arabic is assigned under default in the absence of jussive or subjunctive mood assigner.

(10) ya-bduu ʔanna ħusaam-a yu-ħibb-u
3SG.M.IMP-seem that Husam-ACC 3SG.M.IMP-like-IND
ṭ-ṭaʕaam-a.
the-food-ACC
"It seems that Husam likes the food."

(11)

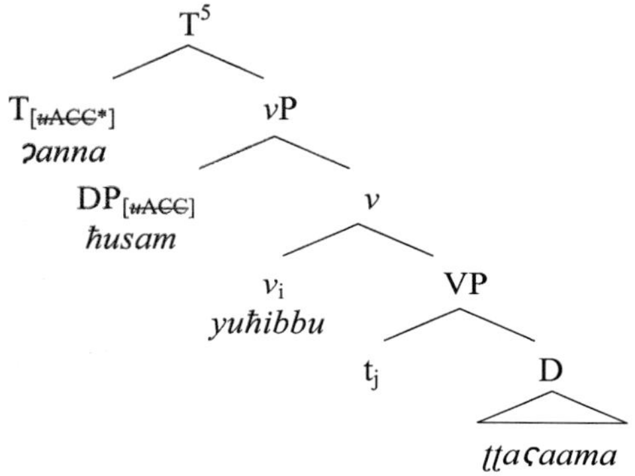

The second analysis I adopt here is that *ʔanna* is a complementizer that occupies C. *ʔanna* carries a strong uninterpretable accusative Case feature, [*u*ACC*], because in its absence, the subject DP receives a default nominative Case. To check this strong feature, the subject that is merged in [Spec,*v*P] is forced to move (Chomsky 1993, 1995 and Roberts & Roussou 2002) to [Spec,TP] to establish locality with the feature to be checked, yielding the non-canonical SVO word order after *ʔanna*. This may sound problematic because locality is satisfied in Spec-head and head-head configurations. This problem could be solved by adopting Chomsky's (2006, 2008) assumption that C has to transfer its features to T. The assumption asserts that C has to transfer its features to something; if T is not present, C cannot transfer its features to *v**. Without T, the derivation crashes. For Chomsky (2008), only CP and *v**P constitute phases. The head of the CP phase, i.e. C, transfers its features to T and the head of the *v**P phrase, i.e. *v**, transfers its features to V. Hence, all the properties of T (e.g., tense, Case, φ-features, etc.) do not belong to T itself; rather, T inherits them from C. In this sense, C transfers its [*u*ACC*] to T, leading to satisfaction of the locality condition. The moved subject DP

[5] The upper projections of the matrix clause of the tree are deleted because they are irrelevant to our analysis. This often applies to other trees throughout the study to save space.

from [Spec,*v*P] establishes locality in a Spec-head relation between [Spec,TP] and the head T. According to this analysis, a sentence such as (10) is derived as in (12):

(12)

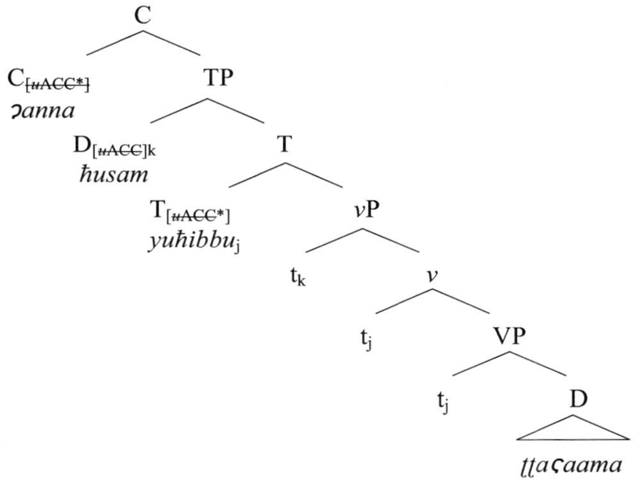

The raising of the subject DP from [Spec,*v*P] to [Spec,TP] becomes obvious if we examine the following two synonymous sentences:

(13) a. ya-bduu ʔanna-hu yu-ħibb-u
3SG.M.IMP-seem that-it 3SG.M.IMP-like-IND
ħusaam-un ṭ-ṭaʕaam-a.
Husam-NOM the-food-ACC

b. ya-bduu ʔanna ħusaam-a
3SG.M.IMP-seem that Husam-ACC
yu-ħibb-u ṭ-ṭaʕaam-a.
3SG.M.IMP-like-IND the-food-ACC
"It seems that Husam likes the food."

In the presence of an expletive pronoun after *ʔanna* (13a), the subject *Husam* remains in situ, i.e. in [Spec,*v*P]. When the expletive does not occur after *ʔanna* (13b), the subject DP *Husam* is forced to raise to [Spec,TP] to check the [*u*ACC*] feature of C.

3.1. *Why Does the First Analysis Fall Short?*

The analysis of *ʔanna* as T falls short for several reasons. First, it will change the long held view that Arabic is a VSO language, implicating that it is always an SVO language. If *ʔanna* occupies T and the following DP occupies [Spec,*v*P], then the verb will be blocked from raising to T to check certain features such as tense, aspect, mood or agreement features. Let us say arguably that it could raise to T and incorporate with *ʔanna*, but why don't we get a VSO order after *ʔanna*? Ouhalla (1994) argues that verb raising is the main way to derive a VSO order of an underlying SVO order. In addition, if one accepts that Arabic is an SVO language, which could be a possibility, one has to account for the different agreement on the verb: full agreement (gender, person, and number) with the subject when the verb follows the subject and partial agreement (only gender and person) with the subject when the verb precedes it (e.g. Mohammad 2000). If the verb cannot raise and remains in situ, how do we expect it to receive its agreement? Whether we adopt Ouhalla's (1994) suggestion that the AGR head is lower than T and higher than [Spec,*v*P] (see also Mohammad 2000: 86-91 for supporting arguments that Agr projects in the syntax of Arabic) or that agreement features are on T (Chomsky 2001), the verb has to raise to AGR or to T to check these features. Then, the subject raises to [Spec,TP] to yield the SVO order that results in full agreement on the verb. The derivations of partial and full agreement in Arabic are beyond the scope of this study.

3.2. **ʔanna** *and the Following DP Are Inseparable Even by Negative Particles*

Another argument in favor of *ʔanna* as a complementizer is that it cannot be followed immediately by a negative expression; the negative expression must follow the DP that follows *ʔanna*. The finiteness that *ʔanna* is imbued with allows it to occur with any of the negative particles in SA that are equal to "not" in English: *maa* and *laa* and its three variants *laysa*, *lam* and *lan*. *laysa* can agree with the subject and it is usually equated with a verb that is used to negate nominal sentences. *lam*, *lan*, and *laa* occur with imperfective verbs. *lam* carries the past tense and assigns the jussive mood to the following verb. *lan* carries the future tense and assigns the subjunctive mood to the following verb. *laa* is the only particle that does not carry tense and does not assign a mood to the following verb; it is followed by the indicative mood (when not preceded by a subjunctive marker such as *ʔan* and *kay* "for"). *maa* can only occur before a perfective verb or a nominal. None of the negative particles can intervene between *ʔanna* and the following DP. Following Benmamoun (1999: 95), negative expressions occupy a Neg head that is between TP and vP. Hence, in order for negation to take place, we need a TP that precedes the negation head Neg and whose specifier is filled by the accusative DP, forcing *ʔanna* to be in C:

(14) a. ya-bduu ʔanna ħusaam-a laa
3SG.M.IMP-seem that Husam-ACC not
yu-ħibb-u ṭ-ṭaʕaam-a.
3SG.M.IMP-like-IND the-food-ACC
b. * ya-bduu ʔanna laa ħusaam-a
3SG.M.IMP-seem that not Husam-ACC
yu-ħibb-u ṭ-ṭaʕaam-a.
3SG.M.IMP-like-IND the-food-ACC
"It seems that Husam does not like the food/Husam does not seem to like the food."

I have mentioned that some negative particles can be used only before imperfective verbs, i.e. *laa* and its two variants *lam* and *lan*. One may argue that the reason for the impossibility of these negatives to intervene between *ʔanna* and the following DP is due to their selection for a verb. However, the following question arises why is it not possible for *maa* and *laysa* to occur in that position since they could be used to negate a nominal sentence, that is, they can occur in sentence initial position before the subject DP? Rather, what is observed is that even these two negative particles cannot precede the subject DP that follows *ʔanna*. If we take examples such as (15a) and (16a) below and embed them after *ʔanna*, as in (15b) and (16b), the result is ungrammatical. Given the assumption that negative particles occupy a position between TP and vP, this result stresses that no negative particle can intervene between *ʔanna* and the accusative DP even those that are allowed sentence initially in nominal sentences and indicates that *ʔanna* selects for a TP complement that is followed by NegP in the presence of negation.

(15) a. laysa ħusaam-un yu-ħibb-u ṭ-ṭaʕaam-a.
not Husam-NOM 3SG.M.IMP-like-IND the-food-ACC
"Husam does not like the food."

b. * ya-bduu ʔanna laysa ħusaam-un
3SG.M.IMP-seem that not Husam-NOM
yu-ħibb-u ṭ-ṭaʕaam-a.
3SG.M.IMP-like-IND the-food-ACC
"It seems that Husam does not like the food."

(16) a. maa ħusaam-un ʃaaʕir-un.
not Husam-NOM poet-NOM
"Husam is not a poet."

b. * ya-bduu ʔanna maa ħusaam-un ʃaaʕir-un.
3SG.M.IMP-seem that not Husam-NOM poet-NOM
"It seems that Husam is not a poet."

Nonetheless, all the negative particles could occur between the subject DP and the predicate. This depends on the tense of the embedded clause because each of the negative particles is compatible with a certain tense or mood or may select for a different syntactic category, which is beyond the scope of this study. For example, *laysa* cannot select for a verb; hence, when it is used to negate the embedded clause after *ʔanna*, what follows it could be another nominal, adverbial (17b), or a prepositional phrase. *laysa* usually occurs sentence initially, as in (17a). When (17a) is embedded after *ʔanna*, the subject DP *Husam* must raise from [Spec,*v*P] to [Spec,TP] for the sentence to be grammatical, both to check the [*u*ACC*] feature of C and to avoid the intervention of a negative particle between *ʔanna* and the following DP.

(17) a. laysa ħusaam-un hunaa.
not Husam-NOM here
"Husam is not here."

b. ya-bduu ʔanna ħusaam-a laysa hunaa.
3SG.M.IMP-seem that Husam-ACC not here
"It seems that Husam is not here."

All the evidence that has been presented so far support the hypothesis that *ʔanna* is a complementizer that selects for a TP complement. *ʔanna* has a strong [*u*ACC*] feature that must be checked by a DP; this strong feature is transferred to T. The subject DP that originates in [Spec,*v*P] must raise to [Spec,TP] to check this Case feature in the absence of another subject/Topic DP, such as an expletive (18b). It has to be the subject DP that raises to [Spec,TP] to check the [*u*ACC*] feature, not the object DP because of Relativized Minimality (Rizzi 1990), (18c), under the assumption that [Spec,TP] is an A-position. If [Spec,TP] is an A'-position, then Relativized Minimality is not the main reason for the impossibility of an object DP to occur in [Spec,TP] after *ɔanna*.

Given Chomsky's (2004) assumption that accusative Case is assigned by *v** to object DPs and that subject DPs receive their Case from C, the subject DP raises to [Spec,TP] to receive its Case since Case like other features of C is transferred to T. This assumption also allows for my hypothesis that the accusative Case assigned by C is a strong feature that is endowed with EPP-like property, requiring raising of the subject DP to [Spec,TP] to check this strong feature; internal-Merge is not triggered by *Agree* (Chomsky 2001) alone. The second assumption is also supported by Pesetsky & Torrego's (2001) Economy Principle (i.e. a head H triggers the minimum number of operations necessary to satisfy the properties (including EPP) of its uninterpretable features).

Thus, moving the subject DP to [Spec,TP] requires fewer operations than moving the object DP to [Spec,TP]. In addition, the second assumption raises the A/A'-position issue after C. In Chomsky (2008), agreement/case systems drive A-movement, whereas *edge feature*, the current term for the generalized version of the EPP introduced in Chomsky (2000), drive A'-movement. This alone does not clarify the issue in SA because both Case and EPP are involved in the subject DP movement to [Spec,TP] after *ɔanna*. To clarify this issue is beyond the scope of this study and should be explored in further research. Under any of these assumptions, *ɔanna* occupies C; verbs that are followed by *ɔanna* take a CP complement.

(18) a. ya-bduu ɔanna ħusaam-a
3SG.M.IMP-seem that Husam-ACC
yu-ħibb-u ʈ-ʈaʕaam-a.
3SG.M.IMP-like-IND the-food-ACC

b. ya-bduu ɔanna-hu yu-ħibb-u
3SG.M.IMP-seem that-it 3SG.M.IMP-like-IND
ħusaam-un ʈ-ʈaʕaam-a.
Husam-NOM the-food-ACC

c. * ya-bduu ɔanna ʈ-ʈaʕaam-a
3SG.M.IMP-seem that-it the-food-ACC
yu-ħibb-u ħusaam-un.
3SG.M.IMP-like-IND Husam-NOM
"It seems that Husam likes the food."

4. Analysis of *ʔan*

This section presents argument against a CP analysis of the *ʔan*-complement and support for a TP analysis of it. First, we explore two possible analyses of the *ʔan*-complement: a CP analysis and then a TP analysis. The subsequent sub-sections provide support for the TP analysis and rejection of the CP analysis: why a CP analysis of *ʔan* falls short, [Spec,TP] does not exist after *ʔan*, Exceptional Case Marking is possible with *ʔan*, and the only negative marker compatible with *ʔan* is *laa*.

4.1. Two Analyses of ʔan*-Complement — as a CP and as a TP*

A CP analysis of the *ʔan*-complement would consider *ʔan* a complementizer that occupies C and selects a TP for its complement. It is not possible for the verb to check the strong uninterpretable subjunctive feature [*u*SUBJ*] in situ under *Agree* (Chomsky 2001) because strong features must be checked in a local configuration, i.e. Spec-head or head-head. Locality with the feature to be checked is achieved by overt movement (Chomsky 1993, 1995 and Roberts & Roussou 2002), not in situ. Thus, the verb raises from V to T to check the strong [*u*SUBJ*] on C in a local head-head configuration. According to this analysis, the structure of (1a) repeated here in (19) is derived as in (20):

(19)	yu-riid-u	ʔan	ya-ʔkul-a	raami
	3SG.M.IMP-want-IND	ʔan	3SG.M.IMP-eat-SUBJ	Rami
	t-tufaħat-a.			
	the-apple-ACC			
	"He wants Rami to eat the apple."			

(20)

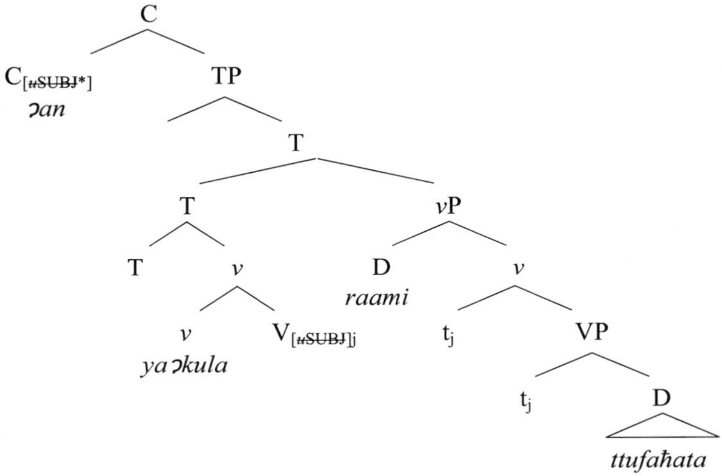

The second analysis that I adopt here suggests that *ʔan* is not a complementizer; it is merely a functional element that selects for a verb in the subjunctive mood; it is more like the infinitival *to*, in that, it occupies the functional head T. Hence, verbs that are followed by *ʔan* take a TP complement. Since Arabic is a VSO language, it is possible that the subject is merged in [Spec,*v*P], and the verb raises to v and the whole v complex raises and incorporates with T to check the strong [*u*SUBJ*] feature in a local head-head configuration. The structure for a sentence like (19) is derived as in (21):

(21)

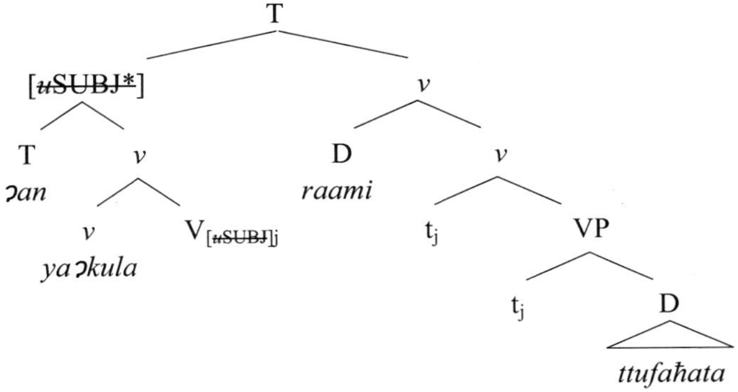

4.2. *Why the First Analysis Falls Short*

A CP analysis of the *ɔan*-complement seems reasonable at first, but it flounders when encountering sentences as (22b), which is ungrammatical because the subject DP of the embedded clause *Rami* intervenes between *ɔan* and the verb. Thus, it is not only that the object DP of the embedded clause, (23), cannot occur between C and the verb but also the subject DP, (22b). In (23), *lkitaab* is an object DP that leads to ungrammaticality because of occurring between *ɔan* and the verb. This is comprehensible because this observation was established in section 4.1 with regards to what could follow C, i.e. [Spec,TP] cannot host an object DP. What is incomprehensible is why the subject DP cannot occur in this position since it is possible in SA for a subject DP to be hosted by [Spec,TP] after C.

(22)	a.	yu-riid-u	ħusaam-un	ɔan	
		3SG.M.IMP-want-IND	Husam-NOM	ɔan	
		ya-ɔkul-a	raami	t-tufaħat-a.	
		3SG.M.IMP-eat-SUBJ	Rami	the-apple-ACC	
	b. *	yu-riid-u	ħusaam-un	ɔan	raami
		3SG.M.IMP-want-IND	Husam-NOM	ɔan	Rami
		ya-ɔkul-a	t-tufaħat-a.		
		3SG.M.IMP-eat-SUBJ	the-apple-ACC		
		"Husam wants Rami to eat the apple."			

(23) *	yu-riid-u	ħusaam-un	ɔan	l-kitab-a
	3SG.M.IMP-want-IND	Husam-NOM	ɔan	the-book-ACC
	yu-nhii.			
	3SG.M.IMP-finish			
	"Husam wants to finish the book."			

The impossibility for a DP whether a subject or an object to occur between *ɔan* and the verb provides very strong evidence that *ɔan* heads a TP complement and selects for a verb in the subjunctive mood, discarding any possibility of a CP complement. It also enforces the idea that *ɔan* and the verb are inseparable and coalesced; the verb raises and incorporate with *ɔan* in T as our account has shown. In this sense, the embedded subject and the matrix subject could check their nominative Case through the operation *Agree* (Chomsky 2001) or they get a nominative Case under default if there is no accusative Case assigner (Ouhalla 1994), as is the case with *ɔanna* that must be followed by a DP in the accusative Case.

This account of *ʔan* is supported by tests adopted from Wurmbrand (2001), which will be explored in section 5.

4.3. Is [Spec,TP] Present after ʔan*?*

We have seen in section 4.2 that *ʔan* could not be in C, otherwise it would be expected for *Rami* in (15b) to be able to occur in [Spec,TP] which is a possible landing site for subject DPs. It is possible in Arabic to have an SVO word order that is derived by raising the subject from [Spec,*v*P] to [Spec,TP]. Since this order is not possible after *ʔan*, there is no reason to believe that there is a TP after it.

Even if we continue to assume that there is a TP, a question arises, what is it that occupies [Spec,TP] that does not allow for a DP to occur there? Could it be a PRO? This is not possible because the embedded sentence already has a subject in [Spec,*v*P], i.e. *Rami*, where it receives its theta role. It has been mentioned before that [Spec,TP] could be a Topic position, i.e. an A′-position. For PRO to occupy [Spec,TP] a theta Criterion violation is incurred. Even if [Spec,TP] is not an A'-position, the precedence of PRO leads to violation of Condition C of the Binding Theory (Chomsky 1981) — an R-expression must be A-free in the domain of its operator. Even if we assume that the DP that occupies [Spec,TP] is the expletive *pro*, how could we explain the possibility of raising subjects from [Spec,*v*P] to [Spec,TP] in some cases and in some cases not? Furthermore, if we assume that the DP occupying [Spec,TP] is a (regular) *pro*, where does it receive its theta role from if [Spec,TP] is an A'-position? In addition, the presence of a *pro* all the time in [Spec,TP] will block the movement of other DPs to [Spec,TP], preventing an SVO order, a possible order in Arabic, to ever occur.

We have seen in section 3 that an SVO order is obligatory after *ʔanna* and that when the overt expletive is not present, the subject DP raises to that position to occupy its place. Even in sentences that do not contain *ʔanna* and have a covert *pro*, the subject DP could raise to replace that *pro*, (24b). Since it is possible to replace *pro* in (24a) with an overt subject, it should be possible to do so if [Spec,TP] exists after *ʔan*, but we have seen that an overt subject DP is not possible after *ʔan*, (22b).

(24) a. *pro* yu-riid-u raami ʔan
3SG.M.IMP-want-IND Rami ʔan
ya-ʔkul-a t-tufaħat-a.
3SG.M.IMP-eat-SUBJ the-apple-ACC

b. raami yu-riid-u ɔan ya-ɔkul-a
Rami 3SG.M.IMP-want-IND ɔan 3SG.M.IMP-eat-SUBJ
t-tufaħat-a.
the-apple-ACC
"Rami wants to eat the apple."

One may further argue that *ɔan* is a C that selects for a TP without an EPP feature, making a filled [Spec,TP] impossible. The verb raises from V to T to check the strong [*u*SUBJ*] feature on C in a head-head configuration. This merely adds an extra projection to the tree, i.e. a CP, as was shown in (20). The addition of one extra projection may not sound very problematic at first sight, but it becomes problematic when it comes to ECM that is possible with *ɔan*.

4.4. Evidence for ECM with ɔan

According to Stowell (1982) and Wurmbrand (2001: 69), ECM is only possible with CP-less infinitives. In ECM constructions in Greek, the subject occupies [Spec,M(ood)P] (Terzi 1997). In this study, I will show that it suffices to have a TP to accommodate the ECM subject, where *ɔan* is situated in T and the subject occupies a position higher than *ɔan*, i.e. [Spec,TP]. The presence of an empty functional head such as T that can be occupied by functional elements (section 5.5) saves us from proposing a further projection such as MP to accommodate *ɔan*, which proves unnecessary and rather non-minimalist. An example of an ECM construction with *ɔan* is (25b).

(25) a. yu-riid-u raami ɔan
3SG.M.IMP-want-NOM Rami ɔan
ta-bdaɔ-a l-mubaaraat-u.
3SG.M.IMP-start-SUBJ the-match-NOM
b. yu-riid-u raami l-mubaaraat-a ɔan
3SG.M.IMP-want-NOM Rami the-match-ACC ɔan
ta-bdaɔ-a.
3SG.M.IMP-start-SUBJ
"Rami wants the match to start."

The change of Case of the noun *lmubaaraat* "the match" in (25b), when raised to the matrix clause, indicates an ECM construction in which the semantic subject of the embedded clause appears in the accusative

Case in the matrix clause. The possibility of the presence of *lmubaaraat* in both the embedded and the matrix clauses makes the structure look like subject-to-object raising unlike English in which the subject of the embedded clause in the ECM constructions is constantly higher than *to*, where it receives an accusative Case from the matrix verb, e.g.

(26) a. Rami wants him to eat the apple.
b. * Rami wants to him eat the apple.

In order for *lmubaaraat* "the match" to occur between the matrix verb and *ʔan*, there must be a position in the tree that can be occupied by a DP, i.e. [Spec,TP]. The position between *ʔan* and the matrix verb cannot be considered a matrix clause object position. The examples in (27) support my view that it is an ECM structure, not a raising-to-object (Salih 1985) structure. In (27a), *lʔawlaad-u* "the children" is the subject DP, indicated by the nominative Case-marker. It follows the verb that shows partial agreement with the subject DP because it precedes the subject. In (27b), the embedded subject *lʔawlaad-a* appears preceding *ʔan* in the accusative Case. In this sentence, the embedded verb shows full agreement with the subject DP, which confirms the existence of ECM in Arabic and that the position between the matrix verb and *ʔan* is [Spec,TP], not an object position of the matrix verb. Full agreement is triggered in Arabic by moving the subject from [Spec,*v*P] to [Spec,TP].

(27) a. yu-riid-u ʔan ya-ktub-a
3SG.M.IMP-want-IND ʔan 3SG.M.IMP-write-SUBJ
l-ʔawlaad-u waaʒib-a-hum.
the-children-NOM homework-ACC-their

b. yu-riid-u l-ʔawlaad-a ʔan
3SG.M.IMP-want-IND the-children-ACC ʔan
ya-ktub-uu waaʒib-a-hum.
3. M.IMP-write-SUBJ.PL homework-ACC-their
"He wants the children to write their homework."

In this sense, a TP should be the complement of the matrix verb, and it is followed by a *v*P. The head T could be a good host for functional categories, and we could suggest that *ʔan* resides in it where it serves a function analogous to the English infinitival *to* that occupies that head. The difference is that in Arabic *ʔan* selects for a verb in the subjunctive mood. This leads to our analysis that could account for the lack of a DP between *ʔan* and the verb and for ECM constructions with *ʔan*.

Ouhalla (1994: 67) argues that ECM is also possible with *ʔanna*, sometimes referring to this construction using the same term used by Salih (1985) 'raising-to-object'. However, in the case of *ʔanna*, a resumptive pronoun must be left behind in the embedded clause:

(28) a. ya-bduu ʔanna ħusaam-a
3SG.M.IMP-seem that Husam-ACC
yu-ħibb-u ṭ-ṭaʕaam-a.
3SG.M.IMP-like-IND the-food-ACC
"It seems that Husam likes the food."

b. ya-bduu ʔanna-**hu** yu-ħibb-u
3SG.M.IMP-seem that-**him** 3SG.M.IMP-like-IND
ṭ-ṭaʕaam-a.
the-food-ACC
"It seems that he likes the food."

This is due to left dislocation, rather than raising to object position because one requirement of left dislocation is for the base-generated matrix DP to have a pronominal copy base-generated in the embedded clause. Coopman (1994: 80) comments on Ouhalla's consideration of this ECM condition with *ʔanna* as movement, indicating that it "cannot be movement in the usual sense" because of the existence of an overt pronominal in the embedded clause with which the moved subject is coindexed. In addition, in ECM constructions one expects the raised subject DP to receive accusative Case in the matrix clause and to have object syntax in addition to its interpretation as the embedded clause subject, which is not the case with *ʔanna*. Rather, the subject DP is semantically the subject of the matrix clause and receives a default nominative Case, indicating that it is base-generated in a Topic position (Ouhalla 1994).

4.5. The Compatibility **of ʔan** *with Negative Markers*

A further argument in support of our account comes from the use of negative markers with *ʔan* and *ʔanna*. It has been mentioned earlier that all the negative markers can occur with *ʔanna*. In contrast, *ʔan* is only compatible with the negative particle *laa* because it is neither a tense carrier nor a mood assigner. *laa* could occur immediately after *ʔan*, i.e. between *ʔan* and the verb (29a), in comparison to *lan* and *lam* (29b).

(29) a. ħaawal-a ħusaam-un ʔan laa ya-ktub-**a**
tried-PRF Husam-NOM ʔan not 3SG.M.IMP-write-**SUBJ**
r-risaalat-a.
the-letter-ACC

b. * ħaawal-a ħusaam-un ʔan lan/lam
tried-PRF Husam-NOM ʔan not
ya-ktub-a/**Ø** r-risaalat-a.
3SG.M.IMP-write-SUBJ/**JUSS** the-letter-ACC
"Husam tried not to write the letter."

The reason that *laa* could occur between *ʔan* + V is that it does not occupy T; it has its own Neg head that is between TP and the verb (Benmamoun 1999: 95). It has also been argued before that the negative particles *lan*, *lam*, and *laysa* that are variants of *laa* could occur after *ʔanna* and its subject, indicating that these negative particles occupy a head that is positioned between TP and the verb. Even *maa*, which according to Benmamoun (1999: 108-109) occupies [Spec,NegP], occurs after *ʔanna* and its subject, suggesting a position between TP and the verb.

Since negative markers in general take a separate head or position in the tree that is not a complementizer position, we could assume the same thing for the subjunctive particle *ʔan*. For example, *lan* is a subjunctive marker like *ʔan* but it occupies a Neg head. Consequently, we should be able to treat *ʔan* in the same way like *lan*, that is, instead of treating it as a complementizer, we could treat it as a functional element that occupies the functional head T. These negative markers have different sub-categorizations (e.g. *lam* [V, *u*NEG*, + Past, *u*JUSS*], *lan* [V, *u*NEG*, + Future, *u*SUBJ*], and so on), and thus different features that must be checked by the verb.

In accordance with the above distribution of the various negative particles, one can further suggest that *ʔanna* occupies C, followed by a TP, followed by a NegP (the Neg head could be specified for both [*u*NEG*] and [*u*SUBJ*] for example) and then a *v*P, whereas *ʔan* occupies T, followed by a NegP and then a *v*P. Following Benmamoun's negative structure (1999: 95), when the negative particle *laa* occurs after *ʔan*, *ʔan* is situated in T and the negative particle heads a NegP below T and above the verb.

Consequently, the verb first raises and incorporates with *laa* in the Neg head, and then the whole Neg complex raises and incorporates with *ʔan* in T for the verb to check the strong [*u*SUBJ*] feature on T as (29a) is depicted in (30):

(30)

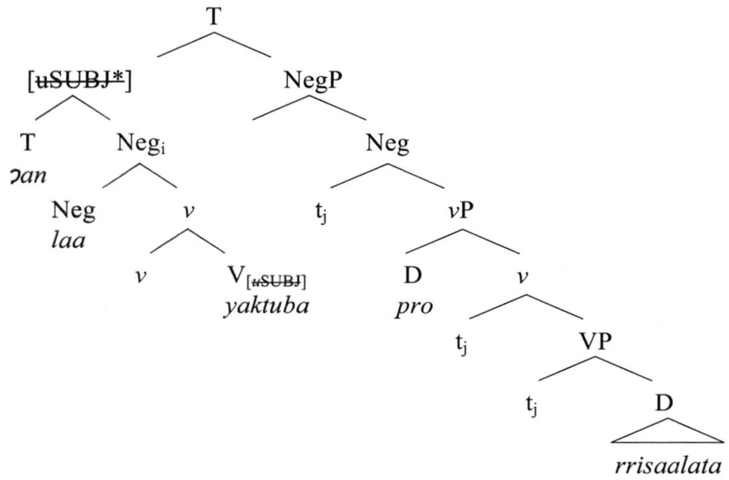

Moreover, the incompatibility of most negative markers with *ʔan* may be due to two reasons. First, negative markers such as *lan* "not" and *lam* "not" are tense carriers, the former carries the future tense and the latter carries the past tense. We will see later (section 5.3) that the *ʔan*-clause has a defective tense: perfective or future tenses are incompatible with it. In contrast, *laa* is not a tense carrier. Second, only the negative marker *laa* "not" is compatible with *ʔan* because *laa*, when not preceded by *ʔan*, can be followed only by verbs in the indicative mood. It is thus not a mood assigner. The two other negative markers are mood assigners: *lan* "not" (subjunctive mood) and *lam* "not" (jussive mood), and this might lead to mood conflict. Since *laa* does not block the verb from receiving its subjunctive mood (29a) when preceded by *ʔan*, this provides strong evidence in support of the derivation given in (30), explaining *laa*'s compatibility with *ʔan* and challenging Ouhalla's (1994:51) suggestion that *laa* blocks V-movement to T.

The incompatibility of *ʔan* with other subjunctive markers and negative markers may raise the following suggestion: all function words, such as mood assigners and negative markers, occupy T, preventing *ʔan* from co-occurring with them because it is probably impossible to have two mood features on T: the [*u*SUBJ*] of *ʔan* and the [*u*JUSS*] and [*u*SUBJ*] of *lam* and *lan* respectively. In the presence of *lam* and *lan*, T will also have tense features which are incompatible with *ʔan* that seems to head a defective tense clause (i.e. non-finite TP) and this will overload T with features. The coalescence of *ʔan* and *laa*, in this case, might be due to competition between the two words to occupy T, but since *laa* does not carry a mood feature or a tense feature, it is not a problem for the two words to occur as one prefixed word in T. However, this suggestion is beyond the scope of this study and requires further investigation.

5. Diagnostics

Wurmbrand (2001) presents a clear distinction between restructuring and non-restructuring structures in German on the one hand and between reduced and full non-restructuring structures on the other hand. Restructuring is the transformation of a bi-clausal structure into a mono-clausal structure (Wurmbrand 2001, adopted from Rizzi 1976); it is equal to a VP.[6] In this sense, the embedded verb forms one complex verb with the matrix verb. Reduced non-restructuring, according to Wurmbrand (2001), is something between restructuring and full non-restructuring, i.e. it is neither a VP nor a CP; rather it is an IP or a *v*P. *v*P assigns an accusative Case to the embedded object. If this object retains its accusative Case when moved from its position, it is an indication that the structure is reduced non-restructuring or full/clausal non-restructuring. If it were restructuring, one would expect the object to receive a nominative Case from [Spec,TP] in the matrix clause in long object movement, a term Wurmbrand uses for passivization. This means that long object movement or long passive is only possible in restructuring structures.

What is relevant to us in this study are the features and operations that distinguish reduced non-restructuring structures (*v*P or TP) from full/clausal non-restructuring structures (CP) (see Table 1 adopted from Wurmbrand's (2001: 3 & 309)).

---

[6] In Colloquial Syrian Arabic (CSA), *ʔan is* deleted most of the time in such constructions (in CSA, *ʔinnu* takes the place of *ʔan* and it is the one deleted), e.g.

(i) badd-uu raami yaa-kul t-tfaħa.
want-3SG.M Rami 3SG.M.IMP-eat the-apple
"Rami wants to eat the apple."

Discussing the structure in (i) is beyond the scope of this study, but it could be an indication that the reduced non-restructuring structure, i.e. a TP, in SA becomes a restructuring structure, i.e. a VP, (Wurmbrand 2001) in CSA by deleting the subjunctive mood marker.

Table 1: Features of German reduced & full non-restructuring infinitives

non-restructuring	structure	properties, distribution	(im)possible operations
reduced	*v*P or TP	embedded (PRO) subject embedded structural case *Possible with:* implicatives, aspectual, irrealis predicates *Possible*: embedded tense embedded negation non-obligatory control	*Possible*: pronoun fronting focus scrambling %extraposition of infinitive *Impossible*: long object movement (non-focus) scrambling relative clause pied-piping
clausal (full)	CP	embedded (PRO) subject embedded structural case embedded tense *Possible with:* all lexical predicates *Obligatory with:* propositional, factive predicates	*Possible*: relative clause pied-piping extraposition of infinitive *Impossible*: long object movement scrambling pronoun fronting %intraposition of infinitive

Since I argue in this study that *ʔan* + V constitute a TP complement and *ʔanna* + DP constitute a CP complement, only operations and properties that show different outcomes with TP and CP complements will be performed. Tests that are not pertinent to our account or on which a TP and a CP behave similarly will be excluded. Long object movement, extraposition, embedded negation, and embedded structural case are possible with both a TP and a CP complement. (Non-focus) scrambling is impossible with both structures. The intraposition test status is somehow marked in the case of a CP and is not highly relevant in the case of a TP. The relative clause pied piping is a German specific structure and proves useless in Arabic. Though embedded tense seems to be possible with both structures, it is obligatory with a CP but only optional with a TP. Therefore, we need this test in the case of *ʔan* and *ʔanna*, which show different distributions with regards to tense. As for the embedded (PRO) subject test, Arabic behaves differently from German; Arabic does not seem to have PRO as an embedded subject as section 5.5 will imply and raise a number of issues for future research about whether the embedded null subject in SA is PRO or *pro* and whether non-obligatory control is raising. Hence, the tests that I will present are: pronoun fronting (section 5.1), (focus) scrambling (section 5.2), tense (section 5.3), implicative vs. factive (section 5.4), and non-obligatory control (section 5.5).

5.1. Pronoun Fronting

Pronoun fronting is an operation in which a pronominal argument originating in the embedded predicate of *try*-infinitive as well as verbs such as *plan* and *decide* can be moved to the left of the matrix subject; the fronting could be from extraposed infinitives (31b) or infinitives in situ (31d) (Wurmbrand 2001: 267-268). In our case, the infinitive is substituted for by *ʔan* + V, and it is not clear if it is extraposition of *ʔan* + V or raising of the embedded subject to the matrix clause in (31a,b). This type of fronting is possible from a vP and TP, but not from a CP and is compatible with NOC (section 5.5), a characteristic of reduced non-restructuring.

(31) a. ħaawal-a ħusaam-un ʔan yu-rsel-a
tried-PRF Husam-NOM ʔan 3SG.M.IMP-send-SUBJ
risaalat-an la-haa.
letter-ACC to-her
"Husam tried to send a letter to her."

b. la-haa ħaawal-a ħusaam-un ʔan
to-her tried-PRF Husam-NOM ʔan
yu-rsel-a risaalat-an.
3SG.M.IMP-send-SUBJ letter-ACC
"To her, Husam tried to send a letter."

c. ħaawal-a ʔan yu-rsel-a
tried-PRF ʔan 3SG.M.IMP-send-SUBJ
ħusaam-un risaalat-an la-haa.
Husam-NOM letter-ACC to-her
"Husam tried to send a letter to her."

d. la-haa ħaawal-a ʔan yu-rsel-a
to-her tried-PRF ʔan 3SG.M.IMP-send-SUBJ
ħusaam-un risaalat-an.
Husam-NOM letter-ACC
"To her, Husam tried to send a letter."

(31b,d) show that pronoun fronting is possible with *ʔan*, supporting our claim that *ʔan* occupies T and is followed by a vP. *ħusaam* c-commands the pronoun before it is fronted in both cases. If the complement were a CP, it would not have been possible to front the pronoun in *la-haa*.

Notice that this kind of pronoun fronting is not possible with *ʔanna*, an indication of a CP complement, as in (32b).

(32) a. ʕalim-a raami ʔanna ħusaam-a
knew-PRF Rami that Husam-ACC
sa-yu-rsel-u risaalat-an la-haa.
will-3SG.M.IMP-send-IND letter-ACC to-her
"Rami knew that Husam will send a letter to her."

b. * la-haa ʕalim-a raami ʔanna ħusaam-a
to-her knew-PRF Rami that Husam-ACC
sa-yu-rsel-u risaalat-an.
will-3SG.M.IMP-send-IND letter-ACC
"To her, Rami knew that Husam will send a letter."

5.2. (Focus) Scrambling

According to Wurmbrand (2001: 269), "[t]he distinction between focus scrambling and non-focus scrambling is [...] shaky." She goes on to say that scrambling to the left is preferred more than scrambling to the right because pre-subject position is "an inherent focus position" (p. 270). In other words, focus scrambling involves a focus interpretation or position, i.e. a C-domain, whereas non-focus scrambling does not have to be in a focus position or have a focus interpretation. We are here concerned with focus scrambling that is possible with reduced but not full non-restructuring constructions.

The idea that focus scrambling involves a C-domain means that the scrambled DP has to be moved to [Spec,CP] across another clause. If focus scrambling is possible, the crossed over clause will be a TP, not a CP; crossing over a CP violates the Phase Interpretability Condition (PIC) (Chomsky 2000, 2001). An example of focus scrambling would be:

(33) a. ħaawal-a ħusaam-un ʔan yu-rsil-a
tried-PRF Husam-NOM ʔan 3SG.M.IMP-send-SUBJ
risaalat-an ʔilaa ranaa.
letter-ACC to Rana
"Husam tried to send a letter to Rana."

b. risaalat-an ħaawal-a ħusaam-un ʔan
letter-ACC tried-PRF Husam-NOM ʔan
yu-rsil-a ʔilaa ranaa.
3SG.M.IMP-send-SUBJ to Rana
"A letter Husam tried to send to Rana."

c. ʔilaa ranaa ħaawal-a ħusaam-un ʔan
to Rana tried-PRF Husam-NOM ʔan
yu-rsil-a risaalat-an.
3SG.M.IMP-send-SUBJ letter-ACC
"To Rana Husam tried to send a letter."

d. ?* ħaawal-a ħusaam-un risaalat-an ʔan
tried-PRF Husam-NOM letter-ACC ʔan
yu-rsil-a ʔilaa ranaa.
3SG.M.IMP-send-SUBJ to Rana
"Husam tried the letter to send to Rana."

In (33b), the direct object DP is scrambled to the focus position. In (33c), the indirect object is scrambled to the focus position. Thus, the possibility of focus scrambling to occur with *ʔan* provides further support for the TP analysis of the *ʔan*-complement. Furthermore, if *ʔan* were a C, we should be able to have focus scrambling immediately before *ʔan*, i.e. in [Spec,CP], but (33d) shows that this is not desirable. On the other hand, focus scrambling seems to be incompatible with *ʔanna*, as (34b,c) reveal, an indication of a CP structure of the *ʔanna*-complement.

(34) a. ʕalim-a-t ranaa ʔanna ħusaam-a
knew-PRF-3SG.F Rana that Husam-ACC
yu-ħibb-u ṭ-ṭaʕaam-a.
3SG.M.IMP-like-IND the-food-ACC
"Rana knew that Husam likes the food."

b. * ṭ-ṭaʕaam-a ʕalim-a-t ranaa ʔanna
the-food-ACC knew-PRF-3SG.F Rana that
ħusaam-a yu-ħibb-u.
Husam-ACC 3SG.M.IMP-like-IND
"The food, Rana knew that Husam likes."

c. * ʕalim-a-t ranaa ṭ-ṭaʕaam-a ʔanna
knew-PRF-3SG.F Rana the-food-ACC that
ħusaam-a yu-ħibb-u.
Husam-ACC 3SG.M.IMP-like-IND
"Rana knew the food that Husam likes."

5.3. Tense

While Fassi Fahri (1993: 141-149) considers Arabic an aspectual language that lacks tense distinctions, I agree with Chung & Timberlake (1985) that all languages express aspect and time to some extent because finiteness is one further feature that distinguishes *ʔanna* from *ʔan*, in that *ʔanna*-clause is finite. *ʔanna* can be followed by the perfective as well as the imperfective (35), whereas *ʔan* can only be followed by the imperfective in the subjunctive mood (36). In section 2, we saw that the *masdar* (deverbal noun), a non-finite complement, can replace *ʔan* + V. In this sense, it should be possible to consider *ʔan* + V as non-finite or as having a defective tense. This further highlights the similarity between *ʔan* + V and the non-finite English TP complement that is headed by the infinitival *to*.

The non-finiteness of the *ʔan*-clause supports Chomsky's (2000, 2001) theory that only C is φ-complete and that T is only φ-complete if selected by C, otherwise it is φ-defective. This assumption encompasses tense and is stressed in Chomsky (2008: 143):

> T manifest the basic tense features if and only if it is selected by C (default agreement aside); if not, it is a raising (or ECM) infinitival, lacking φ-features and basic tense.

This implies that the CP layer is absent when T is tenseless and this is exactly what we encounter with *ʔan* — lack of tense. Given the implications of Chomsky's views, the *ʔan*-clause like any infinitival structure that may exist in other languages lacks a CP layer, reinforcing my proposal that *ʔan* occupies T, rather than C.

(35) ya-bduu ʔanna ħusaam-a
3SG.M.IMP-seem that Husam-ACC
yu-ħibb-u/ʔaħabb-a ṭ-ṭaʕaam-a.
3SG.M.IMP-like-IND/liked-PRF the-food-ACC
"It seems that Husam likes/liked the food."

(36) a. nasiy-a ħusaam-un ʔan ya-ktub-a
forgot-PRF Husam-NOM ʔan 3SG.M.IMP-write-SUBJ
r-risaalat-a.
the-letter-ACC
"Husam forgot to write the letter."

b. * nasiy-a ħusaam-un ʔan katab-a r-risaalat-a.
forgot-PRF Husam-NOM ʔan wrote-PRF the-letter-ACC
"Husam forgot that he wrote the letter."

Furthermore, Noonan (1985: 92) indicates that the subjunctive has a reduced ability to express time/aspect in comparison to the indicative. Persson (2002: 54) also refers to the fact that indicative verbs can "combine with various modifiers to express different time/aspect — and other modifications, the subjunctive is much more limited in this regard." For example, *ʔan* cannot combine with *kaana* "was" (37) that is an auxiliary verb that indicates the past tense nor can it combine with *s–* "will" or *sawfa* "will" (38) that are future markers.

(37) * ħaawal-a ħusaam-un ʔan kaan-a ya-ktub-a
tried-PRF Husam-NOM ʔan was-PRF 3SG.M.IMP-write-SUBJ
r-risaalat-a.
the-letter-ACC
*"Husam tried to was write the letter."

(38) * ħaawal-a ħusaam-un ʔan sa-ya-ktub-a
tried-PRF Husam-NOM ʔan will-3SG.M.IMP-write-SUBJ
r-risaalat-a.
the-letter-ACC
*"Husam tried to will write the letter."

On the other hand, *ʔanna* can be followed by *kaana* (39) and *s–* or *sawfa* (40).

(39) ya-bduu ʔanna ħusaam-a kaana
3SG.M.IMP-seem that Husam-ACC was-PRF
yu-ħibb-u ṭ-ṭaʕaam-a.
3SG.M.IMP-like-IND the-food-ACC
"It seems that Husam likes the food/Husam seems to like the food."

(40) ya-bduu ʔanna ħusaam-a
3SG.M.IMP-seem that Husam-ACC
sa-yu-ħibb-u ṭ-ṭaʕaam-a.
will-3SG.M.IMP-like-IND the-food-ACC
"It seems that Husam likes the food/Husam seems to like the food."

Cantarino (1974/5 II: 234f) also notes the difference between *ʔanna* and *ʔan*: while the former introduces an independent and complete syntactic unit, the latter introduces a statement that is part of a compound. Similarly, Givón (1990: 518) suggests that since *ʔan* and what follows exhibit more dependency on the matrix clause than *ʔanna* and what follows, they are more integrated or incorporated into the main clause or "into a single clause." This dependency refers to time reference dependency, truth-value dependency, and discourse dependency (Persson 2002: 88-89). An example of time dependency is:

(41) a. ħaawal-a ħusaam-un ʔan ya-ktub-a
tried-PRF Husam-NOM ʔan 3SG.M.IMP-write-SUBJ
r-risaalat-a (*ɣad-an).
the-letter-ACC tomorrow
"Husam tried to write the letter tomorrow."

b. ħaawal-a ħusaam-un ʔan ya-ktub-a
tried-PRF Husam-NOM ʔan 3SG.M.IMP-write-SUBJ
r-risaalat-a l-baariħat-a.
the-letter-ACC the-yesterday-ACC
"Husam tried to write the letter yesterday."

Example (41) shows that tense modifiers are allowed with *ʔan*. However, the embedded tense modifier is dependent (Persson 2002: 88) on the tense of the matrix clause as shown in (41a,b) and most likely modifies the matrix verb, not the embedded verb. (41a) shows that the modifier *ɣadan* "tomorrow" cannot co-occur with a matrix verb in the perfective; (41b) shows that a past tense modifier can be used to modify a sentence whose matrix verb is in the perfective, referring to the time *Husam* tried, not to the time he wrote the letter.

Thus, the subjunctive *ʔan*-complement has a defective tense, analogous to Romance languages that have a defective tense subjunctive. This dependency on the matrix clause is observed in other languages. For example, Terzi (1997) points out to the defective tense of the subjunctive in Greek and the tense dependency between the matrix and subordinate clause in the case of subjunctive and to the dependency of the embedded null subject on the matrix subject.

5.4. Implicative vs. Factive

In Table 1, it is stated that reduced non-restructuring structures are possible with implicative and irrealis verbs, whereas full non-restructuring structures are obligatory with propositional and factive verbs. Similar to

German, there are, for example, different verbs of *nasiya* "forgot" in Arabic: implicative and factive. The implicative (42) occurs with reduced non-restructuring, yielding ʔ*an* + V is a TP.

(42) nasiy-a ħusaam-un ʔan ya-ʒtamiʕ-a
forgot-PRF Husam-NOM ʔan 3SG.M.IMP-gather-SUBJ
fii l-maktab-i.
in the-office-GEN
"Husam forgot to gather in the office." (He did not gather.)

On the other hand, the factive (43) occurs with full/clausal non-restructuring, providing evidence that ʔ*anna* + DP is a CP. While (42) implies that *Husam* did not experience the action of gathering, (43) states the fact that the gathering took place.

(43) nasiy-a ħusaam-un ʔanna-hu ʒtamaʕ-a
forgot-PRF Husam-NOM that-he 3SG.M.IMP-gather-SUBJ
fii l-maktab-i.
in the-office-GEN
"Husam forgot that he gathered in the office." (He gathered.)

The use of different types of complement with the verb's two different meanings indicates that the semantics of the verb plays a major role in determining the type of complement that could follow it: a TP (42) or a CP (43).

5.5. *Non-Obligatory Control (NOC)*

According to Table 1, NOC is compatible with a TP complement. (44) shows that only NOC is possible with ʔ*an*. I depict here this NOC with a *pro*, not a PRO, because the null subject (44a) could alternate with an overt subject (44b,c).

(44) a. rafaɖ-a ħusaam-un$_i$ ʔan
refused-PRF Husam-NOM$_i$ ʔan
ya-ktub-a pro$_{i/j}$ waaʒib-a-hu.
3SG.M.IMP-write-SUBJ homework-ACC-his
"Husam$_i$ refused for *pro*$_{i/j}$ to write his homework."

b. rafaɖ-a pro$_{i/j}$ ʔan ya-ktub-a
refused-PRF ʔan 3SG.M.IMP-write-SUBJ
ħusaam-un$_i$ waaʒib-a-hu.
Husam-NOM homework-ACC-his
"*pro*$_{i/j}$ refused for Husam$_i$ to write his homework."

c. rafaɖ-a ħusaam-un ʔan ya-ktub-a
refused-PRF Husam-NOM ʔan 3SG.M.IMP-write-SUBJ
raami waaʒib-a-hu.
raami homework-ACC-his
"Husam refused for Rami to write his homework."
(i.e. Rami's/Husam's homework)

(44a) is synonymous with (44b). If *Husam* could occur in the embedded clause, this would mean that NOC is raising, equating it with the theory of Obligatory Control (OC) as raising (Hornstein 1999).

If raising occurs from the embedded clause, this provides further evidence that *ʔan* heads a TP, not a CP. Otherwise, we would violate PIC (Chomsky 2000, 2001). In addition, the *ʔan*-clause tense defectiveness (section 5.3) implies that it is a raising or ECM structure that lacks a CP layer (Chomsky 2008). Moreover, if it is a reduced non-restructuring structure, the subject of the embedded clause is definitely a *pro*, not PRO because PRO cannot be assigned Case, cannot be governed, and cannot alternate with an overt DP.

It is worth noting here that *ʔanna* constructions do not exhibit control (Salih 1985). They could exhibit raising in Salih's (1985) sense, but it is in my opinion a special kind of raising, copy raising, where the matrix subject is base-generated in a non-thematic Topic position and resumed by a resumptive pronoun that is base-generated as a clitic in the embedded clause. It is beyond the scope of this study to expand on this issue.

6. Conclusion

I have argued in this paper and have been able to show that *ʔan* and *ʔanna* differ with respect to their syntax. *ʔan* is a functional element that heads a TP complement; the embedded verb raises to T to check the strong [*u*SUBJ*] feature on T. On the other hand, *ʔanna* is a complementizer that heads a CP complement; the embedded subject DP raises from [Spec,*v*P] to [Spec,TP] to check the strong [*u*ACC*] of C that transfers this feature to T to satisfy the locality condition of feature checking. The different features of *ʔan* and *ʔanna* and the various tests performed provided evidence in support of a reduced non-restructuring analysis, i.e. TP, of the *ʔan*-complement and a full non-restructuring analysis, i.e. CP, of the *ʔanna*-complement.

These findings par with Chomsky's (2000, 2001, 2004, 2006, 2008) theory that only C and *v** constitute phase heads and that T is φ-defective if not selected by C, as is the case with the *ʔan*-complement that exhibit tense dependency on the matrix clause. Moreover, the findings team up perfectly with the new inheritance/transfer theory (Chomsky 2006, 2008) and its implications with respect to the relationship between C and T. Ample evidence showed that the phase head C must be present for T to have any type of features and that T inherits its features from C. In the absence of C, T is defective. This is evident in the case of *ʔan* that occupies T and lacks tense. When C is present, it transfers its features to T for syntactic operations to take place, particularly internal-Merge. This is evident in the case of *ʔanna* that transfers its [*u*ACC*] feature to T to establish a local Spec-head configuration that allows for this feature to be checked by internal-Merge of the subject DP in [Spec,TP].

The findings of this study lead us to one further conclusion: since Arabic is a VSO language, all that we need is a vP. We need another projection above vP when there is a negative marker, mood marker, AgrS, AgrO, AspP, and so on. All of these heads are equal to TP so to speak because they all function in the same way, assigning some feature. Thus, they should not be treated as CPs. They are just like TPs in being feature assigners. In this sense, it is possible for the functional head T to host some of these functional particles, such as *ʔan*, instead of leaving it empty and projecting another projection, such as MP, that adds one further layer to the structure, which proves unnecessary within the Minimalist Program framework. The existence of TP suffices to accommodate *ʔan* in T and ECM subjects in [Spec,TP].

This study raises many issues that require further investigation, such as the syntactic position of negative markers, i.e. could they occupy T rather than occupying their own Neg head or [Spec,NegP]? They compete with *ʔan* for that position and thus they cannot co-occur adjacent to each other. Section 4.5 has suggested that this could be a possibility. The second issue is whether we really need PRO in NOC structures in SA, given the availability of *pro*. Section 5.3 showed that Arabic like Romance languages has a defective tense subjunctive. This similarity between Arabic and Romance languages could be explored further with regards to the existence of PRO, since Romance languages do not allow PRO to be the null embedded subject in their defective tense subjunctive structures.

The third question that could be raised is whether NOC is raising; if this is the case, control structures do not exist in SA since OC is not possible as well. This realization might extend Hornstein's (1999) theory of OC as raising to NOC. However, the status of PRO, *pro*, and control in Arabic require further investigation.

References

Baalbaki, R. 1999. Coalescence as a grammatical tool in Sībawayhi's *Kitāb*. In Y. Suleiman (ed.), *Arabic Grammar and Linguistics*. Richmond: Curzon Press, 86-102.

Badawi, E., M.G. Carter & A. Gully. 2004. *Modern Written Arabic: A Comprehensive Grammar*. London: Routledge.

Ben Ayad, H. 2003. Mood and functional projections. Ph.D. diss., McGill University, Montreal.

Benmamoun, E. 1999. *The Feature Structure of Functional Categories: A Comparative Study of Arabic Dialects*. New York: Oxford University Press.

Brustad, K. 2000. *The Syntax of Spoken Arabic: A Comparative Study of Moroccan, Egyptian, Syrian, and Kuwaiti Dialects*. Washington, DC: Georgetown University Press.

Cantarino, V. 1974/5. *Syntax of Modern Arabic Prose I-III*. Bloomington, IN: Indiana University Press.

Chomsky, N. 1981. *Lectures on Government and Binding*. Dordrecht: Foris.

Chomsky, N. 1993. A minimalist program for linguistic theory. In K. Hale & S.J. Keyser (eds.), *The View from Building 20: Essays in Linguistics in Honor of Sylvain Bromberger*. Cambridge, MA: MIT Press, 1-52.

Chomsky, N. 1995. *The Minimalist Program*. Cambridge, MA: MIT Press.

Chomsky, N. 2000. Minimalist inquiries: The framework. In R. Martin, D. Michael & J. Uriagereka (eds.), *Step by Step: Essays on Minimalist Syntax in Honour of Howard Lasnik*. Cambridge, MA: MIT Press, 89-115.

Chomsky, N. 2001. Derivation by phase. In M. Kenstowicz (ed.), *Ken Hale: A Life in Language*. Cambridge, MA: MIT Press, 1-52.

Chomsky, N. 2004. Beyond explanatory adequacy. In A. Belletti (ed.), *Structures and Beyond — The Cartography of Syntactic Structures*, vol. 3. New York: Oxford University Press, 104-131.

Chomsky, N. 2006. Turing's thesis. Keynote address delivered at the *InterPhases* conferences, Nicosia.

Chomsky, N. 2008. On phases. In R. Freidin, C.P. Otero & M.L. Zubizarreta (eds.), *Foundational Issues in Linguistic Theory: Essays in Honor of Jean-Roger Vergnaud.* Cambridge, MA: MIT Press, 133-166.

Chomsky, N. & H. Lasnik. 1993. The theory of principles and parameters. In J. Jacobs, A. von Stechow, W. Sternefeld & T. Vennemann (eds.), *Syntax: An International Handbook of Contemporary Research.* Berlin: Walter de Gruyter, 506-569.

Chung, S. & A. Timberlake. 1985. Tense, aspect and mood. In T. Shopen (ed.), *Language Typology and Syntactic Description III.* Cambridge: Cambridge University Press, 202-258.

Coopman, P. 1994. Comments on the paper by Ouhalla. In D. Lightfoot & N. Hornstein (eds.), *Verb Movement.* Cambridge: Cambridge University Press, 73-85.

Fassi Fahri, A. 1993. *Issues in the Structure of Arabic Clauses and Words.* Dordrecht: Kluwer.

Givón, T. 1990. *Syntax: A functional-typological introduction II.* Amsterdam: John Benjamins.

Ingria, R. 1981. Sentential complementation in Modern Greek. Ph.D. diss., MIT, Cambridge.

Letourneau, M.S. 1993. Case-marking and binding of subject clitics in Arabic complement clauses. In M. Eid & C. Holes (eds.), *Perspectives on Arabic Linguistics V: Papers from the Fifth Annual Symposium on Arabic Linguistics*. Amsterdam: John Benjamins, 261-290.

Mohammad, M.A. 1989. *The Sentential Structure of Arabic.* Ph.D. diss., University of Southern California, Los Angeles.

Mohammad, M.A. 2000. *Word Order, Agreement and Pronominalization in Standard and Palestinian Arabic*. Amsterdam: John Benjamins.

Motapanyane, V. 1991. *Theoretical Implications of Complementation in Rumanian*. Ph.D. diss., University of Geneva.

Noonan, M. 1985. Complementation. In T. Shopen (ed.), *Language Typology and Syntactic Description II.* Cambridge: Cambridge University Press, 42-140.

Ouhalla, J. 1994. Verb movement and word order in Arabic. In D. Lightfoot & N. Hornstein (eds.), *Verb Movement.* Cambridge: Cambridge University Press, 41-72.

Ouhalla, J. & U. Shlonsky (eds.). 2002. *Themes in Arabic and Hebrew Syntax*. Dordrecht: Kluwer.

Persson, M. 2002. *Sentential Object Complements in Modern Standard Arabic*. Stockholm: Almqvist & Wiksell.

Pesetsky, D. & E. Torrego. 2001. T-to-C movement: Causes and consequences. In M. Kenstowicz (ed.), *Ken Hale: A Life in Language*. Cambridge, MA: MIT Press, 355-426.

Rivero, M.L. 1994. Clause structure and V-movement in the languages of the Balkans. *Natural Language & Linguistic Theory* 12, 63-120.

Rizzi, L. 1976. Ristrutturazione. *Rivista di Grammatica Generativa* 1.

Rizzi, L. 1990. *Relativized Minimality*. Cambridge, MA: MIT Press.

Roberts, I. & A. Rossou. 2002. The Extended Projection Principle as a condition on the Tense dependency. In P. Svenonius (ed.), *Subjects, Expletives and the EPP*. Oxford: Oxford University Press, 25-55.

Rudin, C. 1983. *Da* and the category *Aux* in Bulgarian. In F. Henry & B. Richards (eds.), *Linguistic Categories: Auxiliaries and Related Puzzles 1*. Dordrecht: Reidel, 3-20.

Salih, M.H. 1985. *Aspects of Clause Structure in Standard Arabic: A Study in Relational Grammar*. Ph.D. diss., SUNY Buffalo.

Sībawayhi, *Kitāb* = Abū Bishr 'Amr b. 'Uthmān Sībawayhi. *al-Kitāb*. Edited by 'Abdalssalām Muħammad Hārūn, 5 vols. Cairo: al-Hay'a l-Miṣriyya l-'Āmmat li-l-Kitāb, 1977.

Sīrāfī, *Sharħ* = Abū Sa'īd al-Ħasan b. 'Abdellāh al-Sīrāfī. *Sharħ Kitāb Sībawayhi*. [In Hārūn's edition of Sībawayhi's *Kitāb*.]

Stowell, T. 1982. The tense of infinitives. *Linguistic Inquiry* 13, 561-570.

Terzi, A. 1991. PRO and obviation in Modern Greek subjunctives. *WCCFL 10: Proceedings of the West Coast Conference on Formal Linguistics 10*, 471-482.

Terzi, A. 1992. *PRO in Finite Clauses: A Study of the Inflectional Heads of the Balkan Languages*. Ph.D. diss., CUNY Graduate Center.

Terzi, A. 1997. PRO and null Case in finite clauses. *The Linguistic Review* 14, 335-360.

Tsimpli, I.-M. 1990. The clause structure and word order in Modern Greek. *UCL Working Papers in Linguistics* 2, 226-255.

Wurmbrand, S. 2001. *Infinitives: Restructuring and Clause structure*. Berlin: Mouton de Gruyter.

CHAPTER EIGHT

INFORMATION-STRUCTURAL RECURSION AT THE PHASE LEVEL

Anna McNay

1. Introduction

1.1. Theoretical Questions and Motivation

The aims of this paper are threefold. Firstly, I address the structural question of what actually constitutes the edge of the phase (Chomsky 1995, 2000, 2001, 2004). I follow Chomsky (2008) in assuming a necessary bifurcation of this domain, but put forward two independent projections — LinkP and AgrP — which I claim are specifically phase edge projections, recurring at the top of each phase, and fulfilling clearly defined feature checking roles within this edge domain. To this end, I introduce the feature [+Link]. Whilst this feature is shown to acquire a particular semantic interpretation at each different phase level, its overarching nature, namely of marking an element as having been selected from a poset (set of possible alternatives), remains constant, thus providing us with a unified definition of the phase.

The second aim of this paper, accordingly, will be to discuss what actually are the phases within a syntactic derivation, and, moreover, how the derivation should proceed. I argue that the phases should be taken to be TP, *v*P, and DP (although I will not exclude the possibility of there being further phases such as AuxP or ModP, following Butler (2004) and Cottell & Henry (2005), and I provide arguments to support this claim, both from pre-existing literature (Dimitrova-Vulchanova & Giusti 1998, Jayaseelan 2001, Belletti 2004, Haegeman 2004, Svenonius 2004) as well as from empirical phenomena I have studied myself (including both VP and NP ellipsis (Gengel & McNay 2006a, 2006b), discontinuous DPs (McNay 2005b, 2007), and 'topicalization', or movement to the *Vorfeld* in German (McNay 2004)).

I then consider the derivational process itself, with particular reference to V2 in German (1), whereby the verb must occur in second position, and thus cannot be preceded by both focus and topic simultaneously, as is possible in Italian (2).

(1)	a.		Hans	hat	das Buch	gelesen.
	b.		Das Buch	hat	Hans	gelesen.
	c.	*	Hans	das Buch	hat	gelesen.
	d.	*	Das Buch	Hans	hat	gelesen.
			the book	Hans	has	read
			"Hans read the book."			

(2)	A	Gianni,	QUESTO,	domani,	gli	dovrete	dire.
	to	Gianni	this	tomorrow	him	you.should	tell
	lit. "Gianni, THIS, tomorrow you should tell him."						

(Rizzi 1997: 291)

This poses a problem for Rizzi's (1997) left peripheral split CP structure, where topic and focus each project their own (possibly recursive) positions. By reducing this periphery to a minimum, as we do here, I argue that this problem can be overcome. Employing the proposed structure, then, I show firstly that a remnant movement analysis (Nilsen 2002, 2003, Müller 2004) is unsuitable, before arguing for an approach with multiple specifiers (Richards 2001) and showing that this is not only compatible with V2, but also accounts for cases of apparent V3 in German.

Finally, with regard to the (somewhat controversial) TP phase level, I show that by adopting the particular edge domain structure proposed here, we are not faced with the problems discussed by Chomsky (2000, 2001, 2004, 2008) and Richards (2007), whereby the derivation would crash if TP were taken to be the phase, because here it will crucially only constitute the domain, with its own LinkP and AgrP edge. That is, LinkP and AgrP, the edge domain projections, make up what we used to think of as the CP phase layer (or split CP), and, at the sentential level, this is actually sandwiched between C and T, with TP therefore representing the actual phase, and CP sitting above this phase as and when needed to host the complementizer.

Whilst the idea of a reiterated information-structural layer at the lower phase levels is by no means new (cf. also Starke 1993 and Butler 2004), this will be a first attempt to unify these projections across all three domains, and to explain what exactly it is which may move to or through the heads and specifiers thereof. As a result, this paper puts forward a clear definition of what a phase is, how its edge is composed, and what the semantic import of this is.

1.2. Outline of Paper

Firstly, in section 2, we deal with the question of what constitutes the edge domain of a phase. Section 2.1 looks at some basic information-structural notions, and, turning to the left periphery or traditional CP layer, and considering German data, points out what it is that unifies the topic and focus elements which may occur there, thus motivating the [+Link] feature and the LinkP projection in which either element may occur. Section 2.2 then looks at the arguments put forward in Chomsky (2008) as to why we need to allow for a second projection within the phase edge and uses this to motivate AgrP. We then turn to the second question at hand, and look at the motivation for and evidence of a recursive edge domain above the lower phase levels as well (section 3). Section 3.1 discusses the vP phase, and section 3.2 moves on to the DP phase. Section 4 turns to the problem of enforcing V2, and considers, firstly, a Remnant Movement approach (section 4.1), before adopting and motivating the alternative of multiple specifiers (section 4.2), which, in section 4.3, is argued to also be able to account for exceptional cases of V3 in German. Section 4.4 shows some sample derivations, before section 4.5 suggests some possible parameters to account for the freer ordering in non V2 languages, including Italian. Finally, section 5 returns to the top of the clause and argues for its being the TP which is the phase, not the CP. Section 6 is a conclusion.

2. Projections in the Left Periphery

2.1. Motivating LinkP

To begin with, let's take a look at the first projection I wish to propose at the phase edge, namely LinkP. The aim of this position, and the feature checked here — [+Link] — is to capture the unifying features between topics and foci which may occur in sentence-initial position, and, as such, it is essentially an information-structural projection.

One of the most important works on information-structure has to be Vallduví's (1993) survey. He takes as a starting point the fact that even though there is some degree of overlap between topic/comment and ground/focus, none of the traditional bipartite divisions of the sentence — e.g. into *theme* and *rheme*, *old/given* and *new*, *topic* and *comment*, and *ground* and *focus* — is capable of capturing the entire range of possibilities which exist for structuring a sentence with regard to the referential status of its parts. As a result, he chooses to use his own system in which he proposes a trinomial hierarchical articulation, where he takes the usual binary distinctions and conflates them into a single schema. For discussion, he takes the example shown in (3) where his schema is given in (3g):

(3) *Valluduvi's Terminology*

a. What about John? What does he drink?
b. [$_{Topic}$ John] [$_{Comment}$ drinks BEER]
c. [$_{Ground}$ John drinks] [$_{Focus}$ BEER]
d. What about John? What does he do?
e. [$_{Topic}$ John] [$_{Comment}$ drinks BEER]
f. [$_{Ground}$ John] [$_{Focus}$ drinks BEER]
g. sentence = {*focus, ground*}
   ground = {*link, tail*}
h. [$_{Ground}$ [$_{Link}$ John] [$_{Tail}$ drinks]] [$_{Focus}$ BEER]

Vallduví takes the human knowledge-store to be a Heimian collection of entity-denoting file cards (Heim 1982), and communication to be a process of updating these cards, with focus completing or altering a record in some way. Thus, in his schema, focus encodes the *actual information* of the sentence, link indicates *where* the information should be entered within the hearer's knowledge-store (this corresponds to *topic*), and tail indicates *how* it fits there.

Choi (1996) further distinguishes between different subtypes of foci on the basis of her observations of violations of the anti-focality constraint which is said to prohibit any focus element from scrambling (Lenerz 1977, Webelhuth 1992). She notes that some focus elements, namely those which appear to occur in contrastive situations, can indeed scramble. She argues that the property which distinguishes these two types of focus is *prominence*, a property also shared by the link or topic:

> 'Topicalization' in English not only encodes the topichood of the fronted element but also expresses the contrastive focality. If we assume that topic and contrastive focus share the same discourse property of being 'prominent', English topicalization can be regarded as a uniform phenomenon, namely, an operation of encoding 'prominence'. (p. 88)

She adds that the topic ought also be conceived of as contrastive since it is being picked out from the set of other potentially topical elements in the discourse, including the tail, as well as sentence-external elements. This notion of a set of possible alternatives is captured by Ward & Birner (2001) who call it the *poset*.

Following from these observations, in McNay (2004, 2005a) I introduce the feature [±Link] to capture the presence or absence of a poset, and assume it is, therefore, valued as positive, at the sentential level, for any kind of topic, as well as for contrastive focus. Based on an analysis of the possible word orders for felicitous question-answer pairs in German, I showed in McNay (2004) that whilst [+Link] elements preferentially occur sentence-initially in the *Vorfeld*, [–Link] elements *cannot* move up this high. Example (4) shows, for example, that either the topic or the contrastive focus may occur in the *Vorfeld* Link position in German:

(4) a. Was hat Hans gegessen?
what has Hans eaten?
b. Hans hat den APFEL gegessen.
Hans has the apple eaten
→ *Topic precedes focus*
c. Den APFEL hat Hans gegessen (, nicht den PFIRSICH).
the apple has Hans eaten not the peach
→ *Focus precedes topic, but, in this case, must be either implicitly or explicitly [+Link] — i.e. contrastive*

Furthermore, expletives may occur sentence-initially in thetic (presentational) sentences, where it is the event as a whole which is being described, and no specific subject is having something predicated of it (for further discussion of the thetic/categorical distinction, cf. Kuroda 1972, Sasse 1987, and Ladusaw 1994, for example):

(5) Es kommt ein Mann aus dem Haus.
it comes a man out the house
"There's a man coming out of the house."

The [+Link] feature captures the commonalities between these different elements — namely, they all constitute what might broadly be termed as *aboutness topics* (cf. Endriss-Hinterwimmer 2006 for a more precise definition). I therefore take the [+Link] feature at this level to be analogous to Rizzi's (2004) [+aboutness] feature. What becomes clear from examples (4) and (5) is that there is a sentence-initial position to which these [+Link] elements must move in order to check this feature, and this is what I refer to as [Spec,LinkP]. Furthermore, since both topic

and contrastive focus may move here, but, crucially, not at the same time, it would seem undesirable and computationally inefficient to maintain the separate projections of TopP and FocP, à la Rizzi (1997.)
Consider now the example in (6) where there are two contrastively focused elements:

(6) a. Wer hat was gegessen?
who has what eaten?
"Who ate what?"
b. *both answers are possible:*
i. HANS hat den APFEL gegessen.
ii. Den APFEL hat HANS gegessen.
the apple has Hans eaten
"Hans ate the apple."

Owing to German being a V2 language, it is not typically possible for both of these [+Link] elements — *HANS* and *den APFEL* — to move to [Spec,LinkP] in the preverbal *Vorfeld*; one necessarily has to remain lower down, arguably in a *v*P focus position (Jayaseelan 2001, Belletti 2004; cf. section 3.1 for further detail). Accordingly, I propose that the [+Link] feature must also be able to be checked at lower levels, and, as such, that the LinkP projection must be recursive. Furthermore, whilst both *HANS* and *den APFEL* are d(iscourse)-linked (i.e. in this case, contrastively focused), only the element in the *Vorfeld* gets further interpreted as being the aboutness topic. Thus, whilst I have compared [+Link$_T$] (the [+Link] feature checked in the sentence-initial position) to Rizzi's (2004) [+aboutness] feature, I additionally argue that [+Link$_v$] must be related to his [+d-linking] feature, or, in the broader sense, mark [+contrast] (cf. the discussion of ellipsis phenomena in section 3.1). Finally, in section 3.2, I will argue that [+Link$_D$] gets the interpretation of [+partitive] (McNay 2005b, 2007).

2.2. Motivating AgrP

Having argued for the need to have a LinkP projection at the top of each phase, we must now consider whether this alone suffices, or whether, akin to the Rizzian tradition, something more complex is required. Whilst it might seem optimal to avoid a split layer — because of the added ease of explaining V2 phenomena — it nevertheless proves to be necessary, once we extend this proposal to recur above the lower phases as well as at the left periphery of the sentence as a whole, to allow for a second projection within the edge domain to which [–Link] elements might move in order to escape from the phase. For example, as we shall see in section 3.2, we need non-partitive nominals to be able to move out of the DP phase without transiting through the [+Link]-marked specifier. We also, of course, need to consider the nature of the *v*P-peripheral, [–Link], completive focus position (assuming that the traditional distinction between such focus types exists; cf. Brunetti 2003 for arguments that it does not). Nevertheless, it remains the case that it would not be efficient to have to compute numerous and iterated empty positions for topic and focus in every sentence, especially since, as already discussed, these elements share more important semantic features in terms of the presence/absence of a poset, and also cannot both occur preverbally in V2 languages.

Chomsky (2008) proposes that each phase head phrase (PHP) selects for what he refers to as a *selected phase head phrase* (PH$_S$P):

(7)

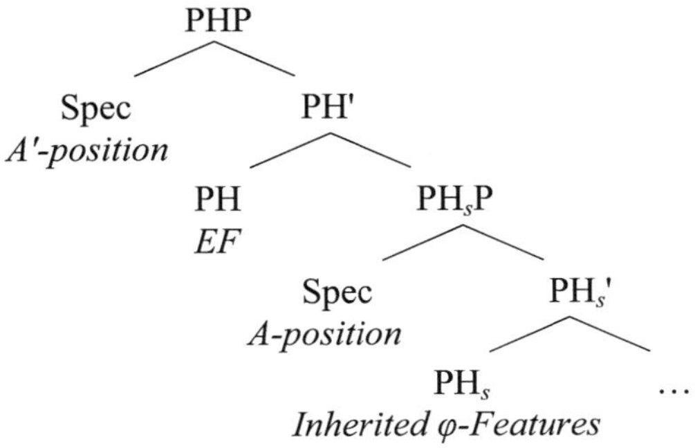

The specifier of the phase head itself corresponds to a traditional A-position, whilst the specifier of the selected phase head corresponds to an A-position. Furthermore, whilst the phase head itself bears the edge features which trigger movement of phrases which want to escape the phase, it is the selected phase head which bears (or, rather, inherits) f features, triggering movement for the purpose of agreement. An example to make this clearer might be given by substituting CP for the phase head phrase, and TP for the selected phase head phrase as in (8). Whilst Chomsky maintains that it is C which is the phase, and which carries the edge features, it appears to be T which ultimately carries the f and tense features, and these features are accordingly checked in [Spec,TP], not [Spec,CP]:

(8) *The CP Phase (Chomsky 2008)*

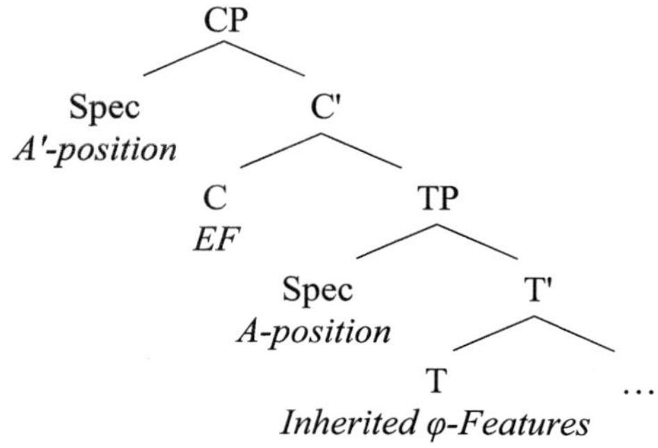

Following from this, I propose a second projection just below LinkP, which I label AgrP, adopted from Richards (2001).[1] It should be noted that Shlonsky (1992) has also suggested the decomposition of CP into CP and AgrP, and Haegeman (1995: 184) also draws such a tree. I shall assume, then, that AgrP checks features such as case, tense, and φ-features, whilst LinkP is operator-like and checks the edge feature [+Link]. All arguments must move through AgrP, but only those carrying the [+Link] feature continue through LinkP. Both projections, however, act as escape hatches from the phase, i.e. they together constitute the minimal edge domain.

The structure of the phase edge domain proposed here is thus always: $[_{LinkP}\ Spec\ Link^{0}\ [_{AgrP}\ Spec\ Agr^{0}\ [_{XP}\ Spec\ X^{0}\ ]]]$.

3. A Recursive Periphery

Before we address the question of how movement through and to these edge positions proceeds, let me give a short overview of some of the further motivation for assuming the 'split CP' information-structural phase edge layer to recur lower down in the sentence, namely above *v*P and DP.

3.1. Motivating the v*P Phase Edge*

With regard to the *v*P level, Belletti (2004) looks at Italian data, including the question/answer pairs in (9), and notes that whilst a

---

1 Richards (2001) actually calls this Agr∀P, since all arguments must move through it to check case. However, to avoid confusion with quantificational elements, I simplify the term to AgrP.

postverbal subject may receive readings as either new completive focus, or as topic (with suitable pragmatic conditions and intonation), a preverbal subject can never be interpreted as completive focus (from Belletti 2004):

(9) a. Chi è partito? / Chi ha parlato? / Che cosa é successo?
who is left who has spoken what thing is happened?
"Who has left? / Who has spoken? / What has happened?"
b. E' partito / ha parlato Gianni.
c. # Gianni è partito / ha parlato.
Gianni is left has spoken
"Gianni has left / spoken."

(10) a. Che cosa ha poi fatto Gianni?
what thing has finally done Gianni?
"What has Gianni finally done?"
b. Ha (poi) parlato, Gianni.
has finally spoken, Gianni
"Gianni has finally spoken."

She argues, therefore, that since the subject in her examples occupies a low structural position (it follows low adverbs), we are led to postulate clause internal topic/focus positions, parallel to those in the left periphery:

> [T]he area immediately above VP displays significant resemblance to the left-periphery of the clause [...] a clause-internal Focus position, surrounded by Topic positions, is identified in the low part of the clause. (Belletti 2004: 17)

Jayaseelan (2001) looks at similar data from Malayalam and various Germanic languages, and draws essentially the same conclusion as Belletti. Although Malayalam is generally assumed, like German, to be a canonically SOV language, Jayaseelan assumes Kayne's (1994) notion of the universal SVO base order, with the surface order derived via movement of the subject and object into higher functional projections: the subject to [Spec,TP], and the object to some position above *v*P but below TP. His observations about Malayalam include the fact that, in *wh*-questions, there is a seemingly strict requirement for the *wh*-word to be immediately to the left of the verb ((11)-(15), from Jayaseelan 2001: 40), and that this thus overrides the SOV requirement, with the *wh*-subject intervening between O and V. Where a clause contains multiple *wh*-words as in (16), however, we find them stacked up together, preverbally.

(11) a. ni**nn**-e aare aTiccu?
you—ACC who beat.PAST
"Who beat you?'
b. * aare ninn-e aTiccu?

(12) a. iwiTe aare uNTe?
here who is
"Who is here?"
b. * aare iwiTe uNTe?

(13) a. awan ewiTe pooyi?
he where went
"Where did he go?"
b. * ewiTe awan pooyi?

(14) a. nii aa pustakam aar-kke koDuttu?
you that book who-DAT gave
"To whom did you gave that book?"
b. * nii aar-kke aa pustakam koDuttu?

(15) a. nii ente aaNe tinn-ate?
you what is ate-NOMINALIZER
"What is that you ate?"
b. * ente nii aaNe tinn-ate?

(16) ii kaaryam aare aar-ooDe eppooL paRaññu enne
this matter who whom-to when said COMP
e**n**i-k'k'e aRiy-illa.
I-DAT know-NEG
"I don't know who told this matter to whom, when."

This, Jayaseelan concludes, is parallel to the multiple *wh*-movement found in languages such as Polish and Hungarian, except that the landing site is not the left periphery of the sentence, but rather some internal periphery, to the left of the verbal complex — a CP heading the *v*P phase.

Finally, Gengel & McNay (2006a, 2006b) discuss the phenomena of VP Ellipsis (17), and Gapping (18), and argue that these can be given a unified analysis, if one adopts the phase edge LinkP and AgrP projections above *v*P, along with a phase based deletion approach (as proposed in Gengel 2006, whereby ellipsis is analyzed as involving deletion of the entire phase domain and not just the phrase at hand):

(17) a. The students will attend the play, but the faculty won't [e].
b. The students should attend the play, but they won't [e].

(18) a. The students should attend the play, and the faculty should [e] the concert.
b. The students should attend the play, but (instead) they will [e] the concert.

(19) The students should attend the play, and the faculty [e] the concert.

In Gapping (19), both the remnant subject and object are necessarily contrastive. We assume, therefore, that they are both marked as [+Link$_v$] (i.e. [+ contrastive d-linking]) and move to specifiers of Link$_v$P. This is then followed by deletion of the entire *v*P domain. The subject is then moved on higher to [Spec,Link$_T$P] to be interpreted as aboutness topic. In cases of Pseudogapping, however, whilst the object must, again, necessarily be contrastive, the subject need not be. When it is, as in (18a), we assume the derivation is basically the same as for Gapping, with movement of both subject and object to specifiers of Link$_v$P, deletion of the entire *v*P domain, further movement of the subject to [Spec,Link$_T$P], and additional insertion of an auxiliary into this final phase. When the subject is not contrastive, however, as in (18b), we assume it only moves as high as [Spec,AgrP] in the *v*P phase periphery, whilst the object still moves further to [Spec,Link$_v$P]. However, since the subject is also marked as [+Link$_T$] (in the sense of being the aboutness topic), it then moves on up from [Spec,Agr$_v$P] to [Spec,Link$_T$P].

Finally, in cases of VP Ellipsis (17), the subject moves up through either just [Spec,Agr$_v$P], if it is not contrastive (17b), or [Spec,Link$_v$P] (17a), to [Spec,Link$_T$P]. The object is not contrastive, and therefore needn't move to check any operator-like features at the *v*P phase edge. It therefore gets deleted along with the rest of the *v*P.[2] *Do*-support is added in the same position as the auxiliary in Pseudogapping. I shall return to these examples and show pictorial derivations for (18a) and (18b) in section 4.4. For now, let it suffice to say that there are, indeed, significant arguments in favour of there being a *v*P level information-structural phasal left periphery, and that its breakdown into LinkP and AgrP, as proposed already for the sentential left periphery, helps provide a unified analysis for a number of cross-linguistic phenomena.

[2] Cf. Gengel & McNay (2006a, 2006b) for further detail, and discussion of how deletion is motivated.

3.2. *Motivating the DP Phase Edge*

Let's turn now to the DP phase edge. As for *v*P, there has been much work already suggesting that there may be some kind of information-structural layer to its left. Haegeman (2004) has looked at data concerning possessors, Dimitrova-Vulchanova & Giusti (1998) have considered topic and focus projections based on evidence from the Balkan languages, and Sauerland (2004) argues for there being an Agr projection above the DP. For reasons of space, however, I shall restrict myself here to a brief summary of Svenonius' (2004) data from Tsez (a Nakh-Daghestanian language), followed by an overview of my own arguments based on discontinuous DPs and NP Ellipsis in German, Dutch, and English.

Firstly, then, we turn to Svenonius (2004), which presents data from Tsez, on the basis of which it is argued convincingly that there must be some DP-internal movement to allow, for example, for cross-clausal agreement as in (20a) where the main verb agrees with the class III noun "bread", and (20a) where it agrees with the class I noun "boy":

(20) a. enir [uza magalu bac`ruli] biyxo.
mother.DAT boy.ERG bread.III.ABS III.eat] III.know
"The mother knows the boy ate the bread."
b. enir [uzi ayruli] iyxo.
mother.DAT boy.I.ABS I.arrive I.know
"The mother knows the boy arrived."

Whilst the DP controlling the agreement need not be overtly at the edge of the embedded clause, Polinsky & Potsdam (2001), from whom the data originates, argue that the controller of agreement does covertly move to a topic position at the periphery of the embedded clause. They also show that when there is cross-clausal agreement, the embedded absolutive is necessarily interpreted as a topic. Svenonius adopts and analyzes this data as showing that it is necessary to move some subpart out of a quantificational DP (or QP) and up to what he calls [Spec,OpP], but which presumably might correspond to my [Spec,LinkP], from where it might remain visible even after the QP spells out. Again, Tsez presents some overt evidence for such movement, in that it has some structures where a topic (Op) head overtly follows the rest of the noun phrase, as in (21):

(21) bikori-n u-za bexursi.
snake-ABS.TOP boy-ERG killed
"As for the snake, the boy killed it."

In McNay (2005b, 2006, 2007), I assume similar movement to the edge of the DP phase to take place in the derivation of discontinuous DPs and NP Ellipsis constructions in German, English, and Dutch. The observation that the adjectives (or quantifiers) licensing both of these phenomena share similar properties goes back to Fanselow (1988) and has recurred in more recent literature (van Hoof 2002, Ntelitheos 2003, 2004), where it is claimed to hold for quite a number of languages. For our purposes here, the type of discontinuous DPs which occur in German and some southern dialects of Dutch (principally Northern Brabantish) most usually come about in cases of split topicalization, where the noun is fronted, but the quantifier remains lower down in the derivation (Split NP Topicalization in the terminology of van Hoof 1997, 2002, 2005). For example, (23a) and (23b) show the fully topicalized and split topicalized versions respectively of the normal German SVO utterance in (22):

(22) Er hat viele Bücher gekauft.
he has many books bought
"He bought many books."

(23) a. Viele Bücher hat er gekauft.
b. Bücher hat er viele gekauft.

Split topicalization in German is a fairly productive phenomenon. In Dutch, it is much less so, and, even in the dialect (Northern Brabantish) where it is permitted, there is a clear need for the involvement of the notion of contrast (van Hoof 2002). Furthermore, if we try to split a DP in Standard Dutch, a number of overt partitive markers (prepositions and R-pronouns) become necessary (Sjef Barbiers, p.c.):

(24) a. Dafna zoekt geen griffioenen.
Dafna seeks no griffins
b. Van griffioenen, *daar* zoekt Dafna *er* geen een van.
of griffins, DAAR seeks Dafna ER no one of

In McNay (2005b, 2006, 2007), I argue that we can turn to the semantic notion of partitivity to explain both the motivation for, and the interpretation of these constructions. We have already seen that, at the most abstract level, the [+Link] feature is used to mark an element selected from a poset. More specifically then, at the DP level, it can be used to mark partitivity, i.e. the selection of a nominal element from a specific wider reference set.

McNay (2007) extends this idea and introduces the notion of pseudo-partitivity. Here, unlike for partitivity, the reference set does not consist of specific tokens, but rather of kinds (cf. Carlson & Pelletier1995: 64). Not only do particular tokens not need to be contextually available, they may, in fact, not even exist. I thus argue that, in the case of splitting, it is pseudo-partitivity, rather than partitivity, which plays a role. This explains why it is possible to use a split construction (but not as easily the fully topicalized counterpart) with both the negative determiner (25a) and a fictional entity (25c), as can be seen from the following German examples:

(25) a. Bücher hat sie keine gekauft.
books has she none bought
"As for books, she bought none."
b. ?# Keine Bücher hat sie gekauft.
no books has she bought
≈ "As for no books, that is what she bought."
→ *pragmatically odd*
c. Einhörner sucht sie keine.
unicorns seeks she none
"As for unicorns, she's not looking for any."
d. ?# Keine Einhörner sucht sie.
no unicorns seeks she
≈ "As for no unicorns, that is what she's looking for."
→ *pragmatically odd*

Now compare the contrast in meaning between the cases of split topicalization, full topicalization, and no topicalization, repeated in (26):

(26) a. *Split Topicalization (pseudo-partitive implicature)*
Bücher hat er viele gekauft.
books has he many bought
"As for books, he bought many (of them)."
b. *Full Topicalization (no pseudo-partitive implicature)*
Viele Bücher hat er gekauft.
many books has he bought
"As for many books, this is what he bought."
c. *No Topicalization (normal word order)*
Er hat viele Bücher gekauft.
he has many books bought
"He bought many books."

Clearly in both cases (26a) and (26b), *Bücher* is a topic (in the sense of an aboutness topic, i.e. [+Link$_T$]), since it would otherwise have no reason to move to the *Vorfeld*. The difference between (26a) and (26b), then, is that the former, through having the N split apart from its quantifier *viele*, acquires a pseudo-partitive reading. The poset from which *books* in (26a) is selected is, therefore, a poset of different kinds, rather than one of different entities or tokens. As generally assumed for pseudo-partitives, we are taking a non-count kind and forcing a measure onto it: *"As for books, he bought many of them."* If the entire DP is selected from a *poset*, as is the case in (26b), however, we do not obtain this pseudo-partitive reading. The interpretation is instead one where we have been talking about a quantity of books already, namely: *"As for many books, this is what he bought."* My claim, then, is that the splitting in discontinuous German DPs is caused when the NP, but not the full DP, is marked [+Link$_D$], and therefore has to move to [Spec,Link$_D$P] to check this feature, as shown by comparing the trees for (26a) and (26b) in (27) and (28).[3] (I return to this example and propose a derivation for the entire sentence in section 4.4.)

(27) *Pseudo-Partitive Split DP*

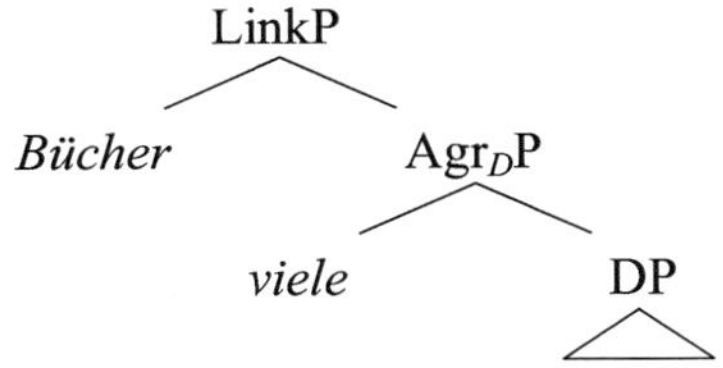

(28) *Non-Pseudo-Partitive Non Split DP*

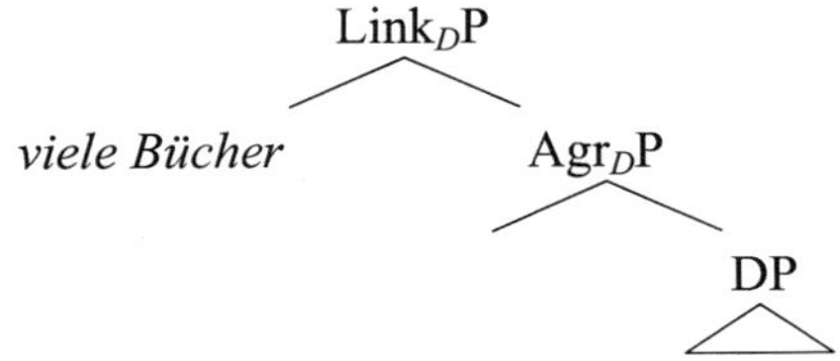

It has also been proposed in the literature (Lobeck 1995, Sleeman 1996) that NP Ellipsis might likewise be licensed by the concept of

---

[3] I abstract away from the mechanisms of movement at this stage, since this remains to be discussed in section 4.

partitivity, thereby explaining the restrictions on which adjectives allow for it without *one*-insertion in English (namely certain quantifiers (29), cardinals (30), deictic determiners (31), possessives (32), comparatives (33a) and superlatives (33b)), and even at all in, for example, French (Sleeman 1996):

(29) John called out the children`s names, and many / few / all / each / *every [e] answered. (Lobeck 1995: 45)

(30) The students attended the play but two [e] went home disappointed. (Kester 1996: 195)

(31) Although she might order these [e], Mary won't buy those books on art history. (Kester 1996: 195)

(32) Although John's friends were late to the rally, Mary's [e] came on time. (Kester 1996: 194)

(33) a. Of the two books available, I will take the larger[e].
b. i. Of the many books available, I will take the largest [e].
ii. Although Helen is the oldest girl in the class, Julie is the tallest. (Quirk et al. 1982)

In these cases, where the interpretation is indeed partitive, I assume that whilst the NP is marked for deletion, and thus remains in situ where it is then elided along with the entire DP domain (thus in a manner parallel to that assumed for VP Ellipsis and its subtypes in section 3.1), the adjective/quantifier/determiner is marked as [+$Link_D$] and thus moves to [Spec,$Link_D$P] to check for this feature. Parallel to the splitting cases just discussed, however, NP Ellipsis may also bring about a pseudo-partitive interpretation, such as in (34) (Gisbert Fanselow, p.c.):

(34) Talking about books, I bought many[e]

In such instances, I propose that the adjective/quantifier/determiner only moves as far as [Spec,Agr_DP], again with the entire DP domain, including the NP, being deleted. As for cases which require overt licensing through *one*-insertion in English (which I take to be an alternative spell out of adjectival inflection in Dutch and German; cf. also Kester 1996 for the same argument), I take this to be motivated through the inherent semantics of the adjective/quantifier/determiner, and whether or not it is able to stand alone in the DP phasal periphery once the domain has been deleted. For reasons of space, I shall not go into further discussion of this here (but see McNay 2006 and Gengel & McNay 2006a for details).

What I hope to have motivated in this brief overview, then, is the need, at the DP level, for both the [+Link] feature to capture the concept of partitivity (again, selection of an element from a set of possible alternatives), as well as for the biphrasal phase periphery, consisting of LinkP (where the [+Link$_D$] feature is checked) and AgrP.

4. V2 in the Germanic Languages

As already noted, the main problem with having more than one projection in the left periphery is how we can then maintain and enforce V2 in Germanic languages. One of the main motivations for simplifying Rizzi's (1997) periphery was to avoid having multiple positions preverbally, in the sentence-initial left periphery. Following standard V2 analyses, such as Holmberg & Platzack (1995) inter alia, the finite verb (Vf) is assumed to move to the highest functional projection of the clause via head movement, before some other element fronts to the specifier of this same projection. Since there is a general ban on adjunction to CP, Vf will always end up in the second position of the clause:

(35) $[_{CP}$ XP$_i$ $[_{CP}$ Vf$_j$ + C $[_{IP}$ ... t$_j$ ... t$_i$ ...]]]

If we have a split CP like Rizzi's, however, the verb, which he assumes to sit in Fin, is preceded by at least four (depending on the recursion of TopP) potential XP landing sites, only one of which may be filled in any given utterance:

(36) $[_{ForceP}$ $[_{TopP*}$ $[_{FocP}$ $[_{TopP*}$ $[_{FinP}$ Vf ...]]]]]

Clearly this requires stipulation, and leads also to redundancy.

4.1. *The (Im)possibility of Remnant Movement*

Firstly, then, let's look at an alternative approach to V2, implemented by Nilsen (2002, 2003) and Müller (2004), namely Remnant Movement. The main point of such an analysis is to avoid analyzing V2 as involving head movement, but rather to see it as fronting of the VP itself, or, rather, of an XP containing the VP. Nilsen ultimately contests the existence of any rigid syntactic structure at all, and furthermore, by denying the distinction between heads and specifiers (cf. also Starke 2004), abolishes head movement altogether, concluding that what we traditionally term a *specifier* is simply whatever element causes XP to project. That is, the structure in (37), where we usually find either the specifier or the head position to be empty anyhow (given the explosion of functional categories in recent minimalist syntax), can now be simplified to the structure in (38):

(37)

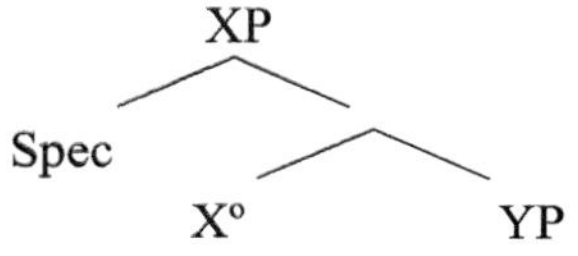

(38)

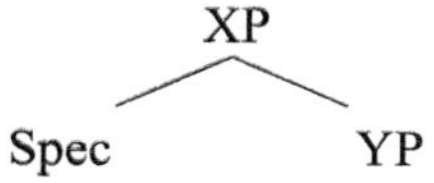

Based on Scandinavian data, Nilsen argues for the following steps to a V2 derivation: firstly, the finite verb is moved out of the VP to a higher FinP projection; secondly, whichever element is going to end up sentence-initially moves to the 'specifier' of what he calls ΣP, above FinP; thirdly, the remnant VP is moved out of this ΣP; and, fourthly, the remnant ΣP is fronted over this moved VP remnant to the top of the sentence.[4] Adverbs can be merged both before and after the VP Remnant Movement:

(39)

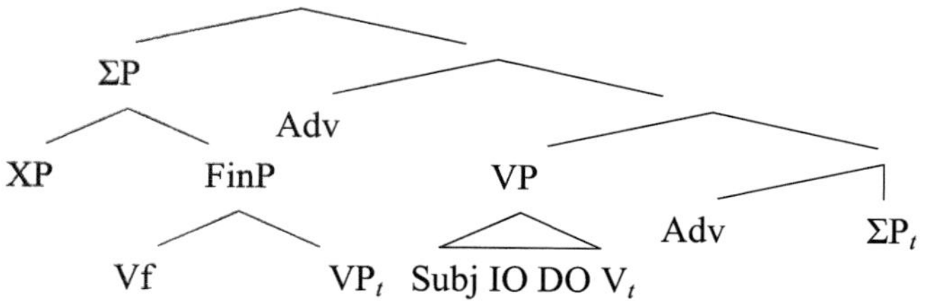

One advantage of such an approach, according to Nilsen, is that the ordering of the arguments is preserved. Furthermore, given the lack of

---

[4] This derivation differs slightly from the ones presented in Nilsen (2002, 2003), but is a more up-to-date version presented by him as part of Máire Noonan's course *Verb-Initial Languages* at the DGfS/GLOW Summer School in Stuttgart (August 2006).

rigid structure, there are additional possibilities for merging adverbs in between the arguments if they are strong DPs as opposed to pronouns. In such an instance it is to be assumed that the sub-VPs (each argument merges and projects to a VP) can move individually, rather than necessarily as a whole. Crucially, however, any VP movement must pied-pipe along with it whatever structure remains lower down, thus retaining the base ordering configuration:

(40)

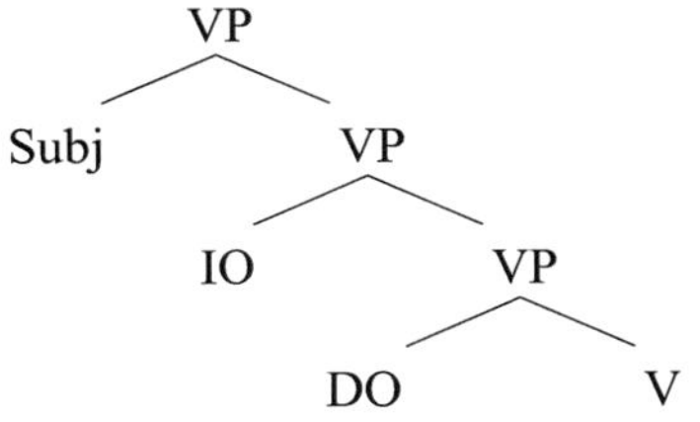

There are a number of problems with this approach, however. Firstly, the assumption about VP movement and order preservation cannot carry over directly to German, since this language allows for the scrambling (reordering) of arguments. This cross-linguistic difference will simply have to be stated. Such inter-argument scrambling also remains unmotivated, since all ΣP evacuation movements are, according to Nilsen, movements to non-labelled, equivalent positions, with no specific interpretative features. As such, we can obtain no syntactic explanation for the different interpretations necessarily associated with scrambling in German. Furthermore, whilst evacuation movement of the VP remnant out of ΣP necessarily involves pied-piping of lower material, prior movement of the ultimately sentence-initial element to [Spec,ΣP] does not pied-pipe the lower VP along. This must also be stipulated. Then there is the question of FinP and ΣP. Whilst the aim here seems to be to avoid rigid structure building, FinP must, nevertheless, always merge directly above VP, and the finite verb must, for whatever reason, always move here. Secondly, although Nilsen does not wish to employ feature driven movement, the element moving to [Spec,ΣP] does, just the same, end up being interpreted as *switch topic* (which seems strikingly reminiscent of my [+Link$_T$] aboutness topic elements), and, importantly, whilst the VP may remnant move in one or more steps, and thus as one or more chunks, only one element may ever move to this [Spec,ΣP] position, and thus only one element may ever end up preverbally. Again, if the goal has been to dissolve the distinction between head and phrasal movement, and to get rid of structure and features altogether, these constraints remain to be stipulated.

Accordingly, it seems as if maintaining a notion of structure, along with associated features to drive the movement, is no more stipulatory than the approach attempted by Nilsen himself. Furthermore, by adopting a recursive and symmetrical structure as proposed here, we reduce the number of stipulations to a minimum, since each phase will be built up in an identical manner. What is more, the structure I propose is both minimal, and also semantically driven. As such, it can explain the interpretative differences brought about by different movements, and thus motivate the scrambling of German arguments as well.

Finally, I argue that we have to reject the notion of Remnant Movement altogether, since it is not compatible with the structure being proposed here at all. Whilst it might, at first blush, still seem possible to argue that V2 word order is brought about by the fronting of a remnant — consisting of the finite verb and the preverbal [+Link] element — to [Spec,Link$_T$P], we face the indissoluble problem of what would actually constitute this remnant. It cannot be just the VP or *v*P, since the arguments will necessarily have moved out of this domain into the Link and Agr *v*P phase edge positions, thus leaving nothing to occur in sentence-initial, preverbal position. Furthermore, if we were to move the entire Link$_v$P phase constituent, we would render the AgrP at the higher phase level (i.e. Agr$_T$P) completely redundant, thus destroying the symmetry built up between the phases, and, with it, the main motivation for such an approach. We would also, crucially, encounter problems with deriving verb final word orders both in subordinate clauses, and when an auxiliary occurs in the finite verb second position, and the phase based deletion approach to ellipsis phenomena (cf. section 3.1 and section 3.2), would also not be compatible with a Remnant Movement approach, since we would want both to delete and to move the selfsame constituent. A final problem with maintaining a Remnant Movement approach would be that we would, again, like Nilsen, require both Remnant Movement, and also prior phrasal and/or head movement of elements to the phase edge. This would seem to complicate, rather than simplify, the derivation, even more so because of the necessity of moving multiple elements to the specifiers of one projection (namely [Spec,Agr$_v$P], if not also [Spec,Link$_v$P]), suggesting a further need for multiple specifiers. Overall, then, it seems undesirable, stipulatory, and unnecessarily complicated to attempt to employ any notion of Remnant Movement in the analysis of V2.

4.2. Head Movement and Multiple Specifiers

Having argued that Remnant Movement cannot play a role, I shall now show how we can go about deriving V2 in the structure proposed here, employing standard head movement of the verb, along with multiple specifiers on the phase edge projections.

The main assumption, then, is that the finite verb, in V2 clauses, must move up through the following positions: V^0 to v^0 to $Agr_v{}^0$ to $Agr_T{}^0$ to, ultimately, $Link_{T'}{}^0$. V^0 to v^0 is a standard assumption. v^0 to Agr^0 is also fairly standard, and, since I have two levels of Agr above the VP, it is clear why the verb must move through both heads. The final landing site of the verb in $Link_T{}^0$, however, is somewhat less obviously motivated and may, unfortunately, require stipulating at this point. It would, however, follow the standard V2 analyses (Holmberg & Platzack 1995) in taking the final landing site of the verb to be the highest functional head, and, furthermore, it would also be a consequence of an extension of Rizzi's (1997) *wh*-criterion, whereby he assumes that if you move something to a specifier position, something else has to be moved to the head.[5]

The second assumption I will make is that the phase edge projections — LinkP and AgrP — may have multiple specifiers.[6] As already mentioned, Richards (2001) assumes that his Agr∀P must have multiple specifiers in order to allow for all arguments to move through and check their features. Since I also need to be able to move all of my arguments through AgrP, I must conclude the same. Naturally, then, following from

---

[5] Petra Sleeman (p.c.), for example, likewise assumes that the finite verb (*sont* in French sentences such as (1)), moves to Top^0, since the subject (here, *ils*) is in [Spec,TopP], the adjective (*rares*) is in [Spec,FocP], and the backgrounded complement (*à avoir des enfants*) is in the lower [Spec,TopP]:

(i) Ils sont rares à avoir des enfants.
they are late to have of.the children
"They are late to have some children."

[6] Christensen (2005: 101) introduces a *Constraint on Multiple Specifiers*, which states that only strong phase heads can license multiple specifiers. He suggests that this is subject to parametric variation, with cross-linguistic differences as to whether or not C is classified as 'strong'.

I assume that no such constraint is necessary, since LinkP and AgrP always have multiple specifiers (cf. ensuing discussion as to how we are still able to account for V2), but that only these phase edge projections are able to have multiple specifiers, specifically *because* they are phase edge projections, and thus lexical and functional projections within the phase domains — i.e. NP, DP, VP, *v*P, TP, and so on — may not license multiple specifiers. Again, this is a feature contributing to the definition of what constitutes the edge of the phase.

the simplest, symmetrical and non-stipulatory approach, if AgrP may have multiple specifiers, so may LinkP. Indeed, this would seem both required and semantically motivated at the DP and *v*P levels, where, for example, as we have seen, it is clear that more than one element out of a given numeration may be contrastively d-linked, and thus require movement through Link_vP, and similarly, at the DP level, both the determiner and/or quantifier and/or adjective and/or noun may be marked as [+Link], and thus move to/through [Spec,Link_DP].

The obvious question that arises now, then, is how we make sure we still only get one element preverbally in V2 situations. Here, I turn firstly to the observation made by Norbert Hornstein (Hornstein & Epstein 1999, Hornstein 2000, and in person teaching the course LSA100 *Advances in Minimalist Syntax*, jointly with Cedric Boeckx, at the LSA Summer Institute, June/July 2005), that "two specifiers of the same projection are equidistant to the same target". That is, in the case of multiple specifiers, each specifier is taken to be the same distance from its head. We have already assumed that the one head can check the required features on multiple elements occurring in its multiple specifiers, namely one Link head can check the [+Link] feature on multiple elements, and one Agr head can check and provide matching agreement on, for example, a row of adjectives.

More importantly, however, this notion of equidistance implies that the head sees its multiple specifiers as if they were part of one *unit* (I refrain from using the term *constituent* here, although it may well boil down to the same thing). This is a semantically well-founded assumption, of course, since all of the elements share the same feature, and, in the case of its being a [+Link] feature, marking selection from a poset, it means that the multiple elements in the multiple specifiers of LinkP form this poset together. Take, for example, the question and answer pair in (41):

(41) a. Was hat er wen gegeben ?
what has he whom given?
"What did he give to whom?"
b. Er hat dem Jungen den Apfel gegeben.
he has the boy the apple given
"He gave the boy the apple / the apple to the boy."

Here, it is clear that the contrastive focus poset is one consisting of both beneficiary and gift, namely both *dem Jungen* and *den Apfel* are contrastively d-linked, and, as such, both move to [Spec,Link_vP], where they form a unit, since it is together that they contrast with the other possible alternative pairs constituting the poset, e.g.:

(42) {{dem Jungen, den Apfel}}
{dem Jungen, die Banane}
{dem Jungen, die Orange}
{dem Jungen, die Trauben}
{dem Mädchen die Apfel}
{dem Mädchen, die Banane}
{ dem Mädchen, die Orange}
{ dem Mädchen, die Trauben}
... }

What is important, however, is that whilst these multiple specifiers indeed do form a unit, the internal structure of this unit has to remain visible and accessible (i.e. not frozen) to higher levels of the derivation, since we still need to be able to (sub-)extract elements and move them up alone. That is, only a subset of the [Spec,$Link_D$P] elements may end up moving up to [Spec,$Link_v$P], and, likewise, only a subset of these will continue up to [Spec,$Link_T$P] (cf. section 4.4). The reason for this accessibility is clear: active features are still at large, namely [+$Link_v$] and [+$Link_T$]. Regarding the latter, Øystein Nilsen[7] claims that there can only ever be one switch topic (which I have already argued to be akin to our aboutness topic, namely the [+$Link_T$] element) per sentence, regardless of how many other 'topical' elements there might be (e.g. weak pronouns, etc.). As such, he imposes a logical semantic restriction on why we can only ever have one element in [Spec,$Link_T$P], thus necessarily giving us V2 in languages such as German. Nevertheless, even in such a strict V2 language as German, there are some instances of what appear to be V3 constructions (cf. especially Müller 2003, 2005, and references therein). This is actually predicted by the approach just outlined, and section 4.3 offers a brief excursus on this point, before we show some sample derivations for German (section 4.4), and consider the possible ways in which to maintain this approach, without losing the empirical coverage offered by Rizzi (1997) for Italian (section 4.5).

4.3. *Instances of Apparent V3 in German*

Following the approach just outlined, then, it ought to be possible to

---

[7] Again, as part of Máire Noonan's course *Verb-Initial Languages* at the DGfS/ GLOW Summer School in Stuttgart (August 2006).

obtain apparent V3, in languages such as German, if there is more than one element marked as [+Link$_T$]. Accordingly, this does seem to be the case. That is, we occasionally do get more than one preverbal element, if and only if these elements together form a unit which constitutes the aboutness topic, thus also sharing a poset.[8] Whilst this will then appear to be a non V2 situation, if we take the multiple preverbal specifiers to build one unit, we see that actually the need for the verb to be the second 'idea' still holds. Consider, for example, the following variation on (41) above:

(43)	a.	WAS	hat	er	WEM	gegeben?		
		what	has	he	whom	given?		
		"What did he give to whom?"						
	b.	HANS	den	APFEL	hat	er	gegeben.	
		Hans	the	apple	has	he	given	
		"To Hans he gave the apple."						

Whilst some speakers seem to reject this outright, others are more or less happy to accept it. And the versions in (44), where the contrastivity of the fronted element is made explicit, seem to be fine all round:[9,10]

---

[8] See also Haider (1982), who proposes that the LF projection of the *Vorfeld* must consist of only one LF constituent, and that the operator in COMP is able to bind only one variable, hence the difference in grammaticality between (iia), where the *wh*-words bind one variable, and (iib), where there remain two variables:

(i)	Gestern	am	Strand	hat	sie	sich	mit	ihm getroffen.
	yesterday	on.the	beach	has	she	REFL	with	him met
	"Yesterday at the beach she met with him."							

(ii)	a.	Wann	und	wo	hat	sie	sich	mit	ihm	getroffen?
		when	and	where	has	she	REFL	with	him	met
		"When and where did she meet with him?"								
	b. *	Wann	und	wer	hat	sich	mit	ihm	getroffen?	
		when	and	who	has	REFL	with	him	met	

[9] Thanks especially to Sabine Mohr and Peter Öhl for pointing out these alternatives to me.

[10] It ought also to be noted that this cannot happen if we only have a transitive verb. That is, both arguments cannot precede the verb if there are only two arguments in total, even if they are both [+Link], as in (ib). I have nothing further to say about this observation at this point, however.

(i)	a.	HANS	den	APFEL	hat	er	gegeben.	
		Hans	the	apple	has	he	given	

(44) a. HANS den APFEL und MARIA die BIRNE hat er gegeben.
lit. "To Hans the apple and to Maria the pear he gave."

b. HANS einen APFEL hat er gegeben, nicht FRITZ eine BIRNE.
lit. "To Hans an apple did he give, not to Fritz a pear."

What is important here, then, is that the multiple preverbal elements *must* form one interpretational unit, and *must*, therefore, share both a poset and the same information-structural interpretation. That is, they must both constitute part of the aboutness topic. For this reason, whilst multiple specifiers of one and the same projection do not cause a problem for us, since they are able to be interpreted together as one unit, specifiers of different focus and topic projections, à la Rizzi (1997), would not be amenable to such an interpretation, and are therefore not possible preverbally in V2 configurations.

4.4. Some Sample Derivations

Now that we have outlined the way in which the derivations ought to take place, namely as involving movement through the heads and multiple specifiers of the phase peripheral Link and Agr positions, let's look at a couple of simple trees to demonstrate.[11] Firstly, let's return to the basic V2 examples from examples (4) and (5), repeated here with their respective trees:

---

b. * ICH den APFEL habe gegessen.
I the apple have eaten

[11] I adopt throughout the base merger structure of UTAH, following Baker (1988) and Ramchand's (2008) First Phase Syntax, namely:

(i)

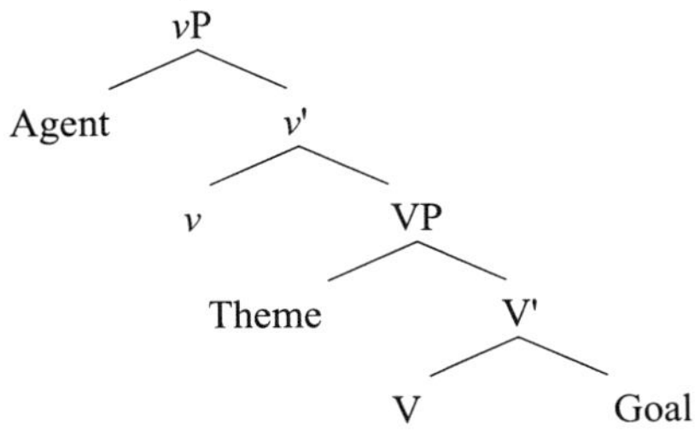

(45) Was hat Hans gegessen?

a. Hans hat den APFEL gegessen.

i. *TP Phase*

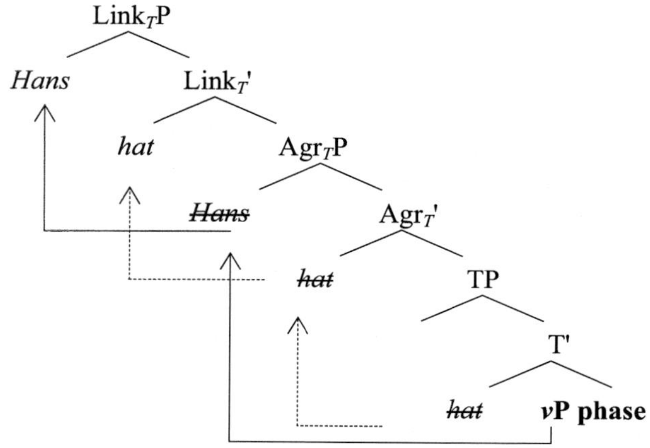

ii. v*P Phase*

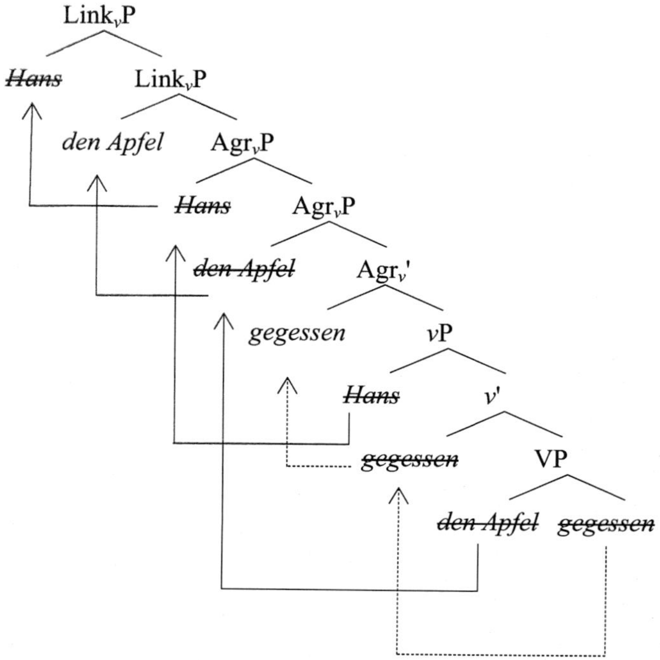

b. Den APFEL hat Hans gegessen.

i. *TP Phase*

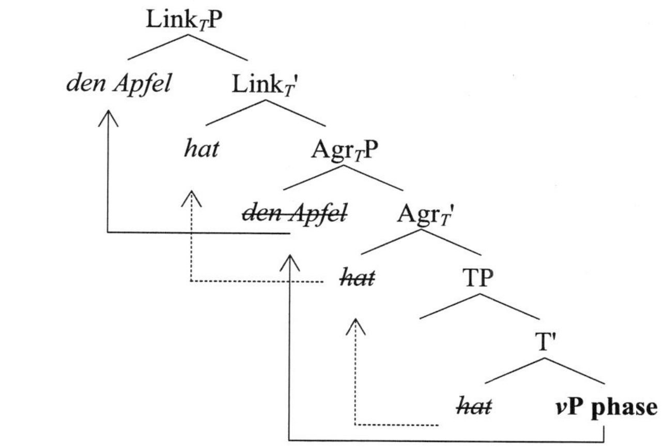

ii. v*P Phase*:

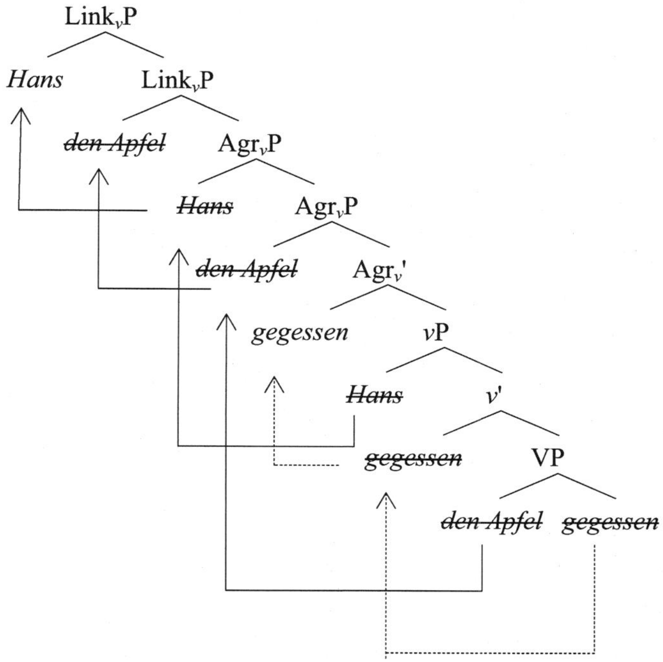

(46) Es kommt ein Mann aus dem Haus.

i. *TP Phase*

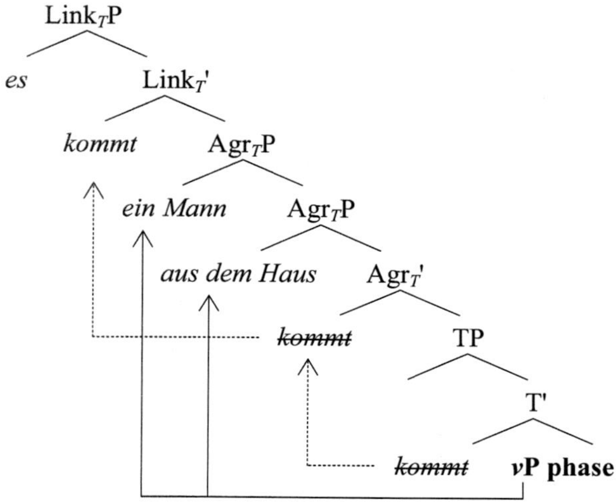

ii. *v*P *Phase*

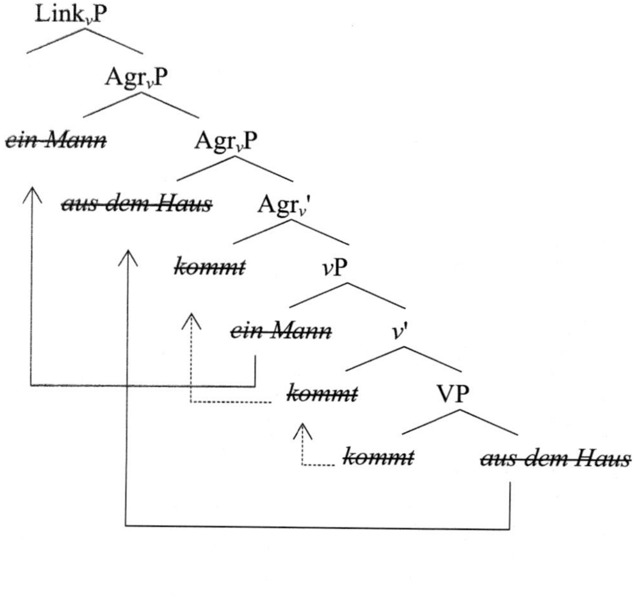

These trees basically show that differences in surface word order can be brought about solely within the TP phase, as a result of different elements being marked as [+Link$_T$]/[+aboutness], even if they are, in these cases, both marked as [+Link$_v$]/[+contrastive d-linking]. However, as we saw for the Pseudogapping examples in section 3.1, there may also be differences at the *v*P level, depending on whether the surface subject is contrastive or not. Examples (18a) and (18b) are repeated here with their respective trees:

(47) a. … the faculty should the concert. *contrastive subject*

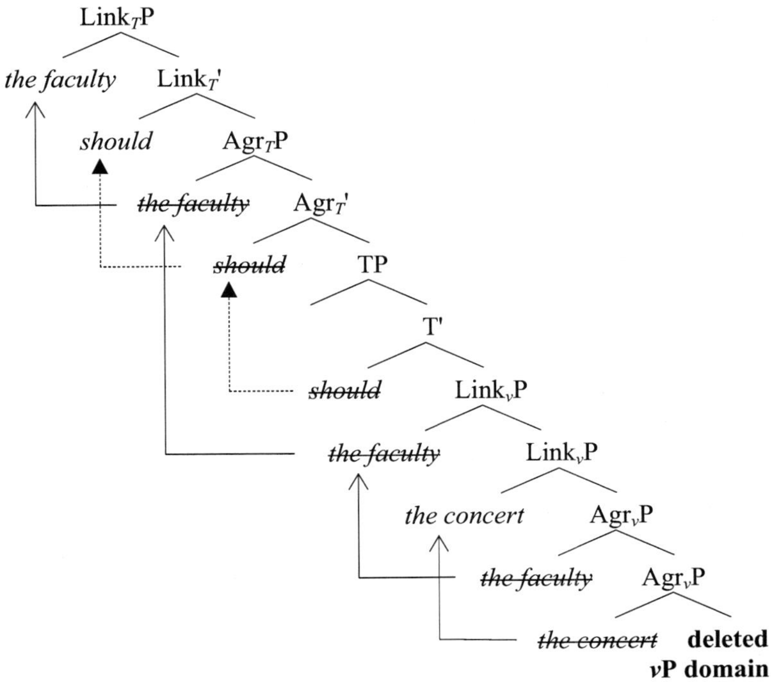

b. … they will the concert. *non-contrastive subject*

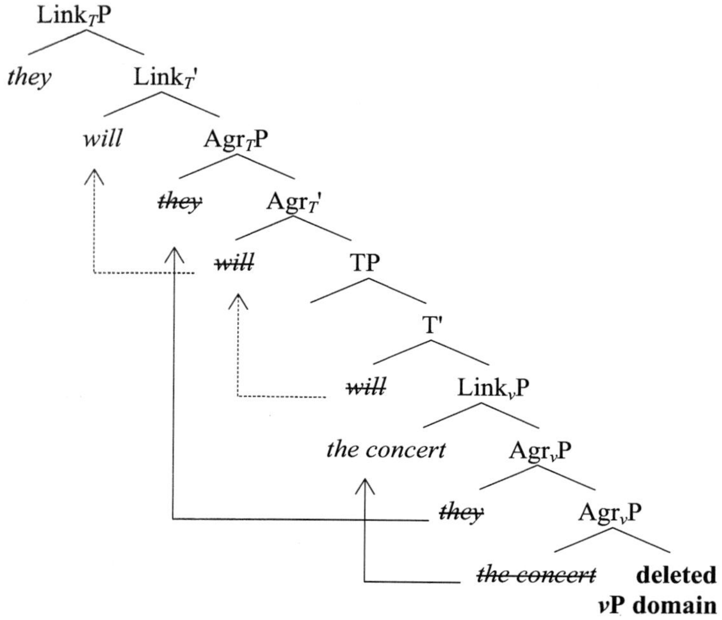

Finally, as we saw in section 3.2, sometimes surface word order can be defined already as low as within the DP phase, as was the case with split DP constructions. The full derivation for (26a) is shown now in (48):[12]

[12] I should mention an issue that I shall leave open for future research, namely the surface position of the past participle *gekauft* in this split DP derivation. In (48), I simply leave it sitting in V, which is not where I believe it should end up. It should presumably move at least to Agr$_v$ in order to check its agreement features. It does, necessarily, however, need to remain in sentence-final position. Accordingly, the same question will hold for the position of the finite verb in V-final (subordinate) clauses.

In such cases, I am tempted to believe that the finite verb still moves up to Link$_T$, and that everything else precedes it in the specifiers of Link$_T$P, possibly even joined later by the finite verb itself, since, to some extent at least, in a clause such as ... *dass er Bücher gekauft hat* "… that he bought books", the entire proposition *er Bücher gekauft hat* can be argued to act together as one unit, and constitute something like an aboutness topic. However, I shall leave further discussion of this point for another paper; cf. section 5, however, with regard to where the complementizer *dass* in such clauses should be merged.

(48) Bücher hat er viele gekauft.

i. *TP Phase*

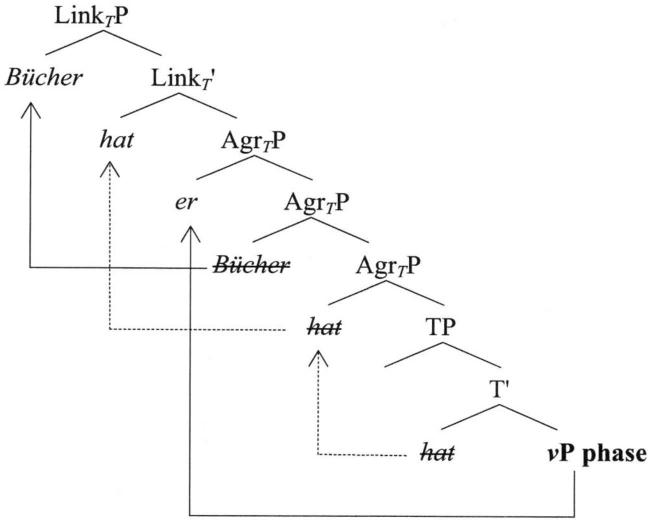

ii.. v*P Phase*

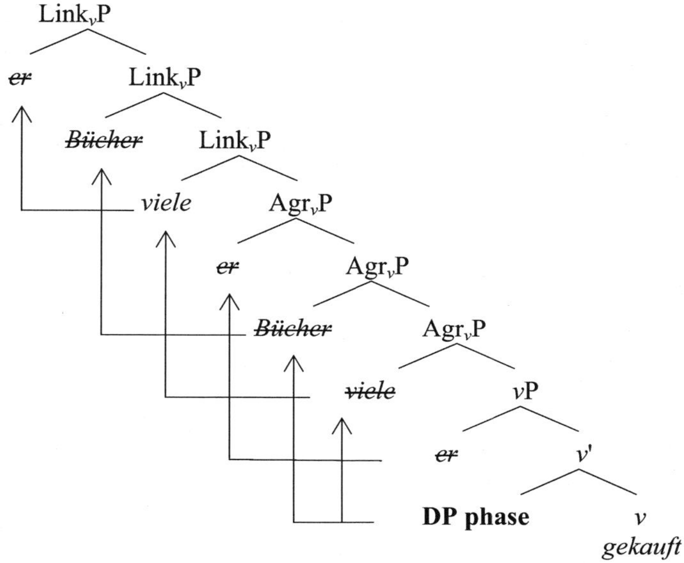

iii. *DP Phase*

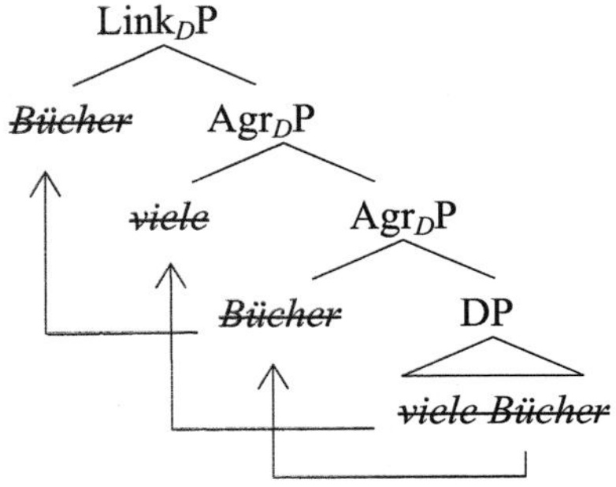

4.5. *Non V2 Languages such as Italian*

I now turn to the question of how to account for the less restricted sentence-initial structure in non V2 languages, such as Italian. That is, if we reject Rizzi's (1997) fine left peripheral structure — that is, roughly, ForceP > TopP(*) > FocP > TopP*> FinP — in favour of one with just the specifiers of LinkP occurring preverbally, how do we explain the empirical data he puts forward in (49), from Rizzi (1997: 296), to show multiple preverbal topic and focus elements? [13]

(49) a. Credo che a Gianni, QUESTO, domain, gli dovremmo dire.
b. Credo che domani, QUESTO, a Gianni, gli dovremmo dire.
c. Credo che domani, a Gianni, QUESTO gli dovremmo dire.
d. Credo che a Gianni, domani, QUESTO gli dovremmo dire.
e. Credo che QUESTO, a Gianni, domani, gli dovremmo dire.
f. Credo che QUESTO, domani, a Gianni, gli dovremmo dire.
I.believe that this tomorrow to Gianni him we.should say

(50) Il libro, a Gianni, domani, glielo darò senz' altro.
the book to Gianni tomorrow him.it I.will.give without doubt

Clearly, whilst in cases just with multiple topics, as in (50), it might be argued that these form a unit, together constituting the aboutness topic element, it is clear that the three elements in the examples in (49) — namely, *a Gianni*, *QUESTO*, and *domani* — are not able to do so, given their different information-structural interpretations (as both topics and

[13] Capitals denote focus; the other preverbal elements are taken to be topics.

focus). It is, however, further important to point out that whilst topic can recurse freely, it is, nevertheless, only possible to have one instance of preverbal focus, as shown in (51). Moreover, this focus must be interpreted as contrastive (data, as (50), taken from Rizzi 1997: 290):

(51) * A GIANNI IL LIBRO darò (non a Piero, l'articolo).
to Gianni the book I.will.give not to Piero, the.article

Additionally, differences in behaviour should be noted between the sentence-initial topic and focus elements. Whilst the former may involve a resumptive clitic within the comment structure (and necessarily do if the topicalized element is the direct object), focalised elements are inconsistent with such a clitic (Cinque 1990: 63; from Rizzi 1997: 289):

(52) a. Il tuo libro, lo ho comprato.
the your book it I.have bought
"Your book, I bought [it]."
b. * Il tuo libro ho compato.

(53) a. * Il TUO LIBRO lo ho comprato (non il suo).
the your book it I.have bought not he his
intended "Your book, I bought [it] (not his)."
b. Il TUO LIBRO ho comprato (non il suo).
the your book I.have bought not he his
"YOUR book I bought (not his)."

As can also be seen from the above examples, the topic, but not the focus constructions, further give rise to the so-called 'comma-intonation'. Both of these observations together make the topic constructions in Italian (and, more generally, in Romance), analogous to what Cinque (1990) terms Clitic Left Dislocation (CLLD). As Rizzi (1997) points out, this construction may also be found in Germanic languages, where a so-called D-pronoun is overtly realised as an anaphoric operator, referring back to the topic (Rizzi 1997: 294):

(54) Den Hans, den kenne ich seit langem.
the Hans him know I since long
"Hans, I have known for a long time."

Crucially, though, this is generally taken to constitute a different type of construction from the ones we have been discussing so far in this paper.

Namely, given both the comma intonation and the resumptive clitic/D-pronoun, one might want to reason that the topicalized element is external to the matrix clause. This is a point I shall pick up on in the next and final section (section 5).

Firstly, however, there is another important point to be made with regard to Rizzi's structure, and that is that Poletto (2000 2005) actually disputes the fact that there is a lower TopP occurring below FocP. She gives a number of arguments (which I shall not go into here), and basically concludes that these lower elements must also be interpreted as foci. Furthermore, she argues that sentence-initial adverbs, such as *domani* in (49) above, should be taken to be scene setting or framing, and thus also to potentially occur outside of/before the standard *Vorfeld*. Again, this is something I shall return to in section 5. For now, however, the crucial point is that we may, even in Italian, only be dealing with the ordering TopP (*) > FocP, and not TopP*> FocP > TopP*.

If this is indeed the case, there are a number of potential ways in which this might be captured, two of which I shall briefly outline now. Firstly, one might want to consider adopting something akin to the Feature Scattering Principle, proposed by Giorgi & Pianesi (1997: 15):

(55) *Feature Scattering Principle*
Each feature can head a projection.

This is claimed to be a cross-linguistically varying parameter, so that, in some languages, features scatter and project independent heads, whereas, in other languages, they fuse and are all checked in multiple specifiers of the one head. Following this, one might assume that, whilst for German, we have fusion, for non V2 languages, such as Italian, we have scattering, and thus the LinkP projects an independent head along with each specifier, thus being able to check not only for aboutness topic, but also for additional contrastive foci. This would, however, require something extra to be said about what extra features (besides the simple [+$Link_T$]) can be checked in this position, thus complicating the situation somewhat.

A second, and perhaps preferable approach, might be to assume that the verb head itself, in Italian, does not move up as far as $Link_T^0$, but only as far as Agr_T^0, or even only as far as one of these projections in the *v*P phase periphery. This would then maintain the old intuition regarding V to T vs. T to C movement as a cross-linguistic parameter. I think this is perhaps the most promising approach, but, at this stage, I leave it aside for further research.

5. CP Recursion or a TP Phase?

So, finally, having motivated the recursive information-structural periphery at the top of each phase, discussed the derivational process itself, and considered possible cross-linguistic alternatives to account for word order difference between Germanic and Romance languages, let me now return to the question of what actually is the highest phase — i.e. is it CP, as is usually claimed, or is it TP? To this end, I turn firstly to discussions of CP recursion by, amongst others, Iatridou & Kroch (1992) and Tallerman (1996).

Iatridou & Kroch (1992) argue for CP recursion to be allowed in certain instances in some of the languages which allow embedded V2, namely Frisian and Danish, but notably not Yiddish or Icelandic. They explain its licensing with respect to the higher CP needing to be transparent and thus deletable at LF (i.e. not *wh*, negative, or irrealis, since these are contentful). Tallerman (1996) also employs the idea of recursive CPs. In her case it is in order to explain what is usually known as the 'mixed' construction, in Welsh, which she refers to as the 'cleft' construction, the major function of which, as exemplified in (56a), is to focus the fronted constituent, although it has also taken on the function of NP topicalization since the demise of the Middle Welsh so-called 'abnormal' construction exemplified in (56b). Two important features, which show that this cannot simply be a form of V2 construction, are that this type of fronting can occur in subordinate clauses, and is, in fact, typically preceded by a complementizer (in embedded clauses as in (56c), but also, historically, in main clauses), and also that the negator is placed before the fronted constituent as in (56d).

(56) a. i. Myfi a gafodd anrheg.
me PRT got.3SG gift
"It was me that got a gift."
ii. Y dynion a werthodd y ci.
the men PRT sold.3SG the dog
"It was the men who sold the dog."

b. i. Myfi a gefais anrheg.
me PRT got.1SG gift
"I got a gift."
ii. Y dynion a werthasant y ci.
the men PRT sold.3PL the dog
"The men sold the dog."

c. Mi wn i mai [yng Nghymru] y mae Gwent.
PRT know I PRT in Wales PRT is Gwent
"I know that it's in Wales that Gwent is."

d. Nid / Dim y dyn a ddaeth.
NEG the man COMP came.3SG
"It wasn't the man who came."

The question she raises then is, if the complementizer is taken to be in the C-slot, where is the fronted material? It cannot now be in [Spec,CP], since it follows, rather than precedes, the complementizer. This is actually a general, cross-linguistic problem, applying to English too, as can be seen in (57):

(57) a. I knew that Irish, she couldn`t speak.
b. * I knew Irish, that she couldn`t speak.

(Tallerman 1996: 106)

Tallerman, like Iatridou & Kroch, thus assumes CP-recursion so that the complementizer may take another CP as its complement. But, again, this has to be subject to a large number of stipulative conditions, and each of the two CPs would have to have quite distinct properties, so as to prevent unlimited recursion. Instead, then, I return to the assumption made by the likes of Baltin (1982) and Lasnik & Saito (1992), that we ought to treat topicalization as adjunction to IP — or, rather, TP. That is, rather than taking our information-structural layer, which includes the landing site for fronting, to either occur above CP, i.e. taking CP to be the phase, or to constitute a split CP, à la Rizzi (1997), we ought, instead, to assume it to occur above TP, which then must be assumed to be the phase. CP, in the cases where we need it (i.e. when there is a complementizer, or such like), may then be merged on top of this periphery as a completely separate projection. This is then analogous to Rizzi's ForceP, occurring above his Topic and Focus phrases. We thus have the structure shown in (58):

(58)

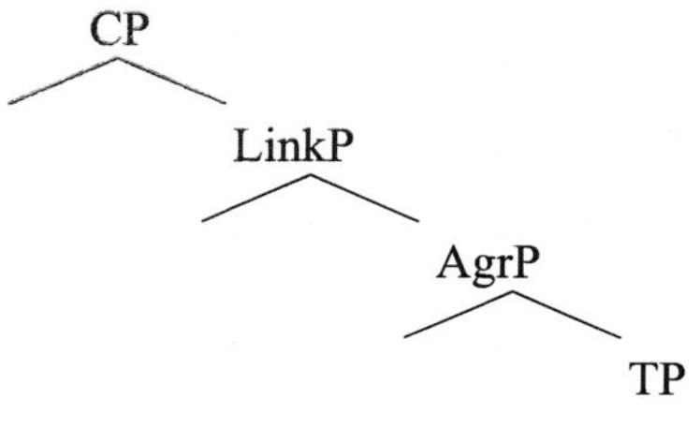

This, then, does not contradict the points made by Chomsky (2000, 2001, 2004, 2008) and Richards (2007), who argue against the TP being able to constitute the phase, since, crucially, we still have the biphrasal edge above the TP itself, and so both φ-features and edge features have their respective positions in which to be checked.

Furthermore, if we take the optional extra CP itself to be a phase, then the extra phasal periphery it would bring with it now also offers a potential position for the topicalized elements in the Germanic D-pronoun constructions such as (54), repeated here as (59):

(59) Den Hans, den kenne ich seit langem.
the Hans him know I since long
"Hans, I have known for a long time."

One might also wish to extend the argument to propose that sentence-initial topics in Italian, when they precede preverbal focused elements taken to sit in [Spec,Link$_T$P], and/or in the CLLD constructions (recall (52) and (53)), may also occur in this CP phase periphery, explaining both the resumptive clitic and the comma intonation. The features of this periphery could then be posited to be something akin to scene setting or framing, thus also offering a place for sentence-initial adverbs, both of the *domani* type, as well as those in the following German examples (Meinunger 2004):

(60) a. Ehrlich (gesagt), ich bin von dir total enttäuscht.
honestly said I am of you total disappointed
"Honestly, I am completely disappointed in you."

b. Nebenbei (bemerkt), ich habe mir die Sache ganz
next.to.it remarked I have me the thing wholly
anders vorgestellt.
different imaginded
"By the way: I had a completely different idea about all this."

This would then pick up on Rizzi's (1997) suggestion that such topic constructions might, in languages such as English, involve a null operator or complementizer. Clearly, however, further research on this point is required, especially since an overt complementizer may also precede these elements (recall (49)).

6. Conclusion

I hope, in the course of this paper, to have provided evidence from numerous people's work, as well as from my own, to show the need for a recursive information-structural layer both in place of a split CP (but not instead of CP itself, which is then merged, as and when needed, above this layer), as well as lower down in the clause — namely above *v*P and DP, two further phase levels. I also hope to have shown that whilst it would be most ideal and minimalist to assume only one projection in this layer, it is, in fact, necessary to allow for two — one to carry edge features, namely LinkP, and one for agreement purposes — namely AgrP. I then proposed that the edge features might be captured cross-phasally by a general [+Link] feature, which, on the whole, marks selection from a poset, but which acquires a more specific flavour at each phase level, namely [+aboutness] at the TP, [+contrastive d-linking] at the *v*P, and [+partitive] at the DP level. Finally, with respect to the actual derivations to and through these phase edge peripheries, I enumerated a number of problems with Remnant Movement approaches, and argued instead that an analysis with multiple specifiers is able to logically account for the data and its restrictions, particularly in V2 languages, but speculatively also cross-linguistically.

References

Baker, M. 1988a. *Incorporation: A Theory of Grammatical Function Changing*. Chicago: University of Chicago Press.

Baker, M. 1988b. Theta theory and the syntax of applicatives in Chichewa. *Natural Language & Linguistic Theory* 6, 353-389.

Baker, M. 1996. *The Polysynthesis Parameter*. New York: Oxford University Press.

Baltin, M. 1982. A landing site theory of movement rules. *Linguistic Inquiry* 13, 1-38.

Belletti, A. 2004. Aspects of the low IP area. In L. Rizzi (ed.), *The Structure of CP and IP — The Cartography of Syntactic Structures*, vol. 2. New York: Oxford University Press, 16-51.

Brunetti, L. 2003. *A Unification of Focus*. Ph.D. diss., University of Padova.

Butler, J. 2004. *Phase Structure, Phrase Structure, and Quantification*. Ph.D. diss., University of York.

Carlson, G.N. & F.J. Pelletier (eds.). 1995. *The Generic Book.* Chicago: University of Chicago Press.

Choi, H.-W. 1996. *Optimizing Structure in Context: Scrambling and Information-structure.* Ph.D. diss., Stanford University.

Chomsky, N. 1995. *The Minimalist Program.* Cambridge, MA: MIT Press.

Chomsky, N. 2000. Minimalist inquiries: The framework. In R. Martin, D. Michael & J. Uriagereka (eds.), *Step by Step: Essays on Minimalist Syntax in Honour of Howard Lasnik.* Cambridge, MA: MIT Press, 89-115.

Chomsky, N. 2001. Derivation by phase. In M. Kenstowicz (ed.), *Ken Hale: A Life in Language*. Cambridge, MA: MIT Press, 1-52.

Chomsky, N. 2004. Beyond explanatory adequacy. In A. Belletti (ed.), *Structures and Beyond — The Cartography of Syntactic Structures*, vol. 3. New York: Oxford University Press, 104-131.

Chomsky, N. 2008. On phases. In R. Freidin, C.P. Otero & M.L. Zubizarreta (eds.), *Foundational Issues in Linguistic Theory: Essays in Honor of Jean-Roger Vergnaud.* Cambridge, MA: MIT Press, 133-166.

Christensen, K.R. 2005. *Interfaces: Negation – Syntax – Brain*. Ph.D. diss., University of Aarhus.

Cinque, G. 1990. *Types of A'- Dependencies*. Cambridge, MA: MIT Press.

Cottell, S. & A. Henry. 2005. Transitive expletives, floating quantifiers and auxiliary positions in an English dialect. Paper presented at the *LAGB Meeting*, Cambridge.

Dimitrova-Vulchanova, M. & G. Giusti. 1988. Fragments of Balkan nominal structure. In A. Alexiadou & C. Wider (eds.), *Possessors, Predicates and Movement in the Determiner Phrase*. Amsterdam: John Benjamins, 333-360.

Epstein, S.D. & N. Hornstein (eds.). 1999. *Working Minimalism.* Cambridge, MA: MIT Press.

Fanselow, G. 1988. Aufspaltung von NPn und das Problem der freien Wortstellung. *Linguistische Berichte* 114, 91-113.

Gengel, K. 2006. Phases and ellipsis, Paper presented at the *Edges in Syntax* conference, Cyprus College, Nicosia.

Gengel, K. & A. McNay. 2006a. Information-structure at the phase level: Ellipsis in the DP. Paper presented at the *Workshop on DP-Internal Information-structure: Topic, Focus and other Illocutionary Forces*, Utrecht University.

Gengel, K. & A. McNay. 2006b. Recursive information-structural layers in syntax: Evidence from the *v*P layer. *Camling 2006: Proceedings of* *the Fourth University of Cambridge Postgraduate Conference in Language Research*, 75-82.

Giorgi, A. & F. Pianessi.1997. *Tense and Aspect: From Semantics to Morphosyntax.* Oxford: Oxford University Press.

Haegeman, L. 1995. *The Syntax of Negation.* Cambridge: Cambridge University Press.

Haegeman, L. 2004 DP-periphery and clausal periphery: Possessor doubling in West Flemish. In D. Adger, C. de Cat & G Tsoulas (eds.), *Peripheries: Syntactic Edges and Their Effects*. Dordrecht: Kluwer, 211-240.

Haider, H. 1982. Dependenzen und Konfigurationen: Zur deutschen V-Projektion. *Groninger Arbeiten zur germanistischen Linguistik* 21: 1-59.

Heim, I. 1982. *The Semantics of Definite and Indefinite Noun Phrases.* Ph.D. diss., University of Massachusetts, Amherst.

Holmberg, A. & C. Platzack. 1995. *The Role of Inflection in Scandinavian Syntax.* New York: Oxford University Press.

Hornstein, N. 2000. *Move! A Minimalist Theory of Construal.* Oxford: Blackwell.

Iatridou, S. & A. Kroch. 1992 The licensing of CP-recursion and its relevance to the Germanic verb-second phenomenon. *Working Papers in Scandinavian Linguistics* 50, 1-25.

Jayaseelan, K.A. 2001. IP-internal topic and focus phrases. *Studia Linguistica* 55, 33-75.

Kayne, R. 1994. *The Antisymmetry of Syntax.* Cambridge, MA: MIT Press.

Kester, E.-P. 1996. *The Nature of Adjectival Inflection.* Ph.D. diss., University of Utrecht.

Kuroda, S.-Y. 1972. The categorical and the thetic judgment: Evidence from Japanese syntax. *Foundations of Language* 9, 153-185.

Ladusaw, W. 1994. Thetic and categorical, stage and individual, weak and strong. *Proceedings of SALT IV*, 220 -229.

Lasnik, H. & M. Saito. 1992. *Move a.* Cambridge, MA: MIT Press.

Lenerz, J. 1997. *Zur Abfolge nominaler Satzglieder im Deutschen.* Tübingen: Niemeyer.

Lobeck, A. 1995. *Ellipsis.* New York: Oxford University Press.

McNay, A. 2005a. Information-structure, word order and quantifiers in German. *Durham and Newcastle Working Papers in Linguistics* 11, 83-96.

McNay, A. 2005b. Split topicalization – Motivating the split. *Oxford University Working Papers in Linguistics, Philology & Phonetics* 10, 41-60.

McNay, A. 2006. Partitivity, splitting, and NPE. Ms., Humboldt University of Berlin.
McNay, A. 2007. Split topicalization and pseudopartitivity. *Proceedings of the 30th Penn Linguistics Colloquium — University of Pennsylvania Working Papers in Linguistics* 13.1, 239-252.
Meinunger, A. 2004. Issues concerning the German left periphery – Parasites in the 'Vorfeld'. Ms., ZAS Berlin.
Müller, G. 2004. Verb-second as *v*P-first. *Journal of Comparative Germanic Linguistics* 7, 179-234.
Müller, S. 2003. Mehrfache Vorfeldbesetzung. *Deutsche Sprache* 31, 29-62.
Müller, S. 2005. Zur Analyse der scheinbar mehrfachen Vorfeldbesetzung. *Linguistiche Berichte* 203, 297-330.
Nilsen, Ø. 2002. V2 and Holmberg`s generalization. In C.J.-W. Zwart & W. Abraham (eds.), *Studies in Comparative Germanic Syntax: Proceedings from the 15th Workshop on Comparative Germanic Syntax*. Amsterdam: John Benjamins, 151-173.
Nilsen, Ø. 2003. *Eliminating Positions*. Ph.D. diss., Utrecht University.
Ntelitheos, D. 2003. The syntax of emphasis: Split DPs and nominal ellipsis. *Proceedings of the 6th International Conference of Greek Linguistics,* Department of Philology University of Crete, Rethymnon.
Ntelitheos, D. 2004. The syntax of elliptical and discontinuous nominals. M.A. thesis, University of California at Los Angeles.
Poletto, C. 2000. *The Higher Functional Field: Evidence from Northern Italian Dialects.* New York: Oxford University Press.
Poletto, C. 2005. Diachronic variation in Romance. Course handout from the 2005 EGG Summer School. Available for download from http://egg.auf.net/05/docs/handouts/Cecilia/eggdiachronicpoletto.pdf.
Polinisky, M. & E. Potsdam. 2001. Long distance agreement and topic in Tsez. *Natural Language & Linguistic Theory* 19, 583-646.
Quirk, R., S. Greenbaum, G. Leech & J. Svartik. 1982. *A Grammar of Contemporary English.* Harlow: Longman.
Ramchand, G. 2008. *Verb Meaning and the Lexicon: A First Phase Syntax*. Cambridge: Cambridge University Press.
Richards, M. 2007. On phases, phase heads, and functional categories. *Nanzan Linguistics* special issue 1, 105-127.
Richards, N. 2001. *Movement* in *Language: Interactions and Architectures.* Oxford: Oxford University Press.
Rizzi, L. 1997. The fine structure of the left periphery. In L. Haegeman (ed.), *Elements of Grammar: Handbook of Generative Syntax.* Dordrecht: Kluwer, 281-337.

Rizzi, L. 2004. Locality and left periphery. In A. Belletti (ed.), *Structures and Beyond — The Cartography of Syntactic Structures*, vol. 3. New York: Oxford University Press, 223-251.

Sasse, H.-J. 1987. The thetic/categorical distinction revisited. *Linguistics* 25, 511-580.

Sauerland, U. 2004. A comprehensive semantics for agreement. Paper presented at the Phi-Workshop, McGill University, Montreal.

Shlonsky, U. 1992. The representation of AGR-in-Comp. *Geneva Generative Papers* 0, 39-52.

Sleeman, P. 1996. *Licensing Empty Nouns in French*. Ph.D. diss., University of Amsterdam.

Starke, M. 1993. En deuxième position en Europe centrale. Ms., University of Geneva.

Starke, M. 2004. On the inexistence of specifiers and the nature of heads. In A. Belletti (ed.), *Structures and Beyond — The Cartography of Syntactic Structures*, vol. 3. New York: Oxford University Press, 252-268.

Svenonius, P. 2004. On the edge. In D. Adger, C. de Cat & G. Tsoulas (eds.), *Peripheries: Syntactic Edges and their Effects*. Dordrecht: Kluwer, 259-287.

Tallerman, M. 1996. Fronting constructions in Welsh. In R.D. Borsley & I. Roberts (eds.), *The Syntax of the Celtic Languages*. Cambridge: Cambridge University Press, 97-124.

Vallduvi, E. 1993. Information packaging: A survey. *Research Paper HCRC/RP-44*, Human Communication Research Centre, University of Edinburgh.

van Hoof, H. 1997. Left dislocation and split topics in Brabant Dutch. In H. van Riemsdijk Anagnostopoulou, E. Anagnostopoulou & F. Zwarts (eds.), *Materials on Left Dislocation*. Amsterdam: John Benjamins, 275-305.

van Hoof, H. 2002. What stranded adjectives reveal about split-NP topicalization. Ms., University of Tübingen.

van Hoof, H. 2005. Split topicalization. In H. van Riemsdijk (ed.), *The Blackwell Companion to Syntax,* vol. IV, ch. 62, Oxford: Blackwell.

Ward, G. & B. Birner. 2001. Discourse and information-structure. In D. Schiffrin, D. Tannen & H.E. Hamilton (eds.), *The Handbook of Discourse Analysis.* Oxford: Blackwell, 119-137.

Webelhuth, G. 1992. *Principles and Parameters of Syntactic Saturation.* New York: Oxford University Press.

CHAPTER NINE

PRAGMATIC MARKERS AS SYNTACTIC HEADS: A CASE STUDY FROM ROMANIAN

Virginia Hill

1. Introduction

Over the last decade — especially after the study on adverbs in Cinque (1999) — the impact of speech acts on the syntactic structure emerged as a key issue for the understanding of how the left periphery works. Two approaches seem to arise from this debate. In one approach, the Complementizer Phrase (CP) field is the layer of discourse features, such as logophoricity, which are crucial for the outcome of the argument structure (Sigurðsson 2004, among others). Accordingly, the cartography of the CP field proposed in Rizzi (1997, 2004) must be revised by introducing logophoric heads under the clause typing Force-head.

The other approach to the left periphery proposes a separate structural segment above ForceP to account for the syntactic effect of some discourse features. For example, tentative studies on the structure of vocatives, such as proposed in Moro (2003), suggest that features related to direct address must be checked above ForceP (i.e. outside the core syntax) in a way that ensures some transparency between the two left peripheral fields, so as to account for logophoricity and binding effects.

Along the same lines, Speas & Tenny (2003), Speas (2004), and Tenny (2005) proceed to an inventory of discourse features with an undeniable effect on syntax. They argue that discourse features (including logophoricity) can be reduced to three pragmatic role features (i.e. *speaker*, *hearer*, *sentience*) saturated in a predicative unit that embeds the utterance. The structural extent of the utterance is not specified (CP or IP?), but if the derivation attains ForceP, the pragmatic predicative unit must be higher than and c-commanding the ForceP.

Basically, all these studies argue for a syntactic computation of speech acts at the highest edge of the clause structure, but differ in deciding which discourse/pragmatic features count for syntax, and, therefore, at what level and in which way they are computed.

As a contribution to this topic, the present chapter presents a case study from Romanian, where the use of some discourse markers coincides with the possibility of having "that"-indicative clauses in root contexts:

(1) a. Hai că tare eşti deşteaptă!
HAI that really are.2SG smart
"You are REALLY smart !" (ironical statement)
b. * Că tare eşti deşteaptă!
that really are.2SG smart

The morpheme *hai* in (1a) is classified as an *injunctive interjection* in traditional grammar (*Gramatica Academiei Române* 1963, Croitor-Balaciu 2006) and as a *pragmatic marker* in discourse studies (e.g. Tschizmarova 2005). The latter label captures the property of such elements to induce a strong speaker-oriented interpretation. Other elements may occur in free alternation with *hai* in (1a), as it will be shown in section 2. The important observation concerns the occurrence of the *că*-indicative clause with *hai* in a construction that qualifies as a root clause. That is, there is no obvious selector or matrix for the *că*-indicative clause in (1a), although *că*-clauses commonly occur in subordinate contexts (i.e. as complement or adjunct). As an interjection, *hai* is not expected to influence the derivation of clauses. However, its exclusion makes the construction ungrammatical, as in (1b). Hence, what is the syntactic impact *hai* and equivalent pragmatic markers have in constructions as in (1), so that their presence or absence decides on the grammaticality of *că*-indicative clauses in root contexts?

This article argues that constructions as in (1a) have the complementizer "that" in the Force-head, so the pragmatic marker (i.e. *hai* or equivalent) merges above ForceP. The analysis accounts for such constructions by pointing out that the pragmatic marker carries the feature cluster [[speech act], [V]], and merges as a Speech Act-head SA^0 that selects ForceP. Thus, Romanian provides empirical evidence for the existence of speech acts as a separate syntactic category, and for their location and impact on the left periphery of the clause.

The characterization of SA^0 as a [+V] element has implications for the theory of the pragmatics-syntax interface. In particular, it supports the analyses that treat the syntactic reflection of the discourse set-up as a predicative unit. That is, if the SA-head has [+V,–N] features and is not part of CP/IP, then it will predictably be computed in the same way full-fledged verbs are, as argued in Speas & Tenny (2003). Any difference in the results does not concern the syntax, but the intrinsic pragmatic or semantic features of the elements involved.

2. Data

The central data in this article are constructions as in (1a), further illustrated in (2), where *că*-indicative clauses follow certain discourse lexical items. Crucially, all these items emphasize the speaker's point of view, so the constructions they initiate have a strong speaker-oriented interpretation (injunctive, evaluative, evidential, epistemic).

(2) a. **Zău** că Maria ne va ajuta!
by.God that Maria us will help
"Maria will help us, cross my heart."
b. **Fireşte** că Maria ne va ajuta!
of.course that Maria us will help
"Of course Maria will help us."
c. **Lasă** că Maria ne va ajuta!
for.sure that Maria us will help
"Maria will help us, for sure."
d. **Trebuie** că ne va ajuta cineva!
must that us will help someone
'Someone will be likely to help us."

The lexical items followed by a "that"-indicative clause may be interjections (2a), adverbs (2b), grammaticalized verbs (2c), and modals (2d). At first sight, constructions as in (2) may spring from a version or a combination of the following configurations:

i. a speaker-oriented root ForceP with an exclamative or injunctive "that" in Force;
ii. a bi-clausal structure in which the matrix verb is suppressed in some way, but it still selects a "that" indicative complement;
ii. a speaker-oriented root ForceP in which "that" is located low (e.g. in FinP).

A closer look at these constructions shows, however, that none of these accounts is plausible. The data to this effect are presented in the next three sections.

2.1. Speaker-Oriented că in Root Clauses

One possible approach to the constructions in (1a) and (2) is to consider *că* "that" as an element with operator-like features that heads a stylistically marked root clause. The preceding item will then be either in the specifier of "that" or adjoined in some form to the root clause.

Indeed, in some Romance languages, the complementizer "that" may head exclamative or injunctive clauses, as shown in (3) for French *que* "that".

(3) a. Qu'il fait beau!
that it does beautiful
"What a beautiful weather!"
b. Qu'il fasse attention!
that he makes attention
"He should pay attention!"

However, Romanian disallows such occurrences of *că*, as shown in (4).

(4)	a.	*	Că frumos! that beautiful "How beautiful!"	a'.	Ce frumos! what beautiful
	b.	*	Că să fie atent! that SBJ be.3SG attentive "He should pay attention!"	b'.	Să fie atent! SBJ be.3SG attentive

Romanian exclamatives make use of interrogative *ce* "what" instead of *că* "that" (4a), whereas root subjunctives with injunctive force display only the marker (i.e. *să*), without a complementizer (4b). Accordingly, the constructions in (1a) and (2), which count as exclamatives, may not be root clauses headed by *că* "that" with operator features.

The interesting observation is that (1a) can be rescued by inserting an item that provides lexical marking for speaker-orientation, as in (4c)[1].

c. Doamne, că frumos mai e azi!
god that nice more is today
"Goodness, what a nice day today!"

In (4c) the insertion of the exclamative noun triggers obligatory inversion between the copula and the adjective and thus, it allows for a *că* "that" exclamative root clause. At first sight, the exclamative noun *doamne* seems to fulfil the same role that *hai* does in (1a); that is, it somehow licenses the *că* "that"-clause in root context.

In conclusion, Romanian *că* "that" does not support operator

[1] I am grateful to an anonymous reviewer for pointing out these data.

features in root clauses, unless it is somehow licensed to occur in such contexts.

2.2. *Bi-Clausal Structures*

Another approach to the constructions in (1a) and (2) is to consider them bi-clausal. So the lexical item preceding "that" belongs to a matrix clause whose predicate selects a regular *că* "that" indicative complement. The examples in (1a) and (2) will be tested for the bi-clausal possibility[2].

2.2.1. Interjections

Consider again the examples with evaluative or evidential reading:

(1) a. Hai că tare eşti deşteaptă!
HAI that really are.2SG smart
"You are REALLY smart !" (ironical statement)

(2) a. **Zău** că Maria ne va ajuta!
by.God that Maria us will help
"Maria will help us, cross my heart."

The elements *hai* (1a) and *zău* (2a) are classified as *interjections*; therefore, they are not expected to be syntactically relevant. However, the well-formedness of (1a) and (2a) compared to (4) signals that such elements have enough syntactic impact to rescue *că* "that" root clauses. Therefore, they either belong to a matrix clause or they close off the "that" phase in a way that allows it to be a root clause.

If these interjections may stand for a matrix clause, then they should also occur alone in out-of-the-blue utterances, as in (5), while maintaining the evaluative reading.

(5) a. # Hai!
b. * Zău!
"Let's go/move!"

Hai is successful in this test with an injunctive reading but it excludes the

---

[2] The assumption is that the complementizer *că* "that" blocks clause union or verb restructuring with the indicative clause, for the same reasons it excludes these processes in other Romance languages (Roberts 1997, among others). So *bi-clausal* in this paper means two distinct *phases* (Chomsky 2001).

relevant evaluative/evidential reading in (1a); *zău* fails completely. Therefore, these two elements cannot constitute separate matrix clauses for (1a) and (2a).[3]

2.2.2. Adverbs

Adverbs preceding the *că*-indicative clause, as in (2b), have an exclusive evidential reading paired with high pitch intonation, the latter distinguishing them from habitual or contrastive focus readings elsewhere in the clause, as in (6).

(2) b. **Fireşte** că Maria ne va ajuta!
of.course that Maria us will help
"Of course Maria will help us."

(6) a. **Sigur** că Maria ne va ajuta!
of.course that Maria us will help
"Of course Maria will help us!"
b. Maria (**sigur**) ne va ajuta (**sigur**).
Maria (certainly) us will help (certainly)
"It is certain that Maria will help us."

Constructions as in (2b) and (6a) are considered bi-clausal in the traditional grammar (Teodorescu 1972). That is, the adverb merges with the copula "be" and selects the *că*-clause; then the copula is suppressed, as in (7a). This analysis is incorrect, as it generates ungrammatical constructions elsewhere, as in (7b); to rescue (7b), the adverb must be replaced with its adjectival equivalent, as in (7c). The confusion in (7a) comes from the homophony of the adjective and the adverb *sigur* 'sure". When homophony does not apply, as in (7b), the adverbial form rules out the copula.

(7) a. (E) **sigur** că Maria ne va ajuta.
(is) sure that Maria us will help
"It is certain that Maria will help us."
b. * E **fireşte** că Maria ne va ajuta.
is of.course that Maria us will help
intended "Of course Maria will help us."

---

[3] An anonymous reviewer points out that the expression *zău aşa* 'really so !" may occur successfully by itself. However, in this expression the self-standing item is not *zău* but the adverb *aşa* 'so" that has *zău* as a modifier.

c. E **firesc** ca Maria să ne ajute.
is natural that Maria us will help
"It is a matter of course that Maria will help us."

Note that changing the adverb with the adjective in (7) modifies not only the structure but also the interpretation, as the evidential reading cannot be preserved in the adjective + copula sequence.

Examples as in (7) indicate that a bi-clausal analysis is not available for constructions as in (2a)[4].

2.2.3. Grammaticalized Verbs

The verb in (2c) is grammaticalized and has evidential interpretation.

(2) c. **Lasă** că Maria ne va ajuta!
for.sure that Maria us will help
"Maria will help us, for sure."

The form *lasă* in (2c) may freely alternate with the plural form *lăsați*; the two forms correspond to the imperative inflection (for 2nd person singular and plural, respectively). There is a full-fledged counterpart, *lăsa*, that means "allow" or "quit, abandon", and has a ditransitive structure. The full-fledged verb selects a DP and/or a subjunctive complement, but not a *că* "that" indicative complement, as shown in (8) for its imperative form.

(8) a. Lasă-l pe Ion în pace!
leave-him PE Ion in peace!
"Leave Ion alone!"
b. Lasă copilul să vină!
let child.the SBJ come.3SG
"Allow the child to come!"
c. Nu-l mai lăsa să vină!
not-him more let SBJ come.3SG
"Don't allow him to come any more!"
d. * Lasă-l pe Ion că vine.
let-him PE Ion that comes
*"Ion comes, for sure."
√"Leave Ion alone, for he'll be coming."

4 For a detailed analysis of constructions as in (2a) we refer the reader to Hill (2007a), where the tests are applied to all classes of 'sentential' adverbs and adverbial expressions.

The imperative forms in (8) have the morphology of the grammaticalized imperative (2c), but not the same syntax. More precisely, the grammaticalized imperative is compatible with a *că*-indicative clause and cannot occur with clitics (pronouns, negation, short adverbs) or with a ditransitive structure, in the intended reading, as shown in (9).

(9) a. Lasă(*-l) că vine!
let(-him) that comes
*"He will come, for sure."
√"Leave him alone, for he'll be coming."
b. (*Nu) lasă că vine!
(not) let that comes
c. (*Mai) lasă că vine!
(more) let that comes
d. * Lasă copilul că vine!
let child.the that comes
*"The child is coming, for sure."
√"Leave the child alone, for he'll be coming."

The examples in (8) and (9) show that the full-fledged verb inflected for imperative and the grammaticalized form with evidential interpretation are in complementary distribution (e.g., ±*că*-complementation) and occupy different locations in the clause. That is, the full-fledged verb is associated with an inflectional phrase, whereas the grammaticalized verb is not, since it cannot support any clitics that are located within IP. Presumably, the two imperative forms of the grammaticalized verb must be two frozen forms merged as such somewhere above IP (see section 4.2). At that level, the grammaticalized *lasă* cannot maintain the ditransitive structure (9d). Therefore, the evidential *lasă*, as in (2c) is not only lacking an IP domain, but a bare ditransitive *v*P structure as well. Accordingly, there is no justification for considering evidential *lasă* as a matrix verb.

2.2.4. Modals

A similar outcome from grammaticalization applies to modals such as "must":

(2) d. **Trebuie** că ne va ajuta cineva!
must that us will help someone
'Someone will be likely to help us."

Notably, when they do not occur with "that" indicative clauses, the modals support clitics (10a) or can be inflected (10b), irrespective of their deontic or epistemic reading.

(10) a. Maria nu mai trebuie să plece.
Maria not more must SBJ leave-3SG
"Maria does not need to leave any longer."
b. Trebuia să fi sosit.
must-PST SBJ be arrived
"It should have arrived." / "It had likely arrived."

In (10) the modal "must" merges in or moves through an IP in which clitic elements such as negation (*nu*) and short adverbs (*mai*) may be spelled out, and where tense marking takes place. These elements are disallowed on the modal that precedes the *că*-clause in (2d), as further shown in (11a). This modal also fails to stand by itself when it has the intended epistemic interpretation, as in (11b).

(11) a. (*Nu mai) **trebuie** că ne va ajuta cineva.
(not more) must that us will help someone
"someone will likely help us."
b. # Trebuie!
"It is necessary!" / *"Likely!"

The modal in (11) lacks the properties that would support an inflectional phrase, so it contrasts with the modal in (10). Hence, the modal in (11) merges outside (and above) CP, and cannot, by itself, stand for a separate matrix clause.

In conclusion, all the lexical items preceding *că* "that" in (1a) and (2) fail the tests for a bi-clausal structure. On the contrary, the data points to a location of these elements at the left edge of the "that"-clause. The diverse traditional classification of these items (i.e. interjections, adverbs, grammaticalized verbs or modals) did not make any difference for the outcome. Since these elements may occur in free alternation with *hai* and have equivalent speaker-oriented effects, they can all be included in the discourse class of *pragmatic markers*.

2.3. The Location of **că**

One may argue that root clauses project to ForceP under stylistic triggers, but this ForceP involves a different *că* "that" than the one introducing sentential complements; in particular, *că* "that" may spell out the low Fin-head (instead of Force). Accordingly, the pragmatic markers preceding *că* "that" in (1a) and (2) would merge directly in the field above Fin, and the absence of a bi-clausal structure is expected.

However, there is evidence that root *că* in (1a) and (2) is the same element as the subordinated *că* in sentential complements, and they both merge in Force. The word order in the following illustrations is assessed according to the cartographic analysis of the CP field in Rizzi (1997, 2004) as summed up in (12).

(12) [Force^0 (*that*) Int^0 Foc^0 Mod^0 Fin^0 [TP ...]]

The hierarchy in (12) contains Romance "that" in Force. Thus, constituents associated with topic, focus, modification, and finiteness must follow "that", in exactly such order, in the constituent sequences. For our purpose, when such constituents follow *că* "that" the location of "that" is in Force^0; if they precede *că* "that", its location is in Fin^0.

2.3.1. Embedded Clauses with că

The test for the position of *că* "that" in embedded clauses involves subjunctive complements where *că* "that" may co-occur with the subjunctive marker *să* located in FinP (e.g. Cornilescu 2000).[5] In such contexts, topic and focus constituents may intervene between *că* and *să* as in (13).

(13) Zice *(**că**) Ion LA EI **să** se instaleze.
says (that) Ion.TOP at them.FOC SBJ REFL install
"S/he says that Ion should move in with THEM."

The word order in (13) maps out the construction with *că* "that" in Force^0, followed by the string Topic-Focus, above *să* in Fin^0. Deletion of *că* "that" is not possible in this context.

2.3.2. The Location of că *in Root Clauses*

The word order in (13) is maintained in constructions with *hai*, as in (14).

[5] The label for this functional head is MoodP in Cornilescu (2000) but its hierarchical location and syntactic effects are equivalent to FinP.

(14) Hai *(**că**) Ion LA EI se instalează.
HAI (that) Ion at them REFL installs
"Finally, Ion is installing himself at their place."

The verb morphology is different in (13) and (14) insofar as the subjunctive marker in Fin^0 is not present in the latter. However, the word order is maintained: *că* "that" – Topic – Focus. Also, the suppression of *că* rules out the root clause, as it does in regular sentential complementation. Therefore, the *că* elements in (13)-(14) must be equally located in $Force^0$.

This analysis of *că* finds confirmation in constructions with a strong speaker-oriented interpretation where features that trigger stylistic inversion add up to the evidential features that trigger derivations as in (1a) and (2). Consider the stylistic inversion in (15).[6]

(15) a. V-o CERTA el_i $preoteasa_i$!
you-will scold.EMPH he.MASC priest's.wife.FEM.
"The priest's wife will scold you, for sure!"
(from Cornilescu 2000: 99)

Hill (2006) argues that in constructions such as (15a), the heavy emphasis on the verb propels it to a high head in the CP field. The subject pronoun is merged directly in TopP, so it may not agree with the constituent that spells out the subject (although it agrees with the verb).[7] High placement of the verb above TopP correctly predicts that focus constituents will be lower than the subject pronoun in the hierarchy (15b).

b. Maria, (*NOUĂ) ne DĂ ea NOUĂ mereu
Maria (to.us.FOC) us gives she.TOP to.us.FOC always
de furcă (nu vouă)!
of fork (not to.you)
"As for Maria, she does make trouble, but for us, not for you."

The relevance of (15b) is that it may occur under *hai că* "that", as in (15c).

c. Hai că v-o CERTA el, preoteasa!
HAI that you-will scold he.MASC priest's.wife-FEM
"The priest's wife will scold you, you'll see!"

---

[6] Examples as in (15) are stylistically marked; versions where the pronoun and the subject DP do not agree are regional.
[7] For more data see Cornilescu (2000) and Hill (2006).

The word order in (15c) is *că* – Verb – TopP (– FocP); hence, *că* merges in the highest head of the CP field, and must be identical to *că* in Force^0 in (13) and (14).[8]

In sum, the element *că* in root clauses as in (1a) and (2) is the same as *că* in sentential complements, and it is merged in the highest functional head of the CP field (i.e. Force^0). Accordingly, the factors that make *că*-indicative clauses compatible with a root context as in (1a) and (2) do not spring from some fluctuation in the properties of *că* but from a different probe at the left periphery. Since such a probe must be higher than ForceP, our attention must now turn to the properties of the pragmatic markers.

3. *Hai* as a Speech Act Head

This section argues that *hai* is visible for syntactic computations as the head of a discourse/pragmatic field, separate from and above ForceP. This head is labelled *speech act* (SA), by adopting the terminology of relevant current studies (Cinque 1999, Speas & Tenny 2003). Here, an SA-head, such as *hai*, is shown to have [V] features and selectional properties.

3.1. The Forms and the Distribution of hai

Hai is a discourse element of Turkish origin widely used in colloquial language. An utterance starting with *hai* conveys the speaker's point of view with the effect of a *speech act*; that is, explicit illocutionary force, directive or expressive (Searle 1969). As a directive, *hai* has strong injunctive force and enhances imperative verbs. As an expressive (E-reading), *hai* has evaluative, evidential or epistemic readings, such as seen in the constructions in (1) and (2).

The Romanian *hai* displays various forms and a consistent distributional pattern that points to its morpho-syntactic properties. In particular, *hai* has a variant *haide* and two inflected forms: *haidem* (where *–m* is the ending for first person plural) and *haideți* (where *–ți* is the ending for second person plural or the politeness singular). These forms may or may not occur in free alternation, depending on the speech act features and on the type of clause they combine with. Table 1 presents the morphological paradigm of *hai* and identifies the speech act potential of each form (i.e. injunctive or E).

---

[8] Hill (2006) proposes a split ForceP for these constructions, where a lower Force-head attracts the verb, whereas the higher Force-head contains the "that" element.

Table 1: The morphological paradigm of hai

Form	**Speech act**		**Person**			**Number**	
	injunctive	**E**	**1**	**2**	**any/generic**	**SG**	**PL**
hai	+	+	+	+	+	+	+
haide	+	–	–	+	+	+	–
haidem[9]	+	–	+	–	–	–	+
haideți	+	+	+	+	–	+	+

The injunctive versus the E-reading follows from the distribution of *hai* in relation to other constituents. That is, an injunctive reading is available when a form of *hai* (i) occurs by itself (16a), (ii) enhances an imperative or an injunctive subjunctive clause (16b-d), or (iii) combines with an adjunct "that"-clause (16e) or an adjunct subjunctive clause (16f).

(16) a. Hai / Haide / Haidem / Haideți!
"Let's..."
b. Hai / haideți plecați!
HAI HAI.2PL go.2PL.IMP
"Go!"
c. Hai să plec / pleci / plece / plecăm / plecați / plece!
HAI SBJ go.1SG 2SG 3SG 1PL 2PL 3PL
"Let me/you/him/her/us/you/them go!"
d. Haidem să începem lucrul!
HAI.1PL SBJ start work
"Let's start the work!"
e. Hai / haideți că e târziu!
HAI HAI.2PL that is late
"Let's go because it is late!"
f. Haide să- mi vezi casa!
HAI SBJ me see.2SG house.the
"Come to see my house!"

The examples in (16) do not display constructions where *că*-indicative clauses merge in a complement position, indicating that an injunctive reading is not compatible with such structures.

Indeed, constructions equivalent to (1a) and (2) have only an E-reading, and they usually occur with the generic *hai*, as in (17a). The form *haideți* is also successful in this context, as in (17b), but not for all the speakers. The form *haidem* is unanimously excluded (17c).

[9] The form *haidem* is sensitive to regional variation; northern regions do not use it.

(17) a. Hai că iar am greşit/s-a greşit!
HAI that again have.1 erred/ARB.SE-has erred
"Damn, I messed it up again." /
"Right, it has been messed up again."

b. Haideţi c-aţi întârziat, ce mai!
HAI.2PL that-have.2PL been.late what else
"Obviously you are late!"

c. * Haidem că iar am greşit!
HAI-1PL that again have.1 erred

To sum up the information, *hai* may appear with person/number endings that look like imperative endings, as shown in Table 1. The compatibility of *hai* with verbal inflection indicates that this element has a [V] feature. The readings available on these forms of *hai* are either injunctive or E. Injunctive readings follow from the context in (16), where *hai* occurs in isolation or enhances an imperative (surrogate imperative) verb. These contexts may support adjunct elements, such as adverbs or adjunct subjunctive or adjunct "that" indicative clauses. On the other hand, the E-reading on *hai* follows from complementation with "that" indicative clauses (17), in which case the range of *hai* forms is restricted. Therefore, in (16) *hai* behaves like an imperative, whereas in (17) it behaves like an exclamative. Is it possible that *hai* underwent lexicalization and turned into a (deficient) verb?

3.2. Hai *Is Not a Lexical Verb*

This section tests the verbal properties of *hai*. If *hai* is a verb, it should be compatible with an inflectional phrase and/or it should behave as a deficient verb with a bare *v*P structure. The data do not meet these criteria.

First, we test *hai* against the clitics associated with IPs. Since *hai* forms may appear by themselves, and have a reading comparable to that of imperative verbs of movement, one may expect them to also support clitic elements as the equivalent imperative verbs do. In (18), *hai* is compared to the imperative form of *pleca* "go", which supports clitic forms of short adverbs and negation.

(18) * mai hai(deţi); *nu hai(deţi)
more HAI not HAI
"Go again!" / "Do not go!"

(18') mai plecaţi; nu plecaţi
more go-2PL not go-2PL

As the examples show, the clitics compatible with imperative verbs of movement (short adverbs, negation) are not supported by *hai*, even when *hai* may have an injunctive movement reading, equivalent to "go". Therefore, *hai* does not project an IP domain.

Is it possible for *hai* to have a bare *v*P structure and behave like a non-argumental verb (e.g., "seem") that selects a "that" indicative clause? If that were the case, lack of an IP would correctly prevent NP-movement, but should not interfere with embedding and should not allow for ambiguities in the illocutionary force of *hai*. The examples in (19) do not meet these expectations.

(19) a. Maria spune că se pare că Ion nu mai vine.
Maria says that ARB-SE seems that Ion not more comes
"Maria says that it seems that Ion is not going to come."
b. * Maria spune că hai că Ion nu mai vine.
Maria says that HAI that Ion not more comes
c. Hai că m-a zăpăcit.
HAI that me-has confused
"Definitely s/he confused me." /
"Let's go because s/he confused me."

Unlike non-argumental verbs, *hai* cannot be embedded (19b) and may have ambiguous readings as either evidential or injunctive (19c). Therefore, *hai* cannot be a non-argumental verb.

The exclusive root property of *hai* indicated in (19b) may suggest a treatment as a bare *v*P with imperative reading, despite the inflectional ending.[10] If that were the case, then *hai* should be unable to appear with adverbs (because adverbs are merged in IP and *hai* has no IP), but it should occur in coordination with other imperative verbs. These predictions are not fulfilled, as shown in (20).

(20) a. Hai / haideți ușurel!
HAI /HAI-2PL slowly
"Come on slowly!"
b. * Haideți și cântați!
HAI.2PL and sing.2PL.IMP[11]

---

[10] A frequently suggested comparison is French *allez* "go", which is seen as a grammaticalized imperative. Such comparison is not fruitful because *allez* does not select a sentential complement; it also projects an IP (e.g., *allez-y* "go-there").
[11] A reviewer points out that in certain contexts, as in (i), coordination between *hai* and imperative verbs is possible:

In (20a) *hai* occurs with an adverb, whereas in (20b) it disallows coordination with imperative verbs (i.e. same imperative reading and spell-out); that is, *hai* displays an opposite behaviour to our predictions, indicating that it is not merged in a bare *v*P structure.

To sum up this section, *hai* is not a regular verb because it does not project an IP. It is not a deficient verb (i.e. a bare *v*P) because it fails to show predictable properties that would classify it either as a non-argumental/non-raising verb, or as a regular imperative. Therefore, *hai* cannot be included in the syntactic category of verbs, despite its [V] feature. This failure can be reduced to lexical properties. In particular, verbs are substantive categories, whereas pragmatic markers are functional categories.

3.3. **Hai** *Is Not an Auxiliary Verb*

Pointing out the functional status of *hai* may suggest a treatment in terms of auxiliary verbs. Indeed, there is a wide cross- and intra-linguistic variation in the merge site for auxiliaries, some of which may head clausal constituents. For example, in Romanian a form of "want" is fused with a subjunctive clause (Avram 1999), as in (21):

(21) a. O să plece.
will SBJ go-3SG
"S/he will go."

This path, however, is not available for *hai*, because there are fundamental syntactic contrasts between *hai* and auxiliaries, as follows:

– *Auxiliaries merge in IP*
(i.e. they occur with clitics, such as the negation in (21b));

b. N-o să plece.
not-will SBJ go-3SG
"S/he will not go."

(i) haideți și ajutați-mă!
come and help-me
"Come and/to help me!"

I argue that contexts as in (i) do not reflect true coordination, but rather an adjunct relation, where "and" introduces a purpose clause (there is no one-to-one mapping between *și* "and" and a coordination structure).

– *Auxiliaries do not interfere with embedding*

c. Spunea că n- o să plece.
said that not will SUBJ go-3sg
"S/he said that s/he will not go."

– *Auxiliaries do not select* că-*indicative clauses*

d. * O că pleacă.
will that go-3SG

Hai yields contrary results in the context of (21); therefore, it does not qualify as an auxiliary.

3.4. **Hai** *Is a Speech Act Head*

So far the analysis has established what *hai* is not: It is not a full-fledged, a deficient, or an auxiliary verb. It is, however, a functional category with a [V] feature whose presence in the derivation is triggered by pragmatic features (i.e. [speech act]). Therefore, where does *hai* merge? How are the inflectional endings recovered for spell-out? What is its syntactic status?

This section will address such questions by investigating the behaviour of the form *haidem*, which is shown in Table 1 to have a very restricted interpretation, namely, first person plural injunction for movement (e.g., "let's go!", "let's leave!"). The distribution of *haidem* indicates a location above ForceP, from which it joins the [V] heads chain of the core structure.

The ending on *haidem* stands for the first person plural; the form has an obligatory injunctive (versus E) reading and displays the following distribution:

(22) a. Haidem!
b. Haidem cu ei / încet / negreşit!
HAI.1PL with them slowly by.all.means
"Let's go with them/slowly/by all means."
c. Haidem să protestăm!
"Let's go to protest!" / *"Let's protest!"
d. Haidem că se protestează!
"Let's go because people are protesting." /
*"Definitely, people are protesting."

As shown in (22), *haidem* may occur in isolation (22a), or it may display adjunct constituents, such as adverbs and adverbial PPs (22b), subjunctive clauses (22c) or "that" indicative clauses (22d). Notably, these constituents are parsed as adjuncts of *haidem* unambiguously.

The first observation is that, despite its imperative reading, *haidem* is not an imperative form. Romanian has only two inflectional forms for imperative: second person singular and plural. For the rest of the person paradigm the imperative borrows the subjunctive forms. This is illustrated in (23) for the verb *veni* "come".

(23) *vino*	"come.2SG.IMP"	=	stem + *o*
veniți	"come.2PL.IMP"	=	stem + *-ți*
să venim	"SBJ come.1PL"	=	subjunctive suppletion
**venim*	"come.1PL.IMP"		

The paradigm in (23) shows *–ți* as an imperative ending (also seen in *haideți*), but not *–m*; the latter appears on the subjunctive form of the verb. How does *hai* receive a subjunctive person ending, when it is not functionally selected by a subjunctive mood-head (i.e. it is not preceded by the mood marker *să*), and there is no evidence of merge in an IP?

The second observation is that *haidem* (as all other forms of *hai*) must be clause-initial when the intonation is fluent (i.e. no significant breaks). For example, constituents as in (22b) cannot precede *haidem,* as shown in (24a), even if they receive a topic or a focus reading.

(24) a. * Cu ei / încet / negreşit haidem!
with them slowly by.all.means HAI-1PL

In (24a) *haidem* cannot support adverbs or adjunct constituents when it occurs at the end of the clause. Such a restriction does not apply to verbs with equivalent injunctive reading, as in (24b).

b. (Să mergem) cu ei / încet / negreşit (să mergem).
(SA go-1PL) with them slowly by.all.means (SA go-1PL)
"Let's go with them/slowly/by all means."

The third observation is a reminder: *Haidem* should not be able to support adverbs or adjunct constituents since it is not a verb, so it does not project an IP in which such constituents are merged. So how to account for (22b)?

These three observations on *haidem* point out that:

i. This marker is situated higher than Topic or Focus (or higher than any position to which constituents might be fronted);
ii. Such a high position must also enable it to be spelled out with the subjunctive ending *–m*;
iii. There is an underlying *v*P/IP structure in which constituents are merged (as adjuncts), although this structure is not generated by *hai*.

Since the previous section has shown that *hai* is not a verb, even in a deficient form, it follows that the *v*P/IP structure responsible for (22) must be projected by a non-lexical verb. Thus, *hai(de)* must be a functional element chain-related to the non-lexical verb, and having the interpretation restricted by this verb, in a configuration as in (25).

(25) [$_{XP\ (=\ SAP)}$ haide**m** [$_{ForceP}$ negreşit Force^0/Fin^0 ~~–**m**~~ [$_{IP}$ I^0 ~~–**m**~~ [$_{VP}$ V^0 ~~"go"~~]]]]

In (25), *haidem* is chain-related to the C/I/V-system and spells out the subjunctive *–m* morphology because the V-head is non-lexical. This non-lexical verb is interpreted as a verb of movement due to the injunctive features on *hai*. The presence of a non-lexical predicative structure as the complement of *haidem* correctly excludes subjunctive or "that" indicative clauses from this position, so only adjuncts are available as sentential constituents.

A configuration as in (25) raises two questions. One concerns the status of *haideţi*: Does the *–ţi* imperative ending follow from the configuration in (25) as well? The other question concerns the status of the head position in which *hai(dem)* merges: Is this position a Force-head, or is it different?

Empirically, both *hai* and *haideţi* occur in contexts identical to that of *haidem* in (25). This is shown in (26a) where *hai/haideţi* are self-standing, they may co-occur with an adverb, and they have an exclusive injunction-for-movement reading.

(26) a. Hai / haideți (uşurel)!
HAI HAI.2PL (slowly)
"Come on slowly!"

The free alternation between *haidem*, *hai* and *haideţi* in the same configuration indicates that all these forms occupy the same position; that is, a position above the complementizer field, since they all select a ForceP as in (25).

However, despite their stable merge site, the forms of *hai* display different selectional properties. More precisely, these forms may have a ForceP complement or not, and when a ForceP complement occurs, it may or may not contain a lexical verb, and if it has a lexical verb, it may come with an imperative, subjunctive or indicative inflection, the latter being introduced by "that". These variations are illustrated in (26b-e).

b. Hai / Haideți plecați odată!
HAI HAI.2PL go.2PL.IMP once
"C"mon, leave!"
c. Hai / Haideți să plecați, că e târziu.
HAI HAI.2PL SA go.2PL that is late
"Let's get you on the way because it's late."
d. Hai / Haideți că tare frumoşi mai sunteți!
HAI HAI.2PL that very handsome more are.2PL
"My-my, you so handsome!"
e. Hai / (*Haideți) că tare frumoşi mai sunt!
HAI (HAI.2PL) that very handsome more are.3PL

In (26b) *hai/haideți* enhance the imperative reading of the verb, adding the injunctive force but not a new event (i.e. "go" versus "go/leave so you can go"). The same takes place in (26c) where the subjunctive is substituted for the imperative form (surrogate imperative). In (26d) *hai/haideți* have an ironical evaluative interpretation. The verb in this latter construction is not imperative, so it should not constrain the person option on *hai*. However, such a constraint applies, since *haideți* is excluded if the person ending on the verb changes, as in (26e); only the morphologically non-marked *hai* may occur there[12].

The paradigm in (26) indicates that *hai/haideți* are connected to the C/I/V-chain, as in the configuration (25), because *haideți* is sensitive to changes in person/number ending on the verb. Therefore, there must be a head-chain agreement process at work. However, the person/number suffix *–ți* may be spelled out both on *hai* and on the verb, whereas the suffix *–m* could be spelled out only once (either on the verb or on *hai*). The difference in the morphological treatment within (25) may reflect a syncretic parsing of the injunctive force feature and the imperative mood feature. So speakers tend to assign morphology to *hai* when an injunctive reading is available. In that case, the imperative form is the default option, whereas the subjunctive (surrogate imperative) form is the marked option.

[12] Some speakers do not accept the form *haideți* in evaluative contexts as in (26d), where they replace it with *hai*.

The default option allows for double spell-out, the marked option does not, being harder to recuperate in an imperative context.

This view on the distribution of the *hai* allows for a uniform account of *hai* constructions, which are all compatible with the configuration in (25). The differences in interpretation between the forms of *hai* follow from the feature specifications on the head in which they are merged (i.e. [injunctive] or [E]) as well as from morpho-syntactic constraints imposed by the complements selected by these features (i.e. imperative morphology selected by [injunctive] features or indicative morphology selected by [E] features).

If the analysis is on the right track, and *hai* is invariably the selector of ForceP in (25), the next task is to define the syntactic status of *hai*. It has been shown that *hai* is the lexical manifestation of a speech act (SA) head that relates to the C/I/V system, but that does not belong to the extended domain of the verb. Although this head has a pragmatic function, it grips on the core sentence by virtue of its [V] feature.

At this point, we know that the SA-head and ForceP are in a selection relation, but we have to determine whether the SA-head is part of the ForceP field or not (e.g., if Force splits in two heads). In this respect, the data indicates separate fields, because:

– hai-*constructions cannot be embedded*

(19) b. * Maria spune că hai că Ion nu mai vine.
Maria says that HAI that Ion not more comes

Since ForceP can be embedded, then *hai* is not within but outside ForceP.

– hai *cannot select interrogative clauses*

(27) # Hai / haideți unde plecați?
HAI HAI.2PL where go.2PL
"C'mon, where are you going?"

If *hai* were a Force-head, then (27) should have allowed for an injunctive or an E-reading on the verb, because *hai* has no [Q]-features to compete with the *wh*-constituent. However, such readings are not available in (27). Instead, the interrogative is parsed as an adjunct, not as a complement of *hai* (i.e. "C'mon, tell me where you are going."). That is, *hai* heads a structure with a non-lexical verb, as in (25), to which the interrogative adjoins. Therefore, *hai* is not part of the interrogative ForceP.

The negative evidence in (19b) and (27) indicates that *hai* belongs to a separate field (the field of speech acts and other pragmatic features), and selects only certain types of ForceP (i.e. imperatives or "that" indicatives). The properties of this higher field need further exploration. For the time being, *hai* provides empirical evidence for the existence of the field, and points out the intrinsic verbal nature of the speech acts.

4. The Category of Speech Acts

As shown in (2), *hai* is not the only lexical manifestation of speech acts. Looking at the type of elements that may alternate with *hai*, one common feature is salient; namely, all these elements (adverbs, modal, or grammaticalized verbs) are intrinsically [+V, –N]. Furthermore, they occur with "that" indicative complements and yield an E-reading, on a par with *hai* constructions. This section argues that all these elements have the same syntactic-pragmatic status as *hai*, and merge as speech act heads. The sub-sections present the tests that indicate their speech act status.

4.1. Adverbs

This section argues that adverbs compatible with the construction in (2b) underwent grammaticalization and became speech act heads that select a "that" indicative clause. The relevant class contains adverbs with evaluative (*bine* "well"), evidential (*normal* "obviously") or epistemic (*probabil* "probably") readings, and includes the interjection *zău* (2a), which may modify an adverb (e.g., *zău aşa* 'very much so"). Consider the adverb *precis* "clearly", "certainly".

(28) a. **Precis** că merge la mare!
clearly that goes to sea
"Clearly s/he's going to the sea shore (I can bet)!"
b. **Precis** merge la mare.
clearly/certainly goes to sea
"I can bet s/he goes to the sea." /
"It is certain that s/he goes to the sea."
c. Se ştie **precis** unde merge.
REFL knows exactly where goes
"It is known exactly where s/he goes."

The evidential reading in (28a) involves high pitch on the adverb; the pitch is lowered for the other readings, irrespective of their propositional (28b) or predicational (28c) scope.[13]

The contrast between the adverbial form in (28a) and the adverbs in (28b-c) is not only prosodic and interpretive, but also syntactic. Thus, modifiers may occur only on the non-evidential versions, as in (29).

(29) a. * [Mai **precis**] că merge la mare!
more clearly that goes to sea
b. Mai **precis** merge la mare.
more exactly goes to sea
"More precisely s/he goes to the sea."
c. Se ştie mai **precis** acum unde merge.
REFL knows more exactly now where goes
"It is known more exactly now where s/he goes."

In (29a) mai "more" cannot modify the evidential but it can modify the punctual version of the adverb. Since the evidential merges in a V-head position, lack of local adverbial modification is expected (i.e. adverbs merge as AdvP in Spec-positions not in head positions).

Furthermore, substitution of the adverb with an adverbial PP (i.e. *în mod precis* "in way precise/exactly") is successful only in the absence of *că* "that":

(30) a. * În mod precis că merge la mare!
in way precise that goes to sea
b. În mod précis merge la mare.
in way precise goes to sea
"I bet s/he goes to the sea." /
"It is certain that s/he goes to the sea."
c. Calculatorul socoteşte în mod precis sumele.
calculator.the calculates in way precise additions.the
"The calculator makes the additions with precision."

In (30) the expression *în mod precis* "in way precise" takes over the interpretation of the adverbs it replaces (i.e. evidential or other), so the ungrammaticality of (30a) cannot be attributed to semantic restrictions, but to the syntax: The PP can be substituted to another XP but not to a non-phrasal category in head position.

In sum, the data show that when the adverb precedes a "that" indicative

[13] High pitch on evidential adverbs is different from the intonation on Focus constituents.

clause, as in (29a), it cannot project a phrasal structure (AdvP) in which adverbial modifiers could merge. This property correctly predicts the ban on adverbial PPs in (30a); that is, free alternation between adverb and PP in (30a) is barred because the adverb preceding *că* "that" is not a syntactic equivalent to the PP (i.e. it is not XP but X)[14]. If the adverbial element in (29a) and (30a) is an X category, then it merges in a head position above *că* "that" (versus the Specifier of "that"). That corresponds to the SA *hai* occupies in (25), hence the possibility of free alternation between these elements, as in (1a) and (2).

4.2. Grammaticalized Verbs and Modals

Sections 2.2.3 and 2.2.4 showed that grammaticalized verbs[15] and modals[16] are unable to generate bi-clausal structures. The arguments are:

- absence of an IP domain, because clitics associated with such a domain are excluded;
- absence of a bare *v*P structure, because the argumental structure and selectional properties of the full-fledged counterpart are lost.

Such observations point out that these verbal forms have a functional versus substantive status, but give no indications of where they merge in the derivation. In particular, these verbal forms merge either in a (split) Force-head above *că* "that", or outside ForceP, in the head of a field with different properties. Restrictions on embedding, as shown in (31), will

---

[14] There are some adverbial expressions that may occur in front of *că* "that" despite their PP structure, e.g. *cu siguranţă că* "with certainty that". These expressions are re-analyzed as one element merged in SA^0. A test with modifiers is telling: If a modifier can occur before the preposition, then the expression works as a head, and the modifier is in the specifier of that head (e.g., [**mai** [cu *siguranţă*]] "more with certainty"); if the modifier occurs after the preposition, then the expression is a true PP (e.g., [în mod [**foarte**] sigur] "in way very certain"). The former can be an SA-head, whereas the latter cannot.

[15] Grammaticalized verbs in ostensive expressions are not relevant to the issue. These verbs retain enough substantive properties to generate bi-clausal structures. E.g., *Uite-l că vine* "look-him that comes" ("Here he comes!"). Ostensive and E-readings follow from different syntactic configurations.

[16] Romanian "can" is compatible with all the instances shown for "must". It is not used for illustrations because it may also appear with an indicative without "that", which makes it difficult to decide when this modal is within or outside ForceP, e.g. *Poate (că) vine* "Perhaps (that) s/he comes" versus *Trebuie *(că) vine* "Probably that s/he comes".

clarify this point.

Embedding is ruled out for these grammaticalized verbs:

(31) a. * Spune că trebuie că vine.
says that must that comes
intended "S/he says that s/he might be coming."
b. * Spune că lasă/lăsați că vine.
says that let let-2pl that comes
intended "S/he says that s/he's definitely coming."

An E-reading, as in (31a-b) is generally compatible with embedding, as in (31c-d).

c. Spune că trebuie să-i fi plăcut.
says that must SBJ-him be pleased
'S/he says that it must have pleased him/her."
d. Spune că precis vrea să vină.
says that undoubtedly wants SBJ comes
"S/he says that undoubtedly s/he wants to come."

In (31c) the grammaticalized modal "must" has an E-reading, comparable to the E-reading on the adverbial form in (31d). The difference between "must" in (31c) and (31a) is that the former is followed by a "that" indicative clause, yielding a recursive ForceP embedding, whereas the latter directly precedes the embedded substantive verb, with no evidence of Force (i.e. "that") intervening between them.

Compatibility of epistemic (31c) and evidential (31d) readings with embedding indicates that the ungrammaticality in (31a-b) does not concern the semantics, but the syntax. More precisely, the presence of the grammaticalized verb forms interferes with the selection of "that"-ForcePs. Hence, the grammaticalized verbs in (31a, b) do not belong to ForceP, but to a higher field.

In sum, the properties of the grammaticalized verbs and modals match the properties of *hai*: There is a cluster of [[V], [speech act]] features and they yield an E-reading in the presence of a "that"-clause. These elements merge above "that"-ForceP, in a configuration compatible with (25).

At this point, one may wonder about examples as in (4c), where an element with clear DP status may also license *că* "that" root clauses. The version of (4c) repeated below indicates that *hai* may also be inserted in this construction.

(4') c. Doamne hai că frumos mai e azi!
god HAI that nice more is today
"Goodness, what a nice day today!"

Syntactically, a DP like *doamne* "god" may merge only in Spec-positions. Its co-occurrence with *hai* indicates the merge site as [Spec,*hai*]. Therefore, constructions as in (4c) show that the SA-head may be optionally spelled-out when another lexical marking is available (e.g., an exclamative DP) for speaker-orientation.[17]

To conclude section 4, adverbial and verbal elements that alternate with *hai*, as in (1a) and (2), display similar interpretive and syntactic properties. Hence, these elements must be classified together not only in the discourse/semantics (i.e. pragmatic markers), but also in the grammar (i.e. speech act heads).

5. Conclusions and Implications

This chapter looked at Romanian constructions where the pragmatic marker *hai* precedes a "that" indicative clause in a root context, as in (1a), and yields an evaluative or evidential reading. Absence or presence of *hai* decides on the grammaticality of the clause (1b). The questions raised for this construction were:

(Q1) Why is the pragmatic marker important for the grammaticality of the clause?
(Q2) What is the left periphery of a "that" indicative clause in a root context?

The analysis answered the first question by defining *hai* as a morpho-pragmatic element with a [V] feature (i.e. it displays person/number endings as in Table 1). The [V] feature clusters with speech act features and yields a speaker-oriented reading that can be injunctive or E(xpressive), according to the type of clause *hai* initiates (i.e. imperative or "that" indicative, respectively). The syntactic behaviour of *hai* (i.e. c-command and selectional properties) provided arguments for defining this element as a Speech Act (SA) head visible in the derivation; the SA-head belongs to a higher (pragmatic) field and selects a ForceP, as in (25). Furthermore, the way in which *hai* may spell out the person/number

[17] For a detailed analysis of constituents in [Spec,SAP] positions, see Hill (2007b).

ending of the subjunctive paradigm (i.e. *haidem*) indicated that the SA-head is connected to the C/I/V local chain in the core (ForceP) structure.

Accordingly, the answer to the second question has to acknowledge the impact of the pragmatic marker on the syntactic derivation. There is no justification for the occurrence of a "that" indicative clause in root context other than the probing from the SA-head. The exact configuration of the left periphery depends on the interaction (i.e. for syntactic checking) between the properties of SA and the morpho-syntax of the substantive verb to which the SA is computationally chained.

Other grammaticalized forms may alternate with *hai* in the context of (1a), allowing for comparable E-readings, as in (2). Despite their varied categorial source (i.e. interjection, adverb, verb), these alternatives to *hai* display a similar feature cluster (i.e. [V], [speech act]) and a similar syntactic behaviour (i.e. X vs. XP elements, c-commanding ForceP). Therefore, *hai* is not an isolated phenomenon, but a member of a class of lexical items that may merge as heads in the speech act field. In discourse/semantics, these items may all be labelled as *pragmatic markers*; in syntax, they belong to the functional category of *speech acts*.

Summing up the findings, the analysis proposed in this article contributes the following information to the debate on the pragmatics-syntax interface:

A. The SA-head has a [V] feature clustered with the SA-features.
B. The SA-head has selectional properties (i.e. [–Q] versus [+Q] sentential complements; imperative clauses)
C. The SA-head is outside ForceP.
D. The SA-head is connected to the V-heads chain in the core syntax (e.g., SA items display spell out copies of endings or verb stems).
E. The injunctive versus E-reading on the SA-head follows from a correlation between speech act features and the CP types available for selection (i.e. imperative or "that"-indicative clauses).

Generalizations stemming from this analysis must account for intra- and cross-linguistic variation in the way in which SA-heads are instantiated. More precisely, when SA-heads are projected (i.e. in speaker-oriented sentences), they occur at the highest level of the left edge and belong to a pragmatic field, distinct from ForceP, but connected to it, as in (25). In such a configuration, the speaker-oriented interpretation follows from the syntactic checking of the [[V], [speech act]] feature cluster. Intra- and cross-linguistic variation is expected in the implementation of the checking process. For example, the SA may be overt or covert; an overt

SA may be realized through direct merge (as seen in all the examples of this paper) or through V-movement to SA. Certain imperative constructions in Romanian, as in (32a), may be seen as cases of V-movement to SA.

(32) a. Ia vino mai repede!
PRT come.IMP.2SG more fast
"Come faster!"
b. Vine-vine!
c. (*nu) / (*mai) vine-vine!
(not) (more) comes-comes
"Coming!"

Hill (2007c) shows that the particle *ia*, as in (32a), is a clitic pragmatic marker for injunctive SA^0. This element belongs to the cluster of proclitics on the verb and triggers V-movement to SA^0 for checking. Furthermore, the reduplication of verbs, associated with high pitch, as in (32b), also points to a V copy in SA^0. As a result of the V-copying in SA^0 (without deletion of the lower copy), elements usually associated with the inflectional field cannot be allowed in the derivation, as shown in (32c).

On the other hand, SA^0 may be covertly checked, through distance Agree with the V-heads in the core structure. That may be the case in languages where V does not move very high in the left periphery, or where lexical pragmatic markers are not available for direct merge. If imperative mood is related to (or licensed by) the [injunctive] features in the SA^0, as it seems to be indicated in the present discussion, then one must reconsider the analysis of imperative constructions in this light, as a possible instantiation of covert checking of the SA-features.

References

Avram, L. 1999. *Auxiliaries and the Structure of Language*. Bucharest: Editura Universității din București.

Chomsky, N. 2001. Derivation by phase. In M. Kenstowicz (ed.), *Ken Hale: A Life in Language*. Cambridge, MA: MIT Press, 1-52.

Cinque, G. 1999. *Adverbs and Functional Heads: A Cross-Linguistic Perspective*. New York: Oxford University Press.

Cornilescu, A. 2000. The double subject construction in Romanian. In V.

Motapanyane (ed.), *Comparative Studies in Romanian Syntax*. Oxford: Elsevier, 83-134.

Croitor-Balaciu, B. 2006 Interjecția. In Institutul de Cercetări Lingvistice (eds), *Gramatica Limbii Române*. Bucharest: Editura Academiei.

Gramatica Academiei Române. 1963. Bucharest: Editura Academiei.

Hill, V. 2006. Stylistic inversion in Romanian. *Studia Linguistica* 60, 156-180.

Hill, V. 2007a. Romanian adverbs and the pragmatic field. *The Linguistic Review* 24, 61-86.

Hill, V. 2007b. Vocatives and the pragmatics-syntax interface. *Lingua* 117, 2077-2105.

Hill, V. 2007c. An imperative marker. In G. Alboiu, L. Avram & D. Isac (eds.), *Pitar Mos: A Building with a View*. Bucharest: Editura Universității din București, 153-166.

Moro, A. 2003, Notes on vocative case: A case study in clause structure. In J. Quer, J. Schroten, M. Scorretti, P. Sleeman & E. Verheugd (eds.), *Romance Languages and Linguistic Theory 2001: Selected Papers from "Going Romance", Amsterdam, 6-8 December 2001*. Amsterdam: John Benjamins, 247-261.

Rizzi, L. 1997. The fine structure of the left periphery. In L. Haegeman (ed.), *Elements of Grammar*. Dordrecht: Kluwer, 281-337.

Rizzi, L. 2004. Locality and left periphery. In A. Belletti (ed.), *Structures and Beyond: The Cartography of Syntactic Structures*, vol. 3. New York: Oxford University Press, 1-27.

Roberts, I. 1997. Restructuring, head movement, and locality. *Linguistic Inquiry* 28, 423-460.

Searl, J.R. 1969. *Speech Acts: An Essay in the Philosophy of Language*. Cambridge: Cambridge University Press.

Sigurðsson, H.Á. 2004. The syntax of person, tense, and speech features. *Rivista di Linguistica* 16, 219-251.

Speas, M. 2004. Evidentiality, logophoricity and the syntactic representation of pragmatic features. *Lingua* 114, 255-276.

Speas, M. & C. Tenny. 2003. Configurational properties of point of view roles. In A.-M. Di Sciullo (ed.), *Asymmetry in Grammar*. Amsterdam: John Benjamins, 315-344.

Tenny, C. 2005. Predicate-argument structure and the grammar of sentience. Paper presented at the *Issues on the Form and Interpretation of Argument Structure* workshop, Harvard University.

Teodorescu, E. 1972. *Propoziția subiectivă*. Bucharest: Editura Științifică.

Tschizmarova, I. 2005. The analysis of the Bulgarian discourse marker *hajde*. *Journal of Pragmatics* 37, 1143-1163.

CHAPTER TEN

ON THE EDGE OF DP: DIFFERENT ARGUMENTS, DIFFERENT EDGES*

Tabea Ihsane

1. Introduction

1.1. General Aims and Proposals

This paper examines some indefinites in French, namely *un*-NPs "a(n)-NP" and *du/des*-NPs "of.the-NPs" in argument positions, in opposition to predicative positions. *Un*-NPs are indefinites with the indefinite article and *du/des*-NPs involve the so-called 'partitive article' *du/des*.

The main aim of the paper is to account for the different interpretations of these indefinites and more precisely to determine how interpretation and structure are related. This implies an analysis of the internal structure of these nominals, in particular of their left periphery.

What I propose in this paper is that the indefinites under study have an extendable telescopic left periphery whose size is related to the feature content of the nominal expression. More precisely, I argue that their left periphery may be of different sizes and contain 3, 2, or 1 projections depending on their interpretation. The size of these noun phrases corresponds to arguments of different semantic types, namely the canonical types <e> and <<e,t>, t> and property-denoting arguments (McNally 1995, 1998, van Geenhoven 1996, Dobrovie-Sorin 1997). In other words, the left periphery of referential indefinites differs from the one of quantificational indefinites which differs from the one of property-denoting arguments. The composition of the left periphery of these indefinites is responsible for several of their characteristics, such as their

---

* The ideas presented in this paper have been developed in my PhD dissertation (Ihsane 2006), published as Ihsane (2008). Warmest thanks to the audience of the conference *Edges in Syntax* for their questions and comments, in particular to Ellen-Petra Kester, Tom Roeper and Petra Sleeman, and to an anonymous reviewer for helpful remarks.

(lack of) scope properties. Assuming that arguments differ structurally from predicates, I argue that the determiners *un* and *du/des* move to the edge of the structure for the nominal to function as an argument.

1.2. Framework

The framework of this paper is that of generative grammar initiated by Chomsky some fifty years ago (Chomsky 1957, 1965, 1981, 1986) and of the theory of Principles and Parameters.

A development in generative grammar adopted here is the so-called 'cartographic approach' to syntax (see Rizzi 1997, 2001, Cinque 1999 as well as the collections of Cinque 2002, Rizzi 2004a, and Belletti 2004, to mention a few references of the last decade), which investigates the make-up of functional categories in the clause, and by extension in nominals. Essentially, it consists in identifying distinct positions in the structure dedicated to different interpretations. At the foundation of the cartographic research is the idea that inflectional morphemes are distributed in the syntax, a view based on the analysis of the English inflectional system (Chomsky 1957). This means that the atoms of syntactic computations can be morphemes, i.e. elements which are not autonomous words.

One idea developed in the cartographic approach is that the nominal structure, on a par with the clausal structure, can be split into three domains, the left periphery, the inflectional domain and the NP/VP-shells:[1]

(1) a. $\underbrace{[_{DP} \ldots [_{DP}}_{\text{Left periphery}} \underbrace{[_{FPadj1} \ldots [_{FPadj2} \ldots}_{\text{Inflectional domain}} \underbrace{[_{nP} \ldots [_{NP} ..]}_{\text{NP/VP-shells}}]]]]]$
b. $[_{CP} \ldots [_{CP} \quad [_{FPadv1} \ldots [_{FPadv2} \ldots \quad [_{vP} \ldots [_{VP} ..]]]]]]$

Left periphery   Inflectional domain   NP/VP-shells

The left periphery generally subsumes notions like topic and focus. In the nominal structure, it is also often associated to features related to the D head such as (in)definiteness, specificity or referentiality. The inflectional domain is the domain where agreement features are checked and where modifiers are generated. Finally, the NP/VP-shells represent the domain

[1] For the clausal left periphery, see Rizzi (1997) and for its nominal counterpart Aboh (2003) to mention but two references. For the thematic domain, see Larson (1988), Chomsky (1995), Grimshaw (1990), and Valois (1991), for example. The tripartite conception represented in (1) parallels the one found in Platzack (2001) and Grohmann (2003) for the clause as well as Grohmann & Haegeman (2003) and Haegeman (2004) for the nominal structure.

where the arguments of the noun or verb are merged, i.e. the thematic domain. Each domain may consist of several discrete functional heads. As a consequence, the DP-layer may be replaced by several functional projections.

Another important assumption in our framework is the theory of Relativized Minimality as formulated in (2) (Rizzi 1990).

(2) … X … Z … Y… (Rizzi 1990:1)

In essence, the idea is that structural relations have to be local. In (2) for example, a local relation between X and Y is impossible if Z has certain characteristics with X and intervenes between X and Y. These shared characteristics have been defined in terms of features and more precisely in classes of features. The typology advocated by Rizzi (2004b) is reported in (3). For a justification of this classification the reader is referred to the original paper.

(3)
a. Argumental: person, number, gender, case
b. Quantificational: Wh, Neg, measure, focus…
c. Modifier: evaluative, epistemic, Neg, frequentative, celerative, measure, manner…
d. Topic

(Rizzi 2004b, (61))

As my analysis focuses on arguments, it will be directly concerned with one aspect of this classification, namely (3)a. In effect, my study of *un*-NPs and *du/des*-NPs will allow me to refine this class of features (section 2.4).

In addition to Relativized Minimality, I adopt two further positions. The first one is that arguments and predicates are structurally different (Higginbotham 1987). One way of formalizing this assumption is reported in (4).

(4) A "nominal expression" is an argument only if it is introduced by a category D. (Longobardi 1994: 620)

However, as in the framework adopted here, DP represents a domain of projections rather than a single layer, (4) needs to be refined. What I propose is (5), which specifies which projection of the nominal left periphery, i.e. of the DP domain, is required to turn a predicate into an argument.

(5) A "nominal expression" is an argument only if it is introduced by the lowest layer of the DP domain (the left periphery).

As for the second assumption, it concerns the syntax-semantics interface. The view adopted here is the one traditionally found in Extended Standard Theory and subsequent work, according to which syntactic structures cannot give rise to ambiguity. In other words, when the semantics gets to interpret a structure, only one reading is possible. In this vein, it predicts that *un*-NPs and *du/des*-NPs with different meanings differ structurally.

The paper is organized as follows. Section 2 concerns the left periphery of *un*-NPs and *du/des*-NPs and section 3 their inflectional domain. Section 2.1 introduces the reader to the three-way typology of indefinites adopted here and to the characteristics of these nominals which will play a role in the analysis put forward. Section 2.2 briefly reports the issues to be addressed. Section 2.3 presents my proposals and some consequences of the analysis advocated. Section 2.4 summarizes the main ideas concerning the left periphery. The aim of the section dealing with the inflectional domain is reported in section 3.1, the analysis proposed for the inflectional domain of *un*-NPs and *du/des*-NPs in section 3.2 and an account for the partitive reading of these indefinites in section 3.3. Section 3.4 summarizes the most important points on the inflectional domain and section 4 is the conclusion of the paper.

2. The Left Periphery

2.1. Introduction: A Three-Way Typology

The study of argumental *un*-NPs and *du/des*-NPs shows that these indefinites may have three readings, and not two as traditionally assumed for indefinites (Milsark 1974, Fodor & Sag 1982, Enç 1991, Diesing 1992). They may be referential, quantificational and interpreted as properties, which corroborates the findings in Dobrovie-Sorin & Beyssade (2004). As the aim here is to determine the relation between interpretation and structure, I will discuss each interpretation in turn, mentioning some of the specificities which will play a role in my analysis. To anticipate, the conception of the syntax-semantics interface adopted here predicts that *un*-NPs and *du/des*-NPs with different meanings have different internal structures. This is because a structure cannot be ambiguous, i.e. it can only give rise to a single reading.

2.1.1. *Referential Noun Phrases*

That indefinite noun phrases may be referential is not new (Donnellan 1978, Wilson 1978, Fodor & Sag 1982, Dobrovie-Sorin & Beyssade 2004). Examples of referential *un*-NPs and *du/des*-NPs are provided in (6) and (7) respectively.

(6) a. Un de mes étudiants a obtenu son doctorat. (*Paul*)
b. A_r student of mine got his Ph.D. (Heim 1991, (135))

(7) Des amis que j'ai rencontrés hier m'ont insulté.
of.the friends whom I have met yesterday me.have offended
(*referential*) (Bosveld-de Smet 1998: 33)

In (6), *un de mes étudiants* refers to Paul if the speaker has this individual in mind. In (7), the referential reading is supported by the presence of the relative clause modifying *des amis*. In both cases, however, the reference of these indefinites depends on the speaker. In other words, these nominals encode speaker's reference (Kripke 1977) in that they refer to an entity the speaker has in mind. This kind of reference typically contrasts with the reference associated with definite noun phrases like *the*-NPs which is rigid.

The reference of *un*-NPs and *du/des*-NPs may also depend on a universal quantifier. This is illustrated in (8), where the members of the Royal Family may co-vary with the students.

(8) Tous les étudiants ont raconté plusieurs histoires qui
all the students have told several stories that
impliquaient des membres de la famille royale.
involved of.the members of the family royal

When the members of the Royal Family co-vary with the students, they can crucially be identified. For example, in a world with three students {1,2,3} and three members of the Royal Family {Lady Diana, Prince Charles, and Camilla Parker-Bowles}, student 1 could tell stories about Lady Diana and Prince Charles, student 2 about Lady Diana, Prince Charles and Camilla Parker-Bowles, and student 3 about Prince Charles and Camilla Parker-Bowles.[2] As the members of the Royal Family can be identified, it means that *des membres de la famille royale*, in this reading,

[2] Of course, the above illustration is not an exhaustive list of the potential combinations of students and members of the Royal Family.

is referential. However, this reference is dependent in the sense that it co-varies with the universal quantifier. More generally, this shows that referential indefinites have a dependent reference. As in most cases, the reference depends on the speaker, I will use the terms S(peaker)-referential.

These referential indefinites are existential in the sense that they assert existence. Consider the following example:

(9)	Jean	aime	une	femme.	(C'est Claire.)
	John	loves	a	woman	it.is Claire

Although (9) has several readings, let us concentrate on the one which states that John loves a particular woman, whose identity seems to be known by the speaker but not by the hearer. If no such woman exists, the sentence is false. This is supported by the paraphrase below:

(10) There is an x, x is a woman, and John loves x.

What (10) does, is, by the means of the semantic formula *there is an x…*, assert that x exists. In other words, S-referential *un*-NPs introduce an entity in the discourse and assert its existence.

As for *du*-NPs, the referential reading is considered as impossible (Bosveld-de Smet 1998: 33, Dobrovie-Sorin & Beyssade 2004). Consider (11):

(11)	*	De l'étoffe	que	j'avais	achetée hier	traînait	par terre.
		of the.material	that	I.had	bought yesterday	lay	on floor

(Bosveld-de Smet 1998: 68)

In (11), *de l'étoffe*, which is mass, cannot be modified by the relative clause, suggesting that it cannot be referential (compare with (7)).

2.1.2. Quantificational Noun Phrases

Indefinites may also be quantificational (Fodor & Sag 1982, Diesing 1992, Dobrovie-Sorin & Beyssade 2004). In this reading they express a subset contrasted with another subset (12a) or a subset of a set which has been previously introduced in the discourse (12b). It is a covert partitive reading. Examples of quantificational indefinites are provided in (12):

(12) a. Des filles étaient blondes, d'autres avaient les
of.the girls were blond of.others had the
cheveux foncés.
hair dark
b. Dans ce champ, du maïs est pollué.
in this field of.the corn is polluted
(Bosveld-de Smet 1998: 15, citing Kleiber 1988)

In (12a), *des filles* is contrasted with *d'autres* and in (12b), *du maïs* is a subset of *ce champ*. Crucially, the blond girls in (12a) cannot be identified.

2.1.3. Property-Denoting Noun Phrases

Finally, argumental *un*-NPs and *du/des*-NPs can be interpreted as properties (Dobrovie-Sorin 1997, Dobrovie-Sorin & Beyssade 2004). This presupposes that properties can function as arguments. That argumental indefinites can be properties has been proposed by Higginbotham (1985) but this approach has only been developed recently in the literature (McNally 1995, van Geenhoven 1996, Dobrovie-Sorin 1996, Farkas & de Swart 2003, Chung & Ladusaw 2004). One characteristic of property-denoting indefinites is that their interpretation is undetermined. Consider (13).

(13) a. Un chien aboie, mais je ne sais pas lequel.
a dog is.barking but I NE know not which.one
b. Des chiens aboient, mais je ne sais pas lequels.
of.the dogs are.barking but I NE know not which.ones

What (13a) tells us is that there is an individual which has the property of being a dog and which is barking. However, it is impossible to identify this individual. The same applies for the plural *des chiens* in (13b).

Another characteristic of property-denoting arguments is that they are associated with narrow scope in examples like (14), all taken or adapted from Bosveld-de Smet (2004, (20)).

(14) a. Il y avait un visiteur tous les jours.
there was a visitor each day
(*each day there is a visitor, but not necessarily the same*)
b. Il y avait de la visite tous les jours.
there were of the people each day
(*each day there are visitors, but not necessarily the same*)

c. Des voyous ont volé deux bicyclettes.
of.the naughty boys have stolen two bicycles
(*no more than two bicycles are involved in the robbery*)

In (14a), for instance, *un visiteur* cannot take scope on *tous les jours*. It has to be in the scope of the universal, i.e. it has 'narrow scope'.[3]

Furthermore, property-denoting indefinites do not necessarily assert existence, a fact often neglected in the literature. This concerns intensional contexts like (15) for example.

(15) a. Jean veut un chat/des chats.
John wants a cat/of.the cats
b. Jean cherche un chat/des chats.
John is.looking.for a cat/of.the cats

Examples like (15) can perfectly be uttered if there is no cat, i.e. if no cat exists. This is not the case with a predicate like *attraper*:

(16) Jean a attrapé un chat/des chats.
John has caught a cat/of.the cats

In (16), *un chat* and *des chats* are existential, i.e. they assert existence. This means that if no cat exists the sentence is false (in opposition to a presupposition failure which would arise with a presuppositional noun phrase). To account for the fact that property-denoting indefinites may be existential (16) or not (15), it has been proposed that the lexical representation of the predicates selecting them should be refined (McNally 1995). The idea is that the lexical representation of some predicates may supply an existential operator to (some of) their variables as shown in (17a) (see also Dobrovie-Sorin 1997). (17b), in contrast, is the representation of *catch* selecting a referential argument. This is possible both in (15) and (16) if the cat (or the cats) in these examples refers to an individual in particular.

(17) a. catch $\Rightarrow \lambda P\ \lambda w\ \lambda x\ \exists y\ (\mathbf{catch}_w\ (x,y) \wedge P_w\ (y))$, where P is a variable of type <s,<e,t>>, w of type s, and x of type e
b. catch $\Rightarrow \lambda w\ \lambda y \lambda x\ (\mathbf{catch}_w\ (x,y))$
(van Geenhoven & Mc Nally 2005: 895)

[3] In section 2.3.1, I suggest that in fact this type of indefinites doesn't have scope properties at all (cf. Enç 1991).

To account for the non-existential reading mentioned for (15), van Geenhoven & McNally propose a semantic decomposition of verbs à la Quine (1960). Quine argues that the complement of verbs of absence like *seek*, *want* and *look for* are interpreted as a proposition and therefore that the verb should be decomposed into a propositional attitude and a relation between individuals, i.e. for example *try* and *find* respectively. In other terms, *seek* means *try to find*. Indefinite complements of *seek* are existential (transparent reading) when they take wide scope with respect to *try*. In contrast, they are not existential (opaque reading) when they take narrow scope with respect to *try*. The latter reading is illustrated in (18).

(18) look for $\Rightarrow \lambda P\ \lambda w\ \lambda x$ (**look for**$_w$ (x,P))
where **look for**$_w$ $(x,P) = 1$ iff in the world of evaluation w an individual x is trying in w to bring it about that there is an individual y in a world w' which x finds in w' and which is P in w'
(van Geenhoven & McNally 2005: 896)

Although the details of (17) and (18) are not relevant for current purposes, what is crucial is that the lexical representation of the predicate may account for the existential reading or lack thereof of property-denoting indefinites.

2.2. *The Puzzle*

The puzzle I will tackle concerning the left periphery of nominals is the following. I would like to provide an analysis of argumental *un*-NPs and *du/des*-NPs which accounts for three of their characteristics, namely their (lack of) existentiality, their (lack of) scope properties and their (lack of) referential/quantificational interpretation. Many of the above issues have been (partially) addressed in the literature. For example, van Geenhoven & McNally (2005) deal with the lack of existential entailment of some indefinites, McNally (1995) with the lack of scope properties of some indefinites, Dobrovie-Sorin & Beyssade (2004) with the categorical difference between indefinites. Although most of them touch upon two of the features mentioned above or sometimes even the three of them, they do not provide a systematic analysis of *all three* characteristics. To combine the three characteristics mentioned is crucial to obtain a clear and fine-grained picture of indefinites and essential as these features are related.

2.3. *The Proposal*

2.3.1. *The Structure*

What I propose is that the composition of the left periphery of *un*-NPs and *du/des*-NPs varies with their different interpretations. More precisely I suggest that the left periphery of these indefinites may comprise one, two or three projections as shown in (19), (21) and (22), where PropP stands for Property Phrase, QP for Quantifier Phrase and SRefP for S-reference Phrase. (19) is the structure I propose for property-denoting *un*-NPs and *du/des*-NPs.

(19) *Property-denoting arguments:* PropP (> NumP…)

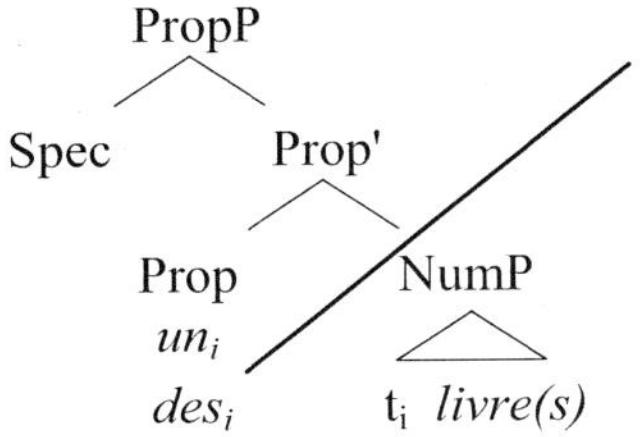

The idea is that the left periphery of property-denoting arguments contains a single projection, labelled Property Phrase (PropP). The function of this layer is to turn a predicative noun phrase, which is a Number Phrase (NumP), into an argument (recall (5)). In other words, what distinguishes properties functioning as arguments from properties functioning as predicates is the presence vs. absence of PropP. Properties functioning as arguments were illustrated in section 2.1.3. (20), in contrast, is an example of properties functioning as predicates.

(20) a. Mon fils est un petit coquin.
my son is a.MASC little.MASC rascal. MASC

b. Ma fille est une petite coquine.
my daughter is a.FEM little.FEM rascal.FEM

c. Mes enfants sont des petits coquins.
my children are of.the little.PL rascals.PL

As *un petit coquin*, *une petite coquine* and *des petits coquins* in (20) agree with *mon fils, ma fille* and *mes enfants* respectively, it shows that these predicative noun phrases encode number, on a par with the properties functioning as arguments (section 2.1.3). The proposal is that only the latter contain a PropP. This projection contains the determiner (*un, du, des*) which has moved from its base-position. The projection encoding number is discussed in section 3.2, as well as the details on the positions where determiners are generated.

As for the left periphery of quantificational arguments, I propose that it is more complex in that it contains the PropP advocated in (19) and a Quantifier Phrase (QP).

(21) *Quantificational arguments:* QP > PropP (> NumP…)

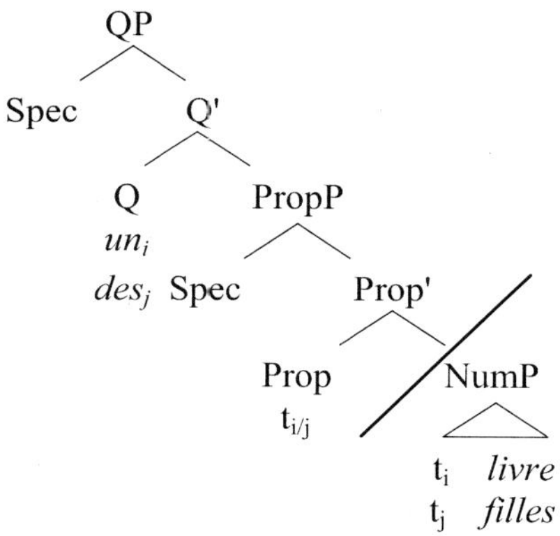

PropP in (21) allows these indefinites to function as arguments, whereas QP encodes the quantificational feature responsible for its quantificational reading. In addition, I propose that it is the presence of this projection which allows us to distinguish between noun phrases which undergo Quantifier Raising (QR) at Logical Form (LF) and those which do not, like property-denoting indefinites (19) (recall (14)). Informally, it means that the QR mechanism will look for a structure containing a QP layer and will move it to a higher position at LF. In (21), the determiner head-moves from its base position to Q, through Prop.

Finally, I argue that the left periphery of S-referential indefinites is even more complex and that it comprises three projections, PropP, QP, and SRefP which encodes speaker's reference (why the SRefP and QP layers cannot be in complementary distribution is addressed in section 2.3.3). The determiner moves to SRef, through Prop and Q.

(22) *S-referential arguments:* SRefP > QP > PropP (> NumP…)

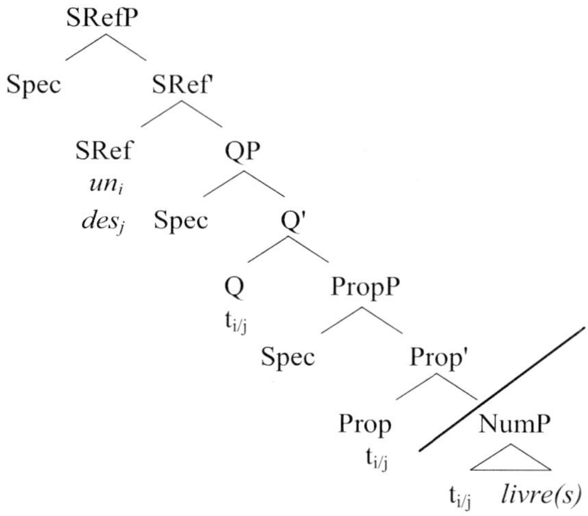

A structure like (22), which contains a QP layer, predicts that these indefinites have scope properties. This prediction is borne out as we will see in section 2.3.3. But before turning to the scope properties of this type of indefinites, let us see what motivates the above structures, namely scope interactions.

2.3.2. Scope Interactions

The analysis presented in the preceding section is motivated by scope interactions. (23) illustrates the interaction between a quantificational indefinite and a property-denoting indefinite. *Sm*, i.e. *some* without the vowels, is a so-called weak indefinite, which is interpreted as our property-denoting arguments. As indicated in parenthesis, *sm* cannot take scope over the universal. In other terms, at LF, the universal quantifier can bypass the property-denoting indefinite (23a) (from Diesing (1992)) whereas the indefinite cannot bypass the universal (23b).

(23) a. Sm cellists played every suite today. (∀> *sm*); *(*sm* > ∀)
     b. Every cellist played sm suite. (∀> *sm*); *(*sm* > ∀)

(24) illustrates the same kind of interaction but between two *un*-NPs in French. *Un violoncelliste* is a property-denoting indefinite whereas *une*

suite is quantificational and is interpreted as *une des suites* "one of.the suites". The only reading of this sentence is a reading where the quantificational *un*-NP takes scope over the property-denoting *un*-NP. This means that the former bypasses the latter at LF.

(24) [$_{PropP}$ Un violoncelliste] a joué [$_{QP}$ une suite] aujourd'hui.
a cellist has played a suite today
(*where* une suite = une des suites *"one of.the suites"*)

(25) illustrates the interaction between two quantificational noun phrases. The interpretation of these examples shows that it is the subject which takes scope over the other quantifier. This means that at LF a quantificational noun phrase cannot bypass another quantificational NP.

(25) a. Tous les étudiants ont lu un livre.
all the students have read a book
($\forall > un_Q$); *($un_Q > \forall$)
b. Un étudiant a acheté tous les journaux.
a student has bought all the newspapers
($un_Q > \forall$); *($\forall > un_Q$)

(26) illustrates the interaction between a quantifier and an S-referential indefinite. As the latter takes scope on the former in both examples, it means that S-referential indefinites may bypass quantifiers at LF (26a) but not the other way round (26b).

(26) a. Tous les étudiants ont lu un livre (*Hamlet*)
all the students have read a (particular) book
($un_{SRef} > \forall$); *($\forall > un_{SRef}$)
b. Un homme a gagné l'estime de tous les étudiants: le doyen.
"A man gained every student's esteem: the Dean."
($un_{SRef} > \forall$); *($\forall > un_{SRef}$)

To account for these facts, I have used a proposal by Starke (2001) based on intervention effects in some islands. The general principle is reported in (27), where the αs and the βs represent semantic features.

(27) a. * $\alpha_i \ldots \alpha_j \ldots \alpha_i$
b. * $\alpha\beta_i \ldots \alpha\beta_j \ldots \alpha\beta_i$
c. * $\alpha \ldots \alpha\beta \ldots \alpha$
d. $\alpha\beta \ldots \alpha \ldots \alpha\beta$ (Starke 2001)

What (27) shows is that an element can bypass another one only if it is semantically heavier (27d). Applied to our indefinites, it implies that quantificational indefinites are semantically heavier than property-denoting indefinites (recall (23)-(24)) and that S-referential indefinites are heavier than quantifiers (recall (26)). Assuming that a projection plays only one role and encodes a single feature in a cartographic spirit, we obtain (28) where QPs contain a PropP layer and SRefPs a QP layer and a PropP layer as proposed in section 2.3.1.

(28)	a.	*	QP	... QP	... QP	(27)a/b
	b.	*	PropP	... QP	... PropP	(27)c
	c.	*	QP	... SRefP	... QP	(27)c
	d.		QP	... PropP	QP	(27)d
	e.		SRefP	... QP	... SRefP	(27)d

(28a) formalizes the fact that a quantifier cannot cross another quantifier (recall (25)), (28b) that a property-denoting indefinite cannot cross a quantifier (recall (23)) and (28c) that a quantifier cannot cross an S-referential indefinite (recall (26)). (28d) in contrast formalizes the fact that a quantifier can cross a property-denoting indefinite (recall (23) and (24)) and (28e) that an S-referential indefinite can cross a quantifier (recall (26)). In short, the extendable telescopic left periphery proposed in this paper for *un*-NPs and *du/des*-NPs accounts for the scope interactions reported in this section.

2.3.3. S-Referential Indefinites and Scope

The analysis proposed in section 2.3.1 predicts that S-referential indefinites have scope properties. This is because their structure contains a QP and because in my account it is this QP which triggers Quantifier Raising. That this type of indefinites has scope properties is illustrated in (29) (=(8)) for *des*-NPs.

(29) a. Tous les étudiants ont raconté plusieurs histoires
all the students have told several stories
qui impliquaient des membres de la famille royale.
that involved of.the members of the family royal

b. des membres de la famille royale > tous les étudiants > plusieurs histoires

c. tous les étudiants > des membres de la famille royale > plusieurs histoires

In section 2.1.1, I mentioned the reading in which the members of the Royal Family in (29) co-vary with the students. This is known as the intermediate scope reading, as *des membres de la famille royale* is in the scope of the universal but takes scope over *plusieurs histoires* (29c). *Des membres de la famille royale* may also take widest scope, i.e. scope over *tous les étudiants* (29b). As the *des*-NP may clearly have different scope properties, it means that it undergoes QR. This is accounted for if its structure contains a QP as proposed here. Crucially, however, the *des*-NP in both (29b-c) is not quantificational as defined in section 2.1.1. It has a dependent reference. When it takes widest scope, its interpretation depends on what the speaker has in mind and when it has intermediate scope, its interpretation co-varies with the universal quantifier. In both cases, the members of the Royal Family can be identified and pointed at[4]. The fact that these indefinites have both scope properties and a dependent reference supports the structure proposed in (22).

The scope properties of the *des*-NP illustrated in (29) show that S-referential indefinites target two different positions at Logical Form. They target the highest projection when they take scope over the universal as in (29b) or the projection immediately following the one hosting the universal quantifier when they co-vary with the universal as in (29c) (cf. Beghelli & Stowell 1997). Following Beghelli & Stowell (1997), I assume that the landing sites of indefinites with widest scope and indefinites with intermediate scope contain an existential operator (∃). In (30), these projections are represented by $FP_{1\text{-}\exists}$ and $FP_{3\text{-}\exists}$ respectively, where FP stands for some functional projection to remain agnostic about labels. The projection hosting the universal quantifier is labelled $FP_{2\text{-}\forall}$. In other words, (30) is a hierarchy of operators, namely $\exists>\forall>\exists$.

(30) $FP_{1\text{-}\exists} > FP_{2\text{-}\forall} > FP_{3\text{-}\exists} > FP_4$

If S-referential indefinites can target two different positions at LF as shown above, one question which arises is what determines their landing site, i.e. what triggers their movement to $FP_{1\text{-}\exists}$ or to $FP_{3\text{-}\exists}$. A first element of answer is that it is not the existential reading of these constituents which triggers their movement. This interpretation rather *results* from movement,

---

[4] This does not mean that a reading in which the members of the Royal Family cannot be identified is not available. *Des membres de la famille royale* could for example be quantificational and thus represent a subset of a set introduced in the discourse. It could also be interpreted as a property-denoting *des*-NP, in which case it wouldn't have any scope properties.

as the landing sites of S-referential indefinites host an existential operator (Beghelli & Stowell 1997).

As for referentiality — more precisely Speaker's reference — I assume that it is encoded in the structure of S-referential expressions, namely in the SRefP layer. This means that S-reference is not a feature to be checked. This is supported by the fact that S-referential indefinites can target two different positions, namely a position above or a position below universal quantifiers. In effect, it seems unlikely that a single feature, for example [+S-referential], could be checked in two different projections. What we have to determine therefore is the interpretative difference between S-referential indefinites which take scope over universals and S-referential indefinites which are in their scope. In my definition of S-reference, I observed that this kind of reference is dependent. It may either depend on the speaker, i.e. on the utterance situation, or co-vary with a universal quantifier. The former interpretation corresponds to (29b), where the indefinite takes scope over the universal, i.e. when it targets $FP_{1-\exists}$. The latter corresponds to (29c), where the indefinite is in the scope of the universal, i.e. when it targets $FP_{3-\exists}$. What I suggest therefore is that it is the kind of dependence of their reference which determines the landing site of S-referential indefinites at LF. The idea is that they move to $FP_{1-\exists}$ when they are deictic and to $FP_{3-\exists}$ when they are not. They are deictic when their reference depends on the speaker. In sum, S-referential expressions take widest scope when they are [+deictic] and move to $FP_{3-\exists}$ when they are not.

2.4. Summary

The analysis proposed in this chapter associates different structures to indefinites of different semantic types. What I have proposed is that the structure of the left periphery of *un*-NPs and *du/des*-NPs varies according to their interpretation. More precisely, their left periphery may comprise one, two or three projections depending on whether the indefinite is property-denoting, quantificational or S-referential respectively (section 2.3.1). Put differently, this telescopic left periphery allows us to account for the (lack of) reference of these indefinites. The other two pieces of our puzzle, namely the (lack of) existential reading and the (lack of) scope properties (section 2.2), follow from my account. The existential reading of some property-denoting indefinites is due to the existential operator supplied by the predicate selecting them and the existential reading of S-referential indefinites is due to the existential operators supplied by their landing sites at LF (sections 2.1.3 and 2.3.3). The fact that property-denoting indefinites may be non-existential in intensional contexts is also accounted for if the lexical representation of the predicates selecting them is refined (section 2.1.3). As for the scope properties of some indefinites, they follow from the structure of their left periphery: When the Quantifier Phrase is projected, these indefinites have scope properties and when QP is not projected, they don't have scope properties (section 2.3).

As this study concentrates on argumental *un*-NPs and *du/des*-NPs and as these indefinites give rise to scope interactions (section 2.3.2), it allows us to refine the typology of features leading to minimality effects (section 1.2). What I suggest is that (3a) be modified as follows:

(31) Argumental$_{indef}$: S-referential, quantificational, (person?, number?, gender?, case?).

(31) takes into account the fact that interpretative features like quantificational and S-referential play a role in intervention effects among indefinites.

Finally, the account presented here argues in favour of a selection in terms of structure (and not in terms of semantic type). This is suggested by the ungrammaticality of sentences like (32).

(32) *John is looking for pretty. (van Geenhoven & McNally 2005: 897)

As verbs like *looking for* typically select property-denoting objects (section 2.1.3), which are of type <e,t>, they should be able to select any complement of type <e,t>, including adjectives. However, the ungrammaticality of (32) shows that this is not the case. To account for such data, I suggest that verbs like *looking for* select a PropP complement and not a complement of type <e,t>. In other words, selection should be defined in terms of structure and not of semantic type[5].

So far, my discussion has concentrated on the edge of some indefinites and on the surface position of *un* and *du/des*. The aim of the next section is to determine the base-position of these determiners.

---

5 An anonymous reviewer observes that another way to consider the selection question would be to say that what verbs like *looking for* select is the extended projection of N.

3. The Inflectional Domain

3.1. The Puzzle

According to the analysis proposed here, the lowest projection of the left periphery has to be projected to allow a noun phrase to function as a predicate (recall (5)). This projection is legitimated by the movement of *un* or *du/des* to its head. Informally, the determiner has to move to Prop for the indefinite to function as an argument and for it to be interpreted as a property. When the indefinite is quantificational or S-referential, the determiner head moves further, to Q or to SRef through Q, respectively. The question which arises is where this determiner is generated in the inflectional domain (recall (1)). The problem is more complex for *du/des* than for *un* as *du* and *des* comprise two components, *de+le/les*. To address this issue, we need to determine which features are encoded in the inflectional domain, i.e. provide a thorough analysis of this portion of the nominal structure.

3.2. The Proposal

The view advocated here for the inflectional domain of *un*-NPs and *du/des*-NPs is reported in (33).[6] This part of the structure may contain three functional projections (FP) encoding different features. It is inspired by Borer (2005) although the conclusions I reach for French differ from the ones in this work.

(33) FP_{number} > $(FP_{quantity})$ > (FP_{count}) > NP

Following Borer (2005), I assume that listemes are not specified for the mass/count distinction in the sense that they are all mass and *become* count in specific contexts, namely in the presence of some functional elements which include the plural morpheme, the indefinite article, and the count *le* "the". However, I depart from Borer's analysis in that I adopt the standard position on plurality, namely that it is a function from individuals. Informally, it means that 'count' is related to individuated elements, i.e. atoms, and not to a division of mass. One reason is that in French it seems that every time a noun phrase is plural there are atoms in its denotation. Intuitively, this is what 'count noun' means, that is, something which can be counted (0, 1, 2, 3…), in contrast with something which is measured for

[6] Note that FP_{number} is another notation for NumP represented in (19), (21), (22).

example. In order to count, you need atoms. The projection responsible for the count reading is labeled FP_{count} in (33). Its projection in a structure leads to an atomized reading.

Although the [+plural] and the [+count] features somehow conflate (plurals are count), the [–plural] and [–count] features do not, as [–plural] noun phrases may be mass (*du pain/le$_{mass}$ pain*) or count (*un pain/le$_{count}$ pain*). This difference leads us to dissociate grammatical number and count reading and to assume that these features are encoded in different projections. I propose that FP_{number} is the projection encoding grammatical number. Grammatical number is what determines the agreement of a verb with its subject, i.e. whether the verb is morphologically singular or plural, or of an adjectives with the noun it modifies, at least in languages with overt number morphology on verbs and adjectives.

Another issue related to plurality and grammatical number is the question of the quantities (or absence thereof) associated with a noun phrase. This issue is delicate in that it is very difficult to determine whether these quantities are due to encyclopedic or pragmatic factors or whether they are encoded in the nominal expressions themselves. Furthermore, in some cases the quantity involved is straightforward whereas in other cases it is not. For instance, *un*-NPs and *le$_{count}$*-NPs clearly imply 1 whereas other examples such as *les*-NPs are not so clear cut (see Borer 2005 for a very detailed and cross linguistic account which is not restricted to *the-* and *a*-NPs). Although we know that the latter constructions mean *more than one*, it is difficult to determine whether this is due to their plurality or to some quantity which is not overtly expressed/morphologically realized. The view advocate here is that quantity is only encoded in a nominal expression when it cannot be inferred from (a combination of) other features. What this means is that *un*-NPs and *le$_{count}$*-NPs imply the cardinality 1 because they are count *and* singular and that *les*-NPs mean *more than one* because they are plural. *Du*-NPs and *le$_{mass}$*-NPs do not mean 1 because they are not count, although they are singular.

The structures obtained for *un pain* "a bread", *le pain$_{mass/count}$* "the bread" and *les pains* "the breads" are reported in (34), where the absence of a projection is represented by X.

(34)		FP_{number}	$FP_{quantity}$	FP_{count}	NP
a.	un pain	un_{sing}	X	un	pain
b.	le $pain_{mass}$	le_{sing}	X	X	pain
c.	le $pain_{count}$	le_{sing}	X	le	pain
d.	les pains	les_{plur}	X	-s	pain

With Borer (2005), I assume that *un*, *le*$_{count}$ and *–s*[7] are generated in the lowest functional projection, i.e. FP$_{count}$ in (34), that this projection is absent from the structure of mass nouns (34b), and that *un* and *le* move to a higher position. In (34), they move to FP$_{number}$ and further to the left periphery when these nominals function as arguments. The above discussion suggests however that FP$_{quantity}$ is projected in neither of the nominals illustrated in (34) whereas FP$_{number}$ is always present.

Applying my analysis to *du/des*-NPs, we obtain (35), which distinguishes quantitative *du/des*-NPs from non-quantitative *du/des*-NPs. This distinction corresponds to the difference between *some bread* and the bare noun *bread* in English.

(35)		FP$_{number}$	FP$_{quantity}$	FP$_{count}$	NP
a.	du pain$_{quantit.}$	le$_{sing}$	√	X	pain
b.	du pain$_{non\text{-}quantit.}$	le$_{sing}$	X	X	pain
c.	des pains$_{quantit.}$	les$_{plur}$	√	-s	pain
d.	des pains$_{non\text{-}quantit.}$	les$_{plur}$	X	-s	pain

As shown in (35), the structure postulated in (33) allows us to account for the difference between quantitative and non-quantitative *du/des*-NPs in that only the former contain the quantity-layer in their structure. The *le/les* component of the *du/des* determiner is generated in FP$_{number}$, on a par with *le*$_{mass}$ and *les* in (34), and encodes grammatical number. The crucial element missing in (35), namely the component *de*, is added in (36).

(36)		FP$_{number}$	FP$_{quantity}$	FP$_{de}$	FP$_{count}$	NP
a.	du pain$_{quantit.}$	de+le$_{sing}$	de	de	X	pain
b.	du pain$_{non\text{-}quantit.}$	de+le$_{sing}$	X	de	X	pain
c.	des pains$_{quantit.}$	de+les$_{plur}$	de	de	-s	pain
d.	des pains$_{non\text{-}quantit.}$	de+les$_{plur}$	X	de	-s	pain

(36) suggests that *de* is generated between the count-layer which hosts the plural *–s* in *des*-NPs and the quantity-layer projected in the structure of quantitative *du/des*-NPs, and that it moves to FP$_{number}$ where it mergers with *le/les*. The complex head *du/des* moves higher up if the nominal is an argument. If this is on the right track, it means that we have identified the base position of the two components of *du/des* and the site where they incorporate.

Another distinction that (33) allows us to make is between the article

[7] Plural affix which attaches to the noun (and not the plural on the determiner).

un and the numeral *un*. The idea is that when *un* is a numeral the structure of the nominal comprises the quantity-layer whereas when *un* is an article $FP_{quantity}$ is not projected.[8] This is illustrated in (37).

(37)			FP_{number}	$FP_{quantity}$	FP_{count}	NP
	a.	un_{art} pain	un_{sing}	X	un	pain
	b.	$un_{numeral}$ pain	un_{sing}	un	un	pain

In short, according to the analysis developed in this paper, *un* in argumental *un*-NPs cyclically moves from FP_{count} to the edge of the nominal expression, which is represented by different projections depending on the interpretation of these indefinites (section 2.3.1). In the same vein, *de* head-moves from its base-position, located between the count-layer and the quantity-layer, to the number-layer, merges with the *le/les* component and further moves to the edge of the nominal expression as a complex head.

In the next section, I turn to the partitive reading often associated with *du/des*-NPs. If as assumed here different interpretations correspond to different structures, I expect this to be reflected in the internal structure of *du/des*-NPs with a partitive reading.

3.3. **du/des-*NPs: A Note on Partitivity***

The element *du/des* is generally referred to as *article partitif* "partitive article" in the literature. Although the term 'partitive' refers to the *part-of* relation, it seems to me that partitive *du/des*-NPs may be classified into two groups, which I call *implicit* and *explicit* partitives. The former express a subset (the set is non-overt) whereas the latter express the set overtly. More precisely, implicit partitive *du/des*-NPs express a subset contrasted with another subset or a subset of a set which has been previously introduced in the discourse. In other words, they correspond to the quantificational reading discussed in section 2.1.2. Recall (12) repeated below as (38) for convenience. The structure proposed for quantificational noun phrases such as *des filles* "of.the girls" and *du maïs* "of.the corn" in (38) is repeated below as (39) (=(21)).

[8] Another distinction between the article *un* and the numeral *un* is a categorial difference: the numeral *un* is probably a maximal projection on a par with other numerals whereas the article is a head.

(38) a. Des filles étaient blondes, d'autres avaient les
of.the girls were blond of.others had the
cheveux foncés.
hair dark

b. Dans ce champ, du maïs est pollué.
in this field of.the corn is polluted

(Bosveld-de Smet 1998: 15, citing Kleiber 1988)

(39) *Quantificational arguments:* QP > PropP (> NumP…)

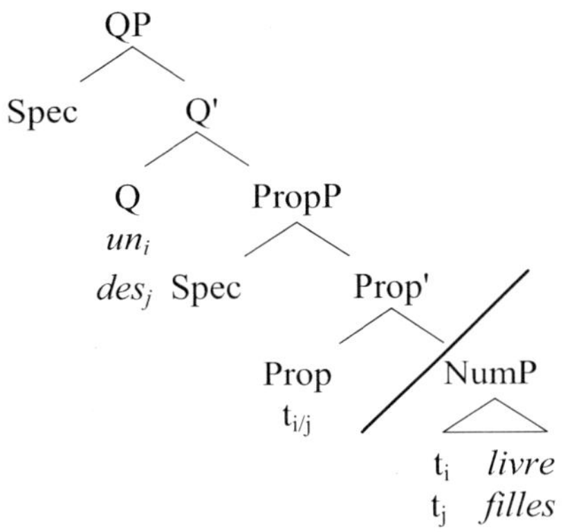

Explicit partitive *du/des*-NPs, in contrast, express the set. As the subset is not expressed overtly, these partitives are sometimes called *bare* partitives. They have a restricted distribution in that they may only occur as complements of fragmentative verbs (Englebert 1992), like *eat* or *drink*:

(40) Elle a mangé **du** gâteau/
she has eaten of.the.MASC cake/
de la tarte/**des** biscuits.
of the.FEM tart/of.the.PL biscuits

According to my analysis, if implicit and explicit partitive *du/des*-NPs may be distinguished, they should have different structures. This prediction seems to be borne out. The intuition is that explicit partitives, contrary to implicit partitives, involve a preposition *de* "of" on a par with bare partitives in English, whose prepositional phrase is not preceded by a quantitative or quantificational element (Kupferman 1979, Milner 1978; the reader is referred to this literature for various tests showing that bare partitives have a preposition in their structure):

(41) a. Jane ate of/from the cake.

b. manger [[∅] $[_{PP}$ de $[_{DP}$ le gâteau]]] eat of the cake

In (41a), the partitive expression, involving the preposition *of/from,* indicates that the object of the verb only partly undergoes the action of eating. The same interpretation characterizes the French example (41b). The idea is that in (41b) *du gâteau* "of.the cake" contains a Prepositional Phrase (PP), *de+le gâteau*, representing the set. The categorical status of this constituent is however not PP. These *du/des*-NPs could for example be PropPs, although this is not the only possibility (see Ihsane 2006 for a more detailed discussion).

Another assumption concerning explicit partitive *du/des*-NPs is that their structure is headed by an empty head, *ec* in (42). This means that these partitives contain two nouns (Jackendoff 1977, Milner 1978), one inside the PP and an empty element in N. Taking these elements into consideration, the structure I suggest for explicit partitive *du/des*-NPs is the following:

(42)

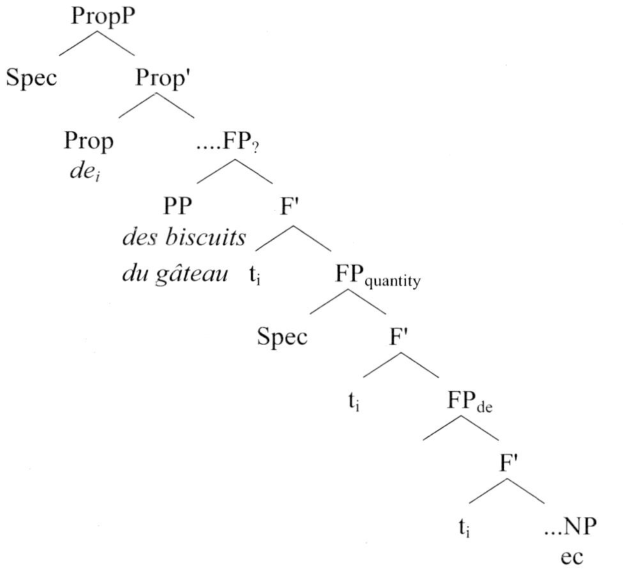

In (42), NP contains an empty category, *ec*, as proposed in the literature. This structure also hosts a PP which represents the set. I tentatively propose that this PP is generated in the specifier position of a

projection dominating $FP_{quantity}$. This projection is in some sense parasitic on the quantity-layer, in that it can only be projected if the quantity-layer is present in the structure. As for the PP, it is a kind of modifier, i.e. it is not selected (see Cardinaletti & Giusti 2005 for a different analysis).

As seen above, (42) differs from the structure of *du/des*-NPs which are not explicit partitives in two ways. The rest of the structure is however identical. In other words, the constitution of the inflectional domain is the same, namely $FP_{number} > (FP_{quantity}) > FP_{de} > (FP_{count}) > NP$. In other words, the element *de* generated in FP_{de} in the structure of *du/des*-NPs which are not explicit partitives is present in (42). This *de* moves to the left periphery to allow these nominals to function as arguments. As a result, explicit partitive *du/des*-NPs contain two *de's*, the one generated in FP_{de} on a par with implicit partitive *du/des*-NPs, and the preposition *de* in the partitive PP. However, as, according to the Grammar of Port-Royal, two successive *de's* are impossible in French because it would give rise to a "cacophony", only one *de* is realised. More generally, we are dealing with an example of haplology (Neeleman & van de Koot 2005). What I suggest is that it is the non-prepositional *de*, i.e. the highest in (42), which is not realised (Gross 1967). Although many issues of this analysis need to be further examined, it shows that different kinds of partitivity correspond to different structures as expected[9]. In other terms, implicit and explicit partitives have different structures.

3.4. *Summary*

The combination of features advocated here for the inflectional domain, namely the features [count], [quantity], and [number] (33), allows us to account for several complex facts, which are much discussed in the literature but for which there is no consensus. It allows us to identify the base position of *de* and *le/les* and to propose a straightforward analysis for the incorporation of these two elements (36). It also allows us to account for the difference between quantitative and non-quantitative *du/des*-NPs (36) and between the article *un* and the numeral *un* (37). In addition, the partitive reading of *du/des*-NPs perfectly fits the analysis developed here (42).

Another consequence of my analysis is that it allows us to make a correlation between the projections $FP_{count,}$ and SRefP. In effect, as referential means pointing at or identifying some individuals, it implies

[9] An anonymous reviewer observes that Roehrs (2006) offers analogous analyses. I was not aware of this work at the time of writing.

that referential nominals have atoms in their extension. This is realized in the structure by the projection of the count-layer, as this projection leads to an atomized reading. Put differently, it means that in order to be S-referential, *un*-NPs and *des*-NPs must have the count-layer in their inflectional domain. This also implies that mass nouns, which don't have the count-layer in their structure, cannot be S-referential: As the inflectional domain of these nominals does not contain the count-layer, they don't have an atomized reading. Consequently, they cannot be S-referential as this reading implies that individuals, i.e. atoms, be pointed at or identified. In other words, the fact that mass *du*-NPs cannot be S-referential follows from my analysis (recall (11)).

4. Conclusion

The analysis developed here also leads me to more general conclusions. The first one concerns the syntax-semantics interface, in the sense that my study shows that syntax drives semantics — and not the other way round. In other words, meaning is shaped by structure. This is striking in my account of S-referential noun phrases as their scope properties are due to a specific aspect of their internal structure.

Related to the previous conclusion, my investigations clearly show that syntax is not about words or morphemes but about features, which allows more subtle distinctions and gives rise to more complex structures. Such a position predicts that structures become more and more complex to encode interpretative features not considered so far.

Furthermore, the assumption that property-denoting noun phrases can function as arguments requires new composition rules, i.e. rules which allow this type of arguments to compose semantically with the predicate selecting them. This means that the semantics of predicates needs to be refined, and more generally, that the study of nominal expressions and the one of predicates should go hand in hand. It also has some consequences on selection which has to be finer-grained than a selection in terms of semantic types. In other words, the analysis proposed here has an impact on the syntax-lexicon interface.

Finally, if the three types of arguments advocated here have a left periphery of different sizes as proposed in this paper, it makes a prediction for languages acquisition. As children seem to acquire smaller structures first, we expect them to use property-denoting nominals first. This seems to be supported by various works in the literature (Roeper 2006, Matthewson & Schaeffer 2000, for example).

This study also raises many questions if only because it concentrates on a restricted number of nominal expressions. This means that other indefinites, *the*-NPs, nominals with demonstratives, possessives, cardinals, or adjectives should be explored in the perspective of the analysis developed here. Other issues like topic, focus, and genericity which have been excluded from this paper should also be looked at in future research.

References

Aboh, E. 2003. *The Morphosyntax of Complement-Head Sequences*. New York: Oxford University Press.

Beghelli, F. & T. Stowell. 1997. Distributivity and negation: The syntax of *each* and *every*. In A. Szabolcsi (ed.), *Ways of Scope Taking*. Dordrecht: Kluwer, 71-108.

Belletti, A. (ed.). 2004. *Structures and Beyond: The Cartography of Syntactic Structures*, vol. 3. New York: Oxford University Press.

Borer, H. 2005. *In Name Only: Structuring Sense*, vol. I. Oxford: Oxford University Press.

Bosveld-de Smet, L. 1998. *On Mass and Plural Quantification: The Case of French "des"/"du"-NPs*. Ph.D. diss., University of Groningen.

Bosveld-de Smet, L. 2004. Towards a uniform characterization of noun phrases with *des* or *du*. In F. Corblin & H. de Swart (eds.), *Handbook of French Semantics*. Stanford, CA: CSLI Publications, 41-55.

Cardinaletti, A. & G. Giusti. 2005. The syntax of quantified phrases and quantitative clitics. In M. Everaert & H. van Riemsdijk (eds.), *Blackwell Companion to Syntax* vol. V. Malden, MA: Blackwell, 23-93.

Chomsky, N. 1957. *Syntactic Structures*. The Hague: Mouton.

Chomsky, N. 1965. *Aspects of the Theory of Syntax*. Cambridge, MA: MIT Press.

Chomsky, N. 1981. *Lectures on Government and Binding*. Dordrecht: Foris.

Chomsky, N. 1986. *Barriers*. Cambridge, MA: MIT Press.

Chomsky, N. 1995. *The Minimalist Program*. Cambridge, MA: MIT Press.

Chung, S. & W.A. Ladusaw. 2004. *Restriction and Saturation*. Cambridge, MA: MIT Press.

Cinque, G. 1999. *Adverbs and Functional Heads*. New York: Oxford University Press.

Cinque, G (ed.). 2002. *Functional Structure in the IP and DP: The Cartography of Syntactic Structures*, vol. 1. New York: Oxford University Press.

Diesing, M. 1992. *Indefinites*. Cambridge, MA: MIT Press.

Dobrovie-Sorin, C. 1996. Syntactic configurations and references: SE/SI in Romance. In K. Zagona (ed.), *Grammatical Theory and Romance Languages*. Amsterdam: John Benjamins, 73-86.

Dobrovie-Sorin, C. 1997. Existential arguments and existential predicates. In A. Lawson (ed.), *Proceedings of SALT VII*. Ithaca, NY: CLC Publications, 117-134.

Dobrovie-Sorin, C. & C. Beyssade. 2004. *Définir les indéfinis*. Paris: CNRS Editions.

Donnellan, K. 1978. Speaker reference, descriptions and anaphora. In P. Cole (ed.), *Pragmatics: Syntax and Semantics*, vol. 9. New York: Academic Press, 47-68.

Enç, M. 1991. The semantics of specificity. *Linguistic Inquiry* 22, 1-25.

Englebert, A. 1992. *Le petit mot DE. Etude de sémantique historique*. Genève: Droz.

Farkas D. & H. de Swart. 2003. *The Semantics of Incorporation*. Stanford, CA: CSLI Publications.

Fodor, J.D. & I.A. Sag. 1982. Referential and quantificational indefinites. *Linguistics & Philosophy* 5, 355-398.

Grimshaw, J. 1990. *Argument Structure*. Cambridge, MA: MIT Press.

Grohmann, K.K. 2003. *Prolific Domains. On the Anti-Locality of Movement Dependencies*. Amsterdam: John Benjamins.

Grohmann, K.K. & L. Haegeman. 2003. Resuming Reflexives. *Proceedings of the 19th Scandinavian Conference of Linguistics — Nordlyd* 31.1, 46-62.

Gross, M. 1967. Sur une règle de cacophonie. *Langages* 7, 105-119.

Haegeman, L. 2004. DP periphery and clausal periphery: Possessor doubling in West Flemish? Relating nominal periphery to clausal periphery. In D. Adger, C. de Cat & G. Tsoulas (eds.), *Peripheries*. Dordrecht: Kluwer, 211-239.

Heim, I. 1991. Artikel und Definitheit. In A. v. Stechow & D. Wunderlich (eds.), *Semantik. Ein internationales Handbuch der zeitgenössischen Forschung*. Berlin: Mouton de Gruyter, 487-535.

Higginbotham, J. 1985. On semantics. *Linguistic Inquiry* 16, 547-593.

Higginbotham, J. 1987. Indefiniteness and predication. In E.J. Reuland & A.G.B. ter Meulen (eds.), *The Representation of (In)definiteness*. Cambridge, MA: MIT Press, 43-70.

Ihsane, T. 2006. *The Construction of the DP Domain: From* un-*NPs and*

du/des-*NPs in French to Bare Nouns in Romance and Germanic*. Ph.D. diss., University of Geneva.
Ihsane, T. 2008. *The Layered DP: Form and Meaning of French Indefinites*. Amsterdam: John Benjamins.
Jackendoff, R. 1977. *X'-Syntax. A Study of Phrase Structure*. Cambridge, MA: MIT Press.
Kleiber, G. 1988. L'opposition *massif/comptable* et les adjectifs. In J. David and G. Kleiber (eds.), 267-292.
Kripke, S. 1977. Speaker's reference and semantic reference. In P.A. French, T.E. Uehling & H.K. Wettstein (eds.), *Contemporary Perspectives in the Philosophy of Language*. Minneapolis : University of Minnesota Press, 6-27.
Kupferman, L. 1979. L'article partitif existe-t-il ?. *Le français moderne* 47, 1-16.
Laenzlinger, C. 2005. Some notes on DP-internal movement. *Generative Grammar in Geneva (GG@G)* 4, 227-260.
Larson, R.K. 1988. On the double object construction. *Linguistic Inquiry* 19, 335-392.
Longobardi, G. 1994. Reference and proper names: A theory of N-movement in syntax and logical form. *Linguistic Inquiry* 25, 609-665.
Matthewson, L. & J. Schaeffer. 2000. Grammar and pragmatics in the acquisition of articles systems. *Language Development and Breakdown — UCLA Working Papers in Linguistics* 5, 1-39.
McNally, L. 1995. Bare plurals in Spanish are interpreted as properties. In G. Morrill & R. Oehrle (eds.), *Formal Grammar*. Barcelona: Universitat Politècnica de Catalunya, 197-222.
McNally, L. 1998. Existential sentences without existential quantification. *Linguistics & Philosophy* 31, 353-392.
Milner, J.-C. 1978. *De la syntaxe à l'interprétation*. Paris: Editions de Seuil.
Milsark, G. 1974. *Existential Sentences in English*. Ph.D. diss., MIT, Cambridge.
Neeleman, A. & H. van de Koot. 2005. Syntactic haplology. In M. Everaert & H. van Riemsdijk (eds.), *Blackwell Companion to Syntax*, vol. IV. Malden, MA: Blackwell, 687-710.
Platzack, C. 2001. Multiple interfaces. In U. Nikanne & E. van der Zee (eds.), *Cognitive Interfaces: Constraints on Linking Cognitive Information*. Oxford: Oxford University Press, 21-53.
Quine, W.V.O. 1960. *Word and Object*. Cambridge, MA: MIT Press.
Rizzi, L. 1990. *Relativized Minimality*. Cambridge, MA: MIT Press.
Rizzi, L. 1997. The fine structure of the left periphery. In L. Haegeman

(ed.), *Elements of Grammar: Handbook of Generative Syntax*. Dordrecht: Kluwer, 281-337.

Rizzi, L. 2001. On the position "Int(errogative)" in the left periphery of the clause. In G. Cinque & G. Salvi (eds.), *Current Studies in Italian Syntax: Esseys Offered to Lorenzo Renzi*. Amsterdam: Elsevier, 287-296.

Rizzi, L (ed.). 2004a. *The Structure of CP and IP: The Cartography of Syntactic Structures*, vol. 2. New York: Oxford University Press.

Rizzi, L. 2004b. Locality and left periphery. In Belletti (ed.), 1-27.

Roehrs, D. 2006. *The Morpho-Syntax of the Germanic Noun Phrase: Determiners Move into the Determiner Phrase*. Ph.D. diss., Indiana University, Bloomington.

Roeper, T. 2006. Watching noun phrases emerge: Seeking compositionality. In V. van Geenhoven (ed.), *Acquisition Meets Semantics*. Dordrecht: Kluwer, 37-64.

Starke, M. 2001. *Move Dissolves into Merge: A Theory of Locality*. Ph.D. diss., University of Geneva.

Valois, D. 1991. *The Internal Syntax of DP*. Ph.D. diss., MIT, Cambridge.

van Geenhoven, V. 1996. *Semantic Incorporation and Indefinite Descriptions: Semantic and Syntactic Aspects of Noun Incorporation in West Greenlandic*. Ph.D. diss., University of Tübingen.

van Geenhoven, V. & L. McNally. 2005. On the property analysis of opaque complements. *Lingua* 115, 885-914.

Wilson, G. 1978. On definite and indefinite descriptions. *Philosophical Review* LXXXVII, 48-76.

CHAPTER ELEVEN

DEMONSTRATIVES, NUMERALS, AND COLOUR TERMS IN (BEIJING) MANDARIN[*]

XUAN DI

1. Introduction

Sometimes, it seems that more than one lexical item with almost the same meaning can be used interchangeably (1a-b). Sometimes, phonological rules may be applied in explaining the relation between different forms (1c). However, when different forms give different semantics (1d), syntactic difference is expected.

(1) a.

Nana	mai	le	**zhe(i)**	ge.
Nana	buy	LE	this(one)	CL_{GE}

"Nana bought this."

b.

yi	shuang	**hong**	**((se)**	**de)**	shoutao
one	CL^{pair}	red	colour	DE	glove

"a pair of red gloves"

c.

yi^{51}	zhi^{55}	wan
one	CL	bowl

"a bowl"

c'.

yi^{35}	ge^{51}	wan
one	CL	bowl

"a bowl"

d.

yi^{51}	wan
one	bowl

"a bowl of"

d'.

yi^{35}	wan
one	bowl

"a bowl"

[NB: tone sandhi of *yi*$^{51/35}$ due to tone of the CL; see section 3]

---

[*] I'm indebted to the encouragement, discussions and comments from Michal Starke, Richard Kayne, Knut Tarald Taraldsen, Klaus Abels, Gillian Ramchand, Lisa Cheng, Rint Sybesma, and Øystein Vangsnes. And many thanks to the audience at the *InterPhases* conference.

In the present contribution, data are arranged around the above Mandarin proximal demonstratives (DEM), colour terms, and numerals (NUM). I am going to show that in fact these interchangeable words have different meanings. Optionality is an illusion which will disappear once we look more carefully into their syntax. Language-internal parameters are also rooted in the lexicon: the complexity of different lexical items decides their syntactic distribution.

The paper is organized as follows. In section 2, I describe two forms of proximal demonstrative (*zhe* and *zhei*), which show different requirements with respect to an immediately following disagreeing classifier (CL) *ge*. This post-DEM *ge* is a disagreeing CL, not because *ge* is a 'default classifier' (Borer 2005) that can be used 'loosely' where one expects an agreeing CL, such a replacement is rarely acceptable among native speakers. I refer to the post-DEM *ge* as disagreeing CL because this is a position where an agreeing CL is not possible. Disagreeing *ge* doesn't license any numerals. Semantically, *zhe* imposes an exclusiveness interpretation.

In section 3, I describe the syntactic property for anti-sandhi numeral *yi* "one" directly preceding a (count) noun: yi^{35}-N. I suggest the derivation for a CL/massifier is a set of operation (restricted ordered movements) that is parallel to the derivation of yi^{35}-N. And I discuss the interaction of numerals, CL and NP. In agreement with Zweig (2005), I show that numerals with different internal structures have different syntax; different from him, I show that there is more than just noun/adjective two types of numerals. Three types of additive number and one type of multiplicative number show different ellipsis pattern of CLs and the weight[1] of the last digit. The type of additives that CL and the lowest weight co-occur, has the parallel derivation as DEM *zhe*.

Section 4 extends *yi*-N style of derivation to "colour base" *SE "COLOUR"*, a morpheme that turns an NP colour term into a DP. The algorithm for selecting count noun in *yi*-N is applicable in deriving non-predicative colour adjectives. If some of the numerals are adjectives, the different derivations of adjectives echo the different derivations for numerals in section 3.

The final section 5 briefly concludes this chapter.

[1] *Weight*, or weight function, here can be understood as a cover term for 10^x in the positional numeral system, corresponding to 10^0, 10^1 "-ty", 10^2 "hundred", etc, without their linguistic content.

2. Demonstrative

2.1. The Required Pointing Gesture

In the answer to a *wh*-question, the reference of the nominal phrase (underlined in (2b)) is new to the hearer. If we define *definite* as a noun phrase whose reference is known to both the speaker and the hearer, the new information NP is not definite[2].

(2)	a.	ni	mai	shenme	le?		
		2SG	buy	what	LE		
		"What did you buy?"					
	b.	wo	mai	le	*si*	*jin*	*xianrenzhang.*
		1SG	buy	LE	four	1/2kilo	cactus
		"I bought two kilos of cacti."					
	c.	wo	mai	le	*xianrenzhang.*		
		1SG	buy	LE	cactus		
		"I bought cacti/cactus."					

On the other hand, the references of the nominals in (2b-c) are known to the speaker; therefore, by definition, this is a position where one finds specific nominals. Ergo, nominals in the answers to (2a) are indefinites specific.

In such a position, we can let the nominal be preceded by a DEM[3], as in (3b-c); interestingly however, we have to add a pointing/showing gesture once we add the DEM[4].

(3)	a.	ni	mai	shenme	le?
		2SG	buy	what	LE
		"What did you buy?"			

[2] No matter whether familiarity is a UG feature, the reference of the numeral-and-classifier preceded nominal phrase (NumP) in (1b) has not been introduced in the discourse, nor has the reference of the bare NP in (1c). Therefore, if the semantic definition of *definite* has familiarity as a necessary component, this position is not definite.

[3] DEM *zhei* "this" does denote proximal. In other Chinese dialects, a range of DEM can be used to modify the distance between the item and the speaker/hearer (S.X. Lü 1990, Q. Mi 1986, Ogawa 1981, Xuefan (W.D. Chen) 1938, J.S. Zhu 1986, Q.Y. Zhu 1988, L. Wang 1944-45, H. Jin 1988). In Beijing Mandarin, DEM only makes a binary distinction between distal (*nei* "that") and proximal.

[4] *Zhei* cannot carry a contrastive stress under this context.

b. wo mai le zhei *si jin xianrenzhang.* *(+ ***pointing***)
1SG buy LE this four 1/2kilo cactus
"I bought these two kilos of cacti"

c. wo mai le zhei (ge) *xianrenzhang.* *(+ *pointing*)
1SG buy LE this CL cactus
"I bought this cactus"

In other words, in an indefinite specific position, DEM must be licensed by pointing. "Pointing" confirms that the DP is specific indefinite. The speaker must know the reference of the entity to be able to point at its location. The hearer doesn't know the reference, otherwise pointing wouldn't be necessary. Before we add the DEM in the nominal position, the reference of the goods purchased doesn't have to be introduced. With a pronounced DEM, the reference of the nominals has to be introduced, by pointing. Crucially the reference cannot be introduced by a DEM alone, i.e. without pointing.

The gesture and DEM co-refer. In this sense, DEM shows the property of an anaphoric pronoun, which calls for an antecedent — here, a pointing/showing gesture which introduces the reference — in a certain domain. The DEM cannot locate an object; this is achieved by the actual body movements required by the DEM[5].

2.2. Two Proximal DEMs and Disagreeing CL under NP Ellipsis

NP ellipsis is possible if the one who did the shopping doesn't know the name of the stuff (s)he got, or if (s)he doesn't want to speak out what the thing is. Three strategies are possible to introduce the reference under NP ellipsis: a bare demonstrative *zhe* "this" (4a), or *zhe* plus a classifier *ge* (4b) or a different form of proximal demonstrative *zhei* "this" together with a classifier *ge*.

(4) a. %? wo mai le *zhe.* + *pointing*
1SG buy LE this

b. wo mai le *zhe ge.* + *pointing*
1SG buy LE this CL
"I bought this."

[5] S.X. Lü (1956:164) classifies two types of demonstrative usages, one of them needs pointing. For more examples in Mandarin on *dependent substitute* see D.Y. Wang (2005). Grohmann & Panagiotidis (2005) also mentioned that Greek DEM also has the dependent substitute usage (i.e. sometimes requires pointing).

c. *	wo	mai	le	*zhei. + pointing*		
	1SG	buy	LE	this		
d.	wo	mai	le	*zhei*	*ge. + pointing*	
	1SG	buy	LE	this	CL	
	"I bought this."					

In all possible cases in (4), the speaker must point to the stuff (s)he bought or show it to the hearer, the same as in the overt NP cases in (3).

The structure that licenses NP ellipsis helps to tell *zhe* "this" and *zhei* "this" apart. The *zhe*, with a tense vowel ɤ, can be used on its own without an overt classifier. The percentage sign represents that some Beijing Mandarin speakers find it preferable to have a following *ge* pronounced for *zhe*. *Zhei*, with a diaphone in its rhyme ɛ(ɪ) — a weakened form of which can be just a lax semi-open vowel in the nuclear — *must* be followed by a classifier *ge*. Even for speakers who find *zhe-ge* preferable than *zhe*, there is a contrast between *zhei-*(ge)* and *zhe-?(ge)*.

We can see the same pattern when the reference of the NP is singular, specified by the preceding bare classifier, the bold faced *ge* in (5).

(5)	a.	wo mai le	***ge***	*xianrenzhang.*	
		1SG buy LE	CL	cactus	
		"I bought a cactus."			
	b.	wo mai le	***ge***	*zhe*	*%?(ge).*
		1SG buy LE	CL	this	CL
	c.	wo mai le	***ge***	*zhei*	**(ge).*
		1SG buy LE	CL	this	CL
		"I bought this."			

Adding numerals (which may change the semantics from singular *one cactus* to plural *four cacti* in (6)) does not change the requirement for the post-DEM CL:

(6)	a.	wo	mai	le	*si / yi*	*ge*	*xianrenzhang.*	
		1SG	buy	LE	four / one	CL	cactus	
		"I bought four cacti/a cactus."						
	b.	wo	mai	le	*si / yi*	*ge*	*zhe*	*%?(ge).*
		1SG	buy	LE	four / one	CL	this	CL
		"I bought this/ four of these."						
	c.	wo	mai	le	*si / yi*	*ge*	*zhei*	**(ge).*
		1SG	buy	LE	four / one	CL	this	CL
		"I bought four of these/this."						

(7) a. wo mai le *si jin* *zhe.* + *pointing*
1SG buy LE four 1/2kilo this
"I bought two kilos of these"
b. wo mai le *si jin* *zhe ge.* + *pointing*
1SG buy LE four 1/2kilo this CL
"I bought two kilos of these."
c. * wo mai le *(si jin)* *zhei.* + *pointing*
1SG buy LE four 1/2kilo this
d. wo mai le *si jin* *zhei ge.* + *pointing*
1SG buy LE four 1/2kilo this CL
"I bought two kilos of these."

Classifiers usually need to agree with the noun. For instance, the classifier for *daxiang* "elephant" is *zhi* (or *tou*), the classifier *ge* is not possible (8); the classifier for *qiang* "gun" is *ba* (or *zhi*), the so-called "default classifier" *ge* is not possible (9).

(8) a. si / yi zhi daxiang.
four / one CL elephant
b. * si / yi ge daxiang.
four / one CL elephant
"four elephants/ an elephant"

(9) a. si / yi ba / zhi qiang.
four / one CL gun
b. * si / yi ge qiang.
four / one CL gun
"four guns/ a gun"

However, for NP ellipsis with a demonstrative, neither classifier has to agree with the noun[6]. In sentence (10c-d), the classifier *ge* can be used even

---

[6] Richard Kayne (p.c.) suggests that the disagreement in NP ellipsis on both CLs recalls in part what he suggested about Hopi (and English) in Kayne (2003): "The fact that the irregular plural morphology of *children* doesn't not carry over:

(i) * They have two seven-year-old ren. [vs. *two seven-year olds*]"

Agreeing CL is not irregular, the number of nouns that requires obligatory CL-N agreement is so high, that if we wish to carry Kayne's suggestion over to Mandarin, his suggestion that "irregular morphology is associated only with the phonological features of a lexical item" may be (better) understood as: the agreement/selection

when the intended noun *daxiang* "elephant" doesn't take *ge* as a classifier.

(10) a. wo mai le *si / yi* *zhi* *daxiang.*
1SG buy LE four / one CL elephant
"I bought four elephants / an elephant."
b. wo mai le *si / yi* *ba* *qiang.*
1SG buy LE four / one CL gun
"I bought four guns / a gun."
c. wo mai le *si / yi* *ge* *zhe %?(ge).*
1SG buy LE four / one CL this CL
"I bought a this / four of this." (can be guns or elephants)
d. wo mai le *si / yi* *ge* *zhei *(ge).*
1SG buy LE four / one CL this CL
"I bought a this / four of this." (can be guns or elephants)

In other words, (10c, 10d) can be used as an equivalent answer to either (10a) or (10b). In the present double-CL condition, the first classifier *doesn't have to* agree with the noun (10c, d); however, it can agree with the unpronounced noun: *ba* agrees with *qiang* "gun"; and *zhi* agrees with *daxiang* "elephant" (11).

(11) a. wo mai le *si / yi* ***ba*** *zhe ?(ge). + showing*
1SG buy LE four / one CL this CL
"I bought a this / four of this." (showing a gun / four guns)
b. wo mai le *si / yi* ***zhi*** *zhe ?(ge).*
1SG buy LE four / one CL this CL
"I bought a this / four of this." (pointing to an elephant / four elephants)
a'. wo mai le *si / yi* ***ba*** *zhei ?(ge).*
1SG buy LE four / one CL this CL
"I bought a this / four of this." (showing a gun/ four guns)
b'. wo mai le **si / yi** **zhi** **zhei ?(ge).**
1SG buy LE four / one CL this CL
"I bought a this / four of this." (pointing to an elephant or four elephants)

For speakers who find *zhe-ge* preferable to a bare *zhe*, some find, under NP ellipsis, a disagreeing pre-DEM CL is also preferred over an agreeing

between two lexical items is licensed by (or directly related to) the step of derivation that licenses NP ellipsis.

CL, i.e. disagreeing all the way down; others see no difference between an agreeing pre-DEM CL and a disagreeing pre-DEM CL.

The second classifier is only visible when the noun is covert. Moreover, the second classifier *cannot* agree with the unpronounced noun, it must be *ge*. In other words, regardless of whether the pre-DEM CL agrees (12) or doesn't agree (13) with the noun, an agreeing post-DEM CL is not possible.

(12)	a. *	wo	mai	le	*si / yi*	*ba*	*zhe*	*ba*	*(qiang).*
		1SG	buy	LE	four / one	CL	this	CL	gun
	b. *	wo	mai	le	*si / yi*	*zhi*	*zhe*	*zhi*	*(qiang).*
		1SG	buy	LE	four / one	CL	this	CL	gun
	a'. *	wo	mai	le	*si / yi*	*ba*	*zhei*	*ba*	*(qiang).*
		1SG	buy	LE	four / one	CL	this	CL	gun
	b'. *	wo	mai	le	*si / yi*	*zhi*	*zhei*	*zhi*	*(qiang).*
		1SG	buy	LE	four / one	CL	this	CL	gun

(13)	a. *	wo	mai	le	*si / yi*	*ge*	*zhe*	*ba*	*(qiang).*
		1SG	buy	LE	four / one	CL	this	CL	gun
	b. *	wo	mai	le	*si / yi*	*ge*	*zhe*	*zhi*	*(qiang).*
		1SG	buy	LE	four / one	CL	this	CL	gun
	a'. *	wo	mai	le	*si / yi*	*ge*	*zhei*	*zhi*	*(qiang).*
		1SG	buy	LE	four / one	CL	this	CL	gun
	b'. *	wo	mai	le	*si / yi*	*ge*	*zhei*	*zhi*	*(qiang).*
		1SG	buy	LE	four / one	CL	this	CL	gun

When the *wh* question focuses on the specifier of an NP, i.e. when the NP is pronounced or is known to both the speaker and the hearer in the context, post-DEM CL can agree with the understood noun.

(14)	wo	mai	le	zhei	zhang.
	1SG	buy	LE	this	CL^{ticket}
	"I got this one."				

Namely, sentence (13), where the post-DEM has agreed with *piao* "ticket", is an appropriate answer to (15) but it is inappropriate to (16).

(15)	a.	wo	mai	le	zhang	Mama Mia,	ni	mai	shenme	le?
		1SG	buy	LE	CL^{ticket}	Mama Mia	2SG	buy	what	LE
		"I bought a ticket of Mamma Mia, what did you get?"								

b. Ni mai le shenme piao?
2SG buy LE what ticket
"What kind of ticket did you get?"

(16) X is just back from a supermarket, Y asks:
ni mai shenme le?
2SG buy what LE
"What did you buy?"

Table 1: zhe(i) *and NUM-CL under NP-Ellipsis*

	Wh	Wh-spec
zhei-ge	OK	OK
zhei-CL_{agree}	#	OK
zhei	*	*
zhe	%?	%?
zhe-ge	OK	OK
zhe-CL_{agree}	**	??*
CL_{agree} zhe(i) ge	$OK_{\%}$	$OK_{\%}$
CL_{agree} zhe(i) CL_{agree}	*	*
ge zhe(i) ge	OK	OK

To sum up (as in Table 1), under the condition of NP ellipsis, NUM-CL *zhe(i)* cannot be followed by a classifier that agrees with the understood noun, it can only be followed by the classifier *ge* that is not agreeing with the noun. *zhe* can be followed by an optional disagreeing classifier *ge*, *zhei* must be followed by an obligatorily disagreeing classifier *ge*.

When there isn't a NUM-CL preceding the DEM, some demonstratives can be followed by an agreeing CL, yet *zhe* prefers not to be followed by any agreeing CL. *zhei* must be followed by an agreeing CL when the *wh*-focus is on the specifier of NP.

There isn't such a thing as a 'basic order' for DEM and NUM-CL; whether a DEM can precede a NUM-CL or not, depends on the internal structure of the DEM. Demonstratives with different internal structures have different semantics, as shown below, each requires a different derivation.

2.3. *Exhaustive* zhe *and the pre-NUM* zhei

Zhe cannot occur in pair-list answer (17b, c).

(17) a. Tamen mai shenme le?
they buy what LE?
"What did they buy?"
b. Tamen mai le zhe*(i) ge, hai you zhe*(i) ge.
they buy LE this CL, yet have this CL
"They bought this, and this."
c. * Nana mai le zhe, Lala mai le zhe. (+ *pointing/showing twice*)
Nana buy LE this, Lala buy LE this
d. Nana mai le zhei ge, Lala mai le zhei ge. + *pointing twice*
Nana buy LE this CL, Lala buy LE this CL
"Nana bought this and Lala bought this."

Abels & Murungi (2007) show that a pair-list can be used as a test for exhaustive focus. The semantics is clear: for instance, in (17c-d) neither the thing that *Nana bought* nor Lala's share is the entire amount of things that they bought. Neither share of the theme exhausts the denotation of the stuff being purchased by some of the agents of *mai* "buy".

Meanwhile, from the speaker's point of view, answering with a sentence in (17d) requires pointing (or showing) twice at different references of things. This multi-event of pointing with the intention of distributing over objects creates a semantic distributive object that is not allowed by *zhe*, whose antecedent denotes the entire (collective) entity of the things being pointed at. Whereas no such number agreeing requirement is needed for *zhei*.

I relate the exhaustive meaning to the fact that *zhe* is normally very non-colloquial when preceding an agreeing CLP.

(18) a. wo xihuan zhe??(i) san duo hua.
I like this three CL flower
"I like these three flowers."
b. wo xihuan zhe??(i) duo hua.
I like this CL flower
"I like this flower."

The CL that can follow *zhe* is the disagreeing *ge*. No numerals can be licensed between the NUM-CL-DEM and *ge*, i.e. this post-DEM *ge* cannot license a numeral. It must be sitting in a position different from pre-DEM agreeing CL that can license a numeral. DEM *zhe* sits in a position that not only blocks the agreement between the CL and the NP, but also blocks the licensing of a NUM.

The interpretation of *zhe-ge*, and *zhei-ge*, can be both singular and plural. An agreeing CL or massifier licenses a numeral. When the numeral is not pronounced, it is interpreted as *yi* "one".

(19)	a.	wo	mai	le	ge / zhi	zhe	(ge).	
		I	buy	LE	CL / CL_{Agree}	this	CL	
		"I bought this."						
	a'.	wo	ma	le	zhe	(ge).		
		I	buy	LE	this	CL		
		"I bought this/these." (e.g. books)						
	b.	wo	mai	le	ge / zhi	zhei	ge.	
		I	buy	LE	CL / CL_{Agree}	this	CL	
	b'.	wo	mai	le	zhei	ge.		
		I	buy	LE	this	CL		

In (19a'-b'), the post-DEM disagreeing CL allows the interpretation of the reference to be both singular and plural. Only an agreeing CL, such as *ge/zhi* in (19a, b), controls the interpretation of the numeral information.

Zhei "this" has a much wider usage than *zhe*. It can precede an agreeing CL (20a), it can precede a bare NP and the phrase renders a singular interpretation (20b), and it can precede NUM-CL (20c).

(20)		wo	mai	le…	
		I	buy	LE	
		"I bought …"			
	a.	… zhei	zhang	chuang.	
		this	CL^{bed}	bed	
		"… this bed."			
	b.	… zhei	chuang.		
		this	bed		
		"… this bed." / *"… these beds."			
	c.	… zhei	si	zhang	chuang.
		this	four	CL^{bed}	bed
		"… these four beds."			

The fact that *zhei* can precede a bare NP and lead to singular interpretation, leads to the hypothesis that *zhei* is a phonologically contracted form of a DEM *zhe* and a *yi* "one" (D.X. Zhu 1982, S.X. Lü 1985 among others).

D.X. Zhu (1982) has noticed some syntactic distributional differences between *zhe* and *zhei*. However, an explicit explanation on the relation between *zhe* and *zhei* is still called for.

I propose that the conditions under which the disagreeing CL *ge* can be omitted reveals the (structural) complexity of the DEM. The question now turns to what exactly the structural difference is. There are three phonologically different forms of *yi* "one", each with its own distinct syntax (to be shown in section 3). If there is a *yi* "one" in *zhei*, we would need to know which *yi* "one" it is.

To sum up, under NP ellipsis, we can find two classifiers in a specific indefinite nominal: the one preceding DEM doesn't have to agree with the noun, but can; pre-DEM CL can license overt NUM or cover *yi* "one" (i.e. when there isn't a NUM, the CL-N is interpreted as *yi*-CL-N). The CL that follows DEM must not agree with the noun. The disagreeing classifier doesn't force a singular reading in the way a bare agreeing classifier does, it doesn't specify number information; and it cannot be preceded by any numerals.

In English, *such a book* and *a book like this* have similar meaning. However, *such* in doesn't agree in number with the NP (*such a book* vs. *such books*); and it precedes *a*, a morpheme that often used to denote singularity but also can be found in a plural denoting phrase *many a student*. Whereas demonstratives do show number agreement: *this* cannot precede an NP that shows number agreement (**this books* vs. *these books*).

The two proximal demonstratives *zhe* and *zhei* have different distributions. *Zhe* cannot precede an agreeing CL (like **this NPs*), whereas *zhei* can.[7] The position of the DEM *zhe* cannot be high (Brugè 2002); because it is not able to precede any agreeing CL or numerals. The position of the DEM *zhei*, on the other hand, cannot be the same as *zhe*. Further derivation needs to be responsible for putting the two overt morphemes *zhe–* "this" and *–i* "one" together. They are not inserted at the same node. In the following section, I will suggest a derivation for *zhe–i* via Merge *and* Move.

3. *yi*^{55} "one", *yi*^{51} "one" and *yi*^{35} "one"

The numeral *yi* "1" has three forms in Northern Mandarin: first tone [55], second tone [35] and fourth tone [51].

---

[7] *Such* must be followed by "a" when preceding a bare NP, but demonstrative *zhei* can precede a bare NP. NP ellipsis can strand *such* (*as such*), but *zhei* requires a CL under NP ellipsis. The closer translation for *such* in Mandarin may be *zhe-me* and *na-me*, with a second morpheme also found in *shen-me* "what", which is historically derived from *wu* "thing".

3.1. Syntactic differences between yi^{51} "one" and yi^{35} "one"

Both *yi*^{35} and *yi*^{51} can precede a classifier. With an overt CL and overt NP, the condition on sandhi is determined by the tone of the CL. A CL that takes a fourth tone [51], only licenses *yi*^{35} (21). CLs of other tones license only *yi*^{51} (22).

(21) a. yi$^{35/*51}$ dao^{51} xue-hen
one stripe blood-stain
"a stripe of blood stain"

b. yi$^{35/*51}$ shan^{51} chuanghu
one CL window
"a window"

(22) a. yi$^{51/*35}$ zhang^{55} zhuo-zi
one CL desk-$_{\text{Nominal suffix}}$
"a desk"

b. yi$^{51/*35}$ tai^{35} PC
one CL PC
"a PC (computer)"

c. yi$^{51/*35}$ ba^{214} yi-zi
one CL chair
"a chair"

When *yi* "one" immediately precedes a lexical item which can be interpreted both as a noun or as a CL (or as a massifier), we can see the difference in the interpretations of the phrase reflected on the tone of *yi* "one".

For instance, when *tong* "bucket" is used as a massifier, the numeral takes the [51] tone, *yi*^{51}; the NP *niunai* "milk" can be pronounced (23a). When *tong* "bucket" is used as a noun, it can be preceded by a bare numeral *yi* "one" (Du YD 1993), and the tone of the numeral *yi* "one" is [35], *yi*^{35} "one" (23b); another NP *niunai* "milk" is then unable to be licensed. As if the English preposition *of* is in *yi*^{51}.

(23) wo mai le…
I buy LE
"I bought…"

a. … yi^{51} tong^{214} (niu nai).
one bucket cow milk
"… a bucket of milk."

b. … yi^{35} tong^{214} (*niu nai).
one bucket cow milk
"… a bucket."

The agreeing CL for *tong* "bucket" is *zhi* [55], and it licenses *yi*^{51}, not *yi*^{35}. Let me propose that when we see *yi*^{35} in (23b), there is an unpronounced disagreeing classifier *ge*^{51}. Again, referring it as disagreeing is because it never agrees with the noun. (Following the convention of using capital letters to indicate unpronounced morphemes.)

(24) yi^{35} GE^{51} tong^{214}
one CL bucket
"a bucket"

Take another example. The classifier for *chuang* "bed" is *zhang*^{55}. *Yi*^{35} is not possible with an overt agreeing classifier that is not of the fourth [51] tone (25a). *yi*^{51} is not possible without the overt agreeing classifier *zhang* (25b). *Yi*^{51} is only possible with an overt classifier, either an agreeing classifier or a non-agreeing amount denoting word (massifier) *chuang* "bed". When *chuang* gives an *amount* meaning (25b' and 25c), it functions as an overt agreeing classifier and blocks the licensing of *yi*^{35}.

(25) wo mai le…
I buy LE
"I bought…"

a. … yi$^{51/*35}$ zhang^{55} chuang.
one CL bed

b. … yi$^{*51/35}$ chuang^{35}.
one bed
"… a bed."

b'. … yi$^{51/*35}$ chuang^{35}.
one bed
"… a bedful." (of something)

c. … yi$^{51/*35}$ chuang^{35} hong-zao-r.
one bed red-date-R
"… a bedful of red-dates."

There are two meanings *yi*-N can provide. The meaning of (25b) and (25b') is roughly as follows:

(26) i. 1 bed
ii. something (e.g. dates), the amount of which is as many as "1 bed" can contain

To get the meaning in (26i), *yi* "one" must take the [35] tone; and the embedded "1 bed" meaning in (26ii), like any case when *yi* precedes a CL, observes the sandhi rule: [51] *yi* precedes all but [51] CL; [51] CL/massifier is preceded by only [35] *yi* (27b).

(27) wo mai le…
I buy LE
"I bought …"
a. … $yi^{51/*35}$ ke^{55} shu.
one CL tree
"… a tree."
b. … $yi^{*51/35}$ shu^{51}.
one tree
"… a tree." or "… a tree of."
c. … $yi^{*51/35}$ shu^{51} (hong-zao-r).
one tree red-date-R
"… a tree (of red dates)."

3.2. *The* yi^{35}-N *conjecture*

The NP that follows an anti-sandhi yi^{35} "one" doesn't undergo NP ellipsis, as (28a) shows. A massifier imposes sandhi of *yi* and allows NP ellipsis, as in (28b).

(28) a. yi^{35} *(shu^{51}/ $chuang^{35}$)
one tree / bed
"a tree / bed" or "a tree / bed of"
b. yi^{35} shu^{51} /yi^{51} $chuang^{35}$ (hong-zao-r)
one tree / one bed red-date-R
"a tree / bed (of red-dates)"

A massifier meaning (embedded amount, as per (26ii)) cannot be interpreted from yi^{35}-N. For instance, the massifier *chuang* doesn't agree with the noun *hong-zao-r*, thus (29b) cannot be interpreted as "a bedful of dates". yi^{35}-N can only be interpreted as the N being counted, i.e. with the meaning in (26i) (agreeing classifiers of *hong-zao-r* "red date" are *ke*, *li-r* or *ge*).

(29) a. yi^{35} qiang
one gun
"a gun" / *"a bed of guns"
b. yi^{35} hong-zao-r
one red-date-R
"a red date" / *"a bed / tree of dates"

yi^{35}-N is used only when the noun is countable, either a count noun or the countable meaning of a noun.

(30) nin neng bang wo mai yi^{35} {shui^{214} / pi^{35} jiu} ma?
2SG can help me buy one water / beer Q.
"Could you help me to get a water/beer?"

For mass nouns that don't come already atomized, deleting the CL is not possible.[8]

(31) nin neng bang wo mai yi^{35} niu^{35}-rou ma?
2SG can help me buy one ox-meat Q.
"Could you help me to get some beef?"
*: at the butcher's (where a butcher cuts and sells)
OK: portioned beef (dishes in restaurant, packages in supermarkets)

The sandhi *yi* "one" doesn't impose the [+count] requirement on the noun. Yi$^{35/51}$ can be followed by a massifier-noun, as well as a CL-N or a Measure unit-N. And the anti-sandhi *yi^{35}* requires a more restrictive environment: i.e. it must be followed by a bare atomized noun.

Not only does the null CL after *yi*^{35} not agree with the noun, also it cannot agree with the noun. If a count noun comes into the derivation pre-atomized, it doesn't necessarily require a CL. And a numeral should be able to specify the amount of the atomized NP directly.

In counting, the numeral *yi* has the first [55] tone (32a). When being used as a noun, the name of the numeral "1", it still has the first tone (32b).

(32) a. yi^{55}
b. **san ge yi^{55}** jia zai yi-qi shi 3.
3 CL 1 add at together be 3
"Adding three one-s together is three."

[8] In dialects of Chinese where *one*-N is not allowed, such as Xiang (Lu Man, p.c.), it seems that their DEM also have different distribution.

The CL for all numerals is *ge* (33). I thus propose that the null GE in *yi*-N is the classifier of a null numeral (34).

(33) a. **san ge er** jia zai yi-qi shi 6.
3 CL 2 add at together be 6
"Adding three two-s together is six."
b. **liu ge yi-bai** shi duoshao?
6 CL $1\text{-}10^2$ be how.much
"How much is six 100 add up to?"

(34) yi^{35} GE YI^{55} NP_{count}
{yi^{55} "one" NP} × 1

The derivation for yi^{35}-N is as (35) and (36). The numeral for the weight 10^0 is *ge* (W.H. Au-Yeung 2005). A countable NP comes into a derivation by Merge with an NP yi^{55} (rather than with the agreeing CL).

(35)

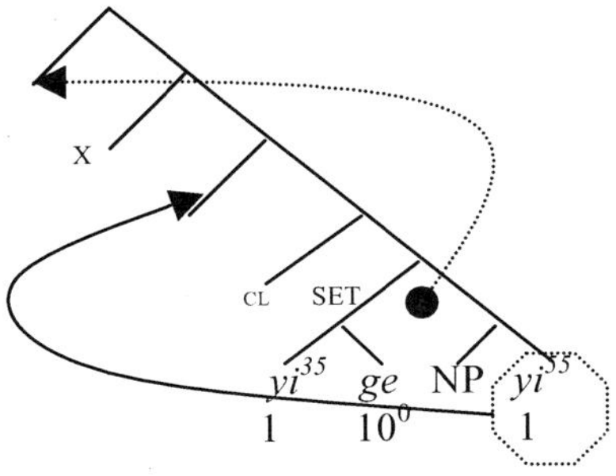

A digit merges with its weight, and the weight projects. In (35), *yi* "1" is the digit and *ge* "10^0", the tree the two forms is labelled as SET, short for weight and super-bases.

NP and yi^{55} are both nouns, the tree they formed is a bare tree (Chomsky 1995). The bigger tree with four terminal nodes merges with a head (CL) that carries number information. The numerical NP daughter of the bare tree, Agree with CL and moves. This step of raising breaks the local symmetry, makes the previously bare tree capable of labelling. I represent the labelling by remnant moving (the arrow with dotted line) the tree to a head (X).

(36)

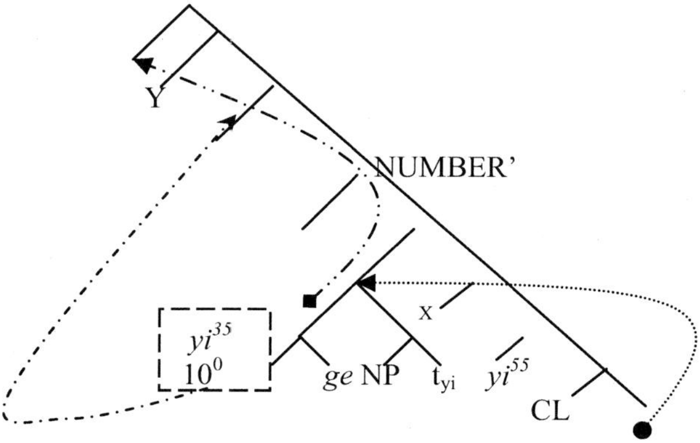

After the labelling of the mother node of NP and *yi*, the node that consist digit, weight, NP and *yi* "1" cannot be labelled, because both of its daughters are labelled. To decide a winner of the daughters, a third head (NUMBER) is merged and the numeral *ge* "10^0" raised via agree. A second round of remnant movement finishes the labelling of the tree (YP).

Yi^{55} and *ge* Move out in due course, leaving out *yi*^{35} and NP to raise to [Spec,YP]. The complement of Y will not be pronounced, only the material in [Spec,YP] will be pronounced (Kayne 2006).

The derivation of yi^{35}-N has two assumptions: (i) principled labelling method and (ii) LCA (Kayne 1994). Crucially different from Cinque (2005), an underlying hierarchical order (such as DEM >> NUM >> (A >>) N) is not a primitive in this system.

As we are going to see in the following sections, the *yi*^{35}-N derivation contains the set of operations that is sufficient in deriving massifiers, numbers and colour term adjectives; and capture the selectional/agreeing relationship among phrases. What's more, the parametrically difference within DEM, NUM, and adjectives can also be captured within this system.

I hereby propose a conjecture of derivation.

***yi*^{35} –N conjecture:**

Every morpheme, covert or overt, is licensed via (cyclically) applying the derivation of yi^{35}*–N, i.e. the representations in (35-36).*

A massifier itself (e.g., *chuang* in *yi-chuang* NP "a bedful of NP") is derived in the same manner as *yi*^{35}*-N* (illustrated in (37)-(38)).

(37)

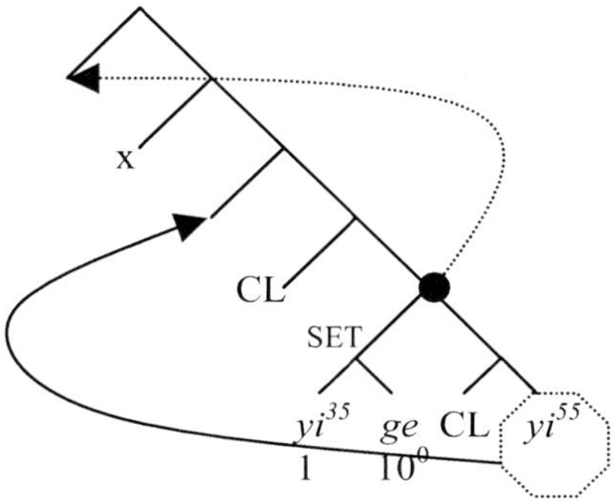

(38)

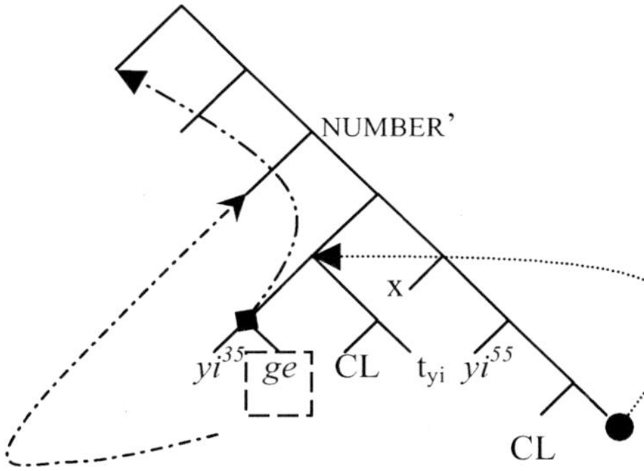

To sum up, *yi^{35}*-N is used only when the N is countable, and the cardinality of the set is "1". Only a singular interpretation is available from *yi^{35}*-N. The anti-sandhi *yi^{35}* is modifying a null disagreeing CL *ge*, also the numeral for the weight 10^0. A massifier in NUM-N_{amount}-NP, which can license numerals and impose tonal constraints on the numeral *yi* "one", doesn't enter any selectional/agreeing relation with the noun. It is a non-agreeing classifier, because it sits in the position of a weight.

3.3. The Weights of Some Additive Numerals

The numeral "1" has [55] tone (39). When *yi* is part of a complex numeral, a weight (e.g. *shi*) doesn't trigger sandhi of a preceding *yi^{55}* (40).

(39) a. shi yi^{55}
10^1 1 (= number 11)

b. san shi yi^{55}
3 10^1 1 (= number 31)

(40) a. er shi yi^{55} wan
[2 10^1 1] 10^4 (= number 210,000)
b. si shi yi^{55} yi
[4 10^1 1] 10^8 (= number 4,100,000,000)

Numerals larger than 9,999 have *wan* 10^4, *yi* 10^8 as the super-base. The weight of the highest digit in a complex numeral (e.g., *bai* "hundred", *qian* "thousand", *wan* 10^4 in (41)), provides the condition for sandhi of *yi* in the way a classifier does. Namely, when 1 directly modifies 10^4, the fourth tone weight *yi*^{51} "10^8" *wan*^{51} "10^4" will licence only *yi*^{35} "1"; *bai*^{214} "10^2", *qian*^{55} "10^3" licence *yi*^{51} "1". Such phonological rules apply no matter whether the entire numeral phrase is used for counting or as part of a NUM-CL phrase.

(41) a. yi^{51} bai^{214} (tiao yu)
1 10^2 CL_{Agree} fish
"one hundred (fish)"
b. yi^{51} $qian^{55}$ (gongjin pangxie)
1 10^3 kilogram crab
"one thousand (kilograms crabs)"

(42) yi^{35} wan^{51} (tai diannao)
1 10^4 CL computer
"ten thousand (computers)"

In an additive numeral, if it is not the highest weight, a middle field weight will not trigger the sandhi of *yi* (43).

(43) a. **yi**$^{\mathbf{51}}$ bai $yi^{55/*51}$ shi $\underline{yi^{55}}$.
1 10^2 1 10 1 (= number 111)
b. yi^{51} qian **yi**$^{\mathbf{55/*51}}$ bai ling $\underline{yi^{55}}$
1 10^3 1 10^2 0 1 (= number 1,101)
c. yi^{35} wan $yi^{55/?51}$ qian **yi**$^{\mathbf{55/*51}}$ bai ling $\underline{yi^{55}}$ (= number 11,101)
1 10^4 1 10^3 1 10^2 0 1

Y.J. Jin (1979) takes the non-sandhi between *yi* and CL to be an argument that the complex numeral forms a constituent itself, with *yi* as part of the numeral phrase and then enters into a relation with the CL. For English and Romance numerals, Kayne (2005) argues that numerals are adjectives, which modifies an unpronounced noun NUMBER first, and then merges with the noun. The two analyses are basically the same, and neither is correct.

We can see that in Mandarin, the sandhi of a numeral *yi* "one" in an additive numeral depends on the position that the *yi* modifies. $110 = 1 \times 10^2 + 1 \times 10^1$ could be considered as having a structure in (44b).

(44) a. yi^{51} bai yi^{55} shi
1 hundred 1 ten (= the number 110)

b.

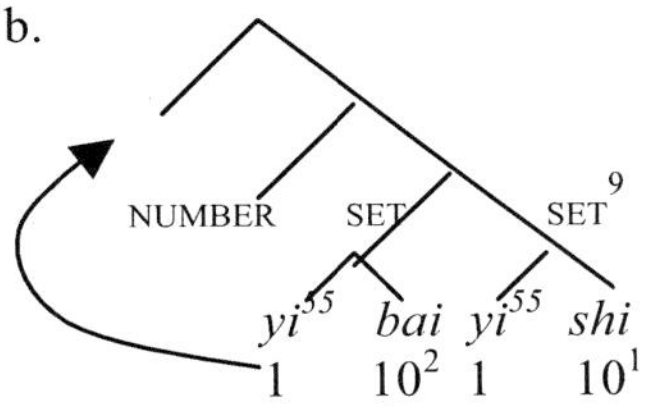

In (44b), the additive numeral move to the specifier of NUMBER to close off a NumeralP, the NumeralP then Merge with the phrase that involves CL and N. However, this simple derivation meets difficulties when a numeral is used as a modifier in a nominal. If a numeral enters a derivation as a constituent (44b), it fails to explain the correlation between having an overt CL and having a lower numeral base (45). Table 2. lists the pattern of ellipsis in NP.

(45) a. ni mai le duo-shao (zhi) niao?
you buy LE how-much CL) bird
"How much birds did you buy?"

b1. – wo mai le yi qian san / yi^{35} wan yi^{55}.
I buy LE 1 10^3 3 / 1 10^4 1
"I bought 1300/11000."

b2. – wo mai le yi qian san **bai** / yi wan yi **qian** zhi (niao).
I buy LE 1 10^3 3 10^2 /1 10^4 1 10^3 **CL** bird

b3. * – wo mai le yi qian san / yi wan yi zhi (niao)
I buy LE 1 10^3 3 / 1 10^4 1 **CL** bird
"I bought 1300/11000 birds."

[9] The head SET is also used in Kayne (2006) which takes some complex numerals to have a SET in their structures. Here, SET means *weight*.

Table 2: Correlation between Overt CL and a Lower Numeral Base

a.	NUM-CL-NP	*yi*^{51} *bai* *yi*^{55} ***shi*** *zhi* *niao* 1 10^2 1 10 CL bird "110 birds"	OK
b.	NP ellipsis: NUM-CL (complete NUM)	*yi*^{51} *bai* *yi*^{55} ***shi*** *zhi* 1 10^2 1 10 CL "110 birds"	OK
c.	NP, CL ellipsis complete NUM	*yi*^{51} *bai* *yi*^{55} ***shi*** 1 10^2 1 10	*
d.	CL ellipsis complete NUM	*yi*^{51} *bai* *yi*^{55} ***shi*** *niao* 1 10^2 1 10 bird	*
e.	NP, CL ellipsis NUM-base ellipsis	*yi*^{51} *bai* *yi*^{55} 1 10^2 1 "110"	OK
f.		*yi*^{51} *bai* *yi*^{55} *{zhi / niao / zhi niao}* 1 10^2 1 CL / bird / CL bird	*

For additive numerals between 109 and 10^8, if there isn't any middle field weight specified as 0, such as 2089, 3005, 100050 etc., and there isn't any digit of the weight 10^0; then the lowest non-10^0 weight, be it *qian* "10^3", *bai* "10^2" or *shi* "10^1" can be omitted. This happens under the condition of NP ellipsis, when the CL (including agreeing CL and massifiers) is also omitted ((45b1), Table 2e). If the CL is *not* omitted, this lower numeral base cannot be omitted ((45b3), Table 2f).

The structure I had in (44b) won't be able to explain why the lower weight has to be pronounced when there is a CL. In that derivation, the weight is too deeply embedded to have any effect on the Merge of a numeral with a CL.

The last middle-field weight should be moved up to have interaction with the CL.

(46)

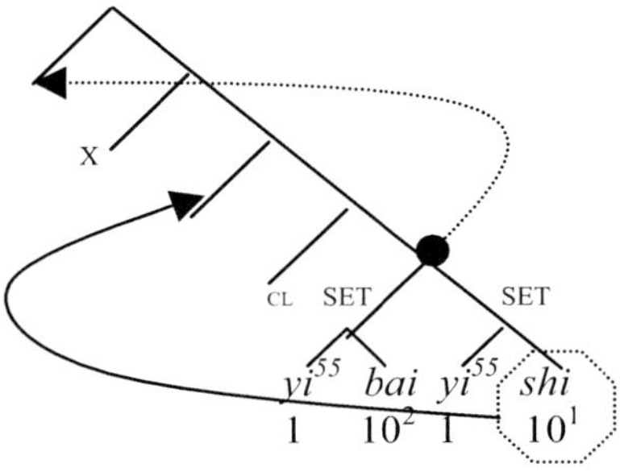

For an additive numeral to form, after each subpart of the numeral is formed, the tree Merges with a CL, which indicates a part-whole relation between 10 and 110. The lower weight (*shi* 10) moves to [Spec,CLP], to let the syntax / semantics know that this low digit is part of a bigger numeral. And then the remnant moves to the specifier of a numeral head, sending the information that now an entire additive number has been created (46).

The NP merges with a CL and then with the structure of an additive numeral, the derivation for NUM-CL-N (e.g. 47a) is illustrated in (47b). Because the CL omission and the weight omission are both under the condition of NP ellipsis, I take the NP to be raised first in (47b).

(47) a. Nana mai le yi bai yi shi zhi yang.
Nana buy LE 1 10^2 1 10^1 CL sheep
"Nana bought 101 sheep."

b.

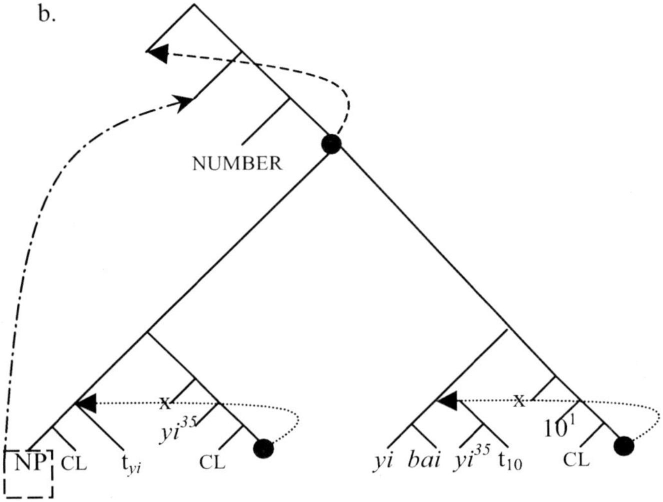

Then the phrase containing the position value *shi* "10^1" raises, triggering the movement of the phrase containing the numeral.

c.

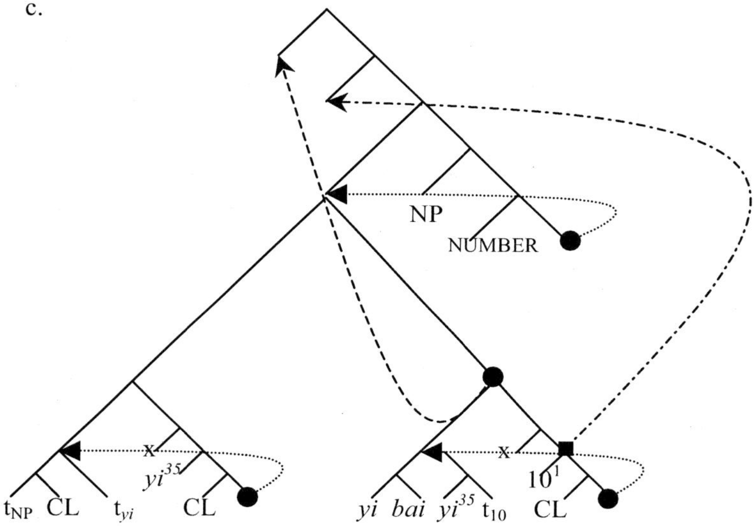

Leaving all Leaving all the traces aside, the word order in (47c) is now NUM-final weight-CL-NP. Once NP is moved up to a non-pronouncing position, namely creating the condition for NP ellipsis, the weight 10^1 and the CL can now be open to an operation that deletes them at the same time.

In this derivation, the weight *shi* "10^1" doesn't enter the derivation as a sister to the noun (Ionin & Matushansky 2004a, b); it takes part in the composition of the numeral internal phrases, it is merged with a digit *yi* "1". Neither does the digit have any direct relation with the NP[10].

In section 2, we have seen that in NP ellipsis, *zhe* allows omitting the disagreeing classifier. The optionally pronounced disagreeing CL (10^0) *ge*, is derived in a manner similar to the optional middle-field numeral base (47c): insert *zhe* in the numeral's position (the tree containing *yi bai yi* t_{10}), *ge* in the raised weight (10^1) position.

[10] Zweig (2005) suggests the digit first merges with NP. Whereas I take the numeral and CL as a tree that undergoes raising.

3.4. *Other Additive Numerals*

With respect to the co-occurrence condition with CL, there are three other types of numerals. Firstly, numerals have empty position(s) (i.e. *ling* "0, and") don't drop their weights and don't like the CL to be omitted (48a). *ling* "0, and" is not a position marker. Because no matter how many empty positions between two weights with specified digits, there is going to be just one *ling* "0, and" (48b).

(48) a. wo mai le liu qian **ling** wu shi? (xiang / ben-r)
I buy LE 6 10^3 **and** 5 10^1 box / CL^{book}
"I bought six thousand **and** fifty (boxes of) books."

b. liu wan **ling** wu (= the number 60,005)
6 10^4 **and** 5

c.

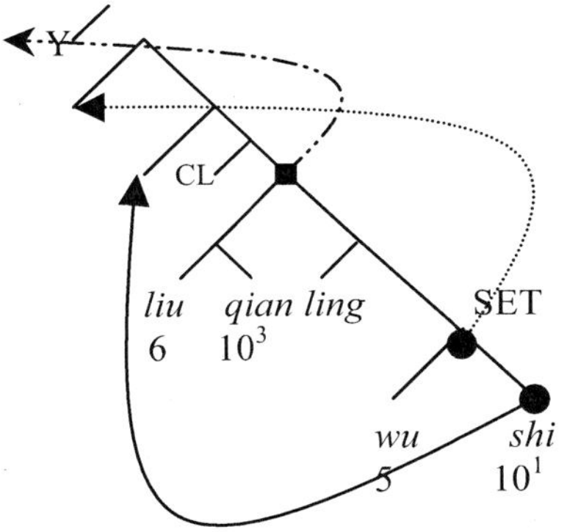

For Mandarin numerals with *ling* "0, and", *ling* "0" is Merged to conjoin the two number phrases *liu-qian* "six thousand" and *wu-shi* "fif-ty" (in English the word *and* is a conjunction, Zweig (2005)). Instead of the weight *shi* "10" raising up, 50 raises up, followed by a remnant movement of [[6000]*ling* t_{50}]. When this X Phrase merges with NP-CL, after NP raising, remnant movement of the [t_{NP} CL] followed by phrasal movement of the [XP $t_{NP\text{-}CL}$]

d.

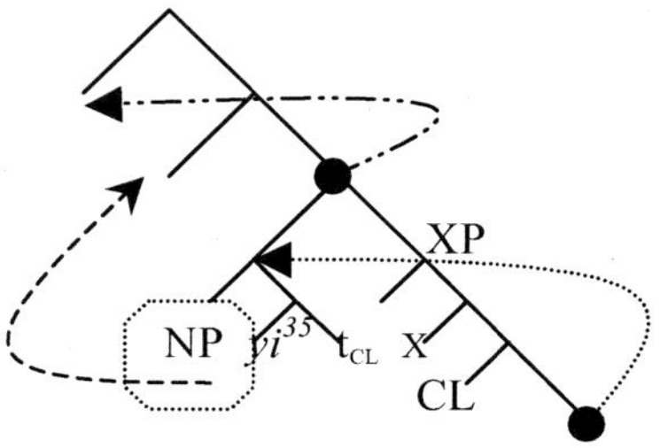

Secondly, numerals with specified 10^0 weight never pronounce its *ge* "10^0", nor do they prefer CL omission (49).

(49) a. wo mai le yi qian san bai wu shi yi[55]?? (xiang / ben-r)
I buy LE 1 10^3 3 10^2 5 10 1 **box / CL[book]**
"I bought 1,351 (boxes of) books."

b. wo mai le yi qian san bai wu shi ba?? (xiang / ben-r)
I buy LE 1 10^3 3 10^2 5 10 8 **box / CL[book]**
"I bought 1,358 (boxes of) books."

This requirement can be captured if the digit of the 10^0 take the weight *ge* that is used in deriving a CL (38) as its weight, directly modifying the *yi* "1"-CL phrases.

c.

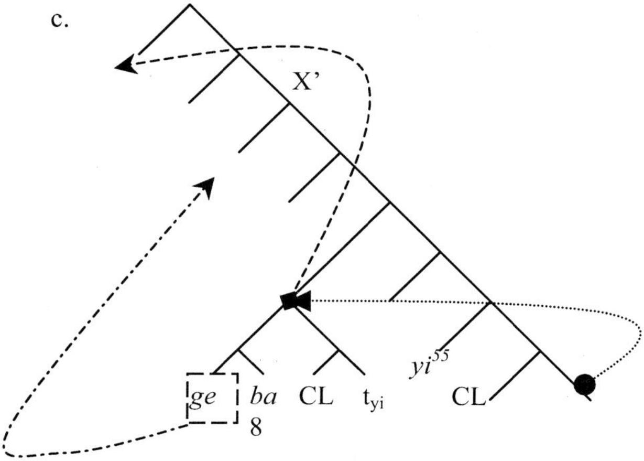

In this way, not only can we capture the generalization that numerals under 109 don't allow CL to be deleted (50a-c); but also the fact that digit modified weight (e.g. *ban* "half, 0.5", digit 5, the weight 10^{-1}), will follow an agreeing CL if there is a higher weight digit (50d).

(50) a. wo mai le yi$^{51/*55}$ *(xiang / ben-r).
I buy LE 1 **box / CL^{book}**
"I bought a (box of) book."
b. wo mai le ba^{55} *(xiang / ben-r).
I buy LE 8 **box / CL^{book}**
"I bought eight (boxes of) books."
c. wo mai le (wu shi) liu *(xiang / ben-r).
I buy LE 5 10^1 6 **box / CL^{book}**
"I bought (fifty) six (boxes of) books."
d. wo mai le liu *(xiang / ben-r) ban (tonghua shu).
I buy LE 6 **box / CL^{book}** half fairytale book
"I bought six and half (boxes of) fairytales."

The NP is separated from the CL in (50d) is also an argument for merging this type of numerals first with the CL, and then have the NUM-CL merge with NP.

3.5. *Multiplicative Numerals and* zhei

Multiplicative numerals allow deleting CL (51a), but don't allow deleting of weights. Semantically deleting the only weight (51b) or deleting a super base (51c) is unrecoverable, no matter in what context.

(51) a. wo mai le liu qian (xiang/ben-r).
I buy LE 6 10^3 **box / CL^{book}**
"I bought six thousand (of books)."
b. wo mai le liu *(qian).
I buy LE 6 10^3
"I bought six thousand."
c. liu qian wu bai *(wan)
(6 10^3 5 10^2) 10^4 (= number 6,500,0000)

Multiplicative numeral doesn't allow weight deletion. The numbers 4-9 don't allow CL deletion. The post-DEM *ge* after *zhei* also cannot be deleted. It is plausible to take *zhe-i* as a numeral with specified 10^0 weight, if we consider *zhe* 'this' as the higher weight and *–i* 'one' as *yi*^{55}. Then *ge* can be taken as a undeletable CL. It is also plausible to consider the *–i* as the digit in a multiplicative numeral (*yi*$^{35/51}$). Then *ge* is the undeletable weight.

However, *ge* doesn't agree with the NP, which make the argument for taking *ge* as weight favourable.

The derivation of DEM *zhei* in a specific indefinite noun with post-DEM disagreeing *ge*, under NP ellipsis, is illustrated in (52, 53).

(52) *differs from (46) in lexical insertion*

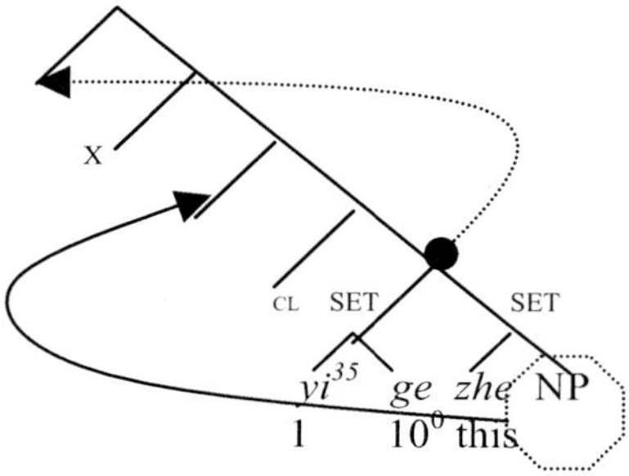

NP raising is followed by Remnant movement. Move *ge* out to a head X, Move the tree that contains the trace of *ge*, the trace of NP, yi^{55} and *zhe* to [Spec,XP]. At this step, *zhe* and yi^{55} move as one constituent, making it phonologically possible to have a contracted *zhei* "this".

(53) *differs from (49c) in lexical insertion*

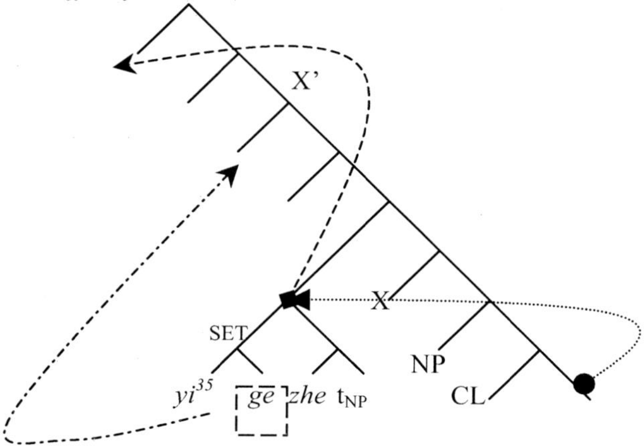

In this derivation, *zhe* doesn't directly modify any QP, thus it doesn't encode a collective reading.

Different internal structures of numerals have different effects on their external derivations (i.e. the omission of CL and pronouncing of weights). The distribution of *zhe* and *zhe-i* are different also because of their internal structures.

In this section, I presented the syntactic difference among three different *yi* "one". Special attention has been paid to the anti-sandhi numeral *yi* "one" directly preceding a (count) noun: *yi*^{35}*-N*. I suggest that the derivation for a CL/massifier is parallel to that of *yi*^{35}*-N*.

I argue that different numerals have different structures, their interaction with their weights, CL and NP are all different. Derivation for *zhe-ge* found only in indefinite specific nominals is taken to be parallel to the additive numerals with omittable weight. DEMonstrative *zhei* in *zhei-ge* has a derivation parallel to a multiplicative numeral. The derivations of the three different additives and the multiplicatives are instances of cyclic application of *yi*^{35}*-N*.

4. Colour Terms

Six different Mandarin lexical items can be translated as *red* in English (54 and 55).

(54) di shang you yi liu-r...
floor up have one CL^{strand}
a. ... **hong** toufa.
red hair
b. ... **hong-de** toufa.
red -de hair
c. ... **hong-se** ***(de)** toufa.
red-colour de hair
d. ... **hong yan-se** ***(de)** toufa.
red colour-colour de hair
"There is a strand of red hair on the floor."

(55) a. wo xihuan **hong** ***(se).**
I like red colour
b. wo xihuan **hong** ***(yan-se).**
I like red colour-colour
"I like red."

Different words for *red* have different syntactic behaviours.

4.1. hong *"red" and* hong-se *"red-colour"*

The bare *hong* "red" can be an adjective modifying some nouns (54a) (see Zhu (1956) for discussions on selective property of non-predicative adjective[11]). *Hong* "red" is also a noun that selects its own classifiers.

(56)	a.	yi	mo	hong	(se)	
		one	CL	red	colour	
		"red"				
	b.	yi	pian	hong	(se)	
		one	$CL^{\text{a large area of}}$	red	colour	
		"red"				
	c.	yi	dian	hong	(se)	
		one	$CL^{\text{a drop of}}$	red	colour	
		"a drop of red"				

But the 'widely' used *ge*, an individualizer classifier (Cheng & Sybesma 1999), cannot be selected by colour terms (57).

(57) *	san	ge	hong	(se)
	three	CL	red	colour

Hong "red" can precede *se* "colour". *Se* "colour" is not a free morpheme (58a), to become a word, either a colour term or a bound morpheme *yan* "colour, face" is required (58b).

(58)	a. *	yi	zhong	se
		one	type	colour
	b.	yi	zhong	yan-se
		one	type	colour-colour
		"a type of colour"		

Hong can directly precede certain nouns, it is a noun that can license its own classifier, and it can modify a bound morpheme *se* "colour". In section 3, we have seen that numeral yi^{35} "one" can directly precede a noun (59a). Yi^{55} "one" is a noun, it can license its own classifier (must be *ge*) (59b); and

[11] In short, non-predicative adjectives (Lü & Rao 1981) are not suffixed by *de*; and they don't freely combine with just any noun. Which non-predicative adjective goes with which noun has been claimed to be random (Zhu 1956), similar to gender marking in Indo-European languages.

some weights are bound morphemes (59c).

(59) a. **yi^{35}** mao^{35} niu^{35}
a hair ox/cow
"a yak"
b1. yi^{35} **ge** yi^{55}
a CL 1
"a 1"
c1. san **ge** yi^{51} bai (= 300)
3 CL one 10^2
"three one hundreds" (three multiplies 100)
c2. * san **ge** bai / qian/ wan
3 CL 10^2 / 10^3 / 10^4

Yi^{55} can be an argument on its own (60a). Although a bare colour term X (let X stands for a colour term) shares the property with *yi^{55}* in being able to select its own classifier, only X-*se* can be a DP (60b).

(60) a. wo de xingyun shuzi shi yi^{55} / *yi$^{51/35}$.
1SG DE lucky number be one
"My lucky number is one."
b. wo de xingyun se shi zi-*(se) / hong-*(se).
1SG DE lucky colour be purple-*(col.) / red-*(col.)
"My lucky colour is purple/red."

Se "colour" serves the function of turning an NP into a DP. X-*se* selects the same set of colour term classifiers as X does (56). Adjective-*se* compounds describing the shade of colour (61), can license the same set of agreeing classifiers as X-*se*.

(61) a. yi pian / mo / dian liang *(se)
one CL bright colour
"bright colour"
b. yi pian / mo / dian qi *(se)
one CL exotic colour
"exotic colour"
c. yi pian / mo / dian ming huang
one CL bright yellow
"bright colour"

Some colour terms don't have free monomorphemic forms, like *yi^{51}*

requires a weight. These colour terms have to co-occur with their "colour base" *–se* (62a), and they can't be degree modified (62b).

(62)	a.		wo	xihuan	nei	mo / dian / pian	zong	*(se)
			1SG	like	that	CL	brown	colour
			"I like that brown."					
	b.	*	hen	zong-(se)				
			very	brown-colour				

Colour terms with obligatory *se* "colour" can't be degree modified. Even for basic colour terms, which have free monomorphemic forms, *se* "colour" cannot occur in degree modification (63).

(63)	a.	hen	hong-(*se)	(de)	
		very	red colour	de	
	b.	hong-hong-(*se) de[12]			
		red-red-colour de			
	c.	hong	tong-tong	(*se)	de
		red	TONG-TONG	colour	de
		"very red"			

I take the ungrammaticality of (64a) to be related to (63), namely, bound

---

[12] Zhu (1961, 1966,1993) argues that the *de* in [XP-de NP] (i) is a contracted form of an adjectival suffix de_2 "-ly", and a nominalizer de_3 "one".

(i)	bai	sheng-sheng	de	li
	white	SHENG-SHENG	-ly.one	pear
	"a white pear"			

This analysis is supported by the fact that in another Northern Mandarin dialect (Shanxi; Zhu 1993), the two morphemes for de_2 and de_3 in reduplication (i) are pronounced differently. The nominalizer analysis leads him to claim that in Chinese, the most common modification is using a noun to modify another noun, and in major European languages noun-noun modification is restricted; that bare adjectives modifying a noun is restricted in Chinese and free in some European languages.

The generalization on the difference between Chinese and other languages is probably too coarse. Why are both bare adjectival modification and Noun modification allowed in one language? Another point that leads to the debate on *de* in the 1960s was that: considering X-*de* as a noun can't capture the intuition that a phrase with deleted noun (A-*de*) doesn't exactly feel like a pronounced full-fledged NP (A-*de*-N). Finally, this analysis can't explain the ungrammaticality of a bare colour term preceding NUMeral classifiers phrase.

colour terms are all modifying an unpronounced *SE* "COLOUR".

(64)	a.	*	zhei	tiao	qunzi	hen	zong.	
			this	CL	skirt	very	brown	
	b.	*	zhei	tiao	qunzi	hen	zong	SE.
			this	CL	skirt	very	brown	COLOUR

A covert *SE* has the same effect as an overt *se* "colour" in their disallowing of degree modification. The covert *SE* requires the overt *se* "colour", that explains why colour terms that cannot be degree modified are bound.

The derivation of the NP *hong* "red" is as follows:

(65)

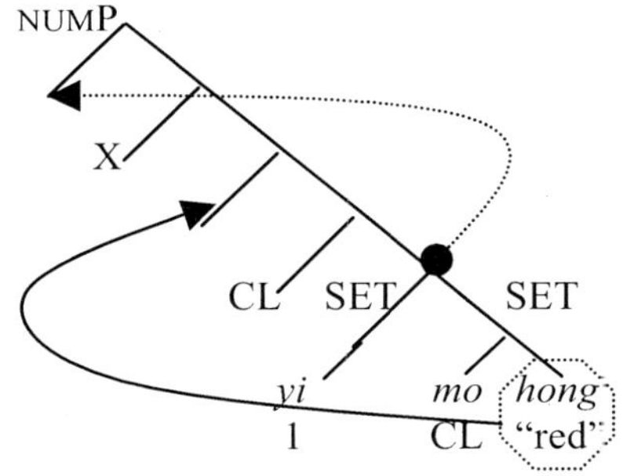

The derivation of the argument DP *hong-se* in "I like red" starts with (66) and carries on as *se* "colour" moves up.

(66)

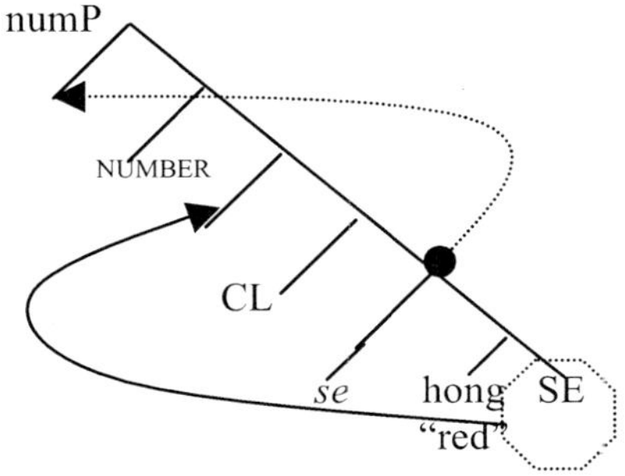

(67)

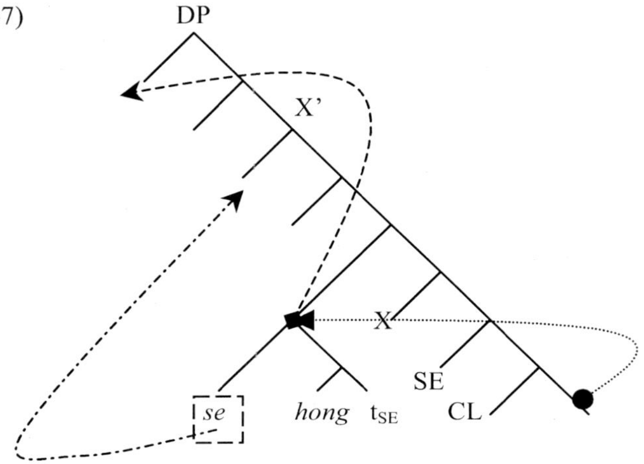

The derivation of non-predicative adjective *hong* "red" should be able to capture the fact that the non-predicative adjective *hong* only directly precedes certain NPs. Namely, there is a selection restriction between the NP and the colour adjective. For instance, *hong* cannot be directly precede the light noun *dongxi* "thing" (68a), nor can any bare colour term; but all free colour terms can precede *shoujuan* "handkerchief" (68b).

(68)	a.	*	hong / huang / lan / bai / hei/ zong	dongxi
			red / yellow / blue / white / black / brown	thing
	b.		hong / huang / lan / bai / hei/ *zong	shoujuan
			red / yellow / blue / white / black / brown	handkerchief
			"red / yellow / blue / white / black / *brown handkerchief(s)"	

The selectional property between a non-predicative adjective and its NP recalls the relation between *yi*[35] and count nouns, which serves as an argument for the existence of the null 'colour base' *se*. NPs that allow colour adjectives to directly precede them have a null colour base in them. The derivation of X-NP is an instance of *yi*-N.

(69)

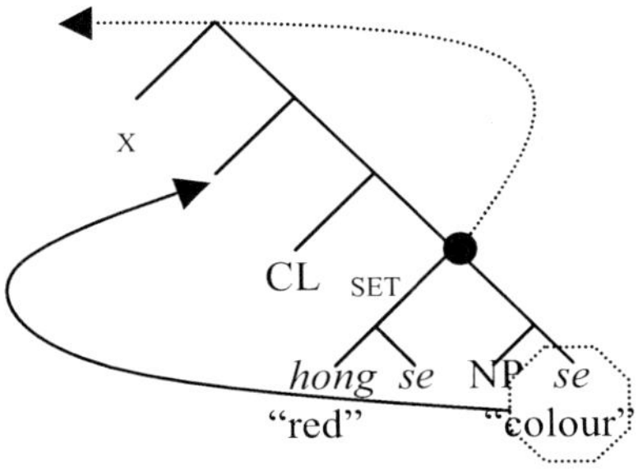

(70)

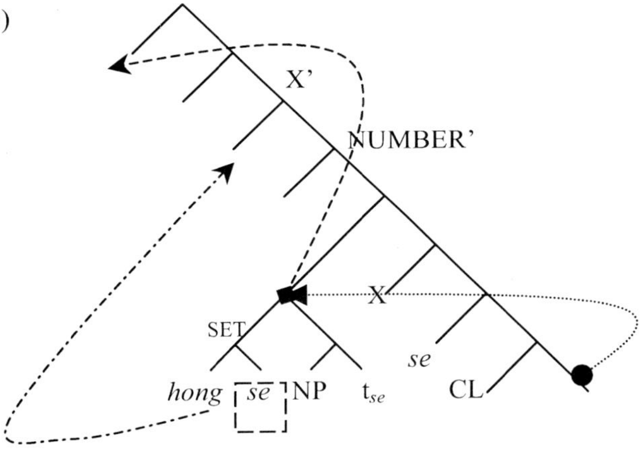

To recap, in this section, I have argued that *hong* as an NP should be analogous to *yi*[55]. And *hong* in *hong-se* is modifying an unpronounced "colour base", *SE* "COLOUR"; a property similar to a sandhi *yi*[35/51] modifying a weight. The overt *se* "colour" is crucial in turning a bare NP colour term into a DP. Non-predicative adjective *hong* "red" in *hong*-N has a derivation that parallel to the anti-sandhi *yi*[35] in *yi*-N.

4.2. de

4.2.1. de *Is Obligatory after a Colour Base*

Bound colour terms (those that require *se* "colour") don't precede an NP directly (71)[13].

(71)	a.	*	Nana	you	si	tiao	zong-se	maoyi.
			Nana	have	four	CL	brown-colour	sweater
	b.	*	Nana	you	si	tiao	hui -se maoyi.	
			Nana	have	four	CL	grey-colour	sweater
	c.	*	Nana	you	si	tiao	fen hong	maoyi.
			Nana	have	four	CL	pink red	sweater

An additional morpheme *de* is required[14].

---

[13] Free colour terms often acquire a figurative meaning with the morpheme *se* "colour". For instance, *huang-se* "yellow" can be a non-predicative adjective, having the interpretation of *erotic*, directly precedes a noun (i-a), but it cannot precede a NUM-CL (i-b) (for recent discussions, see Sio 2006).

(i) a. san ben huang-se xiaoshuo
3 CL^{book} yellow-colour novel
"three erotic novels"
b. * huang-se (nei) san ben xiaoshuo
yellow-colour that 3 CL^{book} novel

An additional morpheme *de* is required to modify a NUM-CL.

(ii) huang-se de ?(nei) san ben xiaoshuo
yellow-colour DE that 3 CL^{book} novel
"those three erotic novels"

X-*se-de* also can be an argument and the condition is the same as on X-*de*.

(iii) Nana xihuan huang-se de.
Nana like yellow-colour DE
"Nana likes {the erotic one(s) / erotic things}."

[14] And it is not just Chinese needs a morpheme to license an overt *colour*. In Hungarian, when *-szìn* "colour" is pronounced, an extra morpheme *-ű* is required for an adjective use (i) (Èva Dèkàny, p.c.).

(i) Var egy szàl vörös (szìn-ű) haj az asztal-om-on.
be one strand scarlet colour-U hair the table-my-on
"There is a strand of scarlet hair on my table."

The analysis for *de* in attributive adjectives is by no means just a "subordinator" as argued in Paul (2005). Nor do her (as well as works therein cited) crucial data

(72) a. Nana you si tiao zong se de maoyi.
Nana have four CL brown colour DE sweater
"Nana has four brown sweaters."
b. Nana you si tiao hui se de maoyi.
Nana have four CL grey colour DE sweater
"Nana has four grey sweaters."
c. Nana you si tiao fen hong se de maoyi.
Nana have four CL pink red colour DE sweater
"Nana has four pink sweaters."

One attempt for *de* would be the *linker* analysis as in den Dikken & Singhaspreecha (2004), further developed in den Dikken (2006). In Mandarin, we can find *de* functioning sometimes as a linker (predicate-linker-argument) and some times as a relator (argument-relator-predicate).

(73) a. hen hong
very red
b. hong de hen [relator]
red DE very
"very red"
c. hong fangzi
red house
d. hong de fangzi [linker]
red DE house
"red house"

It doesn't help much to claim that a word as a linker and relator. However, *de* forces us to investigate into the structure of the phrases it links.

---

stand: *de*-less AN as being compound which is then different from reduced relative A *de* N. The crucial example is that: for some adjectives, it seems that they can stand without a copula.

(ii) Zhangsan zhen congming. (Paul 2005, (3))
Zhangsan really intelligent
"Zhangsan is really intelligent."

However, the sentence stands only due to the fact that there is a degree adverb *zhen* "really". Without this degree adverb, it is not a possible sentence unless used as an answer to "*who is more intelligent, Zhangsan or someone else*?" And this is the same property as that of attributive adjectives.

4.2.2 de *and CL*

Recall that when the anti-sandhi numeral *yi*[35] "1" must be followed by a countable NP without an intervening CL[15]. *de* cannot intervene between a colour noun and its CL. (74) shows that colour adjectives can only modify a colour adjective without *de*.

(74)	a.	yi	mo	zi	(*de)	hong	
		one	CL	purple	de	red	
		"red tinged with purple"					
	b.	yi	mo	lan	(*de)	lü	
		one	CL	blue	de	green	
		"bluish green"					
	c.	yi	mo	hui	(*de)	bai	
		one	CL	gray	de	white	
		"greyish-white"					

When a bare NP modifies colour terms, it cannot be followed by a *de* either (75). However, *de* doesn't block the agreement between a non-colour term NP and its CL (76).

(75)	a.	yi	mo	zhuan	(*de)	hong
		one	CL	brick	de	red
		"brick-red"				
	b.	yi	mo	tian	(*de)	lan
		one	CL	sky	de	blue
		"sky-blue"				
	c.	yi	mo	xue	(*de)	bai
		one	CL	snow	de	white
		"snow-white"				

(76)	a.	yi	kuai	hong	(de)	zhuan
		one	CL	red	de	brick
		"a red brick"				

---

[15] The anti-sandhi *yi* cannot be followed by a weight, nor can the colour base *se* "colour" intervene (i).

(i) *	yi	mo	lan / huang / hui	se	(de)	lü
	one	CL	blue / yellow / grey	colour	de	green

b. yi pian lan (de) tian
one CL blue de sky
"a blue sky"

c. yi dui bai (de) xue
one CL white de snow
"a pile of white snow"

A CL must not follow the anti-sandhi *yi*[35], and *de* must not follow a colour classifier.

Another similarity between an agreeing CL and *de* is that both block the selection between NP and its modifier. When a colour adjective directly precedes an NP, there is also a selectional relation on the NP. However, when there is a CL between the numeral and the noun, there is no restriction on the CL-NP any more. When *de* occurs, X-*de* is allowed to modify any NP (Zhu 1956).

(77) hong de dongxi.
red DE thing
"red things"

Thirdly, an agreeing CL makes NP ellipsis possible when there is a simple numeral (78b). *De* makes NP ellipsis possible where there is an adjective[16].

---

[16] NP ellipsis can take place as long as there is a *de*.

(i) a. Nana xihuan hong *(de)
Nana like red de
"Nana like the red one."

b. Nana xihuan hong se *(de)
Nana like red colour de
"Nana like the red one."

c. Nana xihuan hen hong de
Nana like very red de
"Nana like the very red one."

(ii) a. Nana xihuan zhei pen-r hong *(de)
Nana like this CL^{pot} red de
"Nana like the red flower."

b. Nana xihuan zhei pen-r hong se *(de)
Nana like this CL^{pot} red colour de
"Nana like the red flower."

(78) a. ta mai le hong de.
3SG buy LE red DE
"He bought the red one(s)."
b. ta mai le si duo.
3SG buy LE four CL^{flower}
"He bought four."

Fourthly, as we have seen in section 2, an agreeing CL (but not the disagreeing *ge*) can answer a D-linked *wh*-question. X-*de* is good in an answer to a D-linked *wh*- phrase (79a), infelicitous to a *shenme* "what" question[17]. The sentence in (78), for instance, is not a suitable answer to (79b).

(79) a. Nana xihuan shenme yang de?
Nana like what kind DE
"What kind does Nana like?"
b. Nana xihuan shenme?
Nana like what
"What does Nana like?"

As we have seen in the numeral system, different numerals have different derivational history with respect to the interaction between NUM-CL-N. If *de* is parallel to a CL, there are several kinds of 'numerals' preceding it: adjective *hong* "red", the noun *hong* "red" and the DP *hong-se* "red-colour". Each should render a different derivation.

The derivation for the adjective *hong de* in *hong de hua* "red flower" starts as (81), where *de* is modifying a *yi* "1". This is because X-*de* can precede a DEMP (80). Since there is a *yi* "1" in the derivation of the DEM *zhei* "this" (as well as *nei* "that"), I consider that *de* is merged with a numeral *yi* "1". Again the derivation has the same pattern as *yi*-N.

(80) zhuo shang fang zhe **hong de ??**(zhei / nei) *si* *tiao* qunzi.
table on put ASP **red** DE this / tha *four* *CL* dress
'There are the four RED dresses on the table.'

---

c. Nana xihuan zhei pen-r hen hong de.
Nana like this CL^{pot} very red de
"Nana like the very red flower."

[17] Same as the condition for DEM-CL, the context shouldn't be strong enough to help recovering the NP.

(81) *differs from (46) / (52) in lexical insertion*

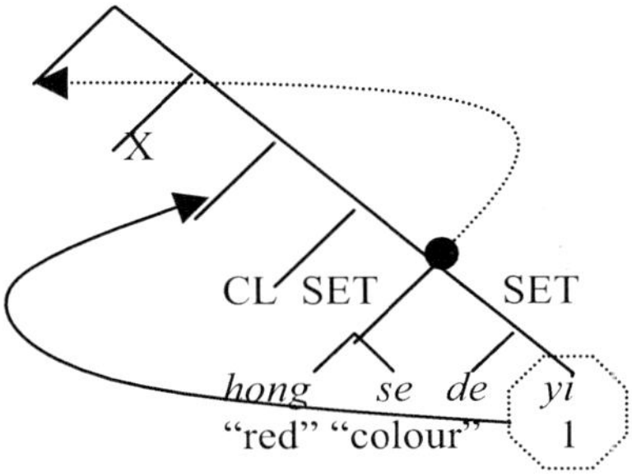

(82)

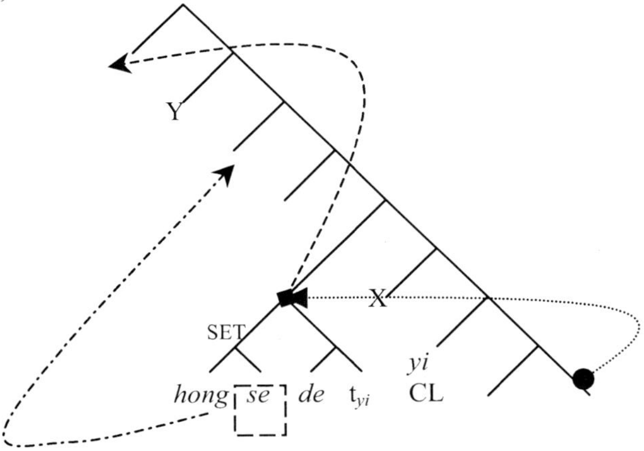

The difference between *hong* and *hong-de* has been described (Jakhontov 1959, Chao 1968) as *hong-de* gives more force to *hong* "red". Zhu (1956) claims with an overt NP, *hong* "red" is subcategorizing the *type of hair*, and *hong de* "red" is describing the *hair*.

That colour terms cannot be preceded by a *de*-Phrase can be linked to the fact that colour terms can never be directly preceded by yi^{35}. If I am on the right track in taking the NP that allows yi^{35}-N in having a covert *GE* (an individualizer in Cheng & Sybesma 1999), then colour terms don't have modify such a morpheme. Colour adjectives in Mandarin modify a colour base *SE* "COLOUR", but colour nouns never spell out a CL

Mandarin colour adjectives don't spell out the weight *GE*, because they cannot enter yi^{35}-*N* construction, i.e. they are not count nouns. They do, however, spell out a colour base *SE*. To sum up this section, colour terms are modifying a colour base *se* "colour", which is a weight in the adjective domain. *De* is merged under the same principle as lexical words.

5. Conclusion

Both *zhe* and *zhei* are generally considered to be proximal demonstratives, whereas yi^{55}, $yi^{35/51}$, and yi^{35} all share the meaning of the numeral "one". Numerals, whether 1400 or 4, are considered to be of one category. *Hong-(de)* "red" and *zong-de* "brown" are both colour adjectives. However, these encyclopaedic synonyms have different syntax.

The derivation of a lexical item and the derivation of a phrase containing the lexical item interweave. Each morpheme needs to be licensed in the syntax. The debate on demonstratives being licensed high or low can result in both sides being right. They may both be right for the DEM they are discussing have different internal structures across languages. This is just like the language-internal parameter that affects the two Mandarin demonstratives: the difference in morphological complexity between *zhe* and *zhei*, determines whether the demonstrative in question can precede a NUM or not. It is not the case that as long as you are a DEM you can then precede NUM. A phrase can precede a NUM if and only if it is derived in such a way that allows it to enter a derivation that finally leads to a higher-than-NUM position. The 'basic word order' is determined by the structural complexity of each lexical item; there isn't such a primitive like 'basic order' in syntax.

The difference between a lexical item (e.g. *hong* "red") and a functional element (e.g. *de*) is not categorical, in terms of their licensing.

For all the data discussed in the present paper, the *yi*-N conjecture holds.

References

Abels, K. & P. Muriungi. 2007. The focus marker in Kıtharaka: Syntax and semantics. Ms., University of Tromsoe.

Au-Yeung, W.-H. 2005. *An Interface Program for Parameterization of Classifiers in Chinese*. Ph.D. diss., Hong Kong University of Science and Technology.

Borer, H. 2005. *In Name Only — Structuring Sense*, vol. I. Oxford: Oxford University Press.

Brugè, L. 2002. The positions of demonstratives in the extended nominal projection. In G. Cinque (ed.), *Functional Structure in DP and IP — The Cartography of Syntactic Structures*, vol. 1. New York: Oxford University Press, 15-53.

Chao, Y.R. 1968. *A Grammar of Spoken Chinese*. Berkeley & Los Angeles: California University Press.

Cheng, L.L.-S. & R. Sybesma. 1999. Bare and not-so-bare nouns and the structure of NP. *Linguistic Inquiry* 30, 509-542.

Chomsky, N. 1995. Bare phrase structure. In G. Webelhuth (ed.), *Government and Binding Theory and the Minimalist Program*. Malden, MA: Blackwell, 383-439.

Cinque, G. 2005. Deriving Greenberg's Universal 20 and its exceptions. *Linguistic Inquiry* 36, 315-332.

den Dikken, M. & P. Singhapreecha. 2004. Complex noun phrases and linkers. *Syntax* 7, 1-54.

den Dikken, M. 2006. *Relators and Linkers: The Syntax of Predication, Predicate Inversion, and copulas*. Cambridge, MA: MIT Press.

Du, Y, 1993. Beijinghua *zhong de* '*yi*+N'. *Zhongguo Yuwen* 233, 142.

Grohmann, K.K. & Phoevos Panagiotidis. 2005. Demonstrative doubling. Ms., University of Cyprus & Cyprus College, Nicosia.

Ionin, T. & O. Matushansky. 2004a. A healthy twelve patients. Paper presented at *GURT 2004*, Georgetown University, Washington, DC.

Ionin, T. & O. Matushansky. 2004b. The non-existence, syntax, and semantics of plurals. Ms., University of Southern California, Los Angeles & CNRS/University of Paris 8/ENS.

Jakhontov, S.E. 1959. *Hanyu de Dongci Fanchou* [On Chinese Verbal Category] (Translated from Russian by C. Konglun). Beijing: Commercial Press.

Jin, H. 1988. Zhishi daici sanfen fa buzheng [More evidence on the ternary distinction of demonstratives]. *Zhongguo Yuwen* 1988, 5.

Jin, Y. 1979 Putonghua yi zi shengdiao de dufa. *Zhongguo Yuwen* 152, 356-358.

Kayne, R.S. 1994. *The Antisymmetry of Syntax*. Cambridge, MA: MIT Press.

Kayne, R.S. 2003. Silent years, silent hours. In L.-O. Delsing, C. Falk, G. Josefsson & H.Á. Sigurðsson (eds.), *Grammar in Focus: Festschrift for Christer Platzack*, vol. 2. Lund: Wallin & Dalholm, 209-226. [Reprinted in Kayne, R.S. 2005. *Movement and Silence*. Oxford: Oxford University Press, 241-260.]

Kayne, R.S. 2005. A note on the syntax of numeral bases. Ms., New York University.

Kayne, R.S. 2006. On parameters and on principles of pronunciation. In J. Koster, N. Corver, U. Kleinhenz & H. Broekhuis (eds.), *Organizing Grammar: Studies in Honor of Henk van Riemsdijk*. Berlin: Mouton de Gruyter, 289-299.

Lü, S. 1956. *Zhongguo Wenfa Yaolüe* [Outline of Chinese Syntax].

Lü, S. 1985. *Jindai Hanyu Zhishi Daici* [Demonstratives of Early Modern Chinese]. *Jiang Lansheng* ed. Shanghai: Xuelin Press.

Lü, S. 1990. Zhishi daici de erfenfa he sanfenfa [Binary and ternary distinction of demonstratives] *Zhongguo Yuwen* 1990.

Lü, S. & C. Rao. 1981. Shilun fei wei xingrongci [On non-predicative adjectives]. *Zhongguo Yuwen* 1981, 81-85.

Mi, Q. 1986. Zhishi daici sanfenfashuo buli [More examples on ternary distinction of demonstratives].

Ogawa, T. 1981. Suzhou fangyan de zhishi daici [Demonstratives in Suzhou dialect]. *Fangyan* 1981.

Paul, W. 2005. Adjectival Modification in Mandarin Chinese and Related Issues. *Linguistics* 43, 757-793.

Pesetsky, D. 1995. *Zero Syntax: Experiencers and Cascades*. Cambridge, MA: MIT Press.

Sio, J. 2006. *Modification and Reference in the Chinese Nominal*. Ph.D. diss., Leiden University.

Wang, D. 2005. *Zhe na de zhishi gongneng yanjiu* [This that and the reference]. Shanghai: Xuelin Chubanshe.

Wang, L. 1945. *Zhongguo Yufa Lilun* [A Theory on Chinese Grammar].

Xuefan (Chen, W.D.). 1938. Biaoshi dongzuo yanxu de liangzhong fangshi [Two ways of expressing verbal duration]. *Yuwen Zhoukan* 2.

Zhu, D. 1956. Xiandai hanyu xingrongci yanjiu [On adjectives in Modern Chinese]. *Yuyan Yanjiu* 1956.1.

Zhu, D. 1961. Shuo de [On *de*]. *Zhongguo Yuwen* 1961.12.

Zhu, D. 1966. Guanyu shuo be [About *On de*]. *Zhongguo Yuwen* 1966.1.

Zhu, D. 1982. *Yufa Jiangyi* [Lecture Notes on Syntax]. Beijing: Commercial Press.

Zhu, D. 1993. Cong lishi he fangyan kan zhuangtai xingrongci de mingcihua [Nominalization of stative adjectives: From synchronic and diachronic perspectives]. *Fangyan* 1993.2.

Zhu, J. 1986. Wuhan de Zhishi daici yeshi sanfen de [Demonstratives in Wuhan dialect are also ternary]. *Zhongguo Yuwen* 1986.6

Zhu, Q. 1988. Wuhan de Zhishi daici bushi sanfen de [Demonstratives in Wuhan dialect are not ternary]. *Zhongguo Yuwen* 1988.5

Zweig, E. 2005. Nouns and adjectives in numeral NPs. *Proceedings of NELS 35*, 663-675.